Fine Homebuilding
REMODELING
IDEAS

Fine Homebuilding
REMODELING IDEAS

The Taunton Press

Photo, p. 1, by Thomas Harboe and Vincent Lepre
Drawing, back cover, by Frances Ashforth

First printing: September 1986
Second printing: April 1987

International Standard Book Number 0-918804-50-7
Library of Congress Catalog Card Number 85-50838
Printed in the United States of America

A FINE HOMEBUILDING Book

FINE HOMEBUILDING® is a trademark of
The Taunton Press, Inc., registered in the
U.S. Patent and Trademark Office.

The Taunton Press, Inc.
63 South Main Street
Box 355
Newtown, Connecticut 06470

Contents

Introduction

In many ways, adapting and preserving existing homes is more challenging and more technically demanding than designing and building a new house on a clean lot. Tearing into walls and roofs inevitably brings surprises, and reinforcing an old foundation to bear the extra weight of an upstairs addition can be dicey work.

To tackle any type of remodeling job with confidence, you need a fairly comprehensive knowledge of older homes and the materials and construction methods used in different places at different times. And it helps considerably to have a wide acquaintance with what others have done to update their clients' houses, add new spaces or restore structures that have historical importance.

That's why we've collected the best articles—43 in all—about remodeling houses from the back issues of *Fine Homebuilding* magazine. We hope you'll find the information here helpful, perhaps inspiring, so that the next time you're stuck for a design idea or rubbing your chin over a construction problem, something from these pages will come to mind.

—The editors

Restorations

Resurrecting the Bolton House

There's more to restoring a Greene and Greene house than following the original plan

by Ken Ross

Black-and-white photos: Courtesy College of Environmental Design, Documents Collection, U.C. Berkeley

When I moved to Pasadena, Calif., in 1974, I saw for the first time several homes designed by Charles and Henry Greene. It was love at first sight. So when one of their houses came on the market in 1979, I bought it without so much as a backward glance.

To my eye, the Greene brothers' work is the ultimate expression of the American Craftsman movement in architecture. Their work brings together several design sources that I admire—oriental architecture, Art Nouveau and the Arts and Crafts movement. And they were able to unify these separate elements and a myriad of highly wrought details to produce cohesive designs in which line and form, texture and color work to make one thing out of many.

The house that I bought (photo facing page, top) was designed and built in 1906 for Dr. William T. Bolton, a Pasadena physician, who died before the house was completed. It was bought and sold many times in the following years. Among the early owners were the Culbertson sisters, for whom the Greenes had designed another home a couple of miles away. The Culbertsons' shrinking inheritance forced them to move from their 10,000-sq. ft. home in Pasadena's Oak Knoll area to the smaller Bolton house (about 5,000 sq. ft. at the time) in the Orange Grove area.

The Culbertson sisters commissioned the Greene brothers to make a number of changes in the house, which ultimately added about 1,000 sq. ft. and which considerably altered the interior. Some changes were good; others

Built in 1906, Greene and Greene's Bolton house suffered neglect and abuse before it was restored by the author, who was able to coordinate the efforts of local builders and craftsmen so that the work they did was equal in quality to the original woodwork, tilework and plastering. In the original entry (facing page, bottom right), the downspouts were made to look like structural elements, lending visual support to the wide overhangs. Missing here is the engaged half-turret to the right of the entry (facing page, top), a later addition designed for new owners by architect Garrett Van Pelt.

were not. The turret stairwell was added in the early 1920s by the Culbertson sisters. It was designed by Garrett Van Pelt, an architect who had earlier worked for the Greenes. The stairwell is similar to one of two that were part of the facade of an earlier house designed for the Culbertsons' father by the Greenes, and built a few blocks away on South Grand St. This addition was built by the original contractor, Peter Hall. The Culbertsons changed the entry hall and writing room, removing some interior brickwork because they thought it was too rustic. Even with all of these changes, the house remained representative of the Greenes' style during the long time the Culbertson sisters lived there.

But the house did not fare so well with subsequent owners. In 1952, it was purchased by people who began a series of transformations that all but effaced the original appearance and character of the house. The new owners went to great lengths to turn a California bungalow into a French Provincial mansion. Their alterations included painting white the cedar and mahogany woodwork, painting over the doors and bookmatched mahogany paneling, removing and discarding all of the Tiffany glass lanterns and oriental-style box beams, and walling over two fireplaces that featured Grueby tiles.

When I bought the house, it had not been used as a residence for many years. After suffering the indignities of French Provincialization, the house had been bought by a local college and used as a warehouse and book depository. Bad things happened inside and out during its sentence as a storage depot. The roof went without maintenance and was allowed to leak. The plumbing wasn't repaired and leaked so profusely that water had rotted large holes through which one could gaze from floor to floor. Carelessly operated hand trucks and forklifts left hundreds of dents, scratches and gouges in floors, walls and trim. Most realtors would have classified it as a "fixer-upper." Indeed, the process that followed is better described as a resurrection

than a restoration. Only a dedicated preservationist or a damn fool would tackle such a project. I qualified on both counts.

Restoring the Bolton house was a challenge and an opportunity. Our principal challenge lay in the fact that most of the original interior features had been entirely stripped away. This left us with the task of determining what the original rooms looked like, and having done that, reproducing their various architectural features. Our principal opportunity was to be found in the freedom to reinterpret creatively and fill in gaps with our own designs.

We were fortunate in finding that several people were interested in the rebirth of the Bolton house. The most recent owner, who had held it for only a few months, had tracked down several sheets of the original blueprints at the Avery Library at Columbia University in New York, as well as copies of all the building permits for the house and its many remodelings. The Greene and Greene library at Gamble House (4 Westmoreland Place, Pasadena, Calif. 91103) provided us with several 1908-vintage photos—both exterior and interior shots like the one of the original dining room below. Other people volunteered bits and pieces of information. All in all, we had quite a lot to go on.

However, having a lot of information is not the same thing as knowing what to do with it. None of us who worked on the project had been involved in a restoration project of this scale before, and restoration is infinitely more time-consuming and difficult than either renovation or new construction. You have to undo all of the old accretions before you can do anything new. You are faced with having to solve innumerable small mysteries before the big jobs can begin. You have to map the electrical, water, sewerage and gas systems before you can do anything with them. You have to reconcile the original blueprints with a structure that has been substantially altered, sometimes in baffling ways. You have to decide which of the original features are worth reproducing and which are not, while still remain-

The original dining room, with its now long-lost custom furniture, was paneled with wide pieces of Honduras mahogany plywood. Unable to find good-quality mahogany plywood in these widths, Ross used standard 4-ft. wide panels and trimmed between with battens.

The kitchen (above), which had been Early-Americanized in the 1950s—knotty-pine cabinets and trim, scalloped copper work and an island range—had to be completely gutted. The window area where the sink stood was removed and the wall there filled in (right), and treated between the tops of the cabinets and the header strip with subway tiles.

ing faithful to your perception of the architects' vision. And, not least important, you have to stay solvent.

Working to high standards—I began the project in a fit of organizational energy. I made flow charts, job descriptions, checklists, spec sheets and budget estimates. I had a wonderful time, but none of these devices seemed to make the job go more smoothly.

There was so much to do that one of my first temptations was to tackle too many tasks at once. We had crews stripping paint, removing the old roof, clearing off the yard, and doing rough carpentry. We had plumbers plumbing, electricians wiring, and dozens of tourists getting in the way and asking questions. Keeping everyone organized, supervised, supplied and paid was tough—at times it was impossible. In the first few months, we went through more than 60 gallons of commercial paint stripper and two heat guns; we used up reams of sandpaper, innumerable other supplies, and lots of patience and goodwill.

In retrospect, I know we'd have been better off with a smaller and more tightly organized crew. Large crews can get work done faster, but they make mistakes faster, too, and sometimes the net result is not positive. Through natural attrition and the outright firing of some workers, our crew gradually shrank to a manageable size, and the overall quality of our work steadily improved.

Certain styles of architecture and interior detailing can be duplicated, more or less, using standard materials, conventional construction techniques and competent workmanship. Not so with Greene and Greene designs. The effect of the whole depends entirely on the near-flawless execution of seemingly insignificant details. Meticulous attention must be paid to wood joinery, to the finish and texture of the expansive wood and plaster surfaces, to the correctly done stained-glass panels, and to many other carefully wrought minutiae. And all these little things, taken together, create the Craftsman look and feel. There's just no such thing as an uncraftsmanly Craftsman house. So it became my responsibility to encourage the highest

possible standards of craftwork, within the constraints of my budget and schedule. I think this is the most important role among the many that an owner-builder can perform.

Encouraging quality is different from demanding it. This kind of encouragement involves making a milieu in which craftsmanship will be the natural result of creative freedom, commitment to an ideal, adequate time and a spirit of cooperation. What this means in practical terms is finding bright, talented people who take pride in their work, and who have the right "chemistry" with each other. Further, it means insisting that such people work on a time-and-materials basis. This last point is an important one. Many trade and craftspeople are capable of much better work than they ordinarily do. But they are so accustomed to competitive bidding and the need to work quickly that they simply won't believe it when you tell them you want a job done right, even if doing it right takes longer and costs more.

Even accomplished craftspeople sometimes need to be convinced that it's okay to do the best work they can. The best way I know of to do this is to insist that they work on a time-and-materials basis, and then to work beside them as much as possible. Working with the crew does three things. It protects you by allowing you to oversee work directly—you don't have to wonder about how something was done, or if it was done. It gives you a chance to communicate your standards, and it establishes a bond of friendship and trust, which is a key ingredient of craftsmanship.

Doing things this way lets you experiment. Time invested experimenting pays dividends in the long run. Our skim-coat technique saved us a bundle. We did several patches right on the wall, varying the formula until we got it right and then proceeding from there. By experimenting we found we could mate old plaster to new drywall and blend them invisibly with a skim coat. This was especially helpful when replacing old ceilings. We also tried various wood finishes and techniques until we arrived at a compromise between ease of application and a good end result.

However, ordinary techniques that work

well in new construction don't always work so well in restoration. The freedom to experiment helped us to solve problems in innovative ways, and saved money in the long run.

In the first several months of work on the house, we reroofed it, rebuilt the mechanical systems and dealt with structural problems. Some previous modifications had left walls with insufficient shear strength, and some modified openings were over-spanned.

The kitchen—The first room in the house to get intense attention was the kitchen. There was general agreement among the crew members that this room transcended bad taste and was better described as an example of "anti-taste," a deliberate, demonic effort to make a pretty thing ugly. It was incomprehensible to us that it had been featured in a 1952 issue of Los Angeles' *Home Magazine* with descriptions of its maple and knotty-pine woodwork, quilted and scalloped copper work, Early American light fixtures and hardware, cork-tile floor and steel casement windows (photo above left). We promptly gutted the room.

We installed a maple floor, one similar to the original. New wood-frame windows were put in place, and we laid up tile on the walls from the floor to a continuous header trim (photo above right). These tiled walls are serviceable, and they're characteristic of the Greenes' kitchens.

In rebuilding the kitchen, our goal was to recreate the style and feel of the original, while at the same time creating a new and functional space with modern amenities. We worked toward this goal in several ways. First, we used a cabinet design patterned after the original but in a different (and expanded) configuration. Both the upper and lower cabinets were modifications of the original design, but close enough to capture their look (photo facing page). This original look was maintained through the faithful retention of many details both large and small: the use of wooden countertops, the elimination of under-the-counter toe space and the use of Craftsman-style joinery (dovetails, finger joints and pegged tenons).

All of the appliances were carefully selected

Construction photos: Ken Ross

The woodwork in the restored kitchen is mostly redwood, and the cabinets are done in a style consonant with the Greene brothers' sense of scale and detailing. The fronts of the dishwasher and refrigerator are paneled, and the countertops are solid wood. Recessed lighting above the work areas concentrates light where it's needed, instead of flooding the whole kitchen with excessive illumination.

and installed to work visually with the overall design. The dishwasher, compacter and refrigerator were wood-paneled in a way that wouldn't attract too much attention to themselves. The refrigerator was flush mounted into a wall. A microwave oven was concealed behind a tambour door. We chose a commercial range for its appropriate scale and for its functional appearance.

The lighting was carefully thought out so as *not* to provide uniform illumination, with the idea that all work and eating areas would be brightly lit, while other non-work areas would

be less so. This adds a degree of drama to the lighting, and also avoids the uniformly bright illumination of most modern kitchens. The cumulative effect of all this attention to detail is a kitchen that is modern and functional, yet entirely in character with the original style and intent of the Greenes' design.

In reworking the kitchen, we used a variety of modern techniques rather than slavishly adhering to old ways. We finished our countertops, for example, with a high-quality, solvent-based polyurethane, and we used a variety of modern sealers and preservatives. We

did the ceiling and upper walls with gypboard, double sheeted and attached with screws. We laid up the wall tile on a plywood base rather than on a cement bed. For this base we used 5/8-in. exterior plywood, secured to the studs with panel cement and ring-shank nails. Instead of using thin-set, we set the tile with type A mastic, a high-quality mastic that's much easier to use and very strong.

For lights, we used a combination of leaded-glass lanterns in the style of the originals, and discreet modern fixtures. Our 2x12 (net dimensions) ceiling joists allowed us to install

The living room, which had been French Provincialized by the same people who remodeled the kitchen, is here being stripped of wallpaper and other accretions. By a stroke of luck, the locations of the original box beams, lanterns, header trim and other features were clearly outlined under the wall coverings. These worked almost like templates for constructing these elements anew.

A copper header with trailing-vine overlay conceals rebar holes above the fireplace lintel.

deeply recessed, museum-style down lights. Equipped with a ribbed black baffle and bezels painted to match the ceiling color, these fixtures faded into the background while at the same time putting light just where we wanted it. Although some preservationists would frown on these techniques, we felt that in almost every case we realized substantial benefits, we saved money and we kept from vitiating the spirit of the Greene brothers' original design.

The living room—After we finished rebuilding the kitchen, we concentrated our efforts on the living room. About the only things left over from the original room were the windows. All of the architectural features had been stripped away in the same remodeling wave that created the Early American kitchen. This room, though, had been redone in a French Provincial style. Even the original sand-finish plaster walls had been covered with canvas, and then papered with a floral print. To our delight, when this canvas was pulled down, it revealed not only the original surface and colors underneath but also the white, unpainted silhouettes of all the original box beams, header trim and other ornamentation, as seen in the photo above left. This allowed us to verify dimensions and details that were unclear from our incomplete set of blueprints. But, our most exciting discovery came when we removed the reproduction French Provincial mantelpiece and chipped a small hole through the plaster behind it. There, covered over for nearly 30 years, was the original fireplace, with its handmade Grueby tiles still in place. Apparently these 1-in. thick tiles had been too hard to remove, so the 1950s remodeling contractor just covered them over with wire lath and plaster.

After photographing the room and carefully measuring the silhouettes, we pulled down the plaster ceiling because it was unsound

and unsafe. We renailed the original wood lath with blue nails and covered it with wire lath, which we attached with heavy-gauge ⅝-in. staples and a pneumatic gun. Then we replastered the ceiling and finished it to get a sand-finish texture. The walls were extensively patched, and then the entire room was skim-coated (except for the new ceiling).

This skim-coating technique (see *FHB #15*, pp. 72-74) worked very well, and we used it extensively throughout the house. This saved us the considerable expense of completely replastering walls that were unsightly but basically sound. Instead of applying commercially prepared skimcoat, we used ordinary premixed latex joint compound and sand, with a little extra water added to help speed troweling. Conventional plaster doesn't work well for skim coating and should not be used. Our joint-compound formula hasn't shown a single crack in the entire house, and it's been in place for about three years now.

We finished the skim-coated walls with one coat of oil-base sealer and one coat of exterior oil-base primer before applying two coats of high-quality latex paint. We modified the oil-base paints with Penetrol and the latex with Floetrol, both made by Flood Co. (Hudson, Ohio 44236). These additives retard the drying time, minimizing lap and roller marks, and give the dried paint a very slight sheen. We painted the room before installing any of the woodwork, thereby avoiding the necessity of cutting in with a brush around innumerable edges and corners.

Restoring the living-room fireplace and hearth turned out to be a major undertaking in itself. Uncovering the original fireplace tiles was really good news. The bad news was that they were covered with mortar and plaster and pierced by two rebar studs, which had been inserted in the masonry to support the plaster. The hearth was missing all its tiles, which had been thrown out and replaced with

marble, and the original copper firebox header was gone.

Then, in another fantastic stroke of luck, a local collector told me he had enough matching Grueby tiles from a demolished house to replace my hearth. Again, this was the good news. The bad news was that these sturdy tiles were still attached, in one monolithic piece, to 8 in. of well-cured concrete.

To make a long story short, we used a hammer and chisel, a water-cooled diamond saw and a lot of sweat to liberate the tiles intact. The tiles were cleaned by repeated scrubbings with a mild muriatic-acid solution and brought back to their original patina with a rubdown using diluted tung oil. We solved the problem of the two stud holes made by the rebar by designing a new copper header with an Art Nouveau trailing-vine overlay (also of copper), which extended up over the tile at the appropriate places and simply covered up the holes (photo above right). We borrowed the trailing-vine motif from the leaded-glass transom light over our front door.

In restoring the living room, we used Port Orford cedar for all the trim, doors, box beams and windows (photo facing page). This wood was a favorite of the Greenes, who selected it for its durability, workability and clear grain. The wood was kiln-dried at the mill and air-dried inside the house for several months. Port Orford cedar is durable and rot-resistant because of its high resin content, but

The restored living room, with its Grueby tile fireplace, stained-glass lanterns and built-in inglenook bench, is almost a copy of the original Greene and Greene living room. The only significant change is the built-in audio cabinet to the right of the fireplace.

it can exude this resin for a long time and did so, right through our meticulously applied finish, in spite of all our precautions.

We used Honduras mahogany, also a Greene and Greene favorite, for cabinets, benches and lanterns. This wood was a pleasure to work, and yielded exceptionally beautiful results.

We began reproducing the woodwork for the living room by building the box beams. These were large heavy structures of various sizes, with radiused edges, arranged in an overlapping oriental design. We built our larger beams with interior ribs, much like a canoe, and attached all of them to the ceiling by nailing them to cleats affixed to the joists with drywall screws. The beams were nailed from the side with a pneumatic gun, firing 2-in. finishing nails. The nail gun was invaluable because it enabled us to do high-quality finish work in close quarters without nicking the plaster on the ceiling or denting the wood.

Before nailing the beams in place, we scribed them to the ceiling, a tedious, time-consuming operation that required us to take them up and down numerous times. The beams had to be brought in through a window, lifted up, held in place using pads and 1-in. by 2-in. braces (used like go-bars), then marked, taken down, planed, sanded and put back up again. Ugh.

One design feature that's truly a Greene and Greene trademark is a continuous wood head-er circling the room and joined at intervals with a pegged scarf joint, like the one in the center photo on the next page. The header joins all the windows and doors, and organizes them into one plane. It also visually lowers the ceiling to a comfortable height. In addition, the header serves as an attachment point for the light fixtures (usually lanterns) and as a picture molding. We installed continuous headers in the living room (and throughout the house), and mortised all the upright trim members—door and window cases—to receive them. Indeed, wherever two pieces of wood came together in this room they were either scarf joined, finger joined, mortised and tenoned or lap joined.

The most time-consuming and difficult woodworking jobs in the living room were the construction of nine wood-and-glass lanterns, an enclosed bookcase, and an inglenook bench. The Japanese-inspired lanterns averaged over 30 separate parts each, and required much meticulous care in construction (photo and drawing, top of next page). These characteristic Greene and Greene style lanterns were attached to an inverted L-shaped bracket, which notched over the header trim and was screwed to both it and the wall below. The screws were recessed in square holes and then hidden behind ebony pegs. This attachment detail is used throughout the house. We don't know exactly how Peter Hall, the Greenes' craftsman builder, executed this detail. We did it by cutting the holes with a square, hollow-chisel mortiser and then tapping in a tapered oversized peg. The pegs were made from a long stick of ebony, milled to the proper size and then sliced like bread; then each one was tapered on a belt sander. Numerous small details like these pegs give a restoration job the stamp of authenticity.

The enclosed bookcase and inglenook bench are two of my favorite pieces. They were both designed along the general lines of the originals (we did not have details) and built out of Honduras mahogany. The framing members in both are joined with mortise and tenon. Panels are allowed to float free in their frames, so that wood movement across the grain of wide pieces wouldn't break the frame joints open. Some of the finger joints and tenons were locked with a screw, which in turn was set in a counterbore and hidden behind a peg. Since there is a gap under the peg, allowance is provided for the screw to move with the wood.

The dining room—By the time we finished the living room, we were really getting good at the kind of joinery and detailing that were such an integral part of Craftsman architecture. Work in the dining room, which was our next focus, went smoothly and quickly in spite of the many details. We had reached our stride. The original dining room had been paneled in Honduras mahogany veneer. In-

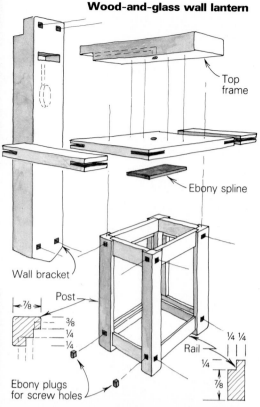

Wood-and-glass wall lantern

Top frame

Ebony spline

Wall bracket

Post

7/8

3/8
1/4
1/4

1/4 1/4

Rail

1/4

7/8

Ebony plugs
for screw holes

stead of trying to reproduce the veneer or buy high-quality mahogany plywood in these widths, we borrowed a pattern from the entry hall that used narrower sections of paneling separated by battens. For the panel sections we used ⅝-in. plywood with a Honduras mahogany face veneer. This was made to order for us by a local company and was surprisingly economical. This paneling was used with solid mahogany trim. We nailed the panels directly to the studs, being careful to align all nails so that they would be covered by the battens. The baseboard and continuous header were mortised to receive the battens, which were then finish-nailed to the panels. After filling, these nail holes were virtually invisible. In this fashion we achieved a tight batten-to-panel fit and also were assured that we would never have an open joint where the battens met the header and baseboard.

We also built a nook complete with window seats for this room. And we made nine more lanterns. The overhead lantern in this room is another one of my favorite pieces. It took almost two weeks to make. Even without the glass this lantern ended up weighing close to 50 lb. We attached it to the ceiling with four lag bolts screwed into the joists.

We achieved a beautiful color and patina on the paneling and other mahogany in this room and throughout the house by means of a technique we developed through experimentation. This technique involved first rubbing in a paste filler (if you don't use this, it will end up looking like lauan), followed by an application of clear sealer. Next came a pure green stain which we mixed ourselves. This stain, when applied over the reddish mahogany, produces a beautiful brown color. After the stain had dried, we applied three coats of a tung-oil base finish, rubbing between coats with 4-0 steel wool. The process is not as time-consuming as it sounds, and produces beautiful results. We used a tung-oil product throughout the house, except on areas that were subject to wear or friction of any kind. In these places we used polyurethane varnish and rubbed it out with steel wool or 3M pads until we got the desired patina. □

Made by Glen Stewart, a Pasadena woodworker, the Greene and Greene style wall lantern, top left, consists of over 30 parts, and is accented by ebony splines and square ebony plugs. The inverted L-shape mounting bracket is notched over the header strip and screwed to the wall, as shown in the drawing.

A signature of Greene and Greene detailing is the double-keyed scarf joint. It is sometimes used structurally, as in the beams, and sometimes used decoratively, as in the header trim, shown in the photo center left. To articulate the connection, the edges of the joining pieces are chamfered, and the keys are left standing proud. The header strip is mortised to house tenons on the vertical battens, and rabbeted to accept the paneling.

Far left, a pegged and chamfered finger joint connects pieces of header trim. Left, detail of the inglenook bench shows how the post is through-tenoned into the arm.

Restoring Fountainhead

Brilliant in form and function but flawed in structure, a Frank Lloyd Wright house is renewed by a thoughtful and thorough architect

by Tim Snyder

When J. Willis Hughes was in college studying geology in 1930, he clipped an article out of the local newspaper in Austin, Tex. It was about a well-known architect, Frank Lloyd Wright, whose ideas on designing houses were unusual and impressive. Almost 20 years passed before Hughes sent Wright the clipping, along with a letter asking the architect to design a house for him and his family in Jackson, Miss. In this span of time Hughes had made a small fortune in oil speculation. Wright, at 81, was at the height of his fame. Although he was busy with plans for the Guggenheim Museum, he invited the Hughes family to visit him at Taliesin East, and agreed to design their house.

By October of 1949 the plans were ready, but the ups and downs of the oil business kept the house from completion until late in 1954. It received a lot of local publicity, and Wright and Mrs. Hughes christened the house Fountainhead, after Ayn Rand's just-published novel, which had been inspired by Wright's career.

Wright hadn't visited the site before drawing up plans for the house. This wasn't an unusual practice for him at the time, but in this case some study of Mississippi's highly expansive soil would have been in order. By the time Robert Adams bought the house from Hughes in 1979, the slab floors had cracked and shifted. Water had leaked in through the roof and damaged large sections of interior woodwork, and many of the large windows had broken with the shifting of floors and walls. Hughes had struggled to repair the buckled floors and broken windows. The untimely death of his wife and a series of dry oilwells brought hard times, and many of his friends urged him to sell the house. More than one developer spoke of razing the house and building a conventional home that could bring a good price. Fortunately Hughes held on to Fountainhead, and in Adams he found an architect whose regard for Wright would ensure a thorough restoration. But rather than start with the house as Adams found it, let's begin with Wright's design.

Breaking out of the box—From the outset, Wright was adamant in his desire to abandon the box-like house with its formal, compart-

Mary Adams scrubs down the chimney in the master bedroom to remove mildew and termite tubes. Leaks in the flat section of roof around the chimney caused moisture damage to wood and concrete, here and elsewhere in the house.

Photo: Robert Parker Adams

mentalized plan. He also insisted on a varied landscape instead of a flat, featureless building site. Before contacting Wright, Hughes had purchased what he considered to be an excellent lot in one of Jackson's best residential sections. It was gently sloping and well drained, with no major site features or trees. Wright rejected it, and told Hughes to find at least an acre of land with some unusual characteristics. Hughes bought up sections of four different lots in an area originally intended to be a cemetery. It was a throwaway site, sloping down steeply from the street toward a gully. Satisfied, Wright agreed to start designing.

In keeping with the fashion of the late 1940s, Mrs. Hughes wanted a split-level house. When the plans arrived by mail, she was astonished. The design was boldly geometric, with walls of concrete and glass, a poured slab floor, and an open, informal plan on one level. It was about as far from the conventional split-level house as one could imagine. But Hughes accepted it, with one reservation. He needed four bedrooms rather than three, as originally requested. Wright had to revise the plan and proportion the spaces anew. Construction got under way in the spring of 1951.

Mastering the grid—Wright designed many of his houses on a strong horizontal grid. The connected squares or rectangles, visible on his plan drawings, were often actually inscribed in the poured slab floors. Window and door locations, wall intersections and roof overhangs all related to this grid, unifying the different parts of the house. Fountainhead is unusual because Wright used a parallelogram as the basic grid unit. It was a shape suggested by the site's contour lines. Two equilateral triangles with a common base form the parallelogram, yielding pairs of 60° and 120° angles. Wright had the parallelogram grid inscribed in the concrete driveway, and carried throughout the house (drawing, facing page). Walls meet at either 60° or 120°, defining spaces that are difficult to measure in conventional terms. As Adams observes, "If you asked me what the square footage of a room is, I couldn't tell you, but I do know that the area and volume feel right, and that's the essence of Wright's designs."

Because parallelograms have two pairs of congruent angles, one would expect an equal number of obtuse and acute intersections throughout the house. But this isn't the case. Where walls meet at 120°, space flows comfortably, and corners can be taken in stride. Acute inside corners are difficult to find. Rather than cramp the interior space, Wright used the 60° angle to create dramatic effects with sharp outside corners, angled shelves and unexpected wedges of space.

The parallelogram module is restated subtly in the unique board-and-batten paneling used throughout the house on walls and ceilings. Unlike conventional square-sided battens, these were rabbeted and ripped at an angle to present a triangular reveal. Adams had to duplicate this detail when he replaced some damaged paneling on one of the bedrooms. The job gave him an appreciation for how time-consuming it must have been to run all that batten stock through a table saw.

Wright also cast the module into the walls of Fountainhead. Before the walls were poured, workers ripped 2x4s diagonally and nailed the resulting 30°-60°-90° triangular strips horizontally inside the forms according to Wright's instructions. The strips created four horizontal rustications—simulated joint lines—in the finished walls. The lowest rustication defines sill height at the back, or private, side of the house; the second line is for sills on the street side; and the third marks the height of doors. The fourth rustication is around the central fireplace mass, the highest wall in the house. It defines the height of the kitchen entries. A sense of horizontal strength was an important part of Wright's style, and here it breaks the otherwise monolithic appearance of the massive walls, and accents the angular grid.

Including a basement was a concession to the sloping site. Wright usually avoided basements because their typically damp, windowless atmosphere ran counter to his sense of livable space. Ironically, the Hughes family actually lived in the basement for a short time while the rest of the house was being completed.

The gallery in the west wing of the house is another unusual feature. The small, triangular panes of glass glazed into the wood-frame west wall transform this back hallway into a display of sunlight.

Construction—The massive concrete walls, some of them 2 ft. thick, were formed and poured without footings. Visitors to the building site at this early stage might easily have mistaken the thick, angular concrete forms for the beginnings of a modern fortress.

The house has a radiant floor of integrally colored concrete, a design feature that Wright had used successfully in many earlier houses. Workers first laid down asphalt-impregnated felt over the compacted soil between the finished walls. Then several inches of pea gravel were spread out as a bed for the cast-iron heating pipes. These were laid out across floor areas throughout the house and welded together, creating a single loop that would later be linked to a furnace-fired water heater. Plumbing supply and waste lines were also roughed in, and a final layer of gravel was added. When the concrete had been poured, workers floated in red pigment and scribed the parallelogram grid in the leveled surface while it was still wet.

Wright knew that cypress is a decay-resistant wood, and the fact that it is native to Mississippi made it even more appropriate for Fountainhead. He specified only clear boards, cut from the heartwood of tidewater red cypress, the densest and most colorful subspecies. This wood was used inside and outside the house for siding, ceilings, interior walls, doors and all of the built-in furniture. Wright used pine boards as a substrate on walls and roof.

On the street side of the house, windows at eye level give privacy as well as a view. In contrast, the garden side of the house has large expanses of glass. The glass doors that open onto the terrace from the living room are nearly 14 ft. high. Fountainhead also has three glass corners, a design that Wright first used in his well-known house, Fallingwater, in 1937.

Wright's fondness for dramatic effect may explain one of Fountainhead's most bizarre details. To create the glass wall that separates the hallway from the dining terrace on the west side of the house, Wright had a large pane of glass cast into the concrete wall. The glass has long since cracked, but Adams intends to restore the original detail.

The cantilevered roof that shades the terrace relies on a hidden steel girder and on the stressed skin of plywood roof sheathing that is held in compression between facing wall sections. Two-by-six rafters were used to frame the roof. The house was built with one small flat section of roof, located around the main chimney mass at the center of the house. Covered with builder's felt and hot asphalt according to Wright's specifications, it was the area where most of the leaks developed.

Inside the house—The angularity of the house made it difficult to furnish. Wright helped solve this problem by designing most of the furniture himself. The long bench against the living-room wall with its adjoining end table was built in, as was the seating in the dining alcove. Ottomans shaped like equilateral triangles took the place of dining-room chairs, and the shape of the dining table was also derived from the

Dwarfed by angular wall sections, workers, below, use a transit to level the ground in preparation for the poured concrete floor. At right, walls without footings and unreinforced joints soon succumbed to the swelling and shrinking of the Mississippi Yazoo clay.

J. Willis Hughes

Neil Arrington

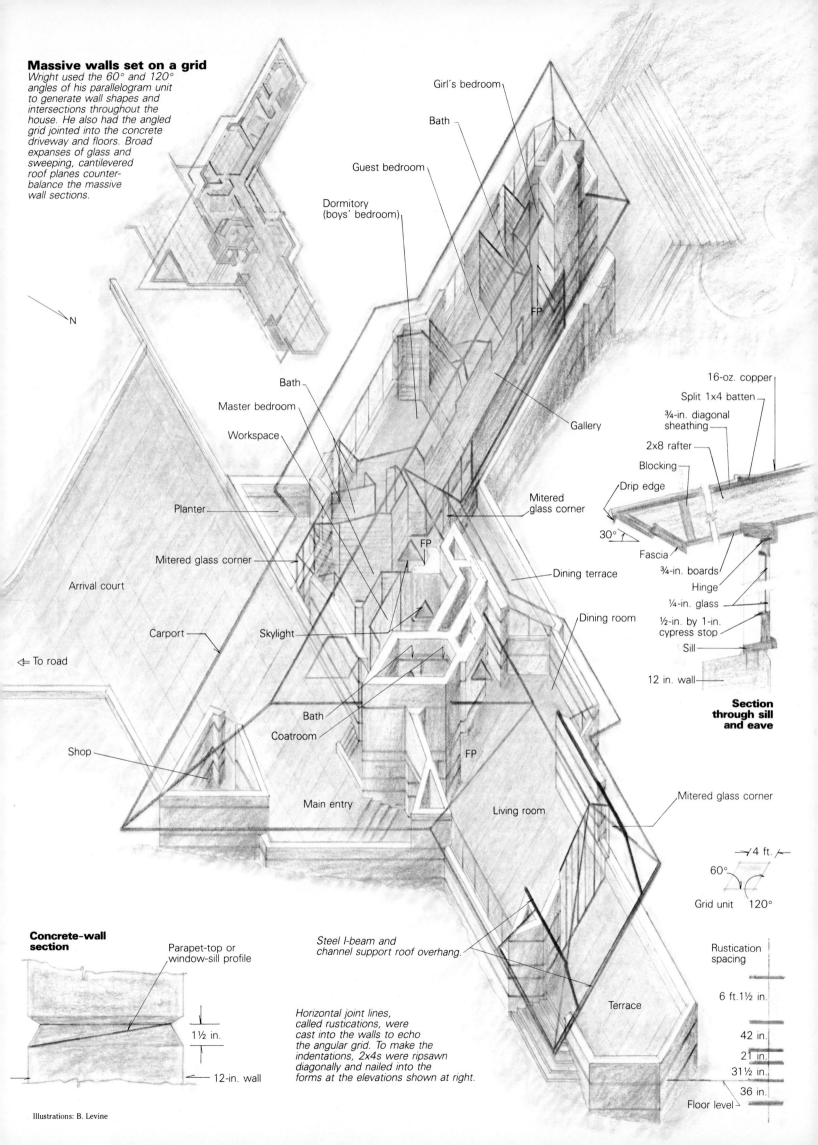

Massive walls set on a grid
Wright used the 60° and 120° angles of his parallelogram unit to generate wall shapes and intersections throughout the house. He also had the angled grid jointed into the concrete driveway and floors. Broad expanses of glass and sweeping, cantilevered roof planes counter- balance the massive wall sections.

N

Girl's bedroom

Bath

Guest bedroom

Dormitory (boys' bedroom)

Bath

Master bedroom

Workspace

Planter

Mitered glass corner

Arrival court

Carport

⇐ To road

Skylight

Bath

Coatroom

Shop

Main entry

Gallery

Mitered glass corner

Dining terrace

Dining room

FP

FP

Living room

Terrace

16-oz. copper

Split 1x4 batten

¾-in. diagonal sheathing

2x8 rafter

Blocking

Drip edge

30°

Fascia

¾-in. boards

Hinge

¼-in. glass

½-in. by 1-in. cypress stop

Sill

12 in. wall

Section through sill and eave

Mitered glass corner

→ 4 ft. ←

60°

Grid unit   120°

Rustication spacing

6 ft.1½ in.

42 in.

21 in.

31½ in.

36 in.

Floor level

Concrete-wall section

Parapet-top or window-sill profile

1½ in.

12-in. wall

Steel I-beam and channel support roof overhang.

Horizontal joint lines, called rustications, were cast into the walls to echo the angular grid. To make the indentations, 2x4s were ripsawn diagonally and nailed into the forms at the elevations shown at right.

Illustrations: B. Levine

Ceilings

Angled cypress battens

Cypress boards

¾-in. board ceiling

⅞-in. pineboard core

Plate from 2x4s

Special batten

⅛-in. by ¼-in. metal strip

Board-and-batten wall

Concrete floor

Section through mullion

Unit or half-unit line

From 1x4

Cypress stop

Glass

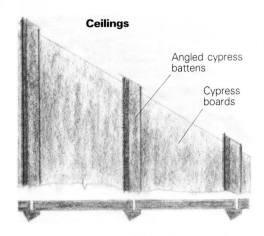

Below, ottomans, chairs (without their cushions) and a built-in bench designed by Wright fill a living-room corner.

Adams restored the kitchen by rescuing the refrigerator with spare parts, replacing the copper countertop, and refinishing the woodwork. Generous work surfaces and open shelving are features that Wright incorporated in many of his houses.

Mitered glass corners (facing page) and glass cast into a wall (above) boldly break down the barrier between interior and exterior space, yet they are structurally unsound.

Beneath geometrically patterned screens designed by Wright, Adams is reconstructing a built-in bed and table from the original plans. This is the back bedroom closest to the pool.

The gallery. This paneled passageway, with its triangular lites and cantilevered shelves, connects the bedroom wing with the living room, dining room, kitchen and main entry.

Still sheltering tools and materials for the restoration, the carport (top photo) also serves as the main entry. The smaller door to the left opens into the kitchen. Living-room windows and the cantilevered roof over the terrace are visible through the opening. Above, a view from the living-room terrace. Set into its sloping lot, angled around the back garden and shaded by trees and roof overhangs, the restored house reflects the unconventional ingenuity of its architect.

parallelogram. The Hughes' bed was built in, and in the boys' bedroom Wright designed a four-bed bunk and an ingenious built-in dresser with parallelogram drawers.

As in most Wright houses, the kitchen is at the core of things, and is close to the hearth. Wright preferred to call the kitchen a workspace, since this word implies a more general use for a part of the house formerly reserved for the housewife or servant. Locating the workspace next to the hearth had another benefit: The chimney could be used as a ventilation stack. Wright raised the ceiling and put in a skylight and vent so that heat and cooking odors could exhaust naturally, eliminating the need for fans or air conditioning.

Wright designed the patterned cypress shutters after the rest of the house was finished. Each 10-in. wide panel is made from two or three separate boards, joined with their grains reversed to counteract warp. Though the unusual pattern contains 60° and 120° angles, its complexity far exceeds that of the grid. Adams sees both Southwestern Indian and Japanese influences in the pattern. Its effect is striking—sun streaks through the small, angled openings, casting a geometry of light and shadow on floors and walls.

Another interesting detail is Wright's use of piano hinges for all of the house's screens and interior doors. With one screw per inch, the brass hardware is painfully tedious to remove and re-install, a fact that Adams discovered when he restored folding kitchen doors that had been hung with more than 300 screws.

The restoration—Soil conditions in Mississippi caused problems for Fountainhead from the start. Yazoo clay, as it is locally known, makes up the greater part of the subsoil and can exert tremendous pressure on a foundation as it swells and shrinks with groundwater changes. Even footings heavily laced with rebar have done the Yazoo shuffle after a few years in the ground, so Wright's lightly reinforced concrete was bound to join the dance. Even before the slab had been poured, some of the wall sections had cracked. The floor slab had fared the worst, however. From 3 in. to 10 in. thick, the concrete floor eventually dropped a total of 18¾ in. from terrace to back bedroom. Plumbing lines and radiant-heating pipes broke, floor and wall sections cracked and settled, and the roof peak above the living room actually separated as walls drifted apart. Buckling floor sections jammed doors shut and broke glass.

Adams tackled these structural problems first when he bought the house. After taking measurements to determine how far out of line the floors and walls were, Adams decided that the only way to raise and stabilize the settled floor sections was by mud-jacking. A liquid mix of mud, cement and sand was pumped beneath the foundation under pressure, forcing the slab upward and filling voids. Adams said that with the first pumping the mud mixture oozed and squirted out of cracks throughout the house. In spite of the resulting mess, this squeeze-out had to be left to dry so that there would be sealed bearing surfaces for subsequent pumping. Hy-

The fountain and pool were added a short time after the house was finished in 1954. Like the walls and floors throughout the house, both had to be repaired by Adams to complete the restoration. Only the original copper roof has survived undamaged.

draulic pressure threatened to force sections of wall apart, so tie-bolts had to be run under the house and through walls to contain the liquid. Nearly 150 cu. yd. of mix was pumped under the slab. Though this raised and consolidated floors and walls, there were still slight variations in floor height and numerous cracks to repair. The broken plumbing lines in the back bathroom were dug out and repaired, and Adams had the original porcelain shower stall reglazed. Even after mud-jacking beneath the slab and leveling skimcoats on top of it, there was no assurance that the expansive Yazoo clay wouldn't cause damage in the future. To keep moisture from collecting in the soil around the house, Adams dug trenches around exterior walls and installed curtain drains.

The splayed rafters in the living room and the leaking flat roof section were other immediate problems. A second ridgeboard, sistered to the original, made up the difference between opposing rafters that had been pulled apart. Adams and his wife, Mary, took down the mildewed cypress paneling, stripped it, and then treated it with bleach to kill the mold. They sanded smooth the raised grain, and then applied a mixture of stain and varnish to duplicate the look of undamaged cypress.

On some sections of the chimney mass, ter-

mite tubes and mildew had to be removed by brushing the concrete down with a dilute solution of muriatic acid. While removing several mildewed cypress boards, Adams discovered that termites had made their way into the fir plywood behind an interior wall, so the damaged sheathing was replaced.

New tar and flashing restored the flat roof section to its original condition, but Adams admits that this part of the roof will require maintenance from time to time to keep water out of the house. The sloped roof on the rest of the house was in good shape, and only a few of the copper seams had to be recrimped.

There were other exterior repairs as well—filling in cracks in the walls and replacing damaged wood siding. It took Adams a long time to find a source for tidewater cypress heartwood. Once the new boards had been nailed in place, they had to be stained in stages to match the original siding.

Wright had considered one oven in the workspace to be insufficient because the Hughes family entertained often, so he designed space for two to be built into the concrete fireplace mass. Today, double ovens are common, but Adams couldn't find units small enough to fit into the openings. Jackhammering the concrete to accommodate the larger ovens took two

weeks. The original brushed-copper countertops were replaced, and Adams was able to rescue the old refrigerator with parts from an identical model found in the basement.

A new pool—As the house was being completed in 1954, Wright added a pool at the end of the gallery, off the back bedroom. Designed as a "pond in a woodland glade," according to Wright, it had its own fountain and waterfall and was surrounded by lush vegetation. But like Fountainhead's concrete floors, the thin pool walls had cracked severely over the years. Pouring a new pool and rebuilding the fountain were Adams' last major reconstruction jobs.

There's still some work to be done on Fountainhead. When visitors come to marvel at the restoration work, Adams can walk through the house and point out small jobs that will get his attention in the months ahead: spot refinishing, painting, landscaping and the like. There's even an old jukebox in the basement, full of 45s from the 1950s, that Adams would like to restore. He admits that the project often seemed impossible in its early stages. But he feels that living and working with the house on such an intense level have brought him close to Wright, perhaps in a way more personal than had they known each other. □

A Greek Revival Restoration

Uncovering the secrets of the Josiah Durkee house

by Gregory Schipa

The Josiah Durkee house, reclaimed, restored and relocated on a knoll at the Bent Hill Settlement in Waitsfield, Vt.

I found the Josiah Durkee house hidden in a pine grove, sinking slowly into the earth of Brookfield, Vt. A small, two-story Greek Revival building, it was not the showy result of an addition to a primitive homestead, but the original creation of local craftsmen who had adapted the popular style to a rural setting. They had retained, even at the late date of 1836, many Federal touches, including moldings and dentils identical to those on older houses in the neighborhood. Josiah Durkee clearly had wanted a stately home in the latest architectural style, but like most of us, he had a limited budget. The result was a genuine piece of folk art, a fine mixture of pride, frugality and romantic whimsey.

Part of my business is dismantling old houses board by board, then transporting, restoring and raising them again at the Bent Hill Settlement in Waitsfield, Vt. We don't sell a building until it is as perfectly detailed as we can make it, so as we disassemble an old structure we look closely for evidence of its original state.

Details—The key to the original detail puzzle often lies in a single 6-in. piece of buried chair rail, baseboard or casing. Durkee, for example, put most of his effort into his best room, where we discovered evidence of beautiful raised panels buried in the plaster under the windows. These I raised anew to match the doors. The window and door casings were built up with three molding cuts: a ¼-in. bead, a ½-in. ogee and a large cove with bead. I matched the casings on the interior of the formal entrance and built up two panels below the side lights. The chair rail we saved intact, a beautiful complement to the casing detail.

Where moldings have been removed, the careful eye will see them mirrored in the grain of the trim they covered. My early assessment of the Durkee house uncovered the complete front pediment detail mirrored in this way, partially covered and protected by asphalt siding. It included crown molding and complete cornice, rake and bed moldings with full dentil work, as well as the frieze and frieze molding. Removing details is best accomplished with at least two patient workers, very sharp, flat bars and good scaffolding. The securing nails cannot be removed without damage until the piece is raised a

bit with pressure from a flat bar driven behind it, and then gently returned to its original position, exposing the nail heads. On the original casement I found an early window detail mirrored in profile on the old sheathing, showing us the original drip cap and molding. It was also the profile on the sheathing that gave me the first evidence of the size of Durkee's remarkable front entrance. The width of the side casings indicated the presence of pilasters. Knowing this, and finding the original double-stud mortises on each side, I could replace the entrance in its original spot. Better yet, the basement shelves yielded the transom and side lights of the old entrance. With the original door still in use, the reconstruction was complete.

Another key detail is the gable treatment. Early gables generally did not overhang, hence the gable's fascia and rake were actually the same piece. This detail is often one of the old house's best-kept secrets, with the seam made by the extension at the gable and creation of the cornice returns very skillfully hidden. Later gable details of the Greek Revival period were often characterized by the full pediment formed by joining the cornice returns. This created a classic look in the Greek style. Josiah Durkee must have wanted this formal look over his magnificent portal, but, a true Yankee, he spent his efforts on the front pediment only. Walking around back, I found a more austere cornice resolved in simple returns.

Windows and doors—On the Durkee house, both sashes and casements of all windows had been changed. The new windows had been left in their original locations on the long-eave side of the house, but they had been too big to fit into the gable ends. Victorian renovators had solved this problem by simply leaving some out. To accurately restore original windowpane size, I merely compared the rough opening to those of neighboring houses built at approximately the same time. In this case they were 6 in. by 6 in. lights in a 12 over 12 configuration. In the pediment, however, I found a large rectangle of new sheathing and widely-spaced gable studs, so I had to make an educated guess. Rectangular, arch and elliptical styles were all appropriate in the Greek Revival

Both Federal and Greek Revival architecture were neoclassical styles, taking inspiration from ancient Greece and Rome. It might be helpful to think of Federal as the merging of the Colonial tradition with England's more sophisticated Late Georgian style, which took the delicate detailing and graceful proportions of Roman domestic architecture as its model. Men like Charles Bulfinch of Boston and Samuel McIntire of Salem created masterpieces incorporating new, functional interior plans with beautifully proportioned details. New England reticence toned down the extravagance of the English style, and the result was the austere dignity that is the hallmark of Federal architecture. Less sophisticated builders, often working from such design books as Asher Benjamin's *The Country Builder's Assistant*, *The Practical House Carpenter*, and early editions of *The American Builder's Companion*, simply added Federal details to houses they had been building along familiar lines, much as modern contractors add popular touches to standard ranch houses.

Federal architecture was widely accepted well into the 19th century, especially in New England, but many influential men wanted little to do with an English-inspired style. Trained architects, a new development in America, consciously searched for a form to suit a young republic. They turned first to a sturdier use of Roman structural systems, and then to what many of them considered the purer classicism of ancient Greece—simple, straightforward, and therefore more appropriate. But while leading architects turned to Greece for intellectual reasons, the style caught on for emotional ones. The rebellion of the modern Greeks against the Turks had captured Americans' imaginations. The country was beginning to feel its Jacksonian oats, and a link with the embattled cradle of democracy satisfied a number of symbolic needs. Naturally, most builders remained more interested in imitating popular details than in attempting to articulate in their work the philosophical underpinnings of the style. Some of them carefully copied classical forms in fashioning the most spectacular examples of what we now know as Greek Revival architecture. Many more simply added a Doric porch or portico to an existing structure, and others built houses that satisfied some superficial convention of the new fashion, while not differing greatly from traditional patterns. This is what Josiah Durkee did when he addressed his formal gable entrance to the small country lane passing by, creating a Greek temple in Brookfield, Vermont.   —*Mark Alvarez*

Development of Greek Revival

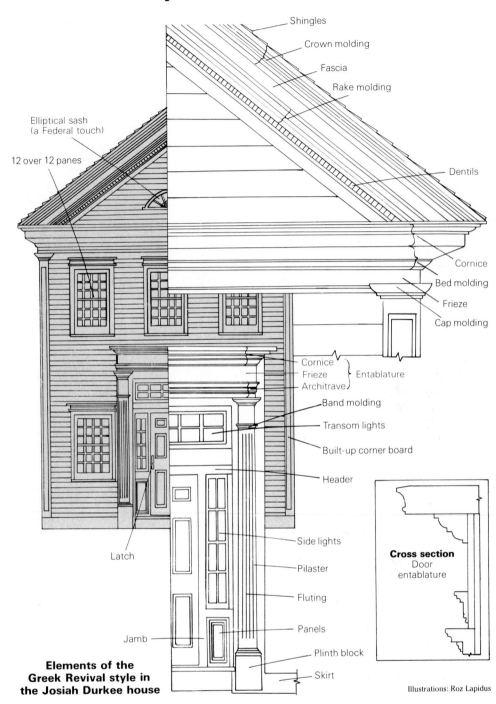

Shingles
Crown molding
Fascia
Rake molding
Dentils
Cornice
Bed molding
Frieze
Cap molding
Elliptical sash (a Federal touch)
12 over 12 panes
Cornice
Frieze
Architrave
Entablature
Band molding
Transom lights
Built-up corner board
Header
Side lights
Pilaster
Fluting
Panels
Plinth block
Skirt
Latch
Jamb

Cross section
Door entablature

Elements of the Greek Revival style in the Josiah Durkee house

Illustrations: Roz Lapidus

---

period. Josiah cut no corners on his formal front, so I chose a nice elliptical window, also appropriate to a transition house. The builders, after all, had certainly been affected by the Federal style they had worked in previously.

Although restorable windows are rare, original doors in decent shape are fairly common. In Durkee's house, I found good, solid six-panel doors on the first floor and matching four-panel doors upstairs. These were handmade raised panels, with thumbnail moldings cut on the stiles and rails. They had only one layer of original milk paint and their latches were intact. Of all the doors in the house, only the exterior ones needed restoration. We pulled all pegs on the

damaged doors, replaced broken stiles or rails and glued the joints. We then replaced the pegs. Although originally doors were not glued, we've found that it tightens them nicely.

Hardware—Old hardware is gold in the restoration and antiques world. As a result, most original hardware has been removed from old houses. It is important to locate and remove all hinges and latches that may have survived; a good blacksmith can reproduce them later. Suffolk latches and Bean latches predate Norfolk latches, which have handles attached to flat metal plates. If latches are original, a careful check will show that they are attached to the

wood beneath the first layer of paint. The sharp eye will more often be forced to observe only the outlines of removed hinges and latches, which can sometimes indicate the style of the original hardware. The Durkee house had all original latches. Better yet, the builder had used Suffolk latches, considerably older than the house, secured with old, blunt-tipped screws first available in the early 1800s. (I like these crooked old screws, especially because their makers never seemed to place the screwdriver slot in the middle.)

Floors—Original floors in the Vermont area are almost always wide, hard, jack-planed pine,

Joists are left exposed in upstairs ceilings (top). Schipa restored the original stairway and balustrade (above), and salvaged the firebox and surround (above right). The transom and side lights of the original entrance (right) were found in the cellar of the old house.

usually painted either red or gray. They are more than 1 in. thick, placed over a ½-in. underlayment of rough pine or spruce. Their edges are always simply butted. Exceptional floors often exhibit invaluable examples of stenciling, grainwork or spatterwork, all conceived to brighten floors before carpets had evolved from the popular bed rug. I discovered to my delight that the front bedchamber of the Durkee house had, under layers of filth, faint black grainwork on gray paint. This, combined with near-perfect original jack-planed

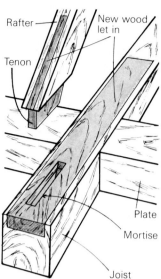

floors, constituted a fabulous find, which was enhanced by the fact that the old maple stairs came out intact and went right back in the restoration, untouched. Original stairs were usually replaced with a straight run when the chimney mass was removed. We always keep a sharp eye out, especially in the cellar hole and attic, for hints of even one original carved or turned baluster or post. An entire balustrade intact is rare indeed, but we found one in perfect condition in the Durkee house. It was extremely simple—hand-planed, and with the classic ogee on the railing—and seemed to predate the house. Perhaps the builder was an old man when he dabbled in Greek Revival, and retained some favorite details of an earlier time. He certainly built with integrity, for the rigid balustrade could only be shifted after complete removal of all wooden pegs.

Roof

Roof—The oldest post-and-beam structures in Vermont are hardwood, usually oak or beech. After 1800, most houses were built of pine, with hardwood bracing and oak pegs. The real key to structural health, however, seems to lie not in the type of wood used in the frame, but in the quality of roof maintenance by the building's previous owners. I don't regard so-called dry rot in the understructure as a serious problem, routinely effecting a complete restoration there. But continuous seepage of water through a disintegrating roof slowly eats through mortise and tenon joints, and the house deteriorates quickly beyond the point of no return. The finest restoration prospects always seem to be those that received metal roofs before abandonment. Many others in excellent shape lasted because of a change to slate roofing in the late 1800s. The Durkee house's old asphalt roof, though way past its prime, was caught just in time. Our repairs were limited to scarfing pieces onto the two-story posts that had been mercilessly hacked out during reckless renovation.

The most damaging leaks are those at the eaves, because they destroy the joint at the rafter base and at the end of the joist or girt,

causing a collapse from the natural outward thrust of the rafter weight. The sensitive point at which the 8x8 attic joists lapped the eave plate on Durkee's house, tying the house together, had taken some moisture on the south side. I let in new wood on the top of each joist, replacing questionable, punky places and creating new, strong mortises. The rafter tenons were in good shape, and could be reused. When they are too far gone, we remove them by cutting right up the middle of the rafter for three or four feet. We then let in a new 2-in. thick hardwood plank to the full depth of the rafter, like replacing the contents of a sandwich. The tenon is then recut at the extending end of this piece.

Chimney mass—The arrival of the efficient wood stove spelled an almost immediate and complete end to the original chimney masses used in Vermont for heating and cooking until the second quarter of the 19th century. Some of the handmade bricks were reused in new stove chimneys and foundation repairs. An old wooden surround found buried in wall plaster or thrown in an attic is often the last remnant of the chimney mass. Once again, the Durkee house proved to be an exception. We discovered its original mass intact, along with a hand-carved soapstone firebox in the parlor and a smaller bedroom fireplace with the original soapstone lintel. Although the formal surround in the parlor was badly damaged, it merited considerable effort. I took it apart and replaced the pilasters and plinth blocks, as well as some molding sections. I also pulled a bad cup out of the frieze board, using 2-in. screws driven into the studs and later covered with reeding. We included a chimney flue in the restoration, but restored the mass by rebuilding it from the old, handmade bricks, many bearing the fingerprints of our ancestors at the brickyard.

Some mysteries of detailing have little to do with historical styles or the ravages of time. When we took down the plaster ceiling of the second floor, we assumed we would find the original split lath. Instead, we discovered new lath, secured by new nails. Careful inspection revealed no other holes or evidence of previous ceiling lath. Without lath, there could have been no plaster. Josiah must have left the attic floor joists exposed in the second-floor ceiling, an inexplicably rough touch in such a formal house. Unless, of course, his frugality had gotten the better of him. I took great glee in leaving the joists exposed in honor of old Josiah Durkee. □

Gregory Schipa restores old houses in the Bent Hill Settlement, Waitsfield, Vt.

The Durkee house was a ruin when Schipa found it. Having suffered from both modernization and neglect, many of its original features were hidden. Schipa carefully dismantled it, unearthed many of its secrets, then rebuilt it using the original frame. (Above photos by the author.)

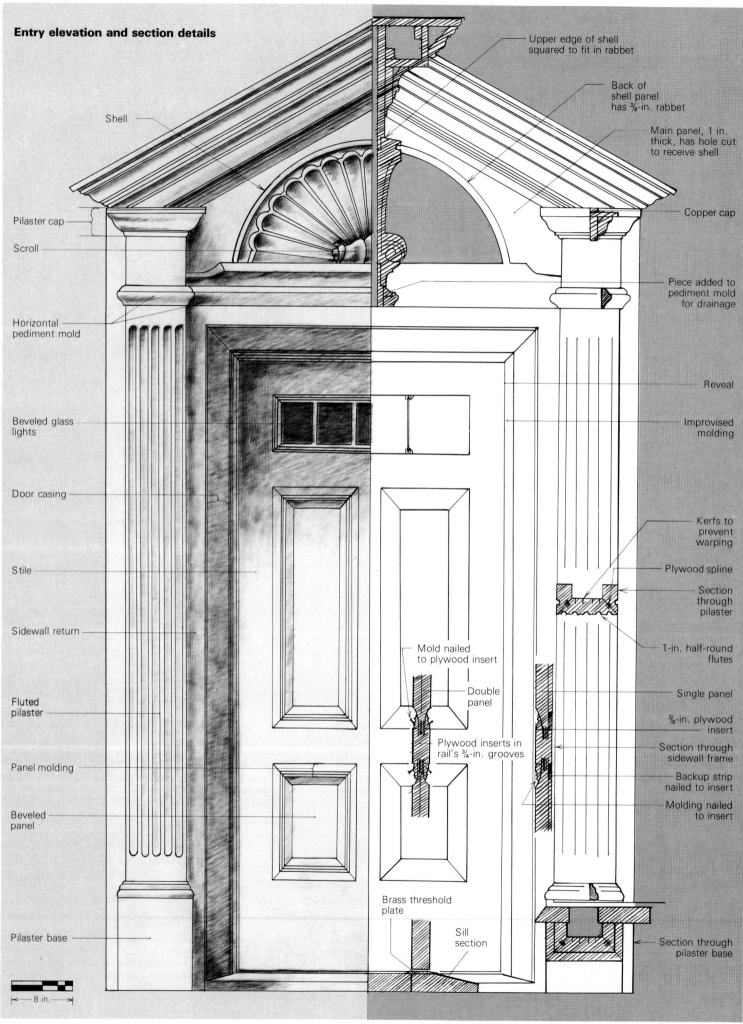

Entry elevation and section details

Shell

Upper edge of shell squared to fit in rabbet

Back of shell panel has ⅜-in. rabbet

Main panel, 1 in. thick, has hole cut to receive shell

Pilaster cap

Scroll

Copper cap

Horizontal pediment mold

Piece added to pediment mold for drainage

Reveal

Beveled glass lights

Improvised molding

Door casing

Kerfs to prevent warping

Plywood spline

Stile

Section through pilaster

Sidewall return

1-in. half-round flutes

Mold nailed to plywood insert

Single panel

Fluted pilaster

Double panel

⅜-in. plywood insert

Section through sidewall frame

Panel molding

Plywood inserts in rail's ¾-in. grooves

Backup strip nailed to insert

Beveled panel

Molding nailed to insert

Brass threshold plate

Pilaster base

Sill section

Section through pilaster base

|← 8 in. →|

Illustrations: Roz Lapidus

A blend of New England architectural elements, the new entryway features custom moldings, a shell carving and a copper-clad roof. The drawing on the facing page details the design.

Formal Entryway

A challenging adaptation of traditional designs

by Sam Bush

It was my pleasure to have been working for Pat Dillon, of Canby, Ore., when Mr. and Mrs. Alfred Herman asked him to build a new entry for their home in Portland. The 18-year-old existing door was not particularly well designed or constructed, and the Hermans wanted to replace it with one that incorporated various traditional elements. Pat often said that the doorway is the most important part of a residence because it introduces the people who live there. Pat and I liked the Hermans, and wanted them to be introduced properly.

We were a good combination of clients and carpenters for work of this sort. Pat is an experienced contractor with high standards for everything he undertakes. My own background is primarily in furnituremaking, cabinetmaking and woodcarving, but I also find enjoyment in challenging finish work. Pat had earned the confidence of the Hermans before I'd come along. It was encouraging to know that they trusted us to do a good job and that our workmanship would be appreciated.

Design and planning—Helen Herman had a pretty clear idea of how she wanted the entry to look: pedimented, with fluted pilasters on either side, and paneled sidewalls. The basic concept was simple elegance. So Pat and I did our research, visiting, photographing and sketching many doorways. This was great fun for me, as I had studied Colonial and Federal work all over New England. We presented our ideas, and after many conversations with Helen we arrived at the proportions and lines that captured what she had in mind. The final design is a personal one, though it is based on traditional elements. We consulted on every part, right down to the panel moldings, which were created with shaper cutters profiled to our drawings. Relying on the good eyes of three people, we strove for balance and attractiveness throughout.

There were two stages of construction: making all the parts in the shop (which took six weeks), and installing them (which took seven days). First came shop drawings and calculations. Pat had made discreet investigations of the substructure of the existing entry without disrupting its appearance too much. We used his measurements for planning and ordering lumber.

For everything but the shell, we used clear, vertical-grain old-stand fir, a wood readily available in the Northwest. It's expensive, but great to work with, except for a tendency to splinter. (One afternoon, as I was working to extract one of a long line of slivers, Pat jokingly accused me of trying to take home wood from the job.)

The frames—Our first job was making the door stiles and rails. All of it was made of 2¼-in. stock, and we chose the pieces very carefully to be sure they would stay straight after installation. All the joints were deep mortise and tenon, haunched top and bottom for strength, and glued. There was also a ¾-in. wide groove run up the inside of every framing member in the lower part of the

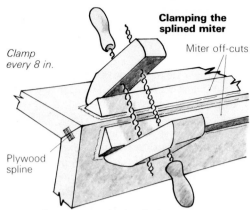

Clamping the splined miter

Clamp every 8 in.

Miter off-cuts

Plywood spline

Layer of newspaper glued to both miter off-cuts and surface allows for easy removal after clamps come off.

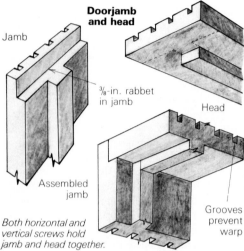

Doorjamb and head

Jamb

⅜-in. rabbet in jamb

Head

Assembled jamb

Grooves prevent warp

Both horizontal and vertical screws hold jamb and head together.

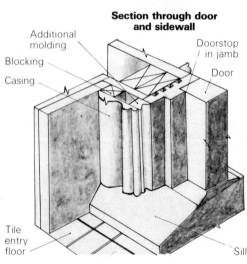

Section through door and sidewall

Additional molding

Blocking

Casing

Doorstop in jamb

Door

Tile entry floor

Sill

Door-frame construction is haunched mortise and tenon; grooves (photo below) will receive plywood inserts for attaching panel moldings. Long ears on door sill (photo bottom) will support door casing. Molding to receive lower right panels is already in place. Other joinery details are shown in the drawings at left.

---

door, to hold the plywood inserts to which panel moldings would be attached. We didn't put a groove in the top panel of the door, since a beveled-glass window would be located there.

Next came the framing for the ceiling and sidewalls, which was made from 1½-in. stock, with mortise-and-tenon construction like the door. We ran ⅜-in. grooves for plywood inserts that would be arranged slightly differently from those in the door. These frames were assembled with a wider stile on the inside so that when the door casing was installed, overlapping it, the remainder showing would be the same size as the outside piece. We also built mitered returns on sidewall and ceiling frames where they would turn and lie on the face sheathing of the building. We decided early on to use as few nails as

possible, knowing their tendency to move and show through, so we joined these miters with ¼-in. plywood splines and glued them with temporary clamp blocks made from the miter off-cuts, as shown in the drawing, top left.

Panels and molding—Door panels could have been made of single 2¼-in. pieces, but we chose to use two thicknesses back-to-back so that they could adjust individually to indoor and outdoor conditions, avoiding the tendency to warp. Each 1⅛-in. thickness was made of two edge-glued boards; we ran the edges on the shaper with a special glue-joint cutter to prevent creep along the joint. Almost every joint in the job was glued with Weldwood resorcinol waterproof glue.

We shaped the panels with a ⅜-in. tongue to

correspond with the plywood inserts. With the other cutter, we ran the molding that would hold the panels in place without inhibiting their natural movement. It was fairly easy to miter the molding on the chop saw and install the panels, which had been treated with wood preservative and primer paint. (All the parts were treated on both sides with two coats of Houston's #3 preservative and one coat of Kelley-Moore exterior primer before final installation.) We used Titebond to glue the molding to the plywood inserts before setting two finish nails on the horizontals and three on the verticals.

The other custom molding for this job was the 4½-in. wide door casing, similar to the panel molding, but larger. We were able to make some of it with shaper and router cutters, but the main line was really handmade, with a few table-saw cuts and a lot of scraping and planing.

Jamb, cornice and pilasters—We used solid stock for the door jamb, and grooved it on the back to prevent possible warp. The sill was screwed to the rabbeted jamb, flat under the door and sloping 5° on the outside, with long ears left on either side for the casings to rest on (photo left). After the jamb and sill were glued and screwed, the door was dimensioned and beveled, leaving a ³⁄₃₂-in. space all around to allow for paint. Hanging involved setting three brass-plated ball-bearing butts, 4½ in. by 4½ in., using a Stanley door guide and a router to make the hinge mortises. We also fitted the brass latch and the Baldwin Lexington-pattern lock hardware, and I can tell you it's an exacting task to get the precise mechanism just right and working smoothly. (And this is no time to drill a hole in the wrong place.) The striker plate was not set into the jamb until later. Making up and nailing on the molding that holds in the beveled glass window completed the door work.

Next, we drew a full-sized plan, on plywood, of one-half the triangular frieze and cornice area. We figured out the length of the roof and the sizes of the box structure to which the cornice would be attached, the main panel, the shell and its moldings. With this information we were able to make up all these parts and get them waterproofed and primed. Since the roof boards over the cornice and the pilaster caps were to be sheathed in copper, they were sent out to the sheet-metal shop for fitting.

The last step before installing the entryway was making the pilasters, which were mitered and splined like the sidewall returns. The major difficulty here was the fluting, which—like everything else—had to be just right: five 1-in. diameter half-round grooves on the face, with exactly ½ in. between them, and one groove on each side surface. I made these on the shaper, relying on a sample block to make the settings. Since the fluting didn't extend to the end of the pilasters, I had to drop the work onto the cutter and pull it off for each cut in accordance with layout lines on the work and the fence. I ran the cuts from both edges. The middle one was quite a reach for Pat's shaper, but everything worked out. The cutter left a peculiar-looking shape where it came out of the work, so I finished the ends of each flute with my carving gouges. After this we cut the pilasters to length and mounted a three-part molding at the top of each. We were finally done in the shop.

Installing the door—While we were doing all this, the tile men had been at the Hermans' laying a 4-in. by 8-in. quarry tile surface on the floor of the new entry. Our first task was to demolish the original finish work. The existing sidewalls were ½-in. plywood with molding nailed on to make them look paneled. Fitting all over was casual, and construction choices were ill considered. In fact, a great deal of water had gotten into the trim and rotted it.

Removing the old doorway was last, and meant we could start rebuilding. It also meant we would be there until the new door was in, since we weren't about to leave for the evening with a big hole in the house. Setting the jamb and sill assembly had to be particularly accurate to fit both the existing interior and the new exterior parts, but the installation was done conventionally. To help take the weight of this heavy door, we ran 3-in. #8 screws through the jamb into the rough framing. These were in the hinge mortises where they would be covered. With the door in place and swinging, I marked and mortised the jamb for the striker plate and dust box. I took special care here, wanting as a matter of pride to have the door close both easily and tightly.

Entry paneling and casing—After the door was installed, we started work on the ceiling unit, the panel of which was pierced to accommodate the overhead lamp. This frame had to be set an exact and uniform distance from the jamb so the door casing would fit evenly. We then leveled, shimmed and nailed it along its left and right edges with as few 16d galvanized finish nails as possible.

The sidewalls were next. Like the ceiling, they were located parallel to the jamb—no margin for error here. They were also scribed to fit both the ceiling (covering its nails) and the pitched tile floor, while showing as a plumb line on the outside face. To prevent rot, we held all our finish work ¼ in. off the tile.

It was at this point that we discovered the only serious mistake of the job. Somewhere back in the calculation stage, I had erred by an inch in the sidewall measurements, making them narrower than they should have been. While the casing fit to the walls, the visible vertical stiles were now of uneven widths, and the balanced effect was spoiled. They say the *real* skill of a carpenter shows in how he gets himself out of the mistakes he gets himself into. Pat earned his money that day, inventing a piece of molded stock that brought out the surface of the jamb and solved the problem. This disaster cost us time, materials and more than a few grey hairs, but as sometimes happens, the adjustment turned out to be an improvement. The additional molding looked natural and made the doorway look even better.

With sidewalls and improvised molding in, and corresponding blocking next to the wall, it was my job to set the handmade casing. There was a lot to keep in mind while I was working: There had to be an even reveal along the door

and perfect fit to the wall; both of the miters had to be tight and meet the corners of the wall and ceiling frames; the side pieces had to be cut at 5° on the bottom to sit on the angled sill—and there was no extra stock.

Around the entry—Next, we moved to the face of the house. We determined where the exterior vertical sticks would rest, and cut the cedar siding to the chalk line using a portable circular saw against a straight board. Likewise we made the angled cuts for the peak, after carefully measuring to ensure that the peak was plumb above the ceiling midline. When the side pieces were laid, they were tight against the siding, with their surfaces in line with the sidewall returns. They were also bedded in a thick corner bead of butyl caulking, which sealed the joint. We later ran another tiny bead of colored caulking along the surface of the siding where it met the side pieces.

Next, we notched the roof boards to fit over the siding, and toenailed them into the sheathing. We screwed blocking under their outer edges, then fit them into their copper covers, working a long flange of the metal up behind the siding. We bent the covers around the roof front edge, where we discreetly nailed it into the blocking with four copper nails. An overlapping, interlocking joint between copper sheets along its apex rendered the roof watertight. Then we mounted the 1-in. thick main panel on shims that brought it out flush with the 1½-in. trim. The back of the shell carving would eventually fit into the space behind the panel, so the shims were placed accordingly.

With the background and roof in place, we fastened the pilasters plumb, leaving an equal width of vertical boards on both sides of each one. The top moldings were already attached, so we needed only to add the angled cap pieces with their matching copper covers. At the base

we nailed on the 1-in. thick spline-mitered base assemblies, after first scribing them to fit the tile. We cut and installed the molding along the tops of the bases to complete the pilasters.

The cornice box went up next, against the roof and backwall blocking, mitered at the top. Putting up the detailed cornice moldings was just about the most trying part of the whole job. A combination of factors—difficult miters inside and outside, close reveals, scribing to the siding, no extra material—left no room for error. But patience and a sharp block plane prevailed, and the parts fit as they were meant to. We used needlepoints, 1¼-in. galvanized finish nails, to fasten these moldings. They hold tightly and don't split the thin molding edges. Driven flush with the surface, they hold paint and don't show. We then installed the two-part detail inside the cornice box and above the shell. The moldings were mitered at the top, and died out against the pilaster caps. The last of the molding work was the strong horizontal piece right above the entry. Compared to the others, this one was simple because it was level, with regular 45° miters. Both Pat and I were glad to be done up above. We had made an unbelievable number of trips up and down the ladders.

The installation was completed except for the shell. We agreed on the lines of its elliptical shape and put up a cardboard mockup to see how it looked, and to get Helen's approval. There had been talk of a fan light or other details above the door in the beginning, but it was the shell that really fit into Helen's idea of the entry. That made me feel pretty good, because it had been my suggestion.

The shell—Back at the shop we used resorcinol to glue up the block from three layers of clear ponderosa pine, which carves nicely. We paid close attention to getting truly flat surfaces, edge and face, laying the boards so their edges did not

To install the entry, the old siding was first removed, left. At right, the entryway complete but for the shell carving—the cardboard mock-up holds its place.

line up. The bottom piece was longer than the main area and was made with an angled top edge glued in an angled rabbet, so the ears on the edges of the shell would have a draining surface. Pat had the further good idea of adding another 1-in. piece to the scroll area so it could project out beyond the rest. This we did, and it added greatly to the finished effect.

I did the carving at home on my basement bench in three-and-a-half days of work. The photos below illustrate the sequence of events. After carefully tracing the pattern onto the wood from the full-sized drawing with carbon paper, I drilled a series of holes of uniform depth very close to each other around the scroll area. This made it possible to remove the wood with chisel and mallet, working always from the outside to the middle and having the long chips break off against the scroll. When the drilled holes started to disappear, it was time to quit at the middle. Other than running my hand back and forth across the dish-shaped depression, feeling for bumps, there was no guide or template to measure the curve. The dark glue-lines showing through were a big help in this respect. The bottom of this area was left angled about 12° for drainage.

The scroll itself was next, a careful sculpting that involved much checking and rechecking to make sure the two halves came out the same size with natural-looking spirals. I established the ends first and then shaped the rest of the block into a balanced, compound-curving mass that looked a bit like a football with its ends cut off. On this bulk, I laid out the lines for the center bump and the ribbon-like strips at the ends. The

careful modeling of the whole block first made it relatively easy to carve in the molded shape and have it come out right. The ends, however, were just plain work. They were difficult to visualize because the spiral shape climbs upward to the tip, and does not lie in a flat plane.

With the scroll complete, I laid out an even spacing around the inside and extended lines from the perimeter to the center with a flexible straightedge. Guided by these sets of tapering lines, I carved the shell flutes with a long-bend gouge. Here again the lamination lines were helpful in establishing depth. The ridges between the flutes were the only part of the dished shape that remained, and I carved these with a slightly concave surface. Then, using a router and straight mortising bit, I reduced the area between the scallops and the edge to a depth of ⅜ in., trimming up the lines with carving tools.

The next move was bandsawing out the block's elliptical shape and the curving ears on each end. I did it with the table on a 12° angle to provide the needed pitch. At this time I also routed a 1-in. deep rim around the back, to allow weathertight mounting of the shell. I was then able to carve the deep concave molding of the base, and carefully sand the whole piece with papers ranging from 60 grit to 120 grit. After a thorough waterproofing during which the wood was lightly heated between coats to maximize absorption, the shell was primed.

Back at the Hermans, mounting involved cutting a hole to receive the shell in the background panel with a reciprocating saw. That allowed the shell's rim and base to lie on the surface of the background panel, so that its profile could be

marked exactly. The shell overlapped the panel by 2 in. We routed out ⅜ in. from the 2-in. overlap with a hand-held router, trimming to the marked outline with chisels where necessary. This left a wide, flat rabbet into which the shell block fit. The bottom edge of its base was worked to correspond with the angled surface of the molding on which it sits. We ran two wide beads of butyl caulk into the rabbet, and permanently mounted the shell with ten large galvanized finish nails in predrilled holes. A thin bead of caulking along the joint between the shell and background panel completed the job.

While I was finishing the shell, Pat got the weatherstrippers to the job to install the brass threshold and brass interlocking trim all around the door. He also installed a copper mail chute the sheet-metal people had made, to carry mail from an extruded brass mail slot to a box located in a closet. This box collects the mail, and is fitted with a door so there isn't heat loss through the mail slot.

That completed our work, except for Pat's overseeing the subcontractors. The concrete men formed up and poured a new set of steps up the bank, and gave them an attractive exposed-aggregate surface. Then the wrought-iron people installed the new railings. And the painters came and finished our work with two coats of exterior oil-base white. For us it was a very successful and satisfying conclusion to a big job. The Hermans were certainly pleased, and said so, and that was our bonus. □

Sam Bush heads the wood program at the Oregon School of Arts and Crafts in Portland.

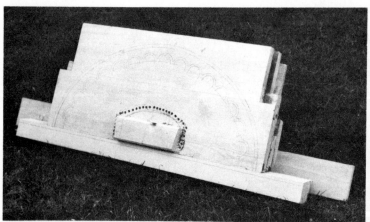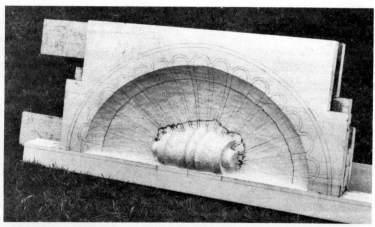

Making the shell begins with gluing up three layers of ponderosa pine, edges staggered for strength, top left. Small block at front is for scroll; holes will aid in carving flutes. Top right, fluting is laid out in dished-out shells; scroll carving is complete. With flutes carved, above left, semicircular groove is routed and block is bandsawn to shape, above right. A concave molding base completes the job.

Frank Lloyd Wright Comes to the Met
How restorers reassembled a Prairie School living room in a museum

by Thomas Harboe and Vincent Lepre

During the summer of 1912, construction began on the Little house, overlooking Lake Minnetonka in Wayzata, Minn. During the last nine months of 1982, we rebuilt the living room of this house in the American Wing of The Metropolitan Museum of Art in New York City, where it remains as a permanent exhibit. It's the most complex and expensive period room ever installed in the Met, and the only one from the 20th century.

Designed by Frank Lloyd Wright, the house was to serve as a summer retreat for Francis W. Little and his family. Though Wright was a close friend of the Littles, there was a running disagreement between architect and clients over various aspects of the house's design, especially the windows. This was a period in Wright's career when he was trying to move away from his Prairie-style houses of the pre-

vious decade. But the Littles liked the look and feel of those earlier houses and wanted something similar. After some thorny times, the differences were resolved, and the house was largely completed in 1914.

By the late 1950s, the house had become the Littles' year-round residence. It remained in the family until maintaining it became too burdensome for Francis Little's daughter and her husband, Raymond Stephenson. They wanted a smaller house, but local zoning laws prohibited building another residence on the property. The Stephensons didn't want to tear the house down, but there was no getting around it.

It was at this point, in 1971, that curators at The Metropolitan Museum of Art learned of the situation and decided to buy the house and its furnishings. During the winter and

spring of 1972, the firm of Kevin Roche, John Dinkeloo Associates inventoried the architectural elements and prepared measured drawings. Soon after, the house was dismantled.

The Met staff had to work fast to meet a deadline for clearing the site. As a result, the documentation was not as thorough as it might have been. A few more rolls of film and a few more detailed drawings would have made our work immeasurably easier. However, the system used by Roche and Dinkeloo to organize and identify the architectural elements for reconstruction worked pretty well. Each piece was numbered with red felt-tipped marker on its back side and keyed to a set of measured drawings, which included elevations, plans and details. The disassembled interior was carefully packed, crated and shipped to the Met, where it was stored for

10 years. Our work was limited to the living room, yet many other of the house's architectural elements still lie in storage at the Met.

Siting the Wright room—The museum's new American Wing is bounded on three sides by Central Park, and the curators chose to rebuild the Wright room near its southern wall. Here a band of windows would allow natural light to give greater impact and dimension to Wright's work.

The room itself is about 28 ft. north to south and 45 ft. east to west. The 15-ft. high coved ceiling hovers above the room, and looks suspended in place. The six skylights in the ceiling dominate the room with the massive beauty of their stained-glass panels. The north and south walls feature 30-ft. bands of windows that form small bays for window seats. Above the main-level windows are bands of clerestory windows. On the west wall is a 12-ft. wide, ceiling-high brick fireplace, which is flanked by a small door and a casement window. The main entrance to the room is on the east wall, to the left of an 8-ft. wide window. All the windows are leaded-glass casements.

The north and south walls are bordered outside by 8-ft. wide corridors from which the public can view the room. A wooden trellis, which cantilevers out from the facade above the main windows, runs for about 38 ft. along the outside of the room. The north and south exterior facades of the living room are reconstructed up to what was the eave of the original roof. The east and west walls, however, are reconstructed on their interior sides only and are backed by walls of adjacent galleries. The windows of the east and west walls frame dioramas that depict, as closely as possible, what one would have seen at the original location of the house.

Reconstructing a room of this complexity requires the skills of many different people. Museum curators, conservators, engineers and restorers had to coordinate their efforts with plasterers, electricians, masons and other tradesmen. Yet most of the construction and installation was done by us and by Jeff Mills, whose father, Ezra Mills, Jr., served as project manager. He also designed many structural and mechanical details that solved problems unique to this project.

Begun in March 1982, the project had to be completed by Dec. 1 of that year. And to complicate things further, we had a second deadline to meet. In order to show the Wright room on the cover of the fall issue of the Museum's *Bulletin*, we had to complete half of the room by Oct. 22 so it could be photographed. Having to trim out one end of the room while unfinished framing remained at our backs seemed a nightmare at first. But things went better than we thought, and we were able to meet the deadline without mishap.

Getting to work—Once closed off from public view, the project site, which measured about 44 ft. by 52 ft., was nothing more than a large concrete bunker with a band of south-facing windows. The floor area was entirely open except for two structural concrete pillars located about 8 ft. from the south wall. These pillars would become structural parts of the corridor walls along the outside of the room.

Several 3-ft. by 4-ft. concrete beams span the ceiling slab east to west. Roche and Dinkeloo, who also designed the new American Wing (which opened in 1980), knew how this space was going to be used, and so they placed the ceiling beams where they would interfere very little with our work. Even so, because the beams were there, the final positioning of the Wright room was determined by laying out the ceiling first and then plumbing down to establish the location of the walls.

Because we were framing a structure to accommodate woodwork, windows and doors that already had fixed dimensions, there was no room for error in our layout. Everything had to be dead on. But there was a kink. To comply with the New York City building code, we had to use fire-resistant wood for framing and sheathing. Because the lumber is immersed in a salt solution to make it fire resistant, it arrived at the Met dripping wet. Our need for stable, accurate framing required us to sticker all the lumber. To hasten drying, we set up a pair of large fans and kept air constantly moving through the stacks. It took about three weeks to dry the lumber thoroughly. Unfortunately, much of the material warped and twisted as it cured, and it had to be straightened before we could use it. So we straightened each board by tacking a wooden straightedge to it and running it through the table saw. Then we ripped each to width. Sometimes we had to glue up several pieces of 2x stock to get the net finished width.

We checked and rechecked our layout lines on the floor and ceiling against the architectural drawings. Then we checked again by measuring and loosely assembling the woodwork. In a sense, we were working backwards from the finished room, subtracting dimensions in order to arrive at a starting point for construction. Each line and plane had to be located with regard to those in the rest of the room. Any one error could cause a multitude of pieces to fit improperly.

Framing walls and ceiling—Although the Little house had been primarily a masonry structure, it was decided to reconstruct the living room with a wood frame. To match the thickness of the original masonry, we built two parallel stud walls and tied them together. We began by bolting the 2x4 plates at 18 in. on center to the concrete-slab floor. The anchor bolts were countersunk so the second 2x4 could be nailed atop the first. We used a double floor plate because a latex-cement cap averaging 1 in. thick would be poured over the concrete slab to level the floor. After this topping was floated in, we installed a second set of floor plates outside of the first set to define the outside face of the walls.

To help the concrete subs pour a level cap, we drilled a grid of holes 4 ft. o. c. in the floor to accept ⅜-in. masonry anchors and bolts. We checked each anchor bolt with a water level, and adjusted each one until its head stopped at precisely the right height. Thus we provided a series of reference points that could be used to guide the screeds. The concrete people were amazed by our concern for 1/16-in. deviation over a 40-ft. floor. We wound up grinding away cured latex cement in some places to get the floor level enough to locate our vertical dimensions.

With the floor plates down and our floor level, we began building the wood frame to provide the inner walls with accurate nailing surfaces for plaster lath and trim.

The ceiling of the Wright room is a flat cove that measures about 22 ft. by 30 ft. As shown in the drawing on the facing page, the ceiling was framed by fastening 4x4 beams to the concrete with bolts in masonry anchors, and by nailing 2x4s to the sides of these beams. The 4x4s are placed 2 ft. o. c. and run north to south across the ceiling slab and down both sides of each of the reinforced concrete ceiling beams (photo facing page). The flat cove, or angled portion of the ceiling, is framed with 2x4s nailed to a ceiling 4x4 and to a 4x4 fastened to the bottom edge of the concrete beams. Plywood gussets strengthen the connection between these members.

It took more than three weeks to fasten the 4x4s across the 1,500 sq.-ft. ceiling (sloping sides included). Even with eye protection and respirators, the work was grueling. We did manage to make drilling the concrete overhead easier by building a simple levering device. We bolted a pair of 2x4s around a single vertical 2x4 so that the hammer drill could be rested, butt down, on a seat at one end of the pair of 2x4s. While one man steadied the drill and pulled the trigger, another pushed down on the opposite end of the lever. As a result, our production was tripled, and our morale was mercifully improved.

Most of the wall area on the north and south walls is taken up by a 30-ft. band of windows. Only the 8-ft. sections at either end of the room, and the east and west walls are floor-to-ceiling stud walls. Plumbing up from the parallel floor plates, we fastened our top plates to the concrete with 2½-in. powder-driven pins.

The stud walls are about 13½ ft. high, but the irregularity of the ceiling meant that each stud had to be cut to a rough length and then scribed to fit. After the studs were in place, the neighboring walls were tied together with ¾-in. plywood gussets, which increase the rigidity of the walls and help keep the studs from bowing in or out.

The kneewalls that support the 30-ft. banks of windows are approximately 18 in. high and 8 in. thick. We framed the kneewalls with 2x8s, which we notched at the top outside edges to accept a cast-concrete sill that fits under the window frames. We capped the kneewall with a double 2x6 plate.

Window walls—Installing the window bays along the north and south walls was our first chance to get our hands on the artwork, as the original material is called. The Douglas fir

Illustration: Frances Ashforth

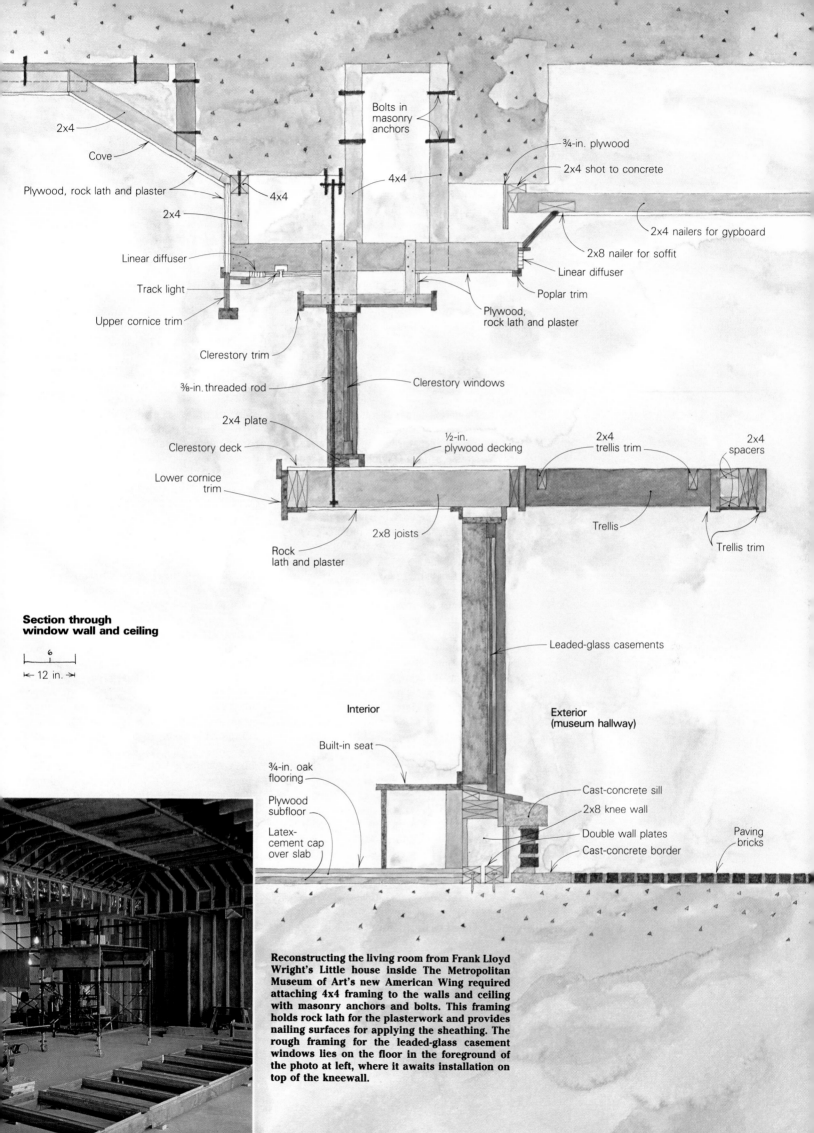

2x4

Cove

Plywood, rock lath and plaster

2x4

Linear diffuser

Track light

Upper cornice trim

Clerestory trim

⅜-in. threaded rod

2x4 plate

Clerestory deck

Lower cornice trim

4x4

Bolts in masonry anchors

4x4

¾-in. plywood

2x4 shot to concrete

2x4 nailers for gypboard

2x8 nailer for soffit

Linear diffuser

Poplar trim

Plywood, rock lath and plaster

Clerestory windows

½-in. plywood decking

2x4 trellis trim

2x4 spacers

Trellis

Trellis trim

2x8 joists

Rock lath and plaster

Section through window wall and ceiling

6

⟵ 12 in. ⟶

Leaded-glass casements

Interior

Exterior (museum hallway)

Built-in seat

¾-in. oak flooring

Plywood subfloor

Latex-cement cap over slab

Cast-concrete sill

2x8 knee wall

Double wall plates

Cast-concrete border

Paving bricks

Reconstructing the living room from Frank Lloyd Wright's Little house inside The Metropolitan Museum of Art's new American Wing required attaching 4x4 framing to the walls and ceiling with masonry anchors and bolts. This framing holds rock lath for the plasterwork and provides nailing surfaces for applying the sheathing. The rough framing for the leaded-glass casement windows lies on the floor in the foreground of the photo at left, where it awaits installation on top of the kneewall.

frames for these windows had been originally constructed in two sections. These butt together at a center mullion and rest atop the kneewalls, which we had just reconstructed. Each 15-ft. section of window frame holds six 2-ft. by 4½-ft. casement sash. A narrow fixed sash at each end of the bay connects the bank of windows with the main walls. Wooden window seats, which were installed in the original house in the 1950s, covered the radiators, and they run the full length of the bays.

At either end of the room, the window frames are secured to the stud walls. We screwed a 2x4 to the window return on each end and then framed it into the walls. The window frames are fastened at the bottom to the kneewall with lag screws (24 in. o. c.) which were inserted from the underside of the 2x8 plates, up into the window sill.

Clerestories—Above the main windows is a band of clerestory windows (photo top left), which sit upon a clerestory deck that runs around the entire inside perimeter of the room at a height of about 6 ft. 6 in. Its plane slices through the wall and becomes the trellis on the outside. Here again is illustrated a key Wrightian principle of integrating the interior and exterior spaces, both structurally and visually. The width of the deck varies. Along the west wall, where it passes in front of the brick fireplace, the deck is barely a foot wide; while in other places, such as the niche above the main entrance at the east wall, it is over 3 ft. wide.

We positioned the 2x8 joists that support the clerestory deck according to the shadows and nail holes left from the original framing. Generally, they are 16 in. o. c. with double joists over each window mullion and over the return at either end. On the north and south walls, these joists are cantilevered in both directions over the window frames.

Inside the room, a double header is nailed to the ends of the clerestory joists to serve as the nailing surface for the oak boards that trim the deck and form the lower of the two cornices in the room.

To construct the clerestory deck over the north and south windows, temporary partitions were erected both inside and outside the room to support the cantilevered joists. The partitions remained in place until we completed the structural work, and decked the joists with ½-in. plywood that extends outside beyond the clerestory windows to the exterior of the main windows.

The clerestory window frames were nailed to a 2x4 plate on top of the plywood deck. In the original construction of the house, a pair

The trellis (left) separates the lower casements from the clerestory windows. The trellis slices through the wall, and on the inside forms the cantilevered clerestory deck (above left). At either end of the trellis is a flitch beam made up of ⅜-in. thick steel plate sandwiched between 2x8s. In the center, the trellis and the clerestory deck are supported by the lower mullions and by lengths of threaded rod, which are suspended from the concrete ceiling.

The original living room was built considerably out of square. The reconstructed room, facing page, was built to the smaller dimension of the original, so the trim could be cut to fit.

of 16-in. I-beams ran above and parallel to the clerestory windows, spanning the 30 ft. between the masonry piers at either end of the room. The evidence (marks in the clerestory mullions) shows that the clerestory deck was suspended from the I-beams with threaded rods. But our design included neither the I-beams nor the masonry piers. Instead, our threaded rods are attached to adjustable steel plates that are bolted at their four corners into the concrete ceiling. Also, the clerestory windows are attached via a complex framing system to the 4x4 nailers on the ceiling.

On the exterior, the trellis (photo bottom left) runs the entire length of the facades on the north and south, and is structurally integrated with the framing of the room. The trellis is supported at either end by a flitch beam made from 10-ft. lengths of ⅜-in. by 6-in. steel sandwiched between a pair of 2x8s.

These beams pass through the walls to form part of the header that supports the clerestory deck of the east and west walls. The 2x8 joists that cantilever into the room from the east and west wall framing are joined to the flitch beam. The finished design of the trellis was achieved by applying additional boards to the frame. The rough texture of these boards matches the original woodwork.

Wall finish—After the framing was in place, we sheathed the walls and ceiling with ¾-in. fire-resistant fir plywood to provide a perfectly flat and stable surface for the masons and plasterers to work on. This sheathing, which we nailed up with 8d commons, also assured us that we would have firm backing for all of the oak trim we would later apply.

In final preparation for plastering, we nailed grounds and lath over the sheathing. Wright's extensive use of wood trim meant that most of our grounds could be applied permanently. The ¾-in. thickness of the lath-and-plaster finish established the thickness of our clear pine grounds, which we ripped to a width of ½ in. less than the trim that would cover it. Having the smooth pine surface to nail the trim to, rather than the rough plaster, proved later to be a great advantage. We found it much more difficult to achieve a satisfactory fit in the instances where we had to nail the trim directly to the roughly textured plaster.

After the grounds were in place, ⅜-in. rock lath was nailed to the sheathing with ring-shank drywall nails. Rock lath, which comes in 16-in. by 48-in. sheets, looks and works much like gypboard, and serves as a scratch coat, which meant that the plastering could be done in only two coats (for more on this technique, see *FHB* #15, pp. 72-74).

To determine the right plaster mix, an analysis of original samples was done. The curatorial staff decided to use a mix that contained two parts sand to one part gypsum plaster. The sand itself contained two parts river sand

to one part #1 blasting sand. In order to match the original textured surface, the plastering was done with a carpeted float. A swatch of low-pile industrial carpet was attached to a piece of ¼-in. plywood, 12 in. by 5 in. The carpet, as it was worked over the surface of the plaster, caught the sharp grains of sand and brought them to the surface.

Skylights—Perhaps the most striking architectural feature of the Frank Lloyd Wright room is the six skylights, which are set in the flat central portion of the ceiling. They have oak-veneered pine frames, and each holds three leaded-glass panels, which are inserted from above. In their original situation, the skylights were artificially illuminated. Seven incandescent fixtures with reflectors were suspended from the attic rafters over each skylight. At the Met, this effect is recreated with seven circular fluorescent fixtures fastened directly to the concrete ceiling slab above each skylight. Several layers of filter paper and gels lie behind the glass panels and help diffuse the fluorescent lighting to simulate incandescence. Clearance was so tight that we had to jackhammer pockets in the concrete to make room for several of the fixtures (photo facing page, top).

The skylights, each of which weighed over 140 lb., had to be installed in a way that would allow them to be removed and rehung for regular maintenance and cleaning. A system using a pair of spring-loaded pulleys at each corner of the skylight allows them to be easily lowered and raised back into place.

We had to locate the skylights accurately to give us lines of reference for the trim on the ceiling and the upper cornice. The pieces applied parallel to the skylights establish a line that is completed by other trim pieces on the vertical-drop portion of the ceiling. Finally, this trim terminates at the blocks applied to the face of the upper cornice.

Installing the trim—We received the quartersawn oak trim in the large paper bundles it had been kept in for 10 years. There were about 30 bundles, some containing hundreds of pieces. Except for some water damage, it was all in good condition, and there were no pieces that we were not able to use. First, we had to sort and inventory the pieces. Then all the woodwork was cleaned and refinished by the Met's Conservation Department. The oak was finished following Wright's original recipe—two parts melted wax (50% beeswax and 50% paraffin), two parts turpentine, and one part boiled linseed oil.

Save for the coved shoe molding covering the joint between the floor and walls, there is no molded trim in the room. Ornamentation is achieved by the interplay and the arrangement of the pieces. Thus, their shape is expressed in the whole of the architecture, and very few of the pieces draw attention to themselves individually. To ensure that all of the original pieces could be trimmed to fit rather than ending up too short and leaving gaps, the Met's room was built to the smaller dimension of the original, which was quite a bit out of square to begin with.

The upper cornice was the first interior woodwork to be applied. Its five members (drawing, p. 27) make it the most complex element of trim in the room. Installing the upper cornice allowed us to trim the ceiling, using it and the skylights as our guides. Watching the geometric shapes take form was one of the really exciting moments of the project. It took several days for two of us, working from our rolling scaffolds, to apply the hundreds of oak strips to the ceiling. Up close, it was hard to gauge the impact of our work, but, at the end of each day we were always excited to see the results from the ground.

Our technique for applying the oak trim was to hold each piece, or group of pieces, in place to check for fit. The unavoidable discrepancies between the original and newly applied plaster meant we had to recut many of the miters. Once a piece was fitted, it was nailed in place. We wanted to avoid scarring the trim with new nail holes, and so tried to reuse the old nail holes by using finishing nails one size larger than the originals. But we found that this did not always give us the firm grab we wanted. Consequently, we made new holes where old ones wouldn't work. In most cases, we predrilled the holes, using a finishing nail chucked in a hand drill. Afterwards, all of the nail holes were filled with a pigmented micro-crystalline wax, which very effectively covered our tracks.

Flooring—The subflooring is ¾-in. plywood nailed on top of the latex-cement cap. In order to ensure that the plywood would be securely fastened, we used 1½-in. and 2-in. masonry nails. The flooring of the room is ¾-in. tongue-and-groove oak taken from the Little house. Wisely, the Met had taken several rooms of flooring from the house, so we had plenty of original material to work with, enabling us to choose only the strips that were in top shape.

Since the flooring was not relaid using the original boards in their original locations, the completed floor had a very uneven surface, and required a heavy sanding. The floor sanding was done with the trim, including the baseboard, in place. The marks left by the sanding machine were covered by the 1-in. shoe molding, which we installed after the floor was finished.

Painting—The plaster surfaces of the room are finished with an oil-base paint, which was applied with rollers and brushes. It is interesting to note that in a large number of Wright's houses the plaster itself was pigmented, not painted. That was not the case in the Little house. Our choice of color was based on analysis of original paint samples taken from the Little house during demolition. One sample of plaster was taken from each level of the original room to record the condition and treatment of the fabric. These samples were set in the east wall of the reconstructed room.

Masonry—As mentioned, the Francis Little house was primarily a masonry structure. It is uncertain how the load-bearing walls were constructed, but the exterior face of brick had been well photographed. The Met's plan for

To match the wide, deeply raked mortar joints of the original masonry, shims were laid between the courses at the outer edge of the bricks, and then removed before the mortar set up hard. The veneer bricks on the outside are original; the firebricks are new.

The leaded-glass skylights in the center of the ceiling were lit by incandescent bulbs in the original house. To simulate that illumination in the Met, circular fluorescent tubes were installed behind filters. The frames are held in place by cables attached to spring-loaded pulleys so that the skylights can be pulled down for maintenance. Clearance was so tight that concrete had to be jackhammered out in places to make room for the fixtures.

reconstructing the room did not include the exterior facades and, as a result, no exterior brick was saved. Enough original brick was taken, however, to face the fireplace.

The fireplace, which is centered on the west wall, was wood-framed and sheathed with ¾-in. plywood. Then the masons laid up the veneer of full brick. Since the fireplace doesn't work, the space behind its facade is used to house electrical components. It also functions as a return-air duct to cool the skylights.

All the cast-concrete architectural elements, like the window sills, were newly fabricated, except for the urn that sits just outside the casement window at the east end of the room.

The exterior walls of the room were sheathed with ¾-in. plywood to provide a solid backing for the brick veneer. As in many of his early houses, Wright employed a running bond with unusually deep and wide horizontal joints in order to emphasize the low, horizontal feeling of the house. The color, texture, form and composition of the original mortar have been reproduced at the Met.

The fireplace was reconstructed with original bricks which had been carefully cleaned. The firebricks laid in the firebox are new, as are the cast-concrete hobs and lintel.

The final masonry project was laying the brick walkways in the corridors adjacent to the north and south walls. At the site in Wayzata, landscaped terraces came right up to the windows. This is where the museum and the room are connected. The brick provides an easy visual transition between the two. □

Restorers Thomas Harboe and Vincent Lepre worked under contract for The Metropolitan Museum of Art. Construction photos by the authors.

Photos: Thomas P. Ford

Restoring a Porch

A fast, inexpensive method that doesn't require house jacks

by Roy F. Cole, Jr.

Some contractors use elaborate house jacks, and plenty of them, to repair two-story porches. Others jack and shore small sections, one at a time, eventually working from one end of the porch to the other. I've found both these methods too expensive because of the costly jacks and extra time involved. By restoring a fair number of two and three-story Charleston porches over the years, I've developed a method for repairing them well and repairing them fast. I shore up the whole porch with timbers, and never use jacks. They are just not necessary. I've done this on one-story porches too, but the challenge of the big ones is more to my liking.

Old Charleston is going through a major resurgence now, and there's plenty of restoration work going on. Luckily, the town was spared Victorian buildings because so few people had

The timber shoring on the porch at left is tied together to prevent workers from knocking it out of place. Cole's method of shoring allows for repair or complete replacement of columns and decking, as in the renovated porch below.

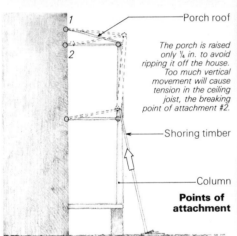

The porch is raised only ¼ in. to avoid ripping it off the house. Too much vertical movement will cause tension in the ceiling joist, the breaking point of attachment #2.

Porch roof

Shoring timber

Column

Points of attachment

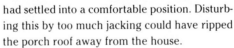

A notch is cut at the upper end of the shoring (top photo) to receive the sill of the second-story deck. Cole places one 4-in. by 6-in. plank next to each column, at left. The base of the shoring sits on a 2-in. by 6-in. plank. Above center, an oak wedge driven between the shoring and the plank raises the second-floor deck. Once weight is off the column, a second wedge is driven under the first and nailed to the plank; then a wood block is nailed to the plank to stabilize the shoring.

any money to spend on houses from the end of the Civil War until the 1930s. So these porches, except for their poor structural condition, are originals. They are elaborate additions to wood or brick houses built after a major fire burned many of the wooden ones in 1861. They also survived an earthquake in the 1880s. Since porches were always popular in Charleston's hot, muggy climate, they were never removed, except for those that removed themselves.

To restore the two-story porch shown on the facing page, we had to replace column bases and plinth, some rotten decking, the sill and damaged hand rails. Luckily, the roof was in good shape, but it was a pretty extensive job nonetheless. We had to raise the second-floor porch deck and roof so the first-floor columns could be removed or lifted for repairs. The trick was to raise the roof no more than absolutely necessary. It was attached to the house at the two points shown in the drawing above, and over the years

had settled into a comfortable position. Disturbing this by too much jacking could have ripped the porch roof away from the house.

My method for taking the weight off the columns by shoring up the whole porch at one time allows us to perform each task only once. This saves a lot of time. Because of the weight involved we use 4-in. by 6-in. shoring timbers of southern yellow pine at each column, as shown directly above. I notch the tops of the timbers (top right photo) to receive the sill beam of the second-story deck. The angle of the notch is not critical. I place the base of the shoring timber on a 2-in. by 6-in. plank about 4 ft. long, and insert an oak wedge between the timber and the plank. The timber should be long enough so that its base is about 4 ft. from the porch; this leaves enough room to work.

Starting at one end of the porch, I tap the wedges with a heavy sledgehammer until each shoring timber relieves the weight on its col-

umn. Upward movement of no more than a fraction of an inch is enough to free the column from the upper-story sill. With the column free, I nail another oak wedge on top of the first and nail a wood block to the plank behind the wedge, as shown in the photo above. Friction between the 4-ft. plank under the shoring and the brick paving prevents the shoring from slipping backward. When no rough paving is available and the shoring must be supported on grass or bare ground, I increase the width and thickness of the planks, depending on the weight of the porch roof to be raised. For instance, I use 3-in. by 8-in. by 4-ft. planks (if the ground is fairly dry) to support shoring for a one-story porch. After all the columns are tapped free, I nail lightweight purlins horizontally to each shoring member to tie them together and prevent accidental movement. Then restoration work begins.

During porch restorations I do not remove columns or any other parts unless it's necessary for

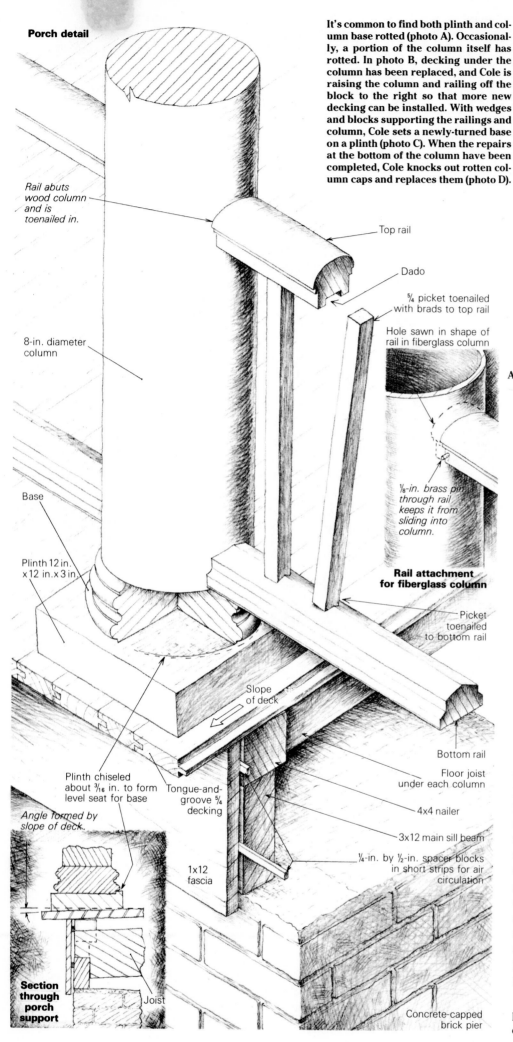

Porch detail

Rail abuts wood column and is toenailed in.

8-in. diameter column

Top rail

Dado

⁵⁄₄ picket toenailed with brads to top rail

Hole sawn in shape of rail in fiberglass column

⅛-in. brass pin through rail keeps it from sliding into column.

Rail attachment for fiberglass column

Base

Plinth 12 in. x 12 in. x 3 in.

Picket toenailed to bottom rail

Slope of deck

Bottom rail

Floor joist under each column

Plinth chiseled about ³⁄₁₆ in. to form level seat for base

Tongue-and-groove ⁵⁄₄ decking

4x4 nailer

3x12 main sill beam

¼-in. by ½-in. spacer blocks in short strips for air circulation

Angle formed by slope of deck.

1x12 fascia

Section through porch support

Joist

Concrete-capped brick pier

It's common to find both plinth and column base rotted (photo A). Occasionally, a portion of the column itself has rotted. In photo B, decking under the column has been replaced, and Cole is raising the column and railing off the block to the right so that more new decking can be installed. With wedges and blocks supporting the railings and column, Cole sets a newly-turned base on a plinth (photo C). When the repairs at the bottom of the column have been completed, Cole knocks out rotten column caps and replaces them (photo D).

A

repairs. Frequently the columns are original to the house; on the porch shown here, they are solid, heavy longleaf pine. When their bottom sections have rotted (as was the case with three columns on this job) they have to be removed. A 1-ft. length is cut off the bottom and the column is sent to a lumberyard to have that foot replaced and turned to match samples of the original. (This costs us about $100 per column.) Once the column has been scraped and repainted it is difficult to tell the old from the new.

There are times I have to completely replace columns. I use hollow, built-up wood columns, which, of course, are not as strong as solid ones that cost from $500 to $750 each. However, there is another replacement: fiberglass columns and plinth covers. When seen up close these columns do not look like wood, so I don't recommend using them in a true restoration. They are strong and rot resistant, but joining the wood rails to the column is a problem. To solve this, we carefully cut holes in the column for the top and bottom rails, slip them in, and pin them in place. (See drawing at left.) Also, because porch decks pitch away from the house for drainage, the plinth also slopes. The vertical column does not sit squarely upon it unless the plinth is beveled or chiseled to form a level seat, or the base of the column is cut on an angle. This is a critical detail to attend to when setting hollow wood and fiberglass columns. If the column does not seat evenly all around, stresses will build up, cause checking and eventually split open the column. The method I use is to put the plinth in place on the deck, then take a level and mark a horizontal line on the side of the plinth. I chisel out the seat for the base to approximate the angle drawn.

If the column is solid and only the base and plinth are rotten (photo A), which is the usual case, only the rotted parts are removed. To do

B

this, we place a block and wedge on each side of the column under the bottom rail. We hammer in the wedge and remove the base and plinth. When the decking under the plinth is also rotten, we remove it and replace it with new decking. Once the new decking is in place, we put a block and wedge directly under the column, transferring the weight to this block and the new decking (photo B). Then the decking on either side of the column is replaced as required.

Weight is placed back on the original blocks once rotten decking has been replaced, and a new base and plinth are slipped under the column (photo C). Then we remove the blocks on either side of the column. At this point, with no weight on the column, we knock out and replace broken caps (photo D). As we complete each column we loosen the shoring until the second story and roof are supported by the column.

If the porch substructure must be changed we do this before replacing the decking. The most common problem here is a rotten 4-in. by 4-in. nailing strip behind the fascia where water gets in. I replace it with treated lumber and put a ½-in. spacer between it and the fascia to allow air circulation, as shown in the drawing at left.

Once all rotten columns, substructure and decking have been replaced and the shoring is removed, handrails are replaced. If rails are missing or destroyed I take samples to a lumberyard that reproduces millwork. New rails are cut to length, and their ends shaped to butt the round columns. They are toenailed in place with countersunk finishing nails. Then the old pickets are tilted and nailed into place as shown in the drawing at left. The porch is painted, and we move on to the next one. □

Roy Cole is a contractor who specializes in house restoration in Charleston, S.C.

C

D

Restoring a Grand Victorian Porch

Mahogany, redwood, and sand paint duplicate the look of weathered brownstone

by David Stenstrom

The Morse-Libby mansion in Portland, Maine, is a National Historic Landmark. Now owned by the Victoria Society of Maine, it was built from 1859 to 1863 and is perhaps the finest and least altered example of a brownstone Italianate villa in the United States. When architect Henry Austin designed the mansion, he chose a rich reddish brownstone for the exterior. Coastal Maine winters, with their cycles of freezes and thaws, were hard on the stone. In warm weather, water poured over the facade, wearing it away. Moisture seeped into the stone and weakened it.

Some of the worst damage was suffered by the large stone porch on the building's main facade, an arrangement of fluted Ionic columns and pilasters supporting a sculpted entablature and balustraded balcony. Without modern drainage or flashing systems, the porch had worn away so badly that some sections were missing two-thirds of their original stone. It was beyond repair. In 1979, the Society for the Preservation of New England Antiquities (S.P.N.E.A.) made measurements, drawings and photographs of the old porch, and had it dismantled before it collapsed.

Contracted to supervise the project, the Society at first planned to replace the porch in stone. But the quarries in Connecticut that had supplied the original stone were under water. A brownstone the right color that would weather well and work easily was no longer to be had in this country. An acceptable stone from England was prohibitively expensive. Finally, it was decided to use wood disguised as stone.

The S.P.N.E.A. drew up the specifications and plans for the new porch. The contractor would be expected to mill and finish wooden columns, pilasters, entablature and balustrades, erect them on a new foundation at the site, and rebuild the floor and roof of the porch with modern flashing and drainage systems. The Society would carve the capitals and turn the balustrades and column bases in its own shop.

I am shop foreman at the Woodward Thomsen Co. in Portland, Maine, which specializes in restorations and architectural woodwork. We knew, though, that this job would require tolerances not normally demanded in building, because historical reproduction is an exact, physi-

cal record of what used to exist. The wooden elements would have to look just like the stone, be finished to fool the eye, then bolted together using spacers and caulking to mimic mortar joints. All of this was a fascinating challenge to the people in our shop. We worked hard to put together a reasonable bid, and we got the job.

We planned to do all the woodworking and painting in the shop, and to erect the components at the mansion in the summer. Work on the entablature began early in 1981. The original had been sculpted from seven large blocks of stone, with moldings, brackets and details as integral parts. Three lower blocks had rested on the columns and pilasters of the porch, supporting the four upper blocks that formed the cornice, which in turn supported the roof and its balustrade. The new entablature would be made of seven wooden boxes built from layered plywood and glue blocks. The details and embellishments would be applied. We talked things over regularly with Morgan Phillips, the architectural conservator of the S.P.N.E.A. Whenever we found that the plans and drawings were not specific enough, we went through the pieces of the old porch, which had been stored behind the mansion.

The Connecticut brownstone of the Morse-Libby mansion's porch was in terrible shape by the 1970s. The porch had to be dismantled and rebuilt shortly before this picture was taken. Because replacement stone was either unavailable or too expensive, the entire porch was restored in wood. Facing page: The first lower entablature block is maneuvered onto the right-hand pilaster and the center column.

Building the blocks—Our first step was to make a cross-sectional model of the entablature, which helped us anticipate problems. It immediately became clear, for example, that the amount of epoxy used to glue the plywood layers added significantly to the dimensions of the finished box. We learned, too, that the long triangular glue blocks called for in the plans would bow or twist as they were sawn. Each box also contained plywood stiffeners along with glue blocks, and these had to be installed before the box was enclosed. But since the finished boxes would be bolted to each other, to the building and to the columns of the porch, each had to have enough room inside it to let us tighten the nuts.

We built the three lower blocks of the entablature first, then the four upper blocks that would form the cornice. Instead of the triangular glue blocks running the length of each box, we used maple 4x4s, jointed on two edges to ensure that the finished box would be square and true. We laid 10-ft. long frames covered with plywood on top of our benches so each box would sit flat as it was glued up. The first layer was either ¾-in. or 1-in. fir plywood glued and screwed to the 4x4 glue blocks. Outside these we glued lengths of Bruynzeel instead of the specified medium-density overlay plywood, which could not be cleaned up at mitered corners because of its outer veneer of paper.

Bruynzeel is a high-quality Dutch plywood made of African mahogany. A veneer-core plywood, it is virtually without voids, and its heavy face veneers are $\frac{1}{16}$ in. thick before they're drum-sanded as a last step in the manufacturing process. It is strong stuff, and highly resistant to water damage. Bruynzeel comes in thicknesses of from 4 mm (about $\frac{1}{6}$ in.) to 40 mm (about 1½ in.), and in sheets from 4x8 to 4x16. We used mostly 4x10 sheets, which cost $235 each. Prices fluctuate rapidly with both inflation and the value of the dollar. Our supplier was Condon Lumber (250 Ferris Ave., White Plains, N.Y. 10603). As we glued up the layers of fir and Bruynzeel, the boxes became heavier and more difficult to move. We suspected that we were simulating not only the shape and look of stone, but its weight as well.

We used a two-part epoxy adhesive made by

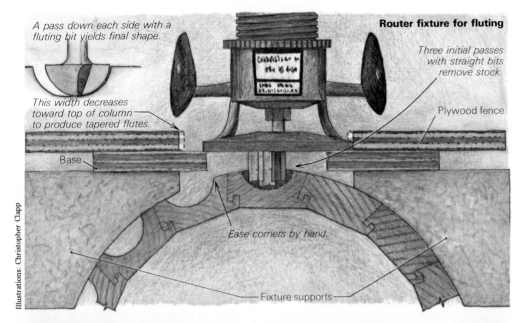

A pass down each side with a fluting bit yields final shape.

Router fixture for fluting

This width decreases toward top of column to produce tapered flutes.

Three initial passes with straight bits remove stock.

Plywood fence

Base

Ease corners by hand.

Fixture supports

The redwood columns were bought unfluted. To cut the flutes, a plywood router fixture like those used by furniture makers, but much longer, was devised. The drawing, top, shows how it works. Fluting the columns removed so much wood that a support system of 6-in. dia. Lally columns (above) with ¼-in. thick steel plates at top and bottom was improvised to take the load.

Columns and pilasters were set over bolts on concrete bases flashed with lead. Stubs of the balustrade's upper rail had been mortised into columns and pilasters. The full rail was later cut to length and screwed and epoxied in place.

Like the other porch elements, the entablature blocks (left) were fabricated in the woodshop. Bruynzeel, a Dutch mahogany plywood, was used on sections exposed to the weather. Fir plywood was used elsewhere, and the gutters were built of solid Honduras mahogany.

the Allied Resin Corp. (Weymouth Industrial Park, P.O. Box A, East Weymouth, Mass. 02189) because it resists moisture and needs only light clamping pressure, unlike resorcinol and some other waterproof glues. When cured, the adhesive is resilient and stable. For fasteners we used drywall screws and concealed them where possible.

The epoxy was thick and cured quickly, so we mixed small batches often. We found we needed a second, thinner epoxy mixture to spread on the large plywood surfaces of each box. We used the thicker formula on the glue blocks, moldings and brackets. Pieces of plastic laminate made good glue spreaders. We removed the excess epoxy that squeezed out of the joints, because when it cured, it became extremely hard, and tooling off hardened epoxy can dull any chisel or plane. The best tool for removing the uncured glue turned out to be a thin, flexible artist's painting knife.

As the boxes were completed, we made a filler of epoxy mixed with microballoons, a grey, flour-like concoction of microscopic, nitrogen-filled, ceramic spheres. (Ecospheres, the brand we used, are available from Emerson and Cummings, 869 Washington St., Canton, Mass. 02021.) With this filler, we patched imperfections and screw holes on the surface of the wood. When the mix cured, we scraped and sanded it as if it were wood. We cut ventilation holes on the back of each entablature box, above what would be the porch's ceiling level. These holes would also let us get in to bolt things together when the porch was erected.

The decorative moldings and brackets of the entablature had to be cut to match those of the original stone. Samples of our work on these pieces, and later on the flutes and railing, were sent to the S.P.N.E.A. office in Boston, where they were examined and approved before we milled the rest. The entablature brackets were bandsawn, then hand-scraped and sanded to finished size.

We ground shaper-knife blanks to produce moldings that would match the profiles of the originals. The solid-wood details were made from Honduras mahogany, which is relatively stable, machines well and is available in thick and wide stock. Finally, we applied the details, and then sanded the seven large entablature blocks to ease the crisp edges of the wood and replicate the worn, rounded edges of the original brownstone.

Support systems—The two round columns and two rectangular pilasters were custom-made by the Hardman Saunders Co. (4340 Bankers Circle, Atlanta, Ga. 30360), using interlocking, staved redwood. These were identical to the originals, except made successively ¾ in. shorter to pitch the copper-lined gutter planned for the new porch.

The flutes in each column tapered from 1¾ in. at the top to 2⅛ in. at the bottom, but remained ¾ in. deep along their whole lengths. The shape of each flute and the size of the lands between them were critical to the balanced appearance of the finished supports.

To cut the flutes we devised a fixture to guide

a router down the length of a column. It's just a big version of the kind cabinetmakers mount over a lathe bed to flute furniture parts. Our fixture consists of a cradle in which the column lies and a plywood guide board, with a wide slot in it for maneuvering the router (drawing, top of facing page). The slot is wider than the router base by just the right amount. We guided the router down one side of the slot to cut one side of the flute and down the other side of the slot to cut the opposite side of the flute. First, most of the waste was removed with straight bits in two separate routers, cutting almost to the final depth. Then, when most of the waste was out of the way, the finished shape was cut with a custom-made, carbide-tipped fluting bit. We cut one side of the flute at a time, holding the router first against one edge of the guide slot, then against the other. Then we rotated the column in the fixture, to cut the next flute.

Working with the redwood was troublesome. Dusty and brittle, it tended to chip and splinter rather than cut cleanly. We used our epoxy-based filler to replace what got torn out. Then we scraped each flute using old plane irons that we ground to shape, and sanded with 80-grit paper stretched over sanding blocks shaped to fit. It took a lot of time and work to achieve the look of stone and the softened edges at the junctures of the flutes and lands.

The fluting removed so much wood from the columns and pilasters that we were concerned about their ability to support the weight of the entablature blocks, roof and upper balustrade. So we decided to reinforce each pilaster and column on the inside with a 6-in. dia. Lally column with ¼-in. steel plates welded top and bottom (photo facing page, center). The bottom plate would fit over bolts in the concrete base. Pouring such bases was also a modification of the plans. But the added weight of the Lally columns might have compressed a wooden base, making it more vulnerable to moisture and rot.

We had originally planned to secure the entablature boxes to each other, to the building and to the capitals of the four columns and pilasters, which would have found their own positions on the floor of the porch. Now that we had to set metal plates over bolts in the foundation, we were locked in to the need for perfect alignment of all pieces. The need for accuracy became almost overwhelming.

Balustrades—The final units we milled and assembled were the upper and lower balustrades. The original lower balustrade had rested on the floor of the porch with its top rail mortised into the fluted surfaces of the columns and pilasters. Our sequence of assembly wouldn't allow us to use the same technique. Instead, in the shop we mortised a stub of the shaped top rail into each column and pilaster at the proper height. The rail itself we left long, to be cut to fit, once the porch supports were in place, and joined to the stubs with epoxy and screws. Epoxy filler and paint would make the joint invisible.

For the sake of good drainage and to keep the wood off the floor, the rectangular bottom rail of the lower balustrade would be mortised to receive steel plates embedded in the bases of

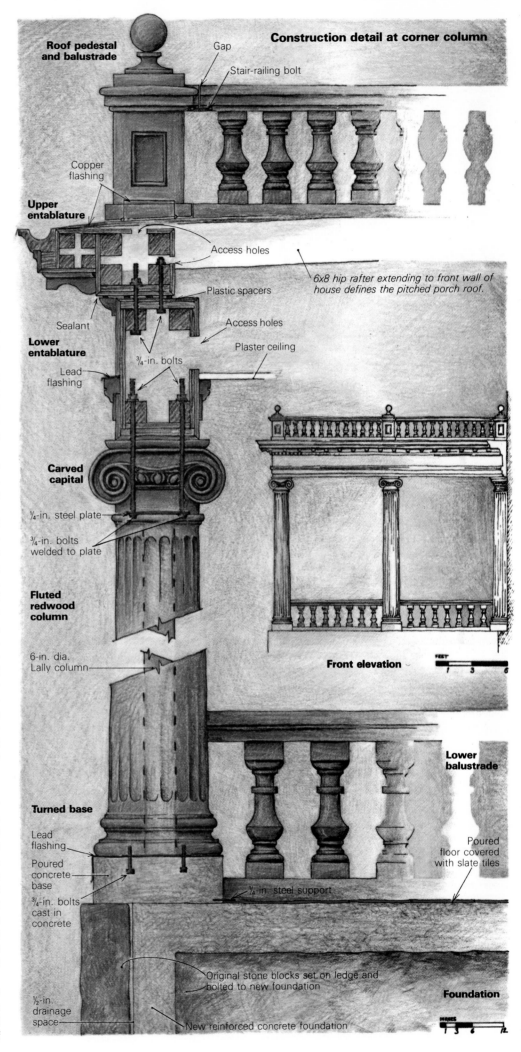

Construction detail at corner column

Roof pedestal and balustrade

Gap

Stair-railing bolt

Copper flashing

Upper entablature

Access holes

6x8 hip rafter extending to front wall of house defines the pitched porch roof.

Plastic spacers

Sealant

Access holes

Lower entablature

Plaster ceiling

¾-in. bolts

Lead flashing

Carved capital

¼-in. steel plate

¾-in. bolts welded to plate

Fluted redwood column

Front elevation

6-in. dia. Lally column

Lower balustrade

Turned base

Lead flashing

Poured concrete base

¾-in. bolts cast in concrete

¼-in. steel support

Poured floor covered with slate tiles

Original stone blocks set on ledge and bolted to new foundation

Foundation

½-in. drainage space

New reinforced concrete foundation

The first upper entablature block with its overhang and gutter is bolted down through ventilation holes.

the pilasters and columns. These plates would position the rail as well as support it.

The shaped top rails of the balustrades were big, and the mahogany stock for them had to be glued up. The blanks had to be perfectly flat and straight. To cut the bevels on the top rails, we shimmed under each edge in turn and passed the blank through the planer. We used the shaper for the molded edges of the rail. The knives of the shaper, planer and joiner did not stand up well to the hard epoxy glue lines in the wood, and we had to resharpen them often.

Final shop work—Once the porch components were fabricated, we began the exacting job of aligning them and working out a fastening system. We set the entablature blocks on six rugged sawhorses in the positions they would occupy on the finished porch. The lower blocks were bolted to each other, and to the upper blocks as well. Plastic-laminate spacers between them simulated mortar joints. The capitals were set under the entablature and positioned to achieve exactly the right projection of the abacus (the top of the capital). We then drilled holes through the capitals into the entablature blocks, corresponding to the bolts welded on top of every Lally column. We also

bored holes in the ends of the entablature pieces that would adjoin the building. The wooden porch would be secured to the stone with ¾-in. anchor bolts, and we used templates to drill holes in the building. The only latitude we would have on the day the porch was erected would come from drilling the holes in the wood ⅛ in. to ¼ in. oversize.

We disassembled the porch components and sealed them with a liberally applied, two-part penetrating epoxy varnish, wiping off the excess to avoid leaving a sheen. This sealer was important—it would weatherproof the wood, make it hard, and fill any microscopic checks, particularly in the outer veneer of Bruynzeel.

Painting, the final step, ultimately gave the wooden parts the look of stone (sidebar, below). We began with two coats of an acrylic artist's paint, custom-mixed to match the original red brownstone, then added beach sand of the correct color to a third coat. As this coat dried, additional sand was thrown on to dry in. Since the sand adhered only to horizontal surfaces, each part of the porch was painted on one side at a time and then rotated.

Foundation—By this time warm weather had come, and work on the foundation for the new porch had started. The original foundation—three large stones about 5 ft. by 10 ft. by 8 in. set on edge above ground to form the base of the porch—was carefully removed, and the brick below grade was dug up. The subcontractor poured a reinforced concrete foundation around the perimeter of the porch with a concrete ledge below grade. The old foundation stones were set on the ledge and blocked up with slate shims, then bolted to the new concrete from inside, leaving a drainage space between the stone and concrete.

A floor slab with a slight pitch for runoff was poured as part of the foundation. Once it had cured, slate tiles 12 in. by 12 in. by ½ in. were laid in mastic and grouted. Then the concrete bases of the columns and pilasters were poured, and flashed with lead to prevent contact with the redwood supports. The bolts and steel plates were cast into the bases.

Assembly—The porch was to be erected in a single day, using a crane to lift the pieces into place. The columns, pilasters, balustrades and entablature blocks were loaded on a flatbed truck and delivered to the site. We were excited and a bit apprehensive.

We had set staging on the floor of the porch for the men who would fasten the pieces as they were lifted into position. First the right-hand pilaster, and then the middle column were set in place and steadied with ropes. The lower entablature block on top of these supports was next. The left pilaster, outside column and the entablature block on top of them followed. The corner block was last. The four upper blocks of the entablature forming the cornice were positioned and bolted, ending with the corner piece. The fit was almost perfect. We had not chipped away enough of the stone quoins on the facade to allow our work to butt tightly against the building. Once this was done, the new porch, seven entablature blocks, four columns and pilasters were in place. Six months of shop work assembled in a day—and it looked like stone. We celebrated.

In the next several weeks the porch was completed. The new roof had to be framed. To slope it, a large hip rafter was let into the masonry and rested upon the lower entablature block. The frame was covered with plywood, and a copper roof with flat soldered seams was installed. Copper was also formed to line the mahogany gutter, and a copper downspout was added. The pedestals of the roof balustrade were set in place over copper-covered flash blocks. To keep the copper from being penetrated, we didn't use screws, nails or bolts. The balustrade itself was fastened to the pedestals with concealed stair-railing bolts. After the porch ceiling had been plastered, we cut and installed the lower balustrade. We filled the spaces between large pieces with silicone caulking to simulate mortar joints. Some paint was touched up, and the job was done. The new porch fits so integrally into the structure of the mansion and so closely resembles stone that most passers-by have forgotten that the old porch ever disappeared. □

Paint for restoration. For some years home owners have felt dissatisfied with exterior house paints. Modern paints do seem to peel and scale off more readily than yesterday's, which were based on white lead and linseed oil. Some attributes of modern paints—the high strength of alkyd resin paints, for example—would probably do more harm than good to aging houses, whose surfaces of weathered wood and old paint are more crumbly every year.

While planning for the Morse-Libby mansion's new portico, we reviewed all the types of paint that might perform better than what is commonly available. We set out to weather-test samples of various paint systems, including lead and linseed oil, applied to the mahogany plywood. At the end of six months, all the samples looked good. We finally chose Liquitex, an artist's quality latex (made by Binney and Smith, 1100 Church Lane, Easton, Pa. 18042), because after the period of weathering, its samples could be immersed in water for ten days and were still highly resistant to scraping with a knife.

The term latex describes the physical form of the paint binder: microscopic spheres of resin dispersed in water, which fuse together as the water evaporates. The resins used vary enormously. The best ones are highly resistant to deterioration. In the Liquitex system, one buys

the acrylic latex binder separately and adds white and color pigments that come dispersed in the same type of binder. The restorer is thus free to formulate the paint according to the needs of the project. The Liquitex color pigments are non-fading iron oxides, good absorbers of the ultraviolet light that would otherwise attack the latex resin.

Why isn't such paint sold in hardware stores? First, its cost would not be competitive. Second, it would probably not perform too well as a regular house-paint because of the difficulty latex paints have in penetrating and binding with weathered or chalky substrates. At the Morse-Libby mansion, we felt we could circumvent this adhesion problem by providing a new, waterproofed and stabilized substrate.

This paint dries very quickly. We had some trouble applying the extra sand to the final coat, because it was setting up so fast and because the sand would fall off any surface that wasn't horizontal. We tried to keep the surfaces flat, and we worked up a technique using troughs to catch and hold sand for difficult elements like the balustrades.

Extra sets of samples on the weathering rack will give us accurate comparisons of durability as time goes on. We need this information. New woodwork of good quality, or old woodwork laboriously reconditioned, deserves better paint. *—Morgan Phillips*

Period Moldings

A primer on these touchstones of Neo-Classical architecture

by Norman L. Vandal

Moldings are structurally non-essential building elements that help ease the transitions between large, primary structural elements. In Classical Greece and Rome, these primary elements were the plinth, the column, the capital, the entablature and the pediment (these and other architectural elements are explained in the Glossary on the next page). Over the years, Classical orders—the interrelationship of the dimension, proportion and location of these elements—were established. Composed of both structural and non-structural elements, they became accepted as proportionately correct and aesthetically pleasing. These strict proportions were adapted much later, when a maturing and increasingly humanistic Europe turned to the Classical past for architectural inspiration.

The Neo-Classical period lasted 150 years or so, and passed through several phases, known in the United States as Georgian (or Colonial), Federal and Greek Revival. There was no abrupt chronological dividing line between these styles, and in some cases overlap

is apparent (see pp. 16-19). The Classical forms were subject to various vernacular interpretations by country builders, who were quick to improvise. A craftsman who owned planes for making Federal moldings wouldn't have been likely to discard these tools and get new ones just because the Greek Revival style happened to be in fashion.

Nonetheless, each of the periods is characterized by the use of particular moldings to embellish essential architectural components. These moldings are distinctly different in each period. On pp. 43-45, the profiles of some of the moldings most characteristic of the different periods are drawn to scale (a profile is the combination of curved and straight parts that form a well-proportioned, graceful whole). They can help you date or restore period structures.

The Greeks and Romans carved their moldings in marble or stone, or cast them in aggregate. The inherent weaknesses in the stone were design determinants, and thus thin edges and steep projections were avoided. As

a result, these moldings were often bold and bulky in section.

When Neo-Classical architecture began to catch on in late 17th-century England, however, wood was the most common material for residential building. All of these moldings were cut with wooden planes that were designed for specific profiles. Some of the simpler configurations were produced on the building site, but the larger, more elaborate ones (bed and cornice moldings and bolections, for example) required specialized planes and the expertise of the shop joiner to make them correct and consistent. Moldings were cut by hand this way until the middle of the 19th century (see *FHB #11*, pp. 36-41). I do a lot of restoration and reproduction work, and I still make and use such planes.

Here's a short primer on the characteristics of the three periods.

Georgian period (c. 1720 to 1790)—At this time, designers and builders in England were abandoning the motifs of the Jacobean period,

Georgian entrances were often elaborate, formal and robust. Builders imitated Roman moldings, and based their details on segments of the circle.

Federal details were still based on sections of the circle, but they were lighter and more delicate. Windows had thinner mullions and, often, semicircular tops.

Greek Revival detailing was based on the ellipse. Architects and builders consciously turned to the cradle of democracy as an appropriate model for American architecture. Columns, pilasters and moldings were larger, but simpler. Facades became grand, often harking back to the Parthenon and other Greek temples.

Glossary

Architectural elements

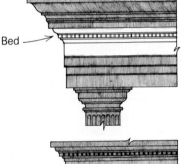

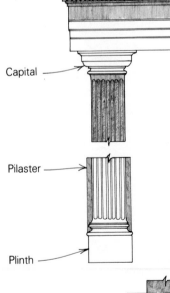

Pediment: The triangular space that forms the gable end of a peaked roof.

Entablature: The horizontal portion of a structure, which is supported by the columns. The entablature, from bottom to top, is composed of the architrave, the frieze, the cornice, and, in some interpretations, the pediment.

Cornice: Outside, the uppermost decoration on a structure, found either at the top edge of the pediment or at the top edge of the entablature where a pediment is not present. Inside, the molding at the intersection of wall and ceiling.

Fascia

Soffit

Fascia: The vertical face of the projecting cornice. The cornice molding is applied to the fascia.

Soffit: The horizontal underside formed by the projecting cornice as it overhangs the frieze.

Bed

Bed: A molded decoration at the intersection of the vertical frieze and the horizontal soffit. In profile a bed molding is similar to or the same as the capital.

Frieze: The portion of the entablature directly below the soffit. At the top edge of the frieze, below the soffit, is the *bed molding*.

Architrave: Outside, the lowest portion of the entablature, directly above the capital or the top of the columns. The moldings that decorate the architrave are often repeated on interior and exterior window and door casings, and these are also called architraves.

Capital

Capital: The molded decoration found at the top of a column or pilaster. It softens the transition between the vertical column and the horizontal entablature.

Pilaster

Pilaster: A vertical element made to resemble a column partly set into the wall.

Plinth

Plinth: The block that the architrave or column sits on.

Chair rail: A molding running around a room at the height of the back chair posts, probably introduced to protect wall surfaces from being marred by furniture, but clearly accepted as a decorative element.

Wainscot: An interior wall treatment using boards or panels to cover the wall from floor to about window-sill height. Wainscot can also be a much broader term used to describe a manner in which boarding is used in various applications, including the construction of a particular form of furniture.

Moldings

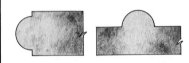

Astragal: A convex, semicircular molding—usually applied—which projects above the surface of a flat plane.

Bead: A small, rounded molding usually found at the edge of a board. It is usually planed or carved, not applied. The most common architectural molding.

Quirk bead: A bead that has a narrow groove along one edge, and so appears to be separate from the surface upon which it is planed. Other moldings, such as ogees, can also be quirked.

Thumbnail bead: A molding in the form of a quarter-round, planed at the edge of a board with a slight step down from the surface upon which it is cut. Usually found on the rails and stiles of Georgian doors and fielded panel walls.

Bolection: A profile or group of moldings that separates two planes and projects from the surface of both. Usually found surrounding Georgian fireplaces.

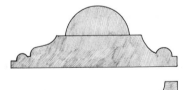

Cove: A rounded, concave molding, sometimes called a *scotia*.

Dentil: A small, rectangular block in a series that project like teeth. Dentils are usually found as elements in a cornice, and are thought to represent purlins projecting beyond rafters.

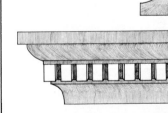

Ogee: A molding that is formed by a continuous double curve, concave below, convex above. Sometimes called *cyma reversa*.

Reverse ogee: Also called *cyma recta*. An S-shaped molding convex below, concave above.

Ovolo: A convex molding—a quarter circle in Roman architecture, but a more elliptical curve in the Greek—which steps down from the surface on which it's planed and has a step at the bottom end of the curve.

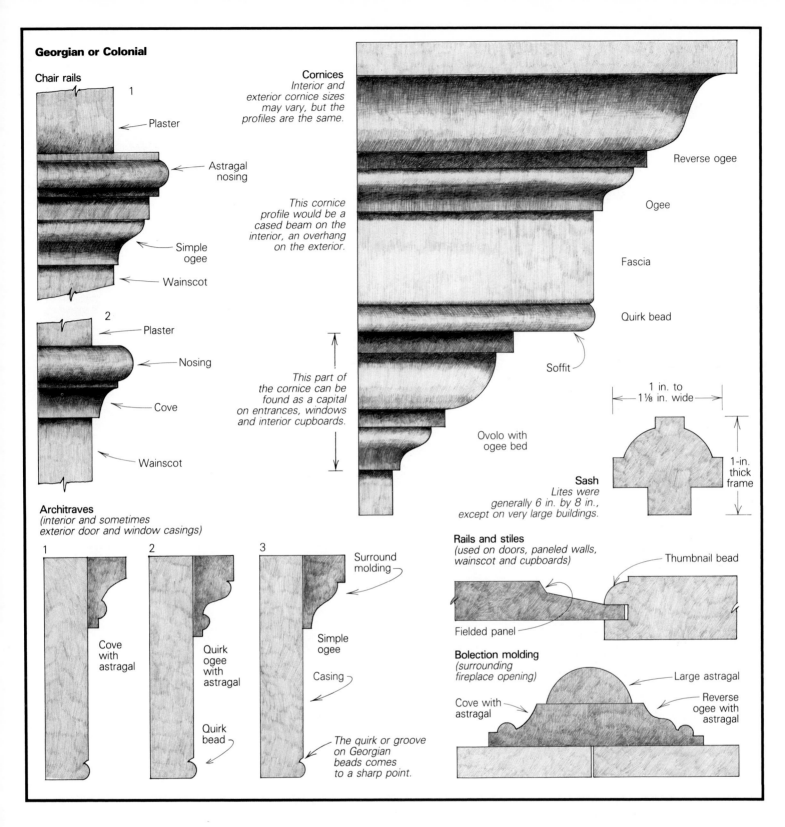

Georgian or Colonial

Chair rails

1

Plaster

Astragal nosing

Simple ogee

Wainscot

2

Plaster

Nosing

Cove

Wainscot

Cornices
Interior and exterior cornice sizes may vary, but the profiles are the same.

This cornice profile would be a cased beam on the interior, an overhang on the exterior.

This part of the cornice can be found as a capital on entrances, windows and interior cupboards.

Reverse ogee

Ogee

Fascia

Quirk bead

Soffit

Ovolo with ogee bed

Sash
Lites were generally 6 in. by 8 in., except on very large buildings.

1 in. to 1⅛ in. wide

1-in. thick frame

Architraves
(interior and sometimes exterior door and window casings)

1

Cove with astragal

2

Quirk ogee with astragal

Quirk bead

3

Surround molding

Simple ogee

Casing

The quirk or groove on Georgian beads comes to a sharp point.

Rails and stiles
(used on doors, paneled walls, wainscot and cupboards)

Thumbnail bead

Fielded panel

Bolection molding
(surrounding fireplace opening)

Cove with astragal

Large astragal

Reverse ogee with astragal

---

which was characterized by the use of stone and masonry in early attempts to imitate the Classical forms. Wooden houses began to replace stone, and this led to more refined Classical lines. Guidebooks were published in England which heralded the new style, called Georgian after the four Hanoverian King Georges whose reigns began in in 1714. The trend crossed the Atlantic and took hold in the increasingly prosperous Colonies, where builders were quick to abandon the older, almost medieval styles.

Georgian buildings were larger and more symmetrical than their predecessors. Elaborate entrances that resembled scaled-down

Classical temples were composed of pilasters, entablatures and ornate pediments. The larger windows were treated with capitals or cornices. Bed and cornice moldings were applied to soffits and fascias. The overall impression was massive, formal and ornate.

Inside, the austerity of the Pilgrim-century house gave way to rich ornamentation, and moldings became an important design element. Posts and girts, formerly left exposed, were cased with pine. Ceilings were plastered. Paneled walls and wainscot came into vogue, along with appropriate Classical moldings. The fireplace wall became a focal point, with the opening surrounded by a large molding

called a bolection. Cornices at the intersection of wall and ceiling were the crowning touch.

The moldings of this period were bold and heavy. Their curves, like those of the Roman moldings they imitated, were based on segments of the circle. American builders interpreted the Classical style literally, and the molding profiles were not really elegant or refined. But this period did signal the acceptance of moldings as necessary elements in architectural ornamentation.

Federal period (c. 1790 to 1825)—This post-Revolution style was also spawned in England, where it is called Adamesque, after

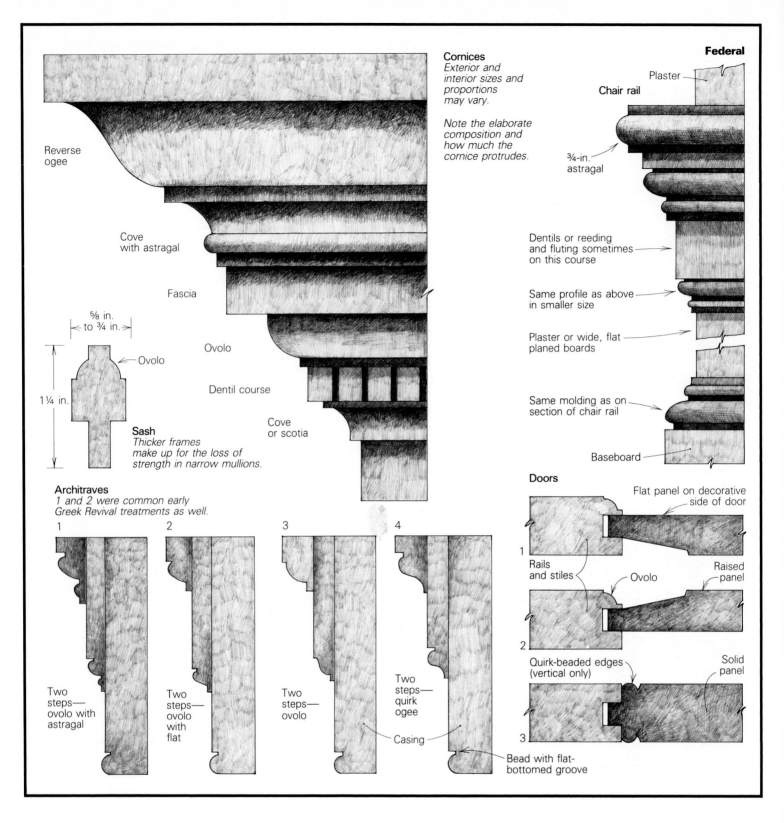

Cornices
Exterior and interior sizes and proportions may vary.

Note the elaborate composition and how much the cornice protrudes.

Reverse ogee

Cove with astragal

Fascia

Ovolo

⅝ in. to ¾ in.

Ovolo

1¼ in.

Dentil course

Cove or scotia

Sash
Thicker frames make up for the loss of strength in narrow mullions.

Architraves
1 and 2 were common early Greek Revival treatments as well.

1

2

3

4

Two steps— ovolo with astragal

Two steps— ovolo with flat

Two steps— ovolo

Two steps— quirk ogee

Casing

Bead with flat-bottomed groove

Federal

Plaster

Chair rail

¾-in. astragal

Dentils or reeding and fluting sometimes on this course

Same profile as above in smaller size

Plaster or wide, flat planed boards

Same molding as on section of chair rail

Baseboard

Doors

Flat panel on decorative side of door

1

Rails and stiles

Ovolo

Raised panel

2

Quirk-beaded edges (vertical only)

Solid panel

3

the brothers, Robert and James Adam. Boston architect Charles Bulfinch brought the new forms back from England and used them in several noted buildings, among them the Massachusetts Capital. Asher Benjamin, a student of Bulfinch's, heralded the new Federal style when he published his builder's guide, *The Country Builder's Assistant,* in 1797.

During this period, the Classical models in molding ornamentation were refined. Joiners took advantage of the fact that wood could be worked to yield thinner edges and flatter projections. Lightness and delicacy became the new guidelines of design.

Buildings were given a lighter and airier feeling. Windows got bigger again. The low, squat appearance of Georgian structures was replaced by a sense of verticality.

The larger window panes had thinner mullion profiles. Federal entrances were reduced in scale, and semicircular gable-end windows became popular.

Inside Federal-style houses, mantelpieces, often with pilasters and carved friezes, became focal points in formal rooms. Plastered surfaces replaced paneling in many parts of the house. Wainscot gradually disappeared, leaving only the molded chair rail and the baseboard. The interior cornice was decorated but lightened. The large expanses of plas-

ter served to set off the lighter and more delicate moldings, and expressed their new importance. Moldings were meant to be noticed and appreciated.

Greek Revival period (c. 1820 to 1840)— This was a time of conscious return to Greek forms, which were considered to be purer than the Roman forms used in earlier periods, and more suitable for the architecture of a young republic. The Greek differs from the Roman in that all parts in the order are larger, and convey a sense of solidity and simplicity. There are fewer ornamental members than in the Roman, which on large structures can be

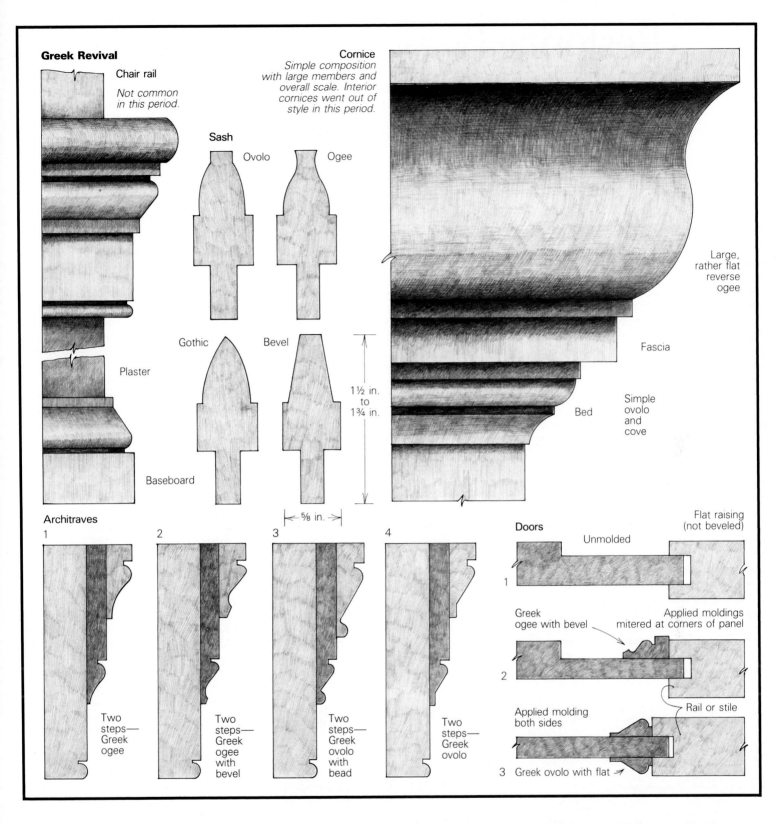

Greek Revival

Chair rail

*Not common
in this period.*

Plaster

Baseboard

Cornice
*Simple composition
with large members and
overall scale. Interior
cornices went out of
style in this period.*

Sash

Ovolo

Ogee

Gothic

Bevel

1½ in.
to
1¾ in.

⅝ in.

Large,
rather flat
reverse
ogee

Fascia

Bed

Simple
ovolo
and
cove

Architraves

1

Two
steps—
Greek
ogee

2

Two
steps—
Greek
ogee
with
bevel

3

Two
steps—
Greek
ovolo
with
bead

4

Two
steps—
Greek
ovolo

Doors

Flat raising
(not beveled)

Unmolded

1

Greek
ogee with bevel

Applied moldings
mitered at corners of panel

2

Applied molding
both sides

Rail or stile

3 Greek ovolo with flat

less confusing. The entablature is larger, with more room for ornamentation.

Roman molding profiles are composed from segments of a circle; Greek moldings from segments of an ellipse. During the Greek Revival period, it was believed that the flatter, elliptically shaped moldings offered a more pleasing reflection of light from their surfaces. The rounder Federal moldings began to fall into disuse. In some rural interpretations of the Greek Revival style, flat, unmolded stock was substituted for moldings, and the effect was quite pleasing.

The new Greek Revival style was a marked departure from the Federal period, and Asher Benjamin kept pace with the times. The sixth edition of his new guide, *The American Builder's Companion* (1827), presented drawings of the Greek orders for the first time, and the impact was tremendous.

On a Greek Revival exterior, the larger proportions of columns and pilasters, the wider entablatures and the larger yet simpler pediments and cornices give Greek Revival structures a solid appearance reminiscent of ancient Greek temples like the Parthenon. The gable end, turned to face the street, became the most important facade. Elliptical sash supplanted the Federal semicircle over entrances and in gable ends. Pedimented entrances lost popularity, and sidelites were used instead of a transom above the door.

The biggest change inside was that the fireplace was replaced by the more efficient woodstove. As a result, the mantel nearly disappeared. Interior cornices were deleted, as were chair rails. A movement to elevate the staircase as the focal point, which had its roots in the Federal period, culminated in the Greek Revival period with the design and execution of the free-standing elliptical staircase, a marvel of Neo-Classical architecture. □

Norman Vandal makes period architectural components and period furniture in Roxbury, Vt.

Restoring Brownstone Facades

Techniques for repairing and replacing 19th-century architectural elements

by Sarah Latham

Brownstone was first commonly used as a building material in New York City during the 1820s and 1830s. Numerous quarries in the East supplied the stone, which was a trim substitute for the more costly marble or limestone. By the 1850s and 1860s, entire rows of townhouses contained brownstone facing or veneer applied to rubble or brick walls. What began as an economic measure had become fashionable.

By the end of the 19th century, however, the use of brownstone as a building material had declined. According to Professor Norman Weiss of the Historic Preservation Program of Columbia University, its waning popularity during the 1880s was due to three causes: a change in public taste, the rise in the use of terra-cotta, and the change in materials selection wrought by the structural needs of multi-story buildings.

Attention shifted to the deterioration of existing brownstone facades, which had become a common and recurring phenomenon. Then, as now, water was the culprit, either as a vehicle for chemicals and salts or in a freeze/thaw cycle. As early as the 1850s articles appeared in building periodicals with remedies for delaminating facades that included the use of linseed oil as a waterproof coating and stabilizer.

Preservation specialists attribute brownstone decay to the nature of the material and the way it was face-bedded on buildings (see "Why stone decays" on the facing page). Brownstone is actually a brown sandstone that consists of multilayer accumulations of water or wind-borne rock. Over long periods of time these sediments became naturally lithified or cemented. When first quarried, brownstone is often pinkish in tone but turns brown as its ferruginous ore oxidizes. It is the iron content that accounts for its color.

Because the brownstone was formed by accreting layers of sediment, it is prone to delamination. On buildings, the layers of stone scale or peel off because the bedding planes were stacked on end (see drawing, facing page). When laid perpendicular to the facade, the surface is less susceptible to delamination or exfoliation. Proper maintenance and cleaning will lengthen the lifetime of brownstone facades (see "Cleaning stone buildings" on p. 49).

If money were no object the most suitable method of restoring brownstone facades would be replacing the damaged material with natural stone from the same or a similar stone quarry. But most of the original brownstone quarries in this country are closed. Currently, sources of supply for replacement brownstone are limited to one dealer of used stone in New Jersey and a sandstone quarry in Ohio. For more information and suppliers, see the list on p. 49.

It is usually more practical to restore the facade by reconstructing the stone surface with either a mortar of cement mixed with crushed brownstone or a mortar dyed to match the existing facade. In practice decayed stone is cut back to a sound substrate and the area is built up with a series of applications of the mortar. This process—known as composite patching or plastic repair—is one of several methods presented here which may be considered for restoring brownstone facades.

Concrete aggregate resurfacing—The most common solution to delaminating brownstone is to remove the damaged stone and resurface the affected area with scratch coats of cement and a finish coat of tinted cement.

Under the direction of Frank Matero of the National Park Service, U.S. Dept. of the Interior, restoration work on the exterior facade of the Theodore Roosevelt Birthplace in New York City included application of a pigmented cement-base composite. The photo below left shows a detailed view of a delaminated brownstone area on the Roosevelt House. The damage was partially caused by the migration of water, which had entered the brownstone surface at the joint line. As seen in the photo below right, mason Dean Korpan of Structural Antiquities Unlimited in Armonk, N.Y., carefully chiseled the deteriorated brownstone. (The use of power-driven tools to remove stone should always be discouraged. They are difficult to control and may inadvertently destroy salvageable stone.)

Once the surface was taken back to a sound substrate, the mason applied the scratch coat surface. At the Theodore Roosevelt Birthplace, small holes were drilled into the surface of the stone to provide a keying bond (photo facing page, top). The scratch coat was forced into the perforations, forming a "toothed" adhesion, then scored in the traditional manner to receive the tinted finish coat. Bonding occurred in this process as the composite mixture (described below) settled into the scored recesses of each preceding coating.

A scratch coat is composed of portland cement and generally will not be tinted. It is usually not less than ¾ in. or more than 3 in. deep. Once the scratch coat has cured, the final or finish coat is then applied.

During the application of the finish coat, the contractor continually moistened the line of contact between the natural stone and the composite patch. As shown in the photo on the bottom of the facing page, this step lessened the chance of rapid shrinkage and helped achieve

Photos, except where noted: Frank G. Matero, National Park Service

A delaminated brownstone facade stone, left, on the Theodore Roosevelt Birthplace in New York City. Delamination has been caused by the migration of water and salts through the face-bedded stone due to improperly maintained mortar joints and the consequent freeze/thaw cycle. At right, mason Dean Korpan removes the deteriorated brownstone. Decayed stone is cut back to a sound substrate in preparation for the application of a scratch coat of cement (see photos, facing page).

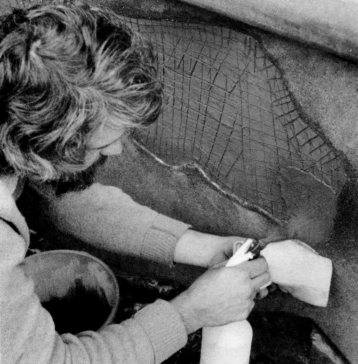

A drilled surface, top, gives the scratch coat a strong, keyed grip on the sound stone substrate. Successive coatings are scored before the finish coat, above, is applied. Korpan continually moistens the contact edges of the natural stone and the brownstone replacement aggregate. This lessens the shrinkage in curing.

Why stone decays

Stone building facades bake in the summer and freeze in the winter. Their cornices glitter with icicles in one season and run with torrential rains in the other three. Stone buildings in cities are cloaked with polluting gases and splashed with salty slush from streets and sidewalks. To survive these ravages, stone buildings demand vigilant care.

Stone deterioration originates with the exertion of some type of unusual pressure from either physical or chemical forces. Water is almost always the source of the problem. Moderate exposure to rainwater is inevitable and, to some extent, beneficial. Damage occurs with cycles of heavy saturation and drying. These cycles may be caused by leaking gutters, ineffective cornices, blocked drains or clinging vegetation. The following are common causes of stone decay.

The freeze/thaw cycle. Water drawn deep into the stone by capillary action causes mechanical stress on the pore walls when it freezes.

Salt crystallization. Soluble salts are carried with water into the pore network, where they form crystals. Because the salts have a larger volume when crystallized than when dissolved, their expansion damages the internal structure of the stone. Frequently salts originate in mortars containing portland cement or from the brick or backing material to which a stone facing is attached. Salts from bird droppings deposited on cornices and sills and sodium chloride scattered to melt ice on steps aggravate stone decay. A telltale sign of a problem in the stone is the formation of efflorescence (salt deposits) on the surface. It frequently appears on new stone facing placed against a damp backing material.

Acidic action. Acids deposited on limestone, marble and some sandstones gradually dissolve the stone. The result is roughening of the surface, separation of bedding planes where soft seams were washed away, erosion around fossil fragments and loss of detail in carvings.

Vegetation. Moss, lichens, vines and even thick shrubbery around a stone foundation trap moisture in stone and prevent evaporation. But probably the greatest damage is caused by roots, which gradually open joints and dislodge particles of mortar through mechanical action.

Structural settlement. In cases of severe settling, sound stones will crack at weak points, such as lintels and sills of doors and windows.

Face bedding. The durability of sedimentary stones such as limestone and sandstone can be drastically affected by the incorrect placement of the blocks. Stone blocks should be laid in the same position as the stone originally laid in the quarry (see the drawing below). On its natural bed, the stone's bedding planes are horizontal. If face-bedded, or laid with bedding planes vertical and parallel to the face of the wall, the surface of the stone will scale in sheets or layers. Face bedding was common in 19th-century construction; stone for columns or door jambs was often placed on end to take advantage of its greater length.

Edge bedding. Edge-bedded stones are laid with bedding planes vertical but perpendicular to the face of the wall. In time, the seams on the exposed surface of the stone may wash out between the lamination. Edge bedding is acceptable on cornices and string courses, which would erode rapidly if the stone were laid on its natural bed.

Open joints. Spaces between stones that are inadequately sealed with mortar allow water to penetrate deep into the masonry. Open joints are caused by settling and by the failure of the mortar to withstand the physical contraction and expansion of stone. This problem frequently arises because too little mortar was used or because the mortar mix did not contain lime, was too hard and eroded.

Rust expansion. Rusting of embedded ironwork is often a problem with railings set into stone steps as well as with concealed metal dowels and clamps inserted during construction. As the iron corrodes, its volume increases and exerts too much pressure on the hole in which it was fitted, causing the stone to split. —*Cornelia Brooke Gilder, a building materials consultant for the Preservation League of New York State.*

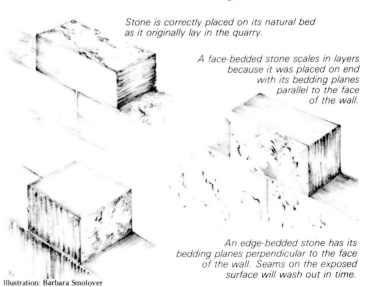

Stone is correctly placed on its natural bed as it originally lay in the quarry.

A face-bedded stone scales in layers because it was placed on end with its bedding planes parallel to the face of the wall.

An edge-bedded stone has its bedding planes perpendicular to the face of the wall. Seams on the exposed surface will wash out in time.

Illustration: Barbara Smolover

Photo: Carl Forster, Landmarks Preservation Commission of New York City

a similarity in texture between the natural stone and the composite patch.

The finish coat is made to resemble brownstone in color and texture through the use of pre-mixed products or a mixture of pre-washed sand and high-calcium lime cement tinted with synthetic pigments or pulverized brownstone. Depending on the nature of the stone to be matched, mica may be added to the recipe as well. The finish coat was steel-troweled and allowed to cure for about six weeks.

Once the finish coat was sufficiently cured, the area was washed down with a weakened solution of muriatic acid. This was followed by a thorough rinsing with water. The acid wash evens out the surface by slightly weathering the finish coat.

Throughout the restoration job on the Theodore Roosevelt Birthplace, Korpan worked in his shirtsleeves. It is important that such work take place only at a constant temperature above 40°F. The use of antifreeze in the mixture should be discouraged, as should the use of artificial heating devices.

In an added attempt to fool the eye, Korpan used wooden screeds to create an artificial joint line between the composite patch and natural stones. Once the composite patching and cast stone elements were keyed in and cured, the wooden screeds were removed. The artificial joint lines were then pointed. This maintains the original appearance of laid stone.

Polymerchemical consolidants—Several attempts have been made to perfect a polymerchemical consolidant to treat damaged stone in situ with a preservative. But methods and materials used to consolidate irreplaceable masonry elements remain in the experimental stages. One obstacle to the use of this process is that the original stone may not accept the chemical consolidant—what Professor Weiss refers to as "transplant rejection."

A few European firms have developed techniques or products for applying polymerchemical consolidants on stone. These methods are primarily used on statuary and in areas that don't have the freeze/thaw conditions we see in the U.S. Consequently, these products have seen little use in this country. In my experience, it is too early to determine the ultimate success of such processes.

Painted portland surface—An inexpensive treatment for delaminating brownstone is to remove the damaged stone and to replace and resurface the facade with untinted portland cement. The cement surface is then painted with a "brownstone" paint, generally a latex paint with sand suspended in the emulsion. Decayed architectural elements can be reconstructed using wood pieces covered with brownstone paint. This process is not usually recommended since once the paint coating wears away, the untinted concrete or wood surface will be exposed. The

To reconstruct the three stoops on W. 119th St. (above), Bill Londino used a shopmade plaster model of each newel post (two pieces), railing (three pieces) and baluster. The cost of making the models and molds was $4,600, and the cost of casting the individual stoop elements was $1,200. All expenses for the new stoops were paid under the provisions of the Facade Improvement Program of the city's Landmarks Preservation Commission, which retained the molds for future use on similar building facades. At the Theodore Roosevelt Birthplace (below), a fractured original coping stone is being drilled to receive Teflon reinforcement rods for its reunion. The small drilled holes provide additional bonding between the surfaces when an epoxide resin adhesive is applied between the surfaces.

Sarah Latham is a former landmarks preservation specialist of the Facade Improvement Program for the Landmarks Preservation Commission of the City of New York.

owner will be faced with a continuing maintenance problem—the repainting of the facade.

Painting—The least successful repair is to paint over the delaminating brownstone surface. This "solution" is merely a cosmetic deferral of the problem. The latex paint coating will soon peel away, exposing the damaged brownstone. If it is ever necessary to remove the paint, the job will be very costly, and in most cases unsuccessful.

Cast-stone elements—Damaged or missing individual stone elements such as foliated door consoles can be replicated in cast stone. When existing elements are in usable condition, a casting is made with a latex mold. This mold is then used to make a plaster negative from which a cement positive is cast. When existing elements are not available, a plaster negative can be created from prefabricated shapes and hand-sculpted parts.

An interchangeable detail that is common to a row of buildings can be economically cast. The initial cost of the mold can be split among several owners, and castings made as needed for each facade. The final product is basically tinted concrete and much less expensive than replacement stone or cast-iron architectural elements.

Cast-stone elements were used to replace missing stoop newels, balusters and handrails for three properties on New York's W. 119th St., under the Facade Improvement Program of the Landmarks Preservation Commission of the City of New York. Bill Londino of Londino Stone Co., Bronx, N.Y., prepared the plaster model and all castings for the project, located in the Mount Morris Historic District. The design was based on sketches and measurements from a nearby stoop, plus some prefabricated parts and hand-sculpted details. After he made a

---

For more information and supplies...

The New York Landmarks Conservancy recently published the results of an extensive study of sandstone restoration techniques in a leaflet for owners of landmark properties. The report is available from the New York Landmarks Conservancy, 330 W. 42nd St., New York, N.Y. 10036; (212) 736-7575.

Preservation and Conservation: Principles and Practices ($17.95), National Trust for Historic Preservation, 1976, and *Introduction to Early American Masonry* ($6.95), by Harley McKee, National Trust and Columbia University, 1973. Both available from Preservation Press, 1785 Massachusetts Ave. NW, Washington, D.C. 20036; (202) 673-4084.

The Cleaning and Waterproof Coating of Masonry Buildings by Robert Mack, AIA. Preservation Brief No. 1. Free from the National Park Service, 440 G St. NW, Washington, D.C. 20243; (202) 343-1100.

Facade Improvement Program of the Landmarks Preservation Commission of the City of New York, 20 Vesey St., New York, N.Y. 10007; (212) 566-7577.

Preservation League of New York State, 307 Hamilton St., Albany, N.Y. 12210; (518) 462-5658.

Reused Connecticut brownstone (a deep red brown), rescued from demolished buildings and inactive quarries, is available from David Anderson, Pascack Valley Stone Co., 401 Demarest Ave., Closter, N.J. 07624; (201) 768-2133.

Quarried sandstone (ranging from chocolate brown to almost black; ask for samples first), used for brownstone repairs and replacements, is available from Ken Taylor, Briar Hill Stone Co., PO Box 398, Glenmont, Ohio 44628; (216) 276-4011.

---

mold of this plaster model, Londino was able to pour a concrete casting. Reinforced with steel bars, the mixture contained synthetic iron oxide pigments that are lime-fast and sun-fast for durability. Sixteen balusters, six rail pieces and four newel-post parts were set on steel pins and joined in place with mortar to create an entire stoop. The color and texture of the completed stoops (photo facing page, top) are uniform. This allows for a natural appearance as the stone weathers and wears in use. Also, there are few joint lines, allowing few avenues for water to enter and cause damage in the future.

Molds for creating cast-stone replacement elements can also be built from wooden forms. Mason Dean Korpan constructed a wooden form to cast a replacement coping stone during the restoration of the exterior facade of the Theodore Roosevelt Birthplace.

Faults can occur if the cast stone is improperly keyed or joined to the natural stone. So Korpan used Teflon rods (photo facing page, bottom), which are not subject to corrosion or damage due to the expansion of the joint and any fissures that develop in the surrounding masonry materials. The natural stone was drilled to receive the Teflon rods, and smaller holes were drilled around them. Drilling provides "teeth" for a successful bonding of the surfaces.

Fiberglass—Fiberglass can also be used to replace ornamental elements. The technique for its use is similar to cast stone in that it uses latex for both negative and positive impressions. But fiberglass replacements are best used only on the higher elevations of a building because there is a marked difference in texture and tint which is evident at street level. Another disadvantage is the potential contusion: One well-aimed rock can craze a fiberglass element.

The advantage of fiberglass as a substitute for sandstone is its lightness of weight. This makes it easy to key in or apply as a cap to existing stone. However, fiberglass as an exterior material is untested for its long-term durability and flame-retardant properties.

Permits and grants programs—The brownstone restoration work discussed in this article was performed on structures in two of the city's 41 designated historic districts. The Theodore Roosevelt Birthplace is also listed in the National Register of Historic Places. When a building is located in a historic district, one must apply for a work permit to perform the needed restoration. The preservation agency or housing authority charged with issuing permits may also have references to masonry contractors who have successfully worked on listed buildings.

Some local authorities have access to federal monies, matching grant programs or state historic preservation funds to pay for restoration work. For instance, the Facade Improvement Program of New York City's Landmarks Preservation Commission provides grants up to $10,000 to cover restoration expenses on building exteriors. These grants are available to owner-occupants whose annual gross income is $13,650 or under and whose buildings are located in a designated historic district. □

Cleaning stone buildings

Various cleaning techniques are available today; the choice must be made on a case-by-case basis. In each instance the proposed method should be tested on different parts of the building in order to determine the most effective technique. It may be necessary to use several cleaning methods on buildings constructed of different kinds of stone or a combination of materials, or in areas where delicate carvings sit amidst massive stone surfaces. Cleaning is particularly important for urban buildings where streaky, uneven accumulations of salt and dirt are not only damaging but may hide other problems such as settlement cracks, open joints and deteriorated stonework.

Water cleaning. In general, this is the most versatile, simplest and cheapest method. Water cleaning involves a low-pressure wash to soften the dirt deposits, followed by scrubbing with bristle brushes or a high-pressure jet for stubborn, heavily soiled patches. The disadvantages of water cleaning are that the work must be completed in frost-free months and that prolonged spraying (which saturates both the facing stone and its backing) may precipitate other problems such as dry rot, rust expansion, and damage to interior plaster, woodwork and paint. However, careful planning can usually overcome these problems.

Steam cleaning. In recent years the popularity of steam cleaning has decreased due to possible danger to the operator, expensive equipment and limited effectiveness. It is still used for cleaning intricately carved areas that would be damaged by brushing, and for removing chewing gum from pavements and floors.

Chemical cleaning. Two general categories of chemical agents, acidic and alkaline, are used for cleaning stone. Their use demands a thorough understanding of the materials to be cleaned. Acidic cleaners are used on granite and some sandstones, but they will erode a limestone lintel or a glazed terra-cotta ornament. Alkaline cleaners can be used on such acid-sensitive stones as marble, limestone and calcareous sandstone. To prevent harmful salt residues, chemical cleaners must be thoroughly washed off with water at the end of the cleaning process. The advantage of chemical cleaning over water is that faster results can be achieved using smaller quantities of water with less risk of staining. On the other hand, rinsing off chemicals with water jets can force the cleaning agents into open cracks and joints.

Mechanical cleaning. Sandblasting or abrasive cleaning with grinders and sanding discs is not recommended for cleaning stone without careful field testing. Relatively soft stones (like limestone and marble) can be damaged under the impact of inappropriately selected aggregates applied at high pressures. Polished stones will become dull and scarred. Mineral grains of even hard granites can be shattered or pulverized by sandblasting, leaving the building without its original sparkle and luster. Mechanical cleaning can be a useful and safe method when understood and conducted with a battery of carefully monitored field tests using a range of aggregates at various pressures.

Maintenance of cleaned surfaces. Properly cleaned, a building should be given regular, light washings (at five-year intervals in urban areas) to prevent dirt build-up. Waterproof coatings and silicone water repellents have not proved effective in dirt inhibition or in stabilization of stone decay. Instead, they may seriously damage masonry by trapping water behind the coating.   —C.B.G.

Molding and Casting Materials

Plaster is still the old master, but rubber by-products give more options

by John Todaro

In restoration work there are times when the only way to reproduce an object is to mold it and pull a cast. This is the case with plaster moldings, ceiling rosettes, cornices, decorative plaster work, friezework, wood carvings and missing metalwork on furniture. With the proper materials it's possible to make a mold of any object: I've even molded high-relief patterned wallpaper. Why go to all the trouble? Usually, the parts are either impossible to get or are too expensive to have made professionally.

In making a mold or negative image of a part to be reproduced, your materials selection depends on factors such as cost, complexity of the part and the number of times you'll use the mold. In casting reproductions from molds, your choice of materials is affected by the surface finish wanted, weight, strength and other factors that vary with each application. The materials list I offer here is by no means definitive, but it should give you a good idea of the range of the products available to the restorer.

Molding materials

Plaster of Paris—Plaster, the all-time classic molding and casting material, is made from gypsum rock that has been heated to drive off the water. The resulting soft rock is crushed into a powder; when water is added, the powder recrystallizes into a solid as hard as the original gypsum rock.

Plaster is cheap, easy to use and doesn't shrink—important where dimensional accuracy is crucial—but large molds and castings can become quite heavy. Although plaster won't stick to the object you're molding or to the castings if you use a mold-release agent, casting objects with severe undercuts may require knockdown molds of several pieces. Because plaster has a short working life, professionals slow setup time by adding lime: generally one-third plaster to two-thirds lime for plastering walls. A teaspoon or so of liquid hide glue or fish glue added to the plaster will slow setup time by about two hours. Opened plaster absorbs moisture from the air and will form lumps when you try to mix it, so don't buy more than you need, and store what

John Todaro, 42, lives in Brooklyn, N.Y. He uses molding and casting techniques to restore ornamental plasterwork in old brownstones.

Ceiling rosette cast in plaster of Paris. (Photo by Jeff Fox.)

you don't use in airtight containers or tightly sealed bags in a dry place.

Moulage—A special molding material commonly used to take impressions from life (or, as the case may be, death), moulage should be used when an object is delicate or when its patina must be preserved. Napoleon's death mask was made using moulage. It captures the finest detail and, best of all, is reusable.

Moulage is usually used to create one master mold from which a more durable mold is made. To do this, heat a block of moulage until it melts. Carefully paint the moulage (while still warm) on the object to be molded, and allow it to cool and set. Before peeling the mold from the object, make a mother mold of plaster or, if the mold is large, from damp sand. This will provide support for the somewhat fragile moulage mold. Make the master cast (plaster is most commonly used) and from the cast make the master mold, using whatever material is most suitable for your purposes. To reuse the moulage, just reheat.

Liquid rubber latex—This material easily can become the restorer's workhorse; it is an excellent molding product that creates light, flexible, durable molds suitable for a variety of casting compounds. It's easy to use, sets quickly, reproduces detail well, doesn't shrink, has inherent release ability (though you may need to use a mold-release agent on complex parts), is tear and crack-resistant, and can be used to make molds of objects of any material. However, if the patina on the object to be molded must be preserved, don't use liquid rubber latex: This material, like plaster, can destroy an object's finish.

Liquid rubber latex comes with a filler; the more you add, the more rigid your mold will be. Since the filler is less expensive than the latex, using more filler will also extend your latex supply. This is a technique developed for mass production where costs are to be kept minimal, but this technique has its limits. I've found that one part latex to three parts filler is an acceptable proportion for molds used to mass produce objects with no undercuts; more filler than this will tend to make the material crumbly. If you are molding a piece with severe undercuts, however, reduce the amount of filler to provide the most flexible mold possible. It's a good idea to experiment. To capture maximum detail on intricate parts you can use the latex without filler for the first coat or two of a mold built up to about five coats, but don't construct the entire mold out of fillerless latex because it will be so flexible that it will lack "memory," and it won't snap back into the shape of the object you have just molded.

RTV silicone rubber—You can make molds of objects of almost any material with RTV (room-temperature-vulcanizing silicone rubber) including low-melt metals, and it is stiff enough so that a mother mold is not needed. It has inherent release ability, but on complex parts it's necessary to use a mold release or graphite. This gentle material won't destroy an object's patina, the way liquid rubber latex and plaster can. It captures finer detail than latex and is stronger, but it is more expensive.

RTV is a two-part medium: a liquid silicone-rubber base and a catalyst or curing agent. Once mixed, it sets quickly and hardens within an hour. It is generally too thick to be brushed on, so you must use a box or a casting jig.

When using RTV silicone rubber, make sure your work area is adequately ventilated, and avoid breathing in fumes. The material may also cause skin irritation, so wear rubber gloves and wash off any compound that you happen to spill. These simple precautions also apply to a few of the other molding and casting materials mentioned here: polyester resin, Monzini compounds, polyurethane foam, and epoxy casting resins. It's essential to read manufacturer's directions and cautions carefully before using any molding or casting material.

Polyester resin—By alternating coats of polyester resin and layers of fiberglass you can build up rigid molds good for hundreds of casts. The advantages of this method are many: You can capture fine detail, molds are lightweight and are excellent for pliable castings, such as from latex rubber. They also work well for thin sheet castings or for large castings with light materials, such as polyurethane foam. This method is also used where RTV would not be economical, or where plaster would be inappropriate or too heavy. However, polyester resin molds are inflexible, and to cast undercuts, you will have to build a knockdown mold of several pieces. Careful preparation of the original with a release agent is imperative.

Polyester resin is used with a catalyst—once mixed it will set up within half an hour, so never mix more than you need. To thicken the polyester resin, add Cab-O-Sil (fumed silica, which comes in the form of light flakes) when mixing the resin and catalyst; it adds bulk and strength to the mold. How much you add depends on how thick you want the material to be. Ideally, it should pour slowly, like heavy honey—use too much Cab-O-Sil and the material won't pour, use to little and it will be runny.

Pour the resin/catalyst/silica mixture on the object, which has been treated with a release agent, and let it set. When the first coat has hardened, apply a layer of fiberglass. Paint or pour more polyester resin on the fiberglass, smooth with a piece of wood or a scraper, and let it set.

If you're making a large sheet mold, a few 2x4s or 2x2s or pieces of pipe will keep it from warping. Lay the braces on the back of the mold, then cover them with polyester resin and strips of fiberglass so that wood will bind to mold. This will also give you something to grip when holding the mold besides the mold's sharp edges. When fiberglass is used with polyester resin, you'll know why they call it fiberglass—all edges of the mold must be filed or sanded to take off the razor sharpness.

Plastilene—Plastilene is used for either small or simple one-time-use molds of objects having no undercuts. It's fine for simple surface impressions. Simply press it evenly onto the object,

making sure that you get a good impression, then peel carefully—you should have a perfect negative of the object, ready for casting. Plastilene gives fair detail, doesn't shrink and is reusable and resonably priced. However, it has poor release ability and may adhere to the object you're molding. It tends to tear and crack if not peeled carefully. Don't handle it too much, because the heat of your hands will soften it and it will be even harder to remove. A little trick in making simple sheet molds is to soften the plastilene in your hands, press it into place and then cool it while it is still on the object. If it is small enough, put it in the refrigerator for ten minutes or so, then peel. If it is not possible to put the mold in the refrigerator, let it stand for an hour or until it feels harder to the touch. Once it firms up, you will be able to remove it from the original with less tearing and cracking.

Plastilene is available in most art-supply stores and comes in hard, medium and soft grades. Medium is the best all-around grade for restoration molding. The soft grade might catch in the detail and rip, or might not hold detail; the hard grade may crack off when you try to remove it.

Casting Materials

Plaster of Paris—Plaster is a fine casting material, and most of the advantages of molding with plaster pertain to casting as well. Plaster can be cast in most molding compounds—even in plaster molds—if you use a mold-release agent. The amount of plaster cast is critical, however. Too heavy a piece may require additional mold support and too thin a piece may be fragile.

If you cast plaster in a plaster mold, here are a few tips. Always use a mold release. Coat all surfaces of the mold, the inside as well as the outside, where plaster might drip and stick. I recommend purchasing inexpensive, commercially

prepared mold release, but you can make your own mold release for plaster by boiling a pound of Ivory soap in about two quarts of water until dissolved, then adding two more quarts of water to thin. Let the brew settle overnight. Thick, glutinous sizing will settle to the bottom, while a clear, syrupy liquid will be at the top. This sizing will be just right to use. Remember, if you don't size the mold before you pour a cast, all you will have is a large plaster doorstop.

A variety of products having characteristics similar to plaster are available for use in casting. Hydrostone, for example, is a mixture of very fine plaster and ground stone. It is stronger and gives finer detail than plaster, and has a sparkly, stonelike look. It comes in terra cotta, black, brown, French buff, grey-green, bronze and crystal white, and you can mix your own colors by adding water-based pigments. Hydrocal, less expensive than Hydrostone (both are more expensive than plaster), gives a dead-white, matte surface. Hydrocal is also stronger than plaster, and gives finer detail.

Latex casting rubber—Despite being sold under a different name, this material seems identical to liquid rubber latex. It is also used with filler, but usually more than is used for moldmaking: Three parts filler to one part latex casting rubber gives a good, rigid cast. Latex casts are flexible and can be cut or trimmed with a sharp knife or razor blade. They can be given a patina or antiqued, and are light enough to mount with white glue (such as Elmer's) or, for a more permanent bond, epoxy adhesive. Latex casting rubber is inexpensive and easy to use in most molds with the proper release agent.

Monzini liquid casting compounds—Monzini compounds have been used by sculptors for

Just wiggle your fingers

How you stir plaster for casting is important, because you don't want air bubbles trapped in the mixture. This is how I learned to do it. Sprinkle plaster in the center of a bowl filled with water (never the other way around). Keep sprinkling until a mound of plaster just rises out of the water. Then put your hand down to the bottom of the bowl and wiggle your fingers so that the plaster is stirred from the bottom and no air bubbles are entrapped. When the plaster has a smooth, slightly-more-than-heavy-cream consistency, you are ready to pour. Plaster is curious stuff: If you sift it into water and don't disturb it, it will not set up quickly. Once mixed it begins to set up normally.

Pour plaster smoothly, without splashing, to avoid trapping air bubbles in the cast. After pouring, but before the plaster sets, vibrate the mold by pounding the table beneath with a rubber mallet, or by tapping the mold sharply a few times. —*J.T.*

years to simulate the textures of bronze, Carrara marble and aluminum. Monzini Bonded Bronze consists of bits of pulverized bronze fused together with bonding liquid. You can cast it in a mold, or apply it to the surface of a previously cast object for a bronze appearance. Carrazini Monzini, the most popular of the compounds, is ivory-colored. To produce the grains and colors of marble, Monzini color pastes are added. Lumizini produces casts that both look like and can be polished like aluminum. All the compounds will reproduce detail as fine as an object's finish, whether matte or polished. Monzini compounds set in under 30 minutes at 75°F, and can be cast in plaster, latex rubber, RTV, metal, wood or Monzini molds, though because of the expense,

casting Monzini in Monzini is impractical. Defects or air bubbles can be repaired simply by filling them with the same material. Monzini compounds won't shrink, and the casts are weatherproof. They can be machined, sanded, drilled, taped and polished. You can weld pieces together using more Monzini compound and clamping the pieces until they set.

Monzini compounds are expensive but worth it. Use Monzini compounds within three months from the date on the label, and be sure to use up however much you mix.

Low-melt metals—The Kindt-Collins Co. distributes Cerro Alloys, a line of six metals with low melting points.

Melt low-melt metals in a double boiler on the kitchen stove. Be sure to use an old pot that you don't need for cooking food, because alloy residue may be difficult to remove completely. Pour the molten metal into your mold and let it cool, and you have a metal cast without going to a foundry. But this convenience doesn't come cheap: Cerro Alloys are sold in two-pound lots, priced by the pound. Prices range from about $10 per pound for Cerrobase 255°F to about $19 for Cerrotru 218°F. A hint for casting low-melt metals: Powder the mold with graphite so the casting pops out of the mold easily.

Polyurethane foam—This material is appropriate where lightweight, bulky castings are

Molding and casting a ceiling bracket

Clean and repair the object to be reproduced and seal its edges with clay (A). Then shellac it, and let it dry. Paint on a coat of fillerless mold rubber, leaving a lip at least 1 in. wide around the object. Brush out any air bubbles. When the rubber has dried, apply the second coat. Let it dry. Mix mold rubber and filler 1:1 in a clean container. Paint on two coats of this mix, drying in between.

Next lay on strips of cheesecloth 2 in. wide by 3 in. to 5 in. long, covering with rubber/filler mix as you go. Cover the object with two or three layers of cheesecloth and rubber/filler (B), allowing drying time between, and finish with a coat of rubber/filler. Let dry, then trim the lip with a mat knife.

Because the weight of a casting can pull even a reinforced mold out of shape, you'll need a mother mold (usually made out of plaster) to support the rubber mold during casting. A simple casting jig made of four pieces of wood and angle irons (see drawing on facing page) will hold the mother mold.

If the object has undercuts, you'll need a two-part mother mold. First, make a shim by cutting a piece of cardboard to the shape of the mold. In places the cardboard won't follow the form, tape pieces of scrap in position and trim to fit. Place this guide on a new piece of heavy cardboard and trace the shape to make the shim. To prevent plaster from running through to the other side, fill open spaces in the shim with clay (C). Apply clay to the side of the shim opposite the side you'll be pouring first.

Place mold and shim in the casting jig, shoring up the sides of the shim with wood supports clamped to the jig with C-clamps. Tape all edges with masking tape to prevent the plaster from leaking into the other side (D). Size the inside of the casting box, the mold and the shim with mold release.

Mix the needed amount of plaster to a heavy-cream consistency. Pour the plaster into the jig until it's an inch or two above the mold (E). Let it set, then remove the shim.

Scoop out three alignment holes (F) with plaster modeling tools or a hooked knife. Then size the mold, casting box and mother mold so

A

B

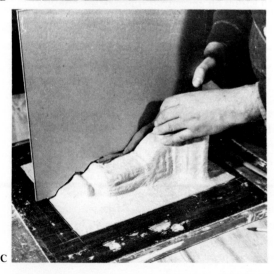

C

D

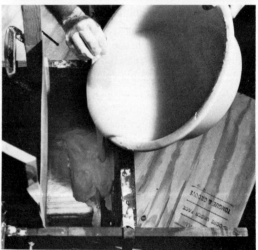

E

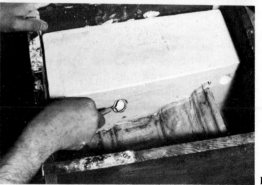

F

needed, such as fake wooden beams and simulated moldings. It can be painted, given a patina, and cut and shaped.

Polyurethane foam is a two-part casting medium that, when mixed, quickly expands approximately 30 times its liquid volume, filling the mold with foam. It's tack-free in about five minutes, and can be removed from the mold in about twenty. You can cast polyurethane foam in plaster, RTV, latex, wooden or metal molds treated with a mold release. Polyurethane foams are available in a range of colors and in three weights: light, medium and dense.

Epoxy casting resin—There are so many different manufacturers and types of epoxy casting

resin that I will touch on only a few of specific interest to the restorer. Emerson and Cuming, Inc., for example, produces the Stycast line of about 70 casting resins, commonly used in the electronics industry. These include general-purpose casting resin (Stycast 2651); a foam epoxy used in aircraft that is so light it floats (Stycast 1090); and a transparent epoxy gel that, when cured, is tough but flexible (Eccogel 1265).

High detail casts, little shrinkage, low cost and ease of use are some of its advantages. Epoxy-resin castings can be machine-cut, drilled and taped; they also adhere to metals, plastics and ceramics. Disadvantages include short pot lives, poor acceptance of paint, and for some, vacuum evacuation for bubble-free casts. □

Sources of supply

Silastic RTV silicone rubber and series 31 RTV rubber: Dow Corning Corp., P.O. Box 1767, Midland, Mich. 48640; also Industrial Plastics Supply, 309 Canal St., New York, N.Y. 10013.

Hydrocal, Hydrostone, moulage, liquid rubber latex, latex casting rubber: Sculpture House, 38 E. 30th St., New York, N.Y. 10016; or Arthur Brown Bros., Inc., 2 W. 46th St., New York, N.Y. 10036.

Adrub RTV rubber, Arte-Vee RTV Kwikset, Adrub RTV Softee, Monzini compounds, polyurethane foam: Adhesive Products Corp., 1660 Boone Ave., Bronx, N.Y. 10460; Industrial Plastics Supply.

Eccosil RTV silicone rubbers, Stycast epoxy casting resins: Emerson & Cuming, Inc., Canton, Mass. 02021.

Low-melt metals: The Kindt-Collins Co., 12651 Elmwood Ave., Cleveland, Ohio 44111.

Cab-O-Sil: Industrial Plastics Supply.

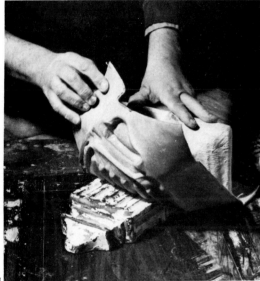

G

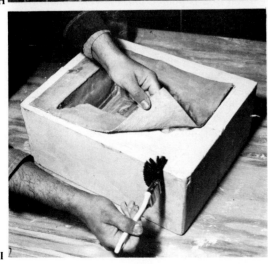

H

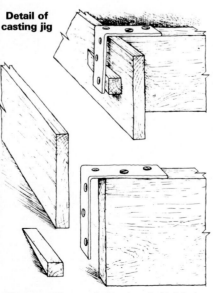

I

that the new plaster will not stick. Pour the other side and let set.

Pry mating halves of the mother mold apart with a spatula. Try to let both sides dry thoroughly before casting (**G**).

Carefully peel back the latex mold from the original object (**H**). Scrub the mold to get rid of any bits of debris that might have accumulated inside. (Liquid rubber latex is notoriously rough on surface patinas.) Dip the mold in very hot water to vulcanize and it's ready for use. (If you don't use the mold until sometime later and find it has become rigid, simply immerse it in hot water until it regains flexibility.)

Place the mold in the mother mold, sizing both mold and mother mold with mold release (**I**). Mix enough plaster for one cast and pour, breaking all the bubbles. Work quickly, and fill the mold before the plaster sets (**J**). Tap the table with a mallet to help release air bubbles from the cast, and smooth out the back of the cast with a straightedge (**K**). Now is the time, while the plaster is setting, to add a hanger or bracket, if necessary for mounting.

When the cast is dry, simply lift it and the mold out of the mother mold and pull the rubber mold back (**L**). Trim off any excess from around the foot of the cast.

Detail of casting jig

All corners slip together and are held tight by wooden wedges.

J

K

L

Decorative Ironwork
Repairing and replacing 19th-century castings

by Rachel Carley

Economical, mass-produced, and available in a fascinating range of patterns, ornamental cast iron was one of the most successful products of the Industrial Revolution in America. Although cast iron was produced by settlers as early as 1664, it wasn't regularly used as a building material on this side of the Atlantic until the early 1800s, when it was introduced to home owners by English and American architectural handbooks. By about 1825, cast-iron gates, fences, balconies, window grilles and other ornamental forms had become commonplace in most major coastal cities.

Readily available through mail-order catalogs, cast-iron details were a ready substitute for more expensive hand-forged, or wrought, iron. The material owed its immense success to low cost and an easy adaptability to the elaborate Victorian design motifs popular at the time. Until the industry was eclipsed by the development of steel at the turn of the century, cast iron had substantial impact on the architectural makeup of the American streetscape, where it often contributed much-needed texture, rhythm and scale. For some examples in New York City and Albany, see the photos on the facing page.

Today, 19th-century cast-iron detailing is an important part of our architectural heritage, and it should be preserved or replaced in kind wherever possible. Although the extensive selection of 19th-century patterns no longer exists, old designs can be copied, and several architectural metals companies are capable of reproducing traditional patterns (see the list of sources on p. 56).

Cast vs. wrought—Wrought iron, which is hand worked rather than mass produced, has a low carbon content (less than 0.3% and usually less than 0.1%). A malleable material, it can be hammered out either hot or cold. You can often recognize wrought iron by the hammer marks and other irregularities that remain on the finished work. The slender stock bars from which the iron is wrought are usually shaped into scrolls or twisted into sinuous designs, rarely displaying the sculptural relief and dimensional depth that cast iron can achieve. Cast iron and wrought iron were sometimes incorporated in the same piece of work, especially on fences and gates, showing off the advantages of both materials.

Cast iron is a commercial alloy of iron and silicon with a relatively high carbon content (usually 2% to 4.5%) and a high melting point (1,200°C to 1,250°C). Although it has good compressive strength, it is a non-malleable material, too brittle to be worked with a hammer. Instead, cast iron is formed by pouring the molten metal into a mold, and can therefore take on almost any shape.

Molds for casting iron are made from sand that is mixed with a binder and usually packed in two halves around a pattern—a master of the shape that was traditionally fashioned from yellow pine or mahogany. Today patterns may be wood, aluminum, urethane, wax, or plaster of Paris. In some cases, the original element to be copied can be used as the pattern. Elaborate patterns can require molds made in several parts.

Once the sand has received the negative impression of the master, the pattern is removed and the halves reassembled. The molten iron is poured into the void (photo left), where it cools and hardens in the shape of the original pattern, though it shrinks slightly as it cools (about ⅛ in. per foot). Then the sand is removed, and the casting is cleaned up by grinding and buffing.

Some cast-iron ornaments, especially those applied to a flat surface, are sculpturally relieved only on the face side. This simplifies the mold-making process because only one of

Photo: Don Quick

Left, foundry workers pour molten iron into a mold of hardened sand. Manufacturing techniques have changed little since the first cast-iron details were produced in this country more than 300 years ago. Cast iron lent itself readily to the ornamental whimsy of the Victorian period, leaving a distinctive mark on the American streetscape, as shown in the photos on the facing page. Fences and gates sometimes combined wrought and cast iron.

Photos facing page: top, and bottom right, Rachel Carley; others, Andrew Dolkart

the halves has to receive an impression from the pattern. Since the same pattern can produce identical pieces over and over again, architectural cast-iron designs can almost always be mass produced.

Dealing with rust—Water is the chief enemy of cast iron; most maintenance is a matter of keeping the metal free from rust. This includes cleaning and painting, which, if done right, doesn't have to be done often.

There are a number of ways to remove rust. On most cast iron, you'll want to remove flaked layers of paint as well as patches of rust, and clean the piece thoroughly so that you'll have a bare metal surface to refinish. Avoid using chemical paint strippers and naval jelly because they have to be washed off with water. Bare cast iron can hold moisture for a long time. If the metal isn't completely dry when it's painted, it will rust, and the paint film will flake off.

Sandblasting can produce good results, and is a reasonable method for cleaning cast iron on a large-scale basis (building codes in some regions prohibit this method, though). Shrubbery and nearby wood or masonry can easily be damaged if you are blasting the cast iron in place, so protect these adjacent areas. And to avoid pitting the cast iron itself, never set the air pressure above 100 psi.

For the small-scale cleaning that most residential jobs demand, rust and old paint are best removed from cast iron with a wire brush and elbow grease, or with a rotary brush chucked in an electric drill. With either method, wear good eye protection.

Once you've worked your way down to bare metal, prime the cast iron immediately to minimize its exposure to dampness. Use an oil-base, rust-prohibitive primer with a high zinc-oxide or red-lead content. Follow two coats of primer with two coats of an exterior-grade, oil-base enamel. Always use primer and paint from the same manufacturer, and don't apply either one if the temperature is below 40°F.

Anchoring cast iron—As iron rusts, it expands. When iron rusts within a masonry or concrete stoop or sidewalk, it can break the stone apart. For this reason, cast-iron anchoring pins should be set in stone with a lead cushioning agent. The lead shields the iron from water and acts as a malleable cushion when stone and iron contract and expand during the freeze-thaw cycle. Unlike lead, quick-setting cement and similar compounds do not provide the necessary give.

The lead is usually melted and then poured around the cast-iron pin, which is centered in a drilled hole, undercut so the lead won't pull away from the masonry. When the lead solidifies, it should be peened with a hammer to tighten the seal. Where it isn't possible to pour molten lead into the masonry, strips of lead can be pounded in around the pin, or bolts and lead expansion shields can be used to fasten cast iron in place.

Large details, like newel posts, are usually held in place with a tension rod. This is just a long rod, fastened into the wall or floor at one end and threaded at the other so that the newel post or similar detail can be bolted down (photos below). The nut is sometimes concealed in a finial or similar cap.

Joining one cast-iron piece to another traditionally called for pins, rivets or bolts. This is still the best way to join cast-iron pieces today. Mating pieces were usually designed with slight channels or overlaps for strength, appearance and ease of assembly. Conventional welding not only obliterates the joint lines, but also can damage the iron since the weld will contract and expand at a different rate from the surrounding metal. When theft and vandalism are problems, nuts can be spot-welded to bolts and pins can be heated and peened over. If welding is unavoidable, then use an arc welder with nickel-cadmium electrodes to keep welding temperatures low. □

Rachel Carley, a former landmarks-preservation specialist for the New York City Landmarks Commission, writes frequently on restoration.

Installation. With most large cast-iron details, many parts make the whole. Tension rods and alignment pins hold the assembly together and anchor it in place. Below left, a tension rod is anchored in concrete with molten lead. The rods extend through balusters and a lower railing section (below right); nuts pull the assembly together. The newel post is installed the same way.

Replacing an Oak Sill
Doing the job on a formal entry without tearing out jambs and trim

by Stephen Sewall

When I undertook the task of repairing the front entry of a Colonial Revival house in Portland, Maine, with its large 3½-ft. by 8-ft. door and side lights, I knew that the most difficult part would be replacing the rotted oak sill. It had suffered the neglect that many do, eventually checking and rotting from exposure to the weather because it hadn't been given periodic coats of sealant. The other repairs—which included replacing the raised panel in the door, replacing the pilaster bases, repairing the side lights and making some crown molding to replace part of the portico trim—were reasonably straightforward, but the sill presented some problems.

It seemed impractical to remove the entire jamb, replace the 7-ft. long sill and then reinstall it as the original (drawing, p. 58) had been. Removing the jamb would require dismantling much of the trim both inside and out, so it would be a big, labor-intensive job. Also, disturbing the entry that much could make refitting the door and side lights more difficult. Finally, I decided it would be best to replace the sill while leaving the jambs—both the inner jambs and the outer jambs at the side lights—intact.

Before the old sill could be removed, though, the door and side lights had to be taken out. The side lights were held in place by stops on four sides. Since all of the trim was in good shape and I wanted to use it over, I was very careful to pry the stops out without damaging them.

The best tool I have found for removing any sort of wood trim is the Hyde #45600 Pry Bar-Nail Puller-Scraper. It has a thin blade that you can insert under almost any piece of trim without damaging either the molding or the surface to which it's attached. The thin end can also be sharpened so that you can cut small wire finish nails by hitting the other end of the bar with a hammer. The curved end of the pry bar can be used to open the joint up further and to scrape down the crusted paint before you reinstall the trim.

The stops of the side lights were inside mitered like most window trim, and because the side stops went in after the top and bottom, they had to be removed first. It's best to start prying at the middle, because the miters lock the ends in place. On each side light, I had to

Stephen Sewall is an architectural woodworker in Portland, Maine. Photos by the author.

The author installed a new sill in this Colonial Revival entryway before going on to replace the raised panel in the door and repair the side lights and part of the portico trim.

cut a few of the nails near the ends of the stop with the pry bar.

As soon as the stops were removed, I marked their back sides so I'd be able to put them back where they belonged. I pulled the remaining nails through from the back so I wouldn't disturb the finish side of the wood. The tools I have found most useful for this are a pair of end snips or end pliers. They shouldn't be too sharp or they will cut the nail instead of pulling it out.

After removing the side lights, I cut plywood panels to fit between the jambs. These would keep the jambs from floating free when I removed the sill. I made the panels short enough so that I'd have room to cut out the old sill underneath them (photo, p. 58). I attached the panels to the inner and outer jambs with drywall screws.

With the door and side lights removed and the jambs locked in place, I was ready to cut out the sill. I used a Sawzall with a 6-in. blade to make cuts through the sill on either side of both inner jambs, and as close to them as possible (drawing, p. 58). I made two more cuts 3 in. from each end of the sill, being careful not to hit the nails coming from the outer jambs into the end grain of the sill. This let

me remove three large chunks of sill, leaving only the four pieces directly under the jambs.

I split out the remaining sections piece by piece with a 2-in. chisel. With all of the wood removed, I was left with 20d nails protruding from the end of the jambs. To get rid of these, I used a metalcutting blade in the Sawzall where I could, and a hand-held hacksaw blade on the less accessible nails.

The old sill had rested on five equally spaced 1-in. strips of wood embedded in mortar and running the width of the sill. I removed them and the mortar so I would be able to slip the new sill under the tenons of the door jambs. I also chipped away the mortar line between the brick and the old sill so that new mortar could be worked in under the outside edge of the new sill once I shimmed it into place.

The new sill—I saved the best section of old sill as a pattern for the new one. After a clean, square cut on the radial-arm saw, I was able to trace a full-size end profile. But even if I could have found a 14½-in. wide piece of 10/4 stock, the replacement sill would have been too hard to make in one piece. The 2-in. raised section under the door meant ¼ in. of stock would have to be removed from the rest of the sill. Making the sill in two sections, one ¼ in. thicker than the other, and splining them together would reduce the work—and the waste.

With the widths of 10/4 oak stock I had available, I made up the sill out of a 6-in. wide piece and an 8½-in. wide piece. The 6-in. section became the part over which the door would sit. This meant that I had only about a 3-in. width over which I'd have to waste ¼ in. of stock. After face-jointing and planing the stock to a net thickness of 2¼ in., I rabbeted out the ¼-in. by 3-in. section on the jointer. (If you haven't got access to a jointer, you could do this on a 10-in. table saw with the blade fully extended.)

The flat, raised section under the door was beveled at 3° to the back of the stock on the table saw. I cut a 45° bevel from the flat under the door to the point at which the finish floor contacts the sill. I used a rabbet plane to cut the small bevel on the other side of the flat.

The 8½-in. wide section needed its front edge ripped at 93° from the face so that it would be plumb when the sill, which would slope slightly toward the outside, was installed. I routed the top front edge with a ball-bearing rounding-over bit. A ⅛-in. by ⅛-in. drip kerf was cut under the front edge of this piece to keep water from finding its way under the sill.

With all of the bevels cut and the front rounded over, I made the cuts for the splines. I cut a ½-in. slot 1 in. deep on each section of the sill, with the top faces held against the fence of the table saw. I epoxied in a piece of Baltic birch for the spline.

The visible parts of the sill needed to be belt-sanded before the wood could be finished. It's worthwhile to scrape off excess epoxy squeeze-out while you're gluing up because it can dull sanding belts in a hurry once it's dry. I find that most putty knives spread the glue on the surface rather than pick it up. The flexible tip of a small artist's paint knife, available at most art-supply stores, works much better.

To finish the sill, I wanted to use something more durable than spar varnish with an ultraviolet filter. In checking our local marine supply, I found that I had a choice of two two-part polyurethane varnishes that are used on the topsides of boats—Petit Durathane (Petit Paint Co., Inc., Borough of Rockaway, N. J. 07866), and Interlux Polythane Super Gloss (International Paint Co., 2270 Morris Ave., Union, N. J. 07083). It is important to buy the thinner recommended for these products. The first coat needs to be thinned down, because the unthinned varnish is a thick syrup that won't penetrate sufficiently. Be sure to use these products in a well-ventilated area. They smell terrible, and the vapors aren't especially good for your health. I applied three coats.

Installing the new sill—The top of the pilaster bases were in the way of installing the sill, and they also needed to be replaced, so I removed them. The bottom of the pilaster itself was also in the way, but the distance between the pilasters was only ¾ in. less than the finish length of the sill. I used my Japanese *azebiki* saw (it has rip teeth on one side, crosscut teeth on the other) to cut small sections out of the pilasters. Its thin, flexible blade makes a clean cut with a narrow kerf. I set the pieces aside to be epoxied back on once the job was complete and the sill and pilaster bases were in place.

I cut the new sill to length with a skillsaw against a homemade guide clamped onto the sill. To fit around the outer jamb framing, I cut 2-in. by 8-in. notches out of the inside ends of the sill. These were cut partway with the skillsaw and then finished off with a handsaw. With these cuts made, the sill could be slid into place.

My new sill was a little thinner than the old one, and the old mortar had been cleared away, so there was room for the sill to slide in under the tenons of the door jambs. With the sill held up snug against the tenons, I marked the mortise locations on the sill. Before I pulled it back out, I took a rough measurement at the back edge to see how much it would have to come up to be at the correct height to the finish floor. This gave me a di-

Side light

Outer jamb

Cut lines

Top scotia and half-round

Middle half-round

Inner jamb (tenoned into sill)

The original sill was set on wood strips bedded in mortar on top of the brick base.

Pilaster

Square base

Doorway with original sill

To start the job, Sewall removed the doorway's side lights and nailed plywood panels in place, with clearance beneath them to slide in the new sill. Then he removed the original sill, which had been resting on 1-in. strips of wood set in a bed of mortar.

Illustrations: Christopher Clapp

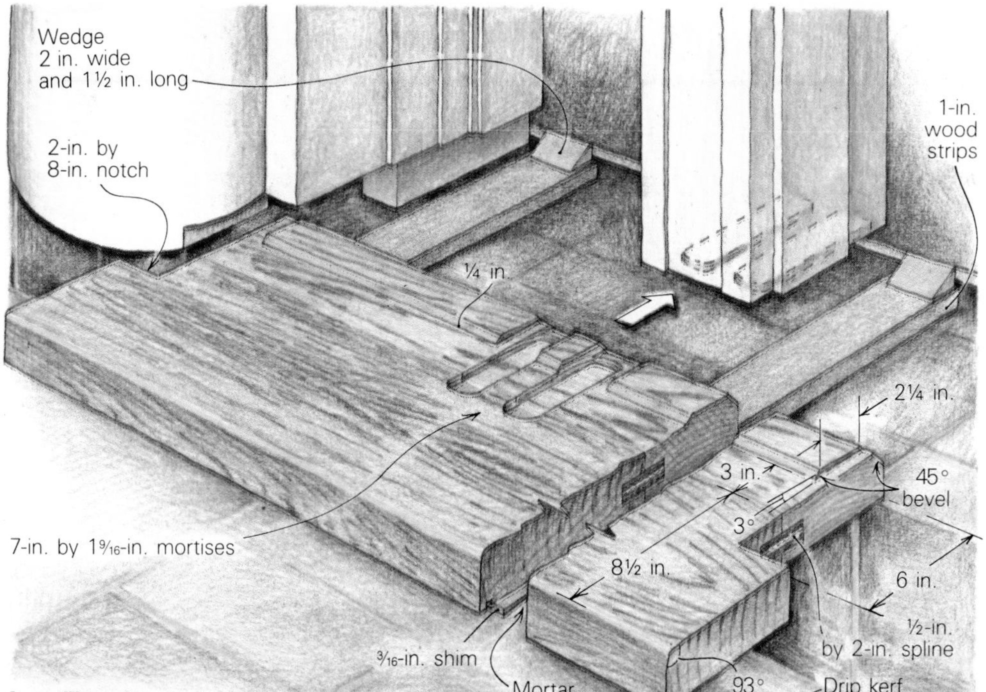
Wedge
2 in. wide
and 1½ in. long
2-in. by
8-in. notch
1-in.
wood
strips
¼ in.
2¼ in.
3 in.
45°
bevel
3°
7-in. by 1⁹⁄₁₆-in. mortises
8½ in.
6 in.
½-in.
by 2-in. spline
³⁄₁₆-in. shim
Mortar
93°
Drip kerf

Installing the new sill

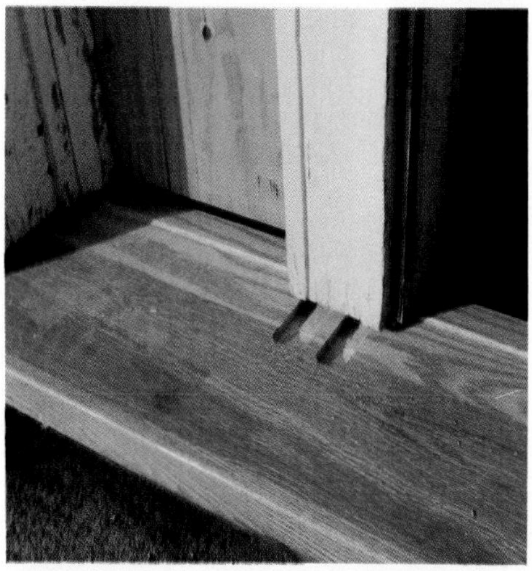

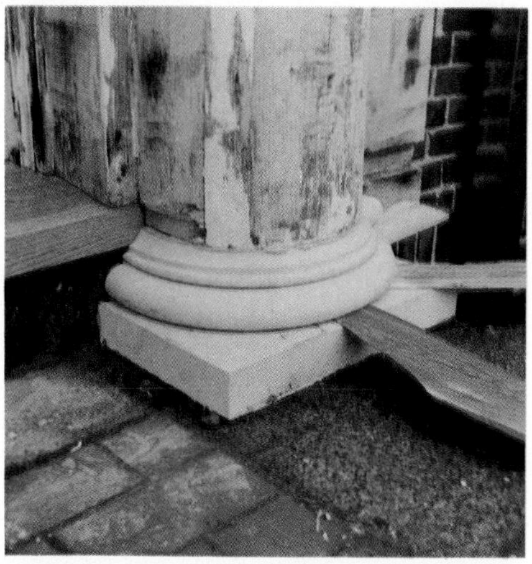

The new sill was splined together from two pieces of 10/4 oak, cut to the dimensions and angles shown in the drawing. The double mortises in the sill received the tenons at the bottom of the door jambs (photo left). Once the sill was in place, the pilaster bases were reinstalled (photo right), using shims to close up the joints between the middle and top half-round sections. The slivers that were cut out of the pilaster so that the sill could slide in were later glued back in place.

mension for the wedges needed to lift the back edge snug into place.

I used a router with a ½-in. straight-face bit to make the four mortises in the sill. I cut the mortises freehand, taking successively deeper cuts until the depth was just over ½ in. Each inner jamb had a double tenon. I cut each mortise ⅛ in. wider than the tenons and extended the mortises through the inside edge (drawing, and photo above left). The extra length was necessary because the wedges would start to push the mortise onto the tenon before the sill was all the way back into place. The extra length would be covered up when the inside plinth block was reinstalled.

I made two wedges out of oak to use for the back edge of the sill. They were 2 in. wide and 1½ in. long. I calculated one to be ⅝ in. high and the other ¾ in. These were set on the subfloor under where the sill would rest when it was slid into place. I used a hand plane to put a slight 45° chamfer under the back edge of the sill so it would slide up more easily on the wedges.

On the second dry fit, the sill slid up the wedges and I got a pretty good fit against the jambs, but one of the wedges needed to be changed to get a perfect fit. With the two wedges adjusted for height, I was ready to make three more to support the entire back edge of the sill. I ran a line from the top of the two wedges and took the measurements at the intermediate locations. With all five wedges in place, I tried a final dry fit. This time I used cedar shingles to shim up the front edge, where the mortar would eventually be packed. I needed to shim up the front edge only about ³⁄₁₆ in.—just right for a good mortar joint.

Before installing the sill, I spread epoxy on the tenons and in the mortises. I also ran a bead of butyl caulk underneath all of the shoulders of the jambs, and spread a stiff batch of mortar between the wedges and as high as I could without interfering with the sill's installation. As the sill rode up on the wedges and came tight to the jambs, the excess butyl and epoxy squeezed out and had to be cleaned off. I reinserted my four shims under the front edge, two at each end and two at the door jambs to lock the sill into place.

During all this, the door jambs were held in position sideways by the plywood in the side-light openings, but they could move in and out slightly in the sill mortises. My next task was to make them plumb so that the front door would close properly. I ran a string on the inside from one outside jamb to the other, then tapped the door jambs into position with a block and hammer. To hold them there, I toe-screwed through them into the sill with 3-in. screws. I also put several toe-screws into the sill at the outside jambs because there was nothing else there to prevent the sill from creeping out, except the cedar shingles and the mortar under the front edge.

I mixed the mortar in a loose batch and worked it under the front edge of the sill. I snapped off the cedar shingles and knocked them in far enough so they would be covered by mortar. With a pointing tool, I worked as much mortar as possible back under the sill. I cleaned up the excess mortar with a stiff brush and water. The butyl caulk was scraped off, and the surface was wiped down with a rag soaked in paint thinner.

Finishing up—The old pilaster bases had been saved for samples so that new ones could be faceplate-turned on the lathe. I used mahogany because it is available in large dimensions and is more resistant to rot than pine. There were three pieces to each base: the square bottom, a half-round middle section and a scotia and half-round on top.

Before I installed the bases, I primed them with oil-base paint. To cushion the wood and to keep the square base from touching the granite below, I covered the base's bottom with butyl caulk and a layer of lead, which was fastened with copper nails.

The top section of the base fit into a rabbet at the bottom of the pilaster, so it could not be slid into place. I caulked the pilaster with butyl and held the upper section in place. With the square section put in place, the middle half round could be slid between the two.

To tighten up the three base sections, I inserted cedar shingles between the bottom two. At some points on the circle no shimming was needed, and at others as much as ⅛ in. was needed. I used 8d galvanized finish nails to pin the sections to each other and the pilaster to the base. The cedar shingles were cut off as far in as possible with a utility knife, and the joint was caulked with butyl. Finally I epoxied and nailed back the slivers that had been cut out of the pilasters so the sill could be slipped between them.

I hung the front door as soon as the epoxy glue in the door jambs had hardened and the mortar under the sill had set. The door fit just as it had when I removed it. The side lights, stops and plinth blocks were reinstalled, and the job was done. □

Trouble Spots in 19th-Century Framing

Old-time workmanship wasn't always what it's cracked up to be. Here's what to watch for if you're rehabilitating an old house

by Dan Desmond

Too many of us involved with preservation work are caught up in a nostalgic reverence for that which never was. Most people who thump the walls of an old house and lament that "they don't build 'em like they used to" have a vision of the old housewright, disciplined master of his craft, who did it right and built it to last. If those walls belong to a 17th or 18th-century house, such confidence is probably warranted, but if the house was built in the 19th century, it may be purest speculation. To some people longevity is admirable in itself. I love old houses, too. But as one who lifts them in the air and has lived to tell the tale, I find occasion to criticize their structures. I manage a project for the Keene (New Hampshire) Housing Authority, which is funded by the Department of Housing and Urban Development to provide public housing through what is appropriately called Substantial Rehabilitation. We work on old houses that have been shunned by the private market, houses that are depressing values in otherwise stable neighborhoods. These are "worst case" examples of neglect—vandalized, dilapidated and

condemned. By rehabilitating them, we provide public housing, eliminate eyesores and demonstrate that few houses are really so far gone that they should be demolished.

In our work, we have uncovered a virtual casebook of 19th-century framing, from about 1830 on. Some of our discoveries are peculiar to New England, but 19th-century framing practice reflects social, economic and technological imperatives that were national in their effect.

The roots of the problem—While many houses in the last century were built with skill and care, many more were not. To understand how this could happen, considering the tradition of craftsmanship that had gone before, remember that 19th-century America was enjoying an unparalleled rate of new commercial and industrial expansion. Timber-frame construction was too slow and expensive for the market, which was gobbling up dimensional lumber as fast as the new steam and water-powered mills could supply it. The Industrial Revolution, with its emphasis on uniformity, high volume and low cost,

made owning a house a new and tantalizing option for the common man. (The first half of the 19th century saw a 300% reduction in the cost of lumber, and an 800% drop in the cost of nails.) Naturally, a lot of people wanted to build houses, including some enterprising do-it-yourselfers and others who were a bit short on experience. And, like many house builders today, they put their money into eye-catchers, paying less than close attention to things buried behind the walls.

During the 1800s, the plasterers and finish joiners were the great craft artists. Their compensatory skills at shimming and feathering covered a multitude of framing irregularities. Exterior appearance and finish work notwithstanding, you may uncover a house that was thrown together and has held together for all the wrong reasons. Accepted standards for framing practice and load bearing were not widely acknowledged by carpenters until late in the century. Even then, old-timers were not always at ease with the balloon frame, and retained random elements of timber-frame design in the houses they built. That's why you will seldom find a

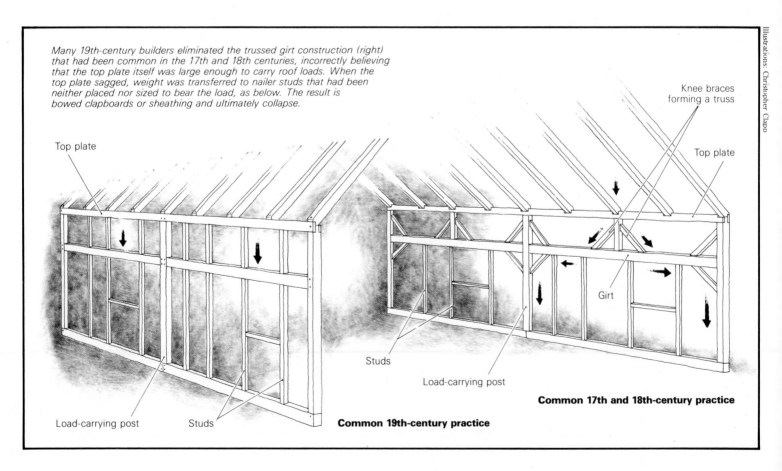

Many 19th-century builders eliminated the trussed girt construction (right) that had been common in the 17th and 18th centuries, incorrectly believing that the top plate itself was large enough to carry roof loads. When the top plate sagged, weight was transferred to nailer studs that had been neither placed nor sized to bear the load, as below. The result is bowed clapboards or sheathing and ultimately collapse.

Top plate

Knee braces forming a truss

Top plate

Girt

Studs

Load-carrying post

Load-carrying post

Studs

Common 19th-century practice

Common 17th and 18th-century practice

Illustrations: Christopher Clapp

pure example of any one framing system like the ones you see in the fix-it books. You can and will find anything behind the walls, and in repairing or rehabilitation, you will have to rely on your skills, not those of someone who might have been in a hurry 150 years ago. You don't want to dig into a vital and usually expensive job and find that what appeared to be a single weakness is inherent in the frame.

Checking the walls—Before beginning any structural repair to a house built 100 or 150 years ago, you've got to know the condition and the composition of its walls. This is especially important if you're facing a repair to some portion of the foundation—the most common job required on a house of this age—because safe and effective lifting and supporting calls for a thorough knowledge of the condition of the frame. This goes far beyond the cursory beam-stabbing ritual practiced by most termite inspectors. An 8x8 sill can be rotted from the outside a good 6 in. and still look fine from the cellar.

For a thorough exterior inspection, carefully examine the sill, and pay particular attention to corner joints. If the house is timber-framed, remove the clapboards and subsheathing from the girt between the first and second floor, both to make sure that the structure is sound and to check that the wall studs or posts are continuous up to the top plate.

The absence of continuous, aligned uprights is not at all uncommon in 19th-century houses. Studs were merely nailers and did not usually bear heavy loads in well-built 17th and 18th-century houses. Their placement wasn't critical. A trussed girt at the top plate carried loads to the large posts that were sized to take them (drawing, facing page). But many 19th-century builders eliminated the time-consuming truss assembly in the belief that the massive top plate would still carry roof loads. As it sagged, this plate put enormous strain on studs that weren't meant to withstand it. Carpenters got away with

this because the clapboard, subsheathing and lath acted as the sides of a box beam, and the arrangement was often strong enough to hold things in place even when the foundation collapsed. Ultimately, of course, such a structure can fail. One easily recognizable sign of this is a conspicuous bowing of clapboards or outside sheathing. Houses have survived for decades in this condition, but might not survive major sill or foundation work unless their frames are first repaired. These problems are less common in late 19th-century houses, after the techniques of balloon framing had become refined.

Check interior walls—Inside, make no assumptions about which partitions are load-bearing. Examine the juncture of wall and ceiling to determine if there is a beam, or even a top plate to carry and distribute loads (photo below left). Since this usually involves removing some plaster and lath, discretion and care are needed to minimize damage. This technique may frighten you if you are repairing a house of architectural or historical importance, but we do it because we believe that it's better to patch a little plaster than to begin work assuming that a partition wall is load-bearing. This mistake is easy to make because of a number of old-time framing practices that you're not likely to see in modern platform construction.

First is the practice of running the floor and ceiling joists parallel to the ridgepole instead of perpendicular to it, the way we do today. This was probably an effort on the part of framers to distribute the floor loads on the gable end of the house, while concentrating the roof loads on the eave end. In Victorian times, the original wood shingle roofs of houses framed this way were often replaced with slate. This put an extraordinary strain on the system. If you're working on a house like this, you should install collar ties as low as possible between its rafters (drawing, right). Be especially careful when insulating or wiring an attic with this type of construction, be-

cause the floorboards act as the bottom chords of a truss with the rafters, and removing too many of them could spring the side walls. I have seen 8x8 top plates split their full length and tie beams broken at the mortise because the insulating contractor saw no reason to renail the floor (photo, below right). If you must gain access to the joist cavity in this kind of frame, lift the boards one at a time, renailing as you go. Also, don't assume that because the joists run in a certain direction on one end of the house, they run the same way on the other. They may alternate, room to room and floor to floor.

The second practice is the persistent use of timber-framing techniques. Despite the increasing popularity of lightweight dimensional lumber, old-school carpenters would set heavy beams in clear span from one side of the house to the other. What we would take for a load-bearing wall is often nothing but slab or waney lumber turned sideways, faced with lath and topped with a thin piece of scrap. Over the years, as the structure settled, these partitions often assumed a role of support they weren't designed for. In our projects, we remove these

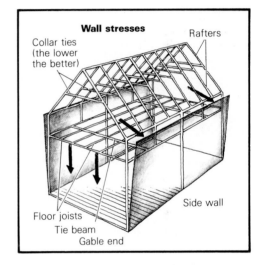

Wall stresses

Collar ties (the lower the better)

Rafters

Floor joists

Tie beam

Gable end

Side wall

In 19th-century houses, walls assumed to be load-bearing often are not. Underneath the plaster and lath, left, boards are simply nailed to the bottom of a light scrap timber. The wall was never meant to support weight. In the old house at right, the attic floor joists run parallel to the ridge. When the floorboards were removed to install insulation, the side walls sprung, splitting the great top plate along its length and breaking the joint between it and the tie beam. The drawing above shows the forces at work, and also the collar ties that would help to hold the system together.

Some 19th-century practices call for 20th-century repairs. Top left, windows and doors cut into a house's heavy sheathing are nailed into place with stud cleats (in this example, the jack studs don't even reach the window frame). In the absence of headers, stresses are transferred to the house's skin, not to its frame. Lifting the house for foundation repairs without bracing such openings can be disastrous. Right, floor joists are face-nailed together. Floorboards (or siding, in the case of spliced wall studs) can hold such joints together, but when this reinforcement is removed during rehabilitation, the frame may fail. In the 19th century, builders sometimes salvaged beams from older structures. Such timbers have often been weakened by previously cut mortises, and if they are in span, like the one above left, they have to be supported if they are to be left in place.

walls and start with new supports and partitions from the ground up. Where preservation is the object, you could install a small-diameter lally column (a steel tube, filled with concrete and cut to length) in the wall to support the sagging beam, providing that the column itself is supported under the floor.

More problems—Two other framing practices were common in the 19th century, and you should always look for them, especially before doing any lifting. First is the failure to use window or door headers in many old houses. Sometimes large wall areas were spanned with a single beam, and windows and doors were cut into the heavy sheathing and nailed into place with stud cleats that often didn't contact the sill and girt (photo top left). This can give you fits if you have to replace, say, the sill in a house with a lot of windows, because during a lift the loads transfer to the lath and clapboards in an unpredictable fashion. If possible, brace doors and windows without headers, remove window sashes to avoid their racking, and concentrate lift points between windows.

The other is the practice of splicing. You will

see this most often in early attempts at balloon framing. Carpenters would fit into place the longest stud that they had. If it didn't reach the plate, they would tack a piece of scrap on the side to complete the support. As I've already mentioned, the tension of the siding or clapboards may be holding a house like this together. If you remove them during a thorough rehabilitation without reinforcing or replacing the splice, the frame might well fail.

The same technique was used on floor joists on occasion (photo above right). Since nails aren't very strong in shear, you have to be careful not to concentrate any new loads on these members without reinforcing the splices.

Another behind-the-wall surprise is the practice of "filling in." In colder areas of the country builders would often fill the outside wall cavity with lath and rough plaster, or occasionally solid brick, to reduce winter air infiltration. This can cause tremendous problems today when you want to wire or insulate the area. Brick-filled walls are especially troublesome if your repairs involve lifting or leveling.

You will also find houses in which most structural members appear to match, and then see a

used timber from a far older structure pieced in. This tells you something about old-time builders: First, they were practical and frugal. Second, they were not nearly as much in love with the practice of hand-hewing as some would have us believe, and were only too happy to get some extended use out of Colonial-era salvage. These members usually worked well as sills or posts, and you can probably leave them in place. In span, though, they often failed because they had been weakened by numerous deep and unfilled mortises. Such timbers should be replaced or reinforced (photo above left).

Economic conditions and a new appreciation for our past will make the purchase and rehabilitation of old houses a growth industry in the 1980s. The necessity for structural repair will expose many new owners to the flip side of old-house charm. Such work is hard, and it's never successful unless it's also safe. That requires a realistic and critical approach to the qualities and styles of workmanship behind the walls. □

Dan Desmond lives in an 1840 timber-framed house in Walpole, N.H. He has been a builder and renovator for 15 years.

Additions

The structure of the studio consists of a welded metal frame, curved box-beams and a wooden connecting framework. Firmly anchored to concrete footings, the metal frame gives strength while the curved beams give form. Framing between the curved beams completes the floor, wall and ceiling skeleton and also adds strength. A temporary diagonal brace holds the curved beam in position until framing is finished.

Sculptural Studio Addition

Striking form and color mask ingenious but straightforward construction methods

by Bart Prince

As we walked around this unique house in Albuquerque, New Mexico, Robert Hanna said, "Visitors to my studio are sometimes at a loss for words." I wasn't surprised, but I knew from the drawings of Bart Prince, the architect, that the construction was less complicated than appearances would indicate. Beneath the unusual surface of Hanna's studio lay a cleverly devised structural system based on standard methods of wood-frame construction.

"Although the methods and sequence of the building were straightforward," explained Hanna, "contractors' bids were excessively high. This forced me to act as general contractor, with

Plexiglas stairs and floor areas, carpeted walls and sweeping curves eliminate standard horizontal and vertical reference points in Hanna's studio. This view shows all four levels.

Prince as the construction supervisor." Together they completed the studio for $30,000 (plus $5,000 for cabinetwork) in 1978.

The total interior square footage is difficult to calculate, because floors and walls merge into one; but the usable horizontal surface is about 500 sq. ft. on four levels. Outside there are two large, cantilevered decks.

Because I was impressed with Prince's ability to find a simple structural solution to a complex form, I asked him to explain his design. Once again, it proved to me how adaptable stick and plywood framing could be in the hands of an inventive designer.
—Editor

Architecture is "building" brought alive. It is this "life" that the architect, working with the client, can bring to any given problem. Every building has functional requirements that must be solved; every building has structural and mechanical problems that have to be worked out so that the building will stand; and every building project has a budget that must be respected if anything is to be finally built. Beyond this, the architect must work with his client to bring imagination and excitement to the design while working within the necessary constraints.

Robert Hanna needed a place to work, think, entertain and generally relax. This space was to be added to his house in Albuquerque, New Mexico. Together we discussed every aspect of his requirements and how they would be incorporated into the studio design. I explained how the building would be placed above the courtyard, rather than on top of his house. This would allow people to walk underneath, and would provide the best views from all levels—a requirement Hanna had stressed.

With the scale and specifications of the plan complete and working drawings prepared, we applied for a building permit. Although the local commission did not fully understand the sculptural quality of the design, they gave their approval and we were allowed to go to work. Hanna and I decided that contractor's expenses would be too high; he elected to act as owner-builder, while my responsibility was to make sure the work progressed smoothly.

Our first job was to fabricate and erect the steel frame that would lift the building up above the courtyard and be its chief means of structural support. We used steel tubing, 5 in. by 5 in. by ½ in., cut and welded to fit the design dimensions. Our fastening system for steel-to-wood joints consisted of paired steel plates (3 in. by 9 in. by ¼ in.) welded to the steel frame and drilled to receive bolts through the wooden members (drawing, p. 67).

When the frame was completed and all fastening plates had been welded on, we slipped the four legs of the assembly over sleeves that had been anchored in footings set 2½ ft. below the floorline of the adjacent garage.

At this point we had some trouble with local zoning officials, who seemed to believe our steel frame was meant to support a large sign of some sort. But by this time the curved box beams were nearly finished, and we were able to convince them to let the work go forward. We had the box beams (p. 67) built in a carpentry shop and trucked to the site. With the help of a crane we fastened them to the steel frame in a day. The fastening bolts were welded and temporary braces held the curved sections in alignment until framing was underway.

We framed in the four horizontal levels first; these floors stiffened the structure and allowed us to work more easily on framing the curved section. We used 2x10s or 2x8s for most of the

First the curved box-beams are secured to the metal frame and held in position with temporary braces (top). Then the rest of the wooden framework goes in, connecting the curved beams and completing floor, wall and roof elements. When the skeleton is complete, the skin goes on (above). All glazing is clear Plexiglas. Japanese tile is glued to curved surfaces and grouted, and the cantilevered deck is covered with indoor-outdoor carpeting. Below, owner-builder Robert Hanna specified clear Plexiglas for certain stair and floor areas in addition to using it for all windows in the studio. The door at the center of the picture gives access to one of the structure's two outside deck areas. Bart Prince, the architect, designed the revolving desk on the upper level for Hanna. Photos: Chuck Johnson

Owner's Perspective

At our first meeting Bart said, "Paper is cheap. Write down everything you can possibly think of that you might want to include in the design." Several pages of thought, suggestions and ideas followed. Every item on my list is in the addition, from my "curved wall to serve as background for portrait photography" to "transparent flooring." He never said, "What you have suggested cannot be done, but I know what you could do instead," as I had often heard from other architects. He expressed the thought that a building should "make a statement" on behalf of its owner. This one does. The building process was as much an event and recreation as occupying it became later. The creative satisfaction and gratification were as unique as the structure.

There is clearly a creative courage contained in the startling new space superimposed upon the comfortable, traditional New Mexican atmosphere in the underlying building. Some Indian people remarked that the addition reminded them of the Zia sun sign, a part of the New Mexico state emblem.

Strangers began to ring my doorbell to ask if they could enter the partly completed building.

I met artists, writers, photographers, travelers and many other individuals. Suddenly the flow of life past my door was diverted into and through my studio, giving me a completely new appreciation for the field of architecture.

I've observed changes in people's moods when they've remained in the studio-office for a long time, a kind of openness and receptivity occurs. Standard reference points are gone. There is an absence of floor, ceiling, wall, inside, outside—even up and down become unclear to the viewer; it's just brand spanking new space.

—*Robert Hanna*

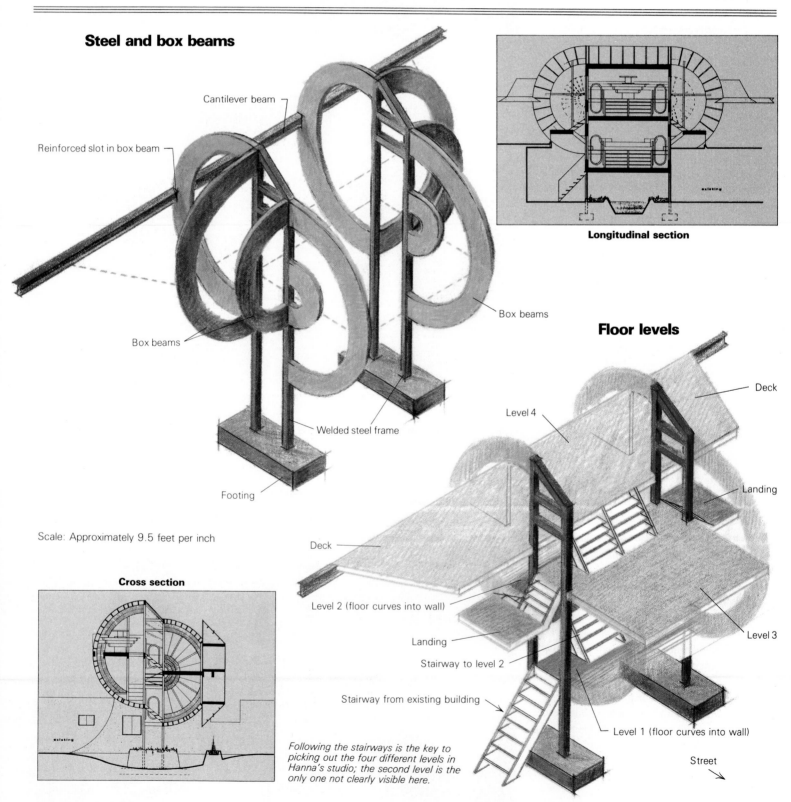

Steel and box beams

Cantilever beam

Reinforced slot in box beam

Box beams

Box beams

Welded steel frame

Footing

Scale: Approximately 9.5 feet per inch

Longitudinal section

Floor levels

Deck

Landing

Level 4

Deck

Level 2 (floor curves into wall)

Landing

Stairway to level 2

Stairway from existing building

Level 3

Level 1 (floor curves into wall)

Street

Cross section

Following the stairways is the key to picking out the four different levels in Hanna's studio; the second level is the only one not clearly visible here.

Building a Curved Box Beam

1. Lay out the plywood on the floor or layout table as shown in the drawing at right. Tack or secure the boards in place so they won't move while you're marking them. To mark the cutting lines, use a rigid arm with its pivot point at the center of the circle. In this case, marks were made on 7-ft. and 9-ft. diameters.

2. When the boards have been marked, you can cut them in place, or remove them and cut each one separately. Cut the beam sections with a sabersaw or bandsaw. Repeat the process for the duplicate sections making up the opposite side.

3. Lay out and cut the double 2x4s as shown in the drawing at right. Glue and nail them together and then glue and nail them to the plywood. (A waterproof resorcinol or plastic resin glue is recommended.) Also glue plywood joints and section-to-section 2x4 joints.

4. Screw angled steel braces to 2x4 joists as shown here. You can make the braces yourself or order them from an ironsmith. The angle will depend on the size of your curved beam.

5. Fill the open center of the beam with insulation if it will be exposed to both interior and exterior space. Then glue, align, and nail the opposite side of box beam in place. Close the edges of the beam by gluing and nailing strips of ⅜-in. exterior plywood to the plywood sides.

6. For this studio, the curved box beams were fastened at their ends to a vertical steel tube to which special flanges had been welded. Double 2x4s at the ends of each beam were fastened to both plywood faces, bolted to adjoining 2x4 sections with metal angle braces (at right), and drilled to receive flange bolts. This is the best way to secure a large (up to 18 ft.) curved box beam.

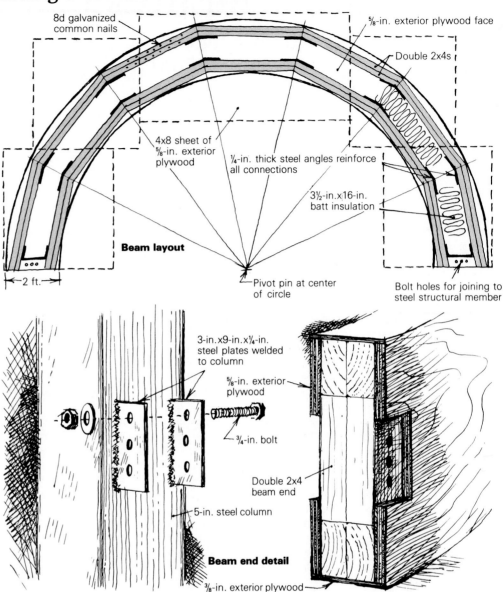

Beam layout

8d galvanized common nails

⅝-in. exterior plywood face

Double 2x4s

4x8 sheet of ⅝-in. exterior plywood

¼-in. thick steel angles reinforce all connections

3½-in.x16-in. batt insulation

Pivot pin at center of circle

Bolt holes for joining to steel structural member

2 ft.

Beam end detail

3-in.x9-in.x¼-in. steel plates welded to column

⅝-in. exterior plywood

¾-in. bolt

Double 2x4 beam end

5-in. steel column

⅜-in. exterior plywood

This scale model, built by Prince as part of the design exercise, shows how the decks are cantilevered over existing adobe structures.

framing, and relied on conventional metal joist hangers for beam-to-frame connections. The deck was cantilevered on an I beam that was sandwiched between standard 2x10 joists and inserted in reinforced slots in two parallel box beams. The I beam was 44 ft. 8 in. long, manufactured to our specifications.

The vertical cylinder housing mechanical components and a revolving closet was made from vertical 2x4s nailed 12 in. on center to a hexagonal frame, and sheathed with ¼-in. plywood. We built it in place, sanded and sealed the exterior, and tiled the surface.

Although the drawing shown here may give the impression of an extremely complex intersection of planes and curving lines, the construction—especially the framing—was really not complicated. We completed most of the work in 6 months. The curved box beams, made of plywood and 2x4s, were easy to build and offered an economical alternative to high-priced laminated or steel beams.

Japanese ceramic tile with brown exterior grout was applied (over frostproof epoxy adhesive) to all curved, exterior wall surfaces. Plexi-glas windows and dark brown indoor-outdoor carpet (glued to floors and walls of the deck) completed the exterior surface treatment.

Finishing the interior took another three months. We used Japanese tiles on the curved beams inside the studio for the same reason we had used them outside: In addition to being a durable, permanent surface treatment, tiles adapt well to the curving lines of the beams, and offer a pleasing sense of pattern and color.

The flat-ceilinged areas under decks and flat floors were covered with cork-bark tiles. Stair treads and portions of the floor were cut from ¾-in. thick Plexiglas, to form transparent areas that break down the distinction between conventional floor and ceiling planes. We covered both floor and wall surfaces with carpeting.

Greg Brown of Palo Alto, Calif., painted a mural on the curving west wall; it enhances the sculptural quality of the building. This is, above all, architecture for the pleasure of the owner, and in this way it is far more successful than a simple room added on to a house could ever be.

Bart Prince, of Albuquerque, is an architect.

Double-Envelope Addition

A greenhouse connector and a barrel-vaulted bedroom heated only by the sun

by Charlie Boldrick

When I set out to design and build a new bedroom, I had two things in mind. I wanted to link the bedroom to the main house with a greenhouse, and I wanted to use passive-solar heating and cooling for the new space. When I first began thinking about an addition, I didn't suspect that I would soon be bending drywall over bowstring trusses, or ratcheting a 500-lb. barrel vault into place.

I did know that I wanted to try something a little different with the 16-ft. by 26-ft. concrete-slab patio that sat beyond the living room. As an architect who designs mostly institutional structures, I knew my best chance to break new ground would be on my own house.

Since the winters here in California are mild, I wanted to try heating the bedroom with a double-envelope, solar-gain system, explained in the sidebar below. This passive-solar approach was pioneered by architect Lee Porter Butler. As far as I know, no one had ever used a double envelope to warm and cool a single room before. The idea of miniaturizing the system fascinated me. So did using a totally passive system, with no conventional heating or cooling devices. After all, the fact that hot air rises should be as useful to the builder as the fact that water flows downhill.

Although many of my decisions about the envelope were instinctive, I did some basic calculating of wall area, air volume and average temperatures. A number of articles critical of early envelope houses have been published in the last several years, notably in the November 1980 issue of *Solar Age*. These articles focused primarily on the problems of storing heat solely in crawl-space earth. But there is a second generation of envelopes that rely strongly on north-wall mass to store heat. My rough calculations convinced me that I could heat and cool my single room with this system even though air drag, something that needs to be minimized in a convection loop, would be proportionally greater in a structure this small. Even so, it occurred to me that using an envelope system on a small addition was a little like hitching a Percheron draft horse to a kid's red wagon.

The layout of the existing house made it necessary to build off the only window wall in the living room, so a greenhouse was the logical link to the new bedroom beyond (drawing, facing page). The greenhouse would allow as much natural light into the living room as before and accommodate both sun and shade-loving plants. They make the view from the living room pleasingly green. Most important to me, a greenhouse functions as a "lung" for the rest of the house, tempering the ambient air during both the long rainy season and the 100°+ heat of summer. Sliding glass doors, jalousie windows, a thermostatically controlled ridgeline fan and gable vents would provide a wide range of choices in ventilating the greenhouse and regulating the air temperature.

Foundation and frame—I began construction with some semi-skilled laborers and a tight budget. I took a sabbatical from my architectural practice to build the addition, and that made both time and money even more precious. Because I'd found a bargain on a stack of weathered fir 4x12s a few months earlier, the frame was to be mostly post-and-beam. We cast reinforced pier foundations for corner posts on the south side of the slab. Along the north side, we sawed through the concrete, dug, and poured a 2-ft. square foundation wall 16 ft. long. It would have to bear the weight of both

---

How a double envelope works

A double envelope is a house within a house. An air space separates the inner shell from the outer shell. The air that circulates in this space moderates the temperature inside the inner shell, preventing wide temperature swings inside. The air in the convection loop is subject to solar heat-gain and heat-loss from the outer shell, which includes a fully glazed south-facing room or passageway and a high-mass storage wall set just inside the insulated north wall. Connecting the two are an attic space, and a crawl space at (or below) grade.

The changing influences on the air in the loop cause it to move. When the sun is shining, the air exposed to the south-side glazing warms up, rises into the attic space, and descends on the opposite side between the north and storage walls, pushed along by more hot air rising behind it. The air passes under the storage wall into the crawl space, to be drawn up into the south passageway again through a floor of spaced decking. This pulling process sets up a rotating belt of solar-heated air whose warmth is stored in the mass wall, which continues to radiate long after the sun goes down.

Early envelope systems relied exclusively on crawl-space earth for solar-gain storage. This often proved insufficient, and resulted in a slowing of the convection loop when the sun wasn't high on the south glazing. The new generation of envelopes have a north-side mass wall, which increases the storage capacity of the house. It also encourages a stronger convection loop. When warm air loses its heat to the storage wall on the north, the air becomes heavier and drops, pushing air ahead of it. This push effect supplements the pulling action of rising warm air on the south side.

The circulation slows and stops at day's end when the air is no longer being heated. As the south room cools rapidly and heat radiates away through the glazing, the air in that room becomes denser and falls into the crawl space, while warmer air is rising from the mass wall on the north. This reverses the flow, but keeps warm air constantly moving around the inner shell, with sunlight as the sole energy source and convection as the only distribution method.

Opening vents at the high point of the loop and low along the north wall cools the bedroom addition during hot summer weather. Hot air rising in the south room sets up a venturi effect as it escapes through the high vents, pulling with it air rising along the storage wall from the low, north vents. The mass wall and the earth of the crawl space act as heat sinks, contributing even further to the cooling effect. —*C.B.*

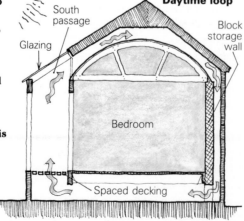

Daytime loop

South passage
Glazing
Block storage wall
Bedroom
Spaced decking

The south passage of this one-room, double-envelope addition, right, is behind the glass doors in the foreground. Acrylic glazing covering the lower half of the addition's roof allows the sun to warm the air in the passage, which begins the convection flow that heats and cools the room. The greenhouse connector (photo below, right), seen from the living room of the house, separates the bedroom addition from the main traffic flow, and allows light in the windows that face it. It also serves as a 'lung,' tempering the ambient air with solar heating in the winter and ventilation in the summer.

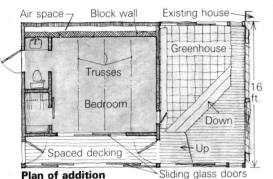

Plan of addition

the exterior stud wall and an interior wall of fully grouted concrete block that would provide much of the structure's mass. However, to complete the convection loop, the air would have to travel through this mass wall and under the floor back to the south side. So we formed a concrete trestle with openings in it to let the air through. It is approximately 30 in. high with openings that measure 12 in. by 20 in. Foundation bolts were cast into the face of the wall for the ledger that would hold the framing of the bedroom floor.

The first wall to be framed was the exterior north wall. Since the air space between this wood-frame wall and the masonry storage wall was to be only 8 in. wide, we had to drywall it before laying up the block for the storage wall. So for a while, a 10-ft. by 16-ft. sheetrocked stud wall stood there alone, and my backyard looked like a drive-in movie theater.

I laid up the mass wall by myself, enjoying the routine of mixing mortar and buttering the blocks. When the wall was done, the blocks were fully grouted to get extra mass, and I used a lot of vertical rebar in the wall for added strength. I live in earthquake country, and this wall is at the head of my bed.

We bolted 4x4 posts to metal saddles set in each pier, and then ran 4x12 girts around the three open sides of the addition, lag-screwing them to the posts. The girts carry the floor joists and are high enough to allow an 18-in. high crawl space underneath for the passage of air. Another set of 4x12s spans the edge of the room at header height, supported by the block wall on the north and 4x4 posts on the south corners. More beams were used to connect this rectangle to the existing house. This defined the greenhouse connector with its raised deck at the living-room sliding glass doors and steps that lead to a tile floor on grade. The open framing, without the obstruction of infill stud walls, was an advantage later on, when it came time to build the barrel vault. The last major framing member was a ridgepiece that canti-

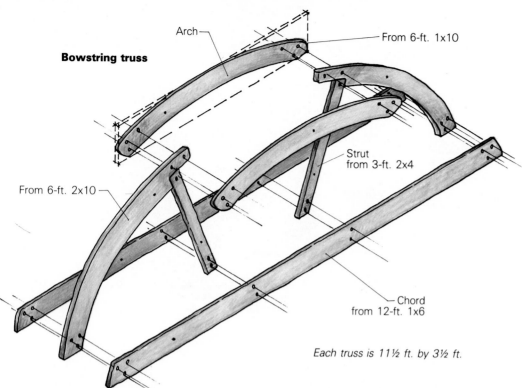

Bowstring truss

Arch

From 6-ft. 1x10

From 6-ft. 2x10

Strut
from 3-ft. 2x4

Chord
from 12-ft. 1x6

Each truss is 11½ ft. by 3½ ft.

Bowstring trusses support the bedroom's vaulted ceiling. The exploded view of a truss, top, shows the short arch segments, designed to use clear vertical-grain fir most economically. The arched ceiling minimizes air drag on the envelope convection loop. It also gives this 10-ft. by 12-ft. room an open and airy feeling.

levers from the bedroom over the greenhouse. This saved me from having to build a structural gable end for the greenhouse at the face of the existing house.

At this point my carpenters, Ron Davis and Angelo Margolis, with 40 years of experience between them, came on the job. Within a few days, we had the bedroom rafters up and sheathed. This formed the lid of the attic air passage. We drywalled the underside of the rafters as a fire-protection measure in this space intended to act as a sort of chimney, and began to work out a ceiling system to close the attic from the room below. A flat ceiling on simple span joists would have been quickest and cheapest, but there were drawbacks to that. First, a flat ceiling over a 10-ft. by 12-ft. room would be depressing. And the prism-shaped volume of air created by the attic above a flat ceiling would impede the flow of air by creating a bottleneck in the loop. It would make for turbulence, and result in more drag on the airflow as it deflects off the floor and ceiling of the convection loop.

Bowstring trusses—I let the natural path of air movement generate the shape of the attic floor—an arch, which in turn, almost demanded a ceiling with the same curve. A vaulted shape would allow the heated air to enter an attic throat of almost uniform cross section, and thus minimize friction in the convection loop. This vaulted ceiling argued for an arched support, which allowed me to indulge a longtime love of the bowstring truss.

Since the arched attic would be no more than 18 in. deep, building the vault in place would have been impossible. Our open post-and-beam frame gave us the solution to this problem—we'd build the ceiling vault on the plywood subfloor, where the absence of stud walls gave us the elbow room to work. Then we would lift it up as an entire unit and secure it in place.

Building the vault was just about as simple as bending gypboard over bowstring trusses. First, I calculated the optimum truss profile on paper: a 42-in. deep chord segment of an 80-in. radius circle. This profile was laid out full-scale in pencil on the subfloor with trammel points, and became the pattern for truss assembly. The truss is a sandwich of 2x material lap-joined with 1xs, and held together with 3½-in. carriage bolts (drawing, above left). I decided to use clear, vertical-grain (quartersawn) Douglas fir for strength and beauty, but because of its high cost, I designed the trusses with short arch segments to use the material most economically. The joints for the arch segments are at each end of the truss, and at points one-third of the way up the curve, where the struts intersect, as shown. Completed, each truss is 11½ ft. long and 3½ ft. high.

We made three bowstring trusses, plus two non-structural fascia arches of similar profile for the end walls of the vault. The number was determined by a guess at the spanning capacity of gypboard bent into a cylindrical section, and by the enthusiasm of the builders. These bowstring trusses were a lot of fun to put together, and we willingly would have produced more of

Raising the vault

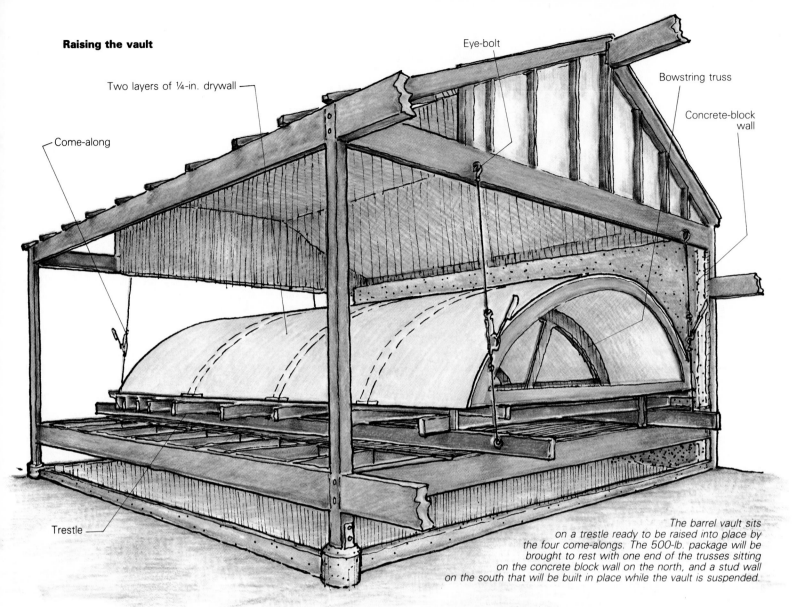

Two layers of ¼-in. drywall

Come-along

Eye-bolt

Bowstring truss

Concrete-block wall

Trestle

The barrel vault sits on a trestle ready to be raised into place by the four come-alongs. The 500-lb. package will be brought to rest with one end of the trusses sitting on the concrete block wall on the north, and a stud wall on the south that will be built in place while the vault is suspended.

them. We finished them on the spot—sanding and two coats of Watco oil—and put them off to one side.

To give us a platform we could use to lift the vault into place, we built a trestle of rough 2x6s on the subfloor, and set the trusses on it. The trusses were temporarily cross-braced, and wrapped in plastic sheeting to protect their finish. Next, we bent ¼-in. gypboard over this frame. We used two layers laminated with panel adhesive. The long dimension of the sheets in the inner layer is parallel to the trusses, with a joint at the crown of the vault. We glued down the outer layer perpendicular to the trusses. Thicker drywall won't bend to this radius without tearing the face paper and fracturing the gypsum inside, but the ¼-in. material bent easily from its own weight when we left it draped on the trusses overnight. In dry climates, misting the back side of the sheets might be necessary to get the paper to bend, but our early-morning summer fog took care of that step for us.

Some experimentation with a pneumatic staple gun at low pressure led us to staple, rather than nail, the gypboard to the trusses. This way, we didn't run the risk of crushing the gypsum with hammer blows. Since the vault would be inaccessible for further work once it was in place, we took the precaution of band-

ing each drywall joint with a belt of 6-in. wide screening spread with panel adhesive. To tighten this belt, we wrapped the ends of the screening around small lengths of lath, and nailed them to the ends of the trusses. This extra step gave us a little added assurance that the drywall won't pull away from the top surface of the trusses.

Raising the vault—The rest of this phase of the work was simple to the point of anticlimax. A large screw-eye was put into each corner of the trestle, and another into the beam directly above each corner. Each pair of points was connected with a ratcheting come-along (drawing, above). As we worked the four come-alongs simultaneously (if somewhat gingerly), the vault ascended into place with no problem.

On the north side of the room, the ends of the trusses were made to rest on top of the mass storage wall. We then built a stud wall, which separates the bedroom and the glazed, south passageway, to support the south side of the vault. The vault and trestle weighed no more than 500 lb., so we could do this without hurrying. In fact, people became intrigued by the hanging structure, and would stroll bemused beneath it, while it was still cable-supported. Not dangerous, but not recommended, either.

Once in place, the vault and the bedroom

face of the storage wall were finished with a texture coat of joint compound and painted. The vaulted ceiling is a source of satisfaction every day. It was well worth the extra $1,500 in materials and labor over the cost of building a flat ceiling.

Although I moved in months ago, the addition still needs the odd trim piece and a few days of painting to be complete. It's receiving attention only on weekends since the constraints of time and money forced me to go back to my office work early. The important thing to me is that the experiment happened. The envelope is working adequately, and has become what I wanted—an unobstrusive system that operates without much maintenance or thought. It only requires opening the top and bottom vents for summer, and closing them for winter. A system on this scale would probably not work in a cold climate, but larger versions of the double envelope do.

Experimental structures like my addition are perhaps better examples of approach than product. Problems encountered on a unique project often generate equally unique solutions, and therein may lie some economy or unexpected beauty. □

Charlie Boldrick lives in Fairfax, Calif., and works as an architect in San Francisco.

Adding Up
A new second story on independent footings straddles an old house

by Eric K. Rekdahl

In my neighborhood, second-story additions are sprouting like weeds. The reason is simple enough: few people can afford to buy a larger home in today's inflated housing market, and adding a few rooms to a small house can be a solution for the growing family with limited funds. Usually, the easiest way to expand a home is horizontally, but many houses, especially in cities, are on tiny lots that won't allow spreading out. Building up is the only other way to go.

My client, Tom Rankin, faced a similar dilemma in deciding where to add about 600 sq. ft. of living space to his pre-war bungalow. As a self-employed lawyer with his office at home, Tom needed more space for both work and family. His house had a box-car floor plan that suited the shape of its urban lot. Adding to the back end was out of the question because it would further accentuate the long, narrow plan and severely complicate the traffic pattern within the house. Equally important, such an addition would have engulfed the small backyard.

It was clear that a second floor would be the best solution to Tom's remodeling problem, as well as a thoughtful response to the design of the existing house and its place in the neighborhood. We decided to extend the original one-room second story over the entire first floor to gain space for a bedroom, a study, a guest room and a bath. The extension would have an exposed ridge beam, skylights and a cathedral ceiling throughout, all of which would make for a spacious feeling.

Downstairs, the living room was too small for living and the dining room too big for eating, so we planned to remove the partition between them and combine their functions. The floors would be linked by a new stairway from the dining room to the new upstairs study. Leaving the stairwell open would also let some much needed light penetrate to the first floor.

The plan we developed was straightforward and modest. But building the addition economically and in compliance with local building codes would require solutions to three distinct problems. The foundation would have to be enlarged; a cathedral ceiling without benefit of collar ties or interior bearing walls would have to be engineered; and the requirements for racking resistance for the added structure in this earthquake-prone area would have to be calculated and resolved.

New piers—Two-story houses require footings that are both wider and deeper than single-story houses do. Since it is rare for a one-story house to be constructed on more than a minimal foundation, most existing houses need beefed-up footings to support a second floor. Tom's house was no exception. We investigated removing the original perimeter foundation and replacing it with a two-story version, but the cost was so high that we devised an alternate plan. We decided to make the second story entirely self-supporting. This meant enveloping the downstairs with an independent framework of posts and footings and tying these to the old house for structural and visual integrity. Built above and around the old house, the new structure would stand like a spider holding its prey underneath, while supporting

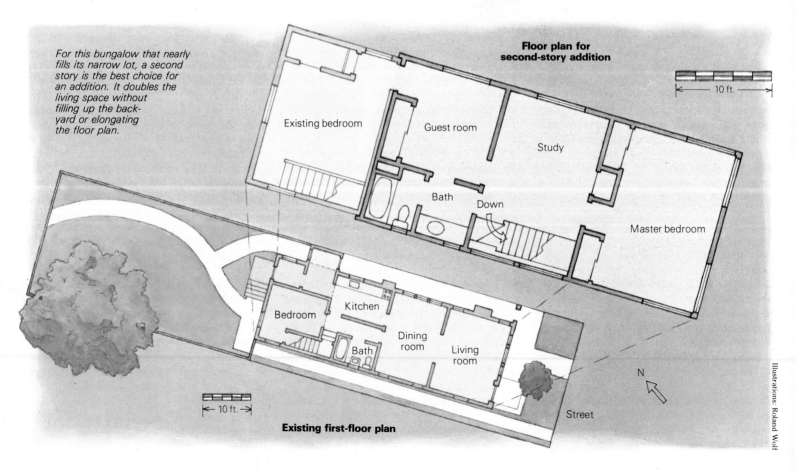

For this bungalow that nearly fills its narrow lot, a second story is the best choice for an addition. It doubles the living space without filling up the backyard or elongating the floor plan.

Floor plan for second-story addition

Existing bedroom · Guest room · Study · Bath · Down · Master bedroom

10 ft.

Bedroom · Kitchen · Bath · Dining room · Living room · Street

10 ft.

N

Existing first-floor plan

New piers

Simpson hold-downs

½-in. by 7-in. lag screws, through 4x8 post, 2 ft. o.c.

2x redwood sill

5/8-in. by 10-in. J-bolts

6 in. min.

18 in. min.

Varies from 3½ ft. to 5 ft.

3½ ft.

Original foundation

#4 rebar, 12-in. grid set in new pier

An independent post-and-beam skeleton.
Lag-bolted to the first-floor framing, 4x8 posts rest on individual piers (drawing and photo, left). Atop the posts, 4x16 beams form a structural perimeter to hold floor joists and walls of the second story (inset, above). The badly deteriorated original stucco finish has been removed from the first-floor walls (top). They will be restuccoed. The exterior on the new second story will be board and batten.

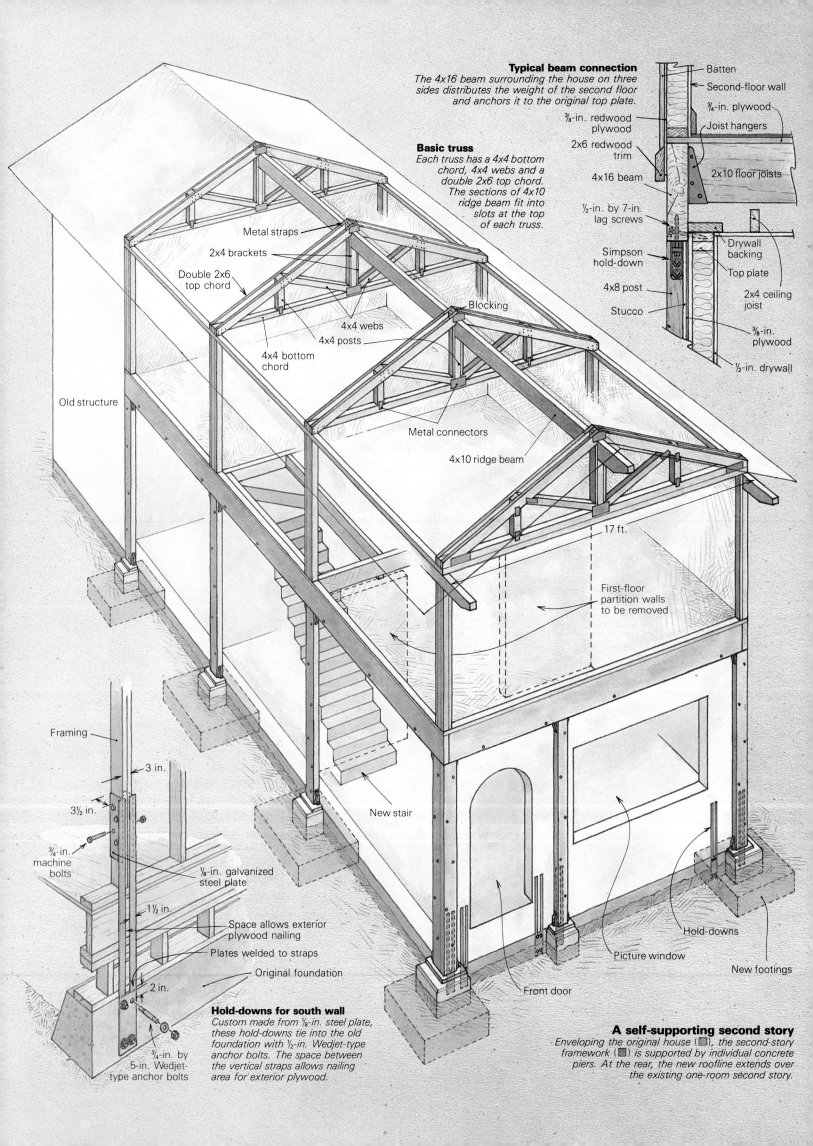

Typical beam connection
The 4x16 beam surrounding the house on three sides distributes the weight of the second floor and anchors it to the original top plate.

Batten
Second-floor wall
¾-in. plywood
Joist hangers
⅜-in. redwood plywood
2x6 redwood trim
4x16 beam
½-in. by 7-in. lag screws
Simpson hold-down
4x8 post
Stucco
2x10 floor joists
Drywall backing
Top plate
2x4 ceiling joist
⅜-in. plywood
½-in. drywall

Basic truss
Each truss has a 4x4 bottom chord, 4x4 webs and a double 2x6 top chord. The sections of 4x10 ridge beam fit into slots at the top of each truss.

Metal straps
2x4 brackets
Double 2x6 top chord
4x4 webs
4x4 posts
4x4 bottom chord
Blocking
Metal connectors
4x10 ridge beam

Old structure

17 ft.

First-floor partition walls to be removed

New stair

Framing

3 in.

3½ in.

¾-in. machine bolts

⅛-in. galvanized steel plate

1½ in.

Space allows exterior plywood nailing

Plates welded to straps

Original foundation

2 in.

¾-in. by 5-in. Wedjet-type anchor bolts

Front door

Picture window

Hold-downs

New footings

Hold-downs for south wall
Custom made from ⅛-in. steel plate, these hold-downs tie into the old foundation with ½-in. Wedjet-type anchor bolts. The space between the vertical straps allows nailing area for exterior plywood.

A self-supporting second story
Enveloping the original house (▢), the second-story framework (▨) is supported by individual concrete piers. At the rear, the new roofline extends over the existing one-room second story.

the combined weight on its 4x8 legs. (Try using that explanation on a building inspector.)

Our structural engineer, Gene St. Onge, calculated the combined live and dead loads of the addition, and designed concrete piers to support the new load. Placement of the piers was influenced by the need to anchor the new posts to the original framing. We figured that the most likely place to find sturdy connections was the partition framing the intersections of interior walls and the exterior bearing walls.

Each pier had to extend under the existing foundation for 16 in., which meant undermining the original footing in sections up to 5 ft. in length. Before excavating for the piers, the builders removed the old roof to lessen the load on the foundation. Our guess that the stucco and sheathing on the walls would act as a beam to distribute the loads over the unsupported parts of the foundation proved to be correct. There were no problems with cracking or settling before the new concrete was poured to fill the voids.

When the builders tried to lag-bolt the posts to the existing partition studding, it became apparent that the studs we expected to tie into just weren't there. They removed the stucco to find an odd assortment of blocking, lath nailers and dry rot where we expected plate-to-plate framing. Other excavations into the stucco revealed thriving colonies of termites, so the builders removed the entire layer of stucco rather than settle for an equally costly patch job, and repaired or replaced the missing or damaged framing.

To carry the weight of the addition and to help connect the original framing to the second floor, 4x16 beams were set on the new posts. A 4x16 is deep enough to accommodate the new 2x10 floor joists of the addition at the top and still cover the original 2x4 first-story ceiling joists and top plate on the bottom. These beams were anchored securely to the 4x8 posts with lag screws and two steel angle braces per post. The same 7-in. lag screws were angled through the beam into the top plate of the first floor.

With the skeleton built up to the second-floor level, work could start on the floor framing and walls of the new addition. Two-by-ten floor joists 16 in. on center were laid across the 17-ft. width of the house. They were fastened to the 4x16 beams with joist hangers. To frame the opening for the new stairway, 4x10 joists were used for extra strength.

Once the ¾-in. plywood subfloor had been nailed down, wall framing began. The builders used 2x4 studs throughout, but doubled up at the corners and above each 4x8 post. These built-up posts on the second floor would hold the roof trusses for the cathedral ceiling. Aligning the first and second-floor posts ensured that the roof load would be transferred directly to the new piers below.

Trusses—The decision to build a cathedral ceiling with an exposed ridge beam meant some rearranging of the usual flat ceiling layout. In the typical flat ceiling, the ceiling joists act as collar ties to prevent the load of the roof from pushing the walls apart. Without collar ties or joists, a ridge beam has to carry half the roof load. Usually such a structural ridge beam is supported at various points by interior posts, but Tom's house lacked adequate foundations under the center of the house to carry the ridge beam. Instead, our engineer designed trusses, which could be built from standard framing lumber, to carry the ridge-beam load to the outside walls, then to the new footings.

So they could deliver their concentrated loads, the trusses were located directly over the new posts. Since the posts are in line with the existing partition walls, the spacing of the original floor plan could be carried upstairs. We were also able to put the upstairs bathroom over the first-floor bath, reducing plumbing runs.

Tying the addition to the ground—The second-floor addition made the house slightly top-heavy, a condition that can be dangerous in this part of the country. The forces generated by an earthquake or by high wind are erratic and can vary rapidly in direction and intensity. These forces can cause the two levels of the house to respond in different ways. This oscillating, alternating pattern of motion between the upper and lower floor can produce racking and

uplifting forces in magnitudes the original house never had to resist.

The east and west walls are longer than they are high, and had enough shear value in the stucco and sheathing to cope with any second-floor gyrations, but the south wall presented the biggest problem. We wanted to keep the original front door (3 ft. wide) and the picture window (8 ft. wide), which left only three narrow panels to resist any east/west movement. Tremendous uplift develops at the lower corners of these slender panels during a racking motion. To restrain this uplift, our engineer devised an elaborate hold-down for each corner. These custom steel hold-down plates were to be made at a local metal shop.

Enveloping the original house with an essentially independent structure accomplished several goals. For one, the concrete piers cost a little less than $3,000, well below the $8,000 to $10,000 estimates for shoring up the house and replacing the original foundation. Second, the entire addition was framed and secured before the first-floor ceiling needed opening for stairs and service connections, which left the downstairs largely undisturbed during much of the construction. And finally, changes still to come on the first floor can now be accomplished without concern for the loads induced by a new second story.   □

Eric Rekdahl is a partner in the design/build firm of Rekdahl & Tellefsen in Berkeley, Calif.

Cottage Sunspace

Stock materials and used brick
turn a sagging porch into a bright living space

by William Stokes

My brother's house in southwestern Connecticut began life as a vacation cottage with a southern exposure and a great view of the lake below. It was remodeled and winterized years ago, but by last year the front porch and the roof above it were sagging (photo left). Jack and Karen also needed more room. They decided to solve both problems by replacing the dilapidated veranda with a sunspace. They asked me to work out a design and help with the construction. Tight purse strings meant that we'd have to stick with stock materials. We also wanted to make sure that the new sun room would blend in with both the house and the hillside neighborhood.

I live in New Hampshire, and developing the design meant lots of phone calls, a number of trips to the post office and, finally, a trip south. What I came up with (photo below) was a south wall of fixed glass above low awning windows, an entrance with a similar look on the east and an insulated west wall with a double awning window. Jack decided to remove the door and windows on the existing

exterior wall of the house and install a sliding glass door between the living room and the new addition. The floor would be used brick over a concrete slab.

I relied on a number of details to incorporate this large expanse of glass into the existing house. Setting the glazing deep within the 2x6s of the wall keeps it out of the wet weather and the hot summer sun. It also creates strong shadow lines that give the wall a sense of depth, thereby avoiding the faceless glare that so much glass can create. We agreed to angle the trim at the upper corners of the fixed lites so they wouldn't look like stark rectangles, and to use wide pine trim to help the bright glass front merge with and complement the rest of the house's external trim.

I decided to use standard insulated sliding-door replacement panels for the fixed lites. Those across the front are 34 in. by 76 in., and the larger one next to the entry door is 46 in. by 76 in. We bought them at a discount through a factory outlet, and their dimensions determined the sizes of the wooden awning

The house, originally built as a summer cottage (above), had been winterized for year-round use. The front porch, sagging because its piers hadn't been sunk below the frost line, was converted to a sun room (below). Fixed sliding-door replacement sash was installed over wooden awning windows. Inside, a slab was poured and covered with used brick, and a new patio door was cut through into the living room. The sunspace remains cool in the summer, collects heat in the winter, and provides more space throughout the year.

windows that we planned to fit underneath. We finally got two of the sizes we needed—Brosco 241411s for under the smaller replacement panels along the front, and a Hurd 2719 double-awning for the west wall—through Rivco, a big distributor in Pennacook, N.H. I came to Connecticut thinking we'd have to get the awning to go under the large fixed lite on the east wall custom-milled, but a local lumberyard suggested a Norco 41611. The awnings weren't cheap. At $90 to $160, each awning window cost more than twice as much as one of our fixed glass panels.

Jack began by shoring up the roof (photo below) with timbers notched at their tops to fit the top plate, and wedged tightly to fit at their bottoms, as described on p. 32. Then he dismantled the deck and dug out the concrete piers that had unsuccessfully borne its weight. They hadn't been sunk below the frost line, and their heaving had caused all the porch's problems. As the porch sagged, so had the roofline above it. He restored a level fascia line with a 25-ton hydraulic jack.

Having poured footings—below the frost line—for a perimeter wall, Jack then laid up the concrete-block foundation. Next, he insulated inside the walls with 2-in. rigid foam board, backfilled, laid down a 6-in. layer of crushed rock and poured a 4-in. concrete slab over wire mesh and rebar.

Once the slab had cured, I arrived from New Hampshire, and together Jack and I put up the rough frame. Because there was still some variation in height across the front of the house, we decided to cut and toenail each stud individually. There weren't many studs involved, so it went quickly.

The concrete slab was level and the framing

was now fairly accurate, but I knew from my previous experiences installing a series of horizontal elements, like the sills supporting the fixed lites, that a very small variation between them can give the job an undulating look. So, instead of measuring the height of each window sill individually from the bottom plate, we shot the proper height on the two outside corners with a transit and snapped a chalkline across the studs. By holding the sills to this mark we made sure that they'd come out in a straight line.

In installing them we also used a split jack at the jambs rather than a single, continuous trimmer stud, which is used more frequently because it is less labor intensive. Instead of relying solely on the tensile strength of the nails between the trimmer and the rough sill, the split jack locks the sill in place and provides support under each end (drawing below). This was especially important, because I wanted to prevent any twisting that could crack a large glass panel.

I also had to double the rough sill, since the awning windows below precluded any cripple or jack studs to support this span. The glass itself was installed in a fairly standard manner, using neoprene setting blocks and silicone caulk.

The awning windows beneath the large fixed panels were installed next, followed by the window over the door. The door itself had been special ordered at a 6-ft. 6-in. height, instead of the more common 6 ft. 8 in. This gave us the extra 2 in. we needed to squeeze in the standard-size window above it.

A word of caution for those contemplating a similar design. Building codes generally call for tempered safety glass or plastic in win-

dows placed as low as our awning units, something we had overlooked but which our building inspector did not. A check back with the distributor confirmed that safety glass was unavailable. We wound up screwing Plexiglas to the inside sash, which worked out well because it gave us the added benefit of triple glazing, as well as making it safe for my 10-month-old niece to press her nose against the new windows in exploratory delight.

After the framing was completed, I returned to New Hampshire. Jack closed in the room by early April and finished the inside with cedar. The room was a cheerfully bright and comfortable space all last summer. The 16-in. overhang blocked out the hot sun, while the careful placement of awning vents kept air moving steadily.

Winter, of course, was the true test of the room. Last January, daytime temperatures inside the sunspace averaged in the high 80s. Jack and Karen vented the excess warmth into the house by opening the sliding-glass doors. At dusk, foam shutters were placed over the windows until morning, when they were removed and stored in two brick storage bins whose wooden lids double as plant shelves. With the shutters in place, the early-morning temperatures are in the high 40s.

The sparkling glass face has quietly been given neighborhood approval. At least we think it has. In the land of the Connecticut Yankee, such indications can be quite subtle. A nod as people drive slowly by, or a few words from the postman are all you're likely to get. □

William Stokes is a designer-builder in Canterbury, N.H.

With the porch roof propped up with 2x6s, above, the old porch and its piers were demolished. Then a block perimeter wall was laid up and a slab poured. The roof was forced back into level with a 25-ton hydraulic jack. Framing up the rough openings for the lites, the author used split jacks, shown in the drawing, to lock the sills into place, rather than the more common trimmer stud.

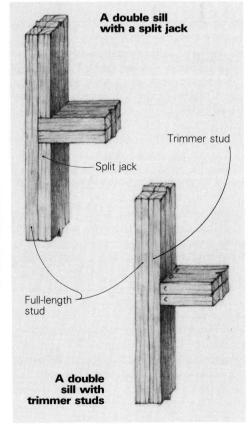

A double sill with a split jack

Trimmer stud

Split jack

Full-length stud

A double sill with trimmer studs

Smokehouse

A small outbuilding becomes a home through a series of additions

by Edward Nichols

The house that my wife and I live in began its life as a 12-ft. by 16-ft. smokehouse on my family's farm in the early part of this century. This small structure (photo right) had a partition wall dividing the smoking room from the aging room, where for years hams and sausages were hung to cure. During the Great Depression, a 10-ft. by 16-ft. lean-to was added on and used as a commissary where bulk foods were stored for the families living on the farm. By the early 1960s, none of these rooms was being used for its original purpose.

I returned to Mississippi in 1973 and decided to live and work on the land that my great-great-grandfather had settled in the 1830s. The old mule barn caught my attention first, but I didn't want to deal with 3,600 sq. ft. of space. I then cast my eye on the smokehouse, a building that was beginning to deteriorate but was still salvageable.

Saving the roof and ceiling—Though darkened from use, the smokehouse ceiling was in good shape. It had been built with two layers of planks to keep the smoke in, and I think the smoke must have preserved the wood better than it cured the meat. The roof over the planks was also sound, but the original structure had an earthen floor, and the sides of the building were in poor condition. Attending to these problems was my first job. I took the board-and-batten walls off on three sides, and then I braced up the roof with 2x6s and removed the original studs on these three walls. This left the roof supported by the only remaining wall and my 2x6 braces. Though it looked strange, this arrangement enabled me to form and pour a slab foundation with the roof still in place. After the concrete had cured, I built the walls in place, spiked them to the rafters, removed the 2x6 braces and then tore down the remaining original wall along with the old commissary attached to it.

Some of my framing lumber was bought new; the rest I got from a nearby wrecking yard and from an old house that I had dismantled on the property. Much of the original siding I had removed in taking down the old walls was good enough to be re-used. These old boards had been painted with a home-brewed mixture of used motor oil collected from farm vehicles during the winter and red lead pigment purchased from the local farm-supply store. Though the paint has peeled after 30 or more years to the weather, most of

Humble beginnings. Little changed since its construction some 80 years ago, this 12-ft. by 16-ft. smokehouse became the core of a 1,300-sq.-ft. house. The porch was the structure's first addition; after that came the master bedroom, dining room, greenhouse and sauna.

the boards are still so oil-saturated that they won't hold store-bought paint.

I poured a slab where the commissary had been, joining it to the smokehouse slab. Then I rebuilt the lean-to, widening it by 2 ft. The smokehouse became my bedroom and living room, while the lean-to held the kitchen and bathroom—a total of just under 400 sq. ft.

Adding on—The first addition, in the summer of 1974, was a screened-in front porch. Porches were a virtual institution in the South at one time, but with the advent of TV and air conditioning, they've fallen into disuse. Having neither of these modern conveniences, I knew that the porch would be a pleasant place to sit at the end of a day's work.

Adding a long (12-ft. by 24-ft.) room on the west end of the smokehouse was next. I envisioned it as a dining and work room, and that's how it turned out. I removed the lower part of the original west wall to expose the slab, then formed and poured a new slab up to it. With a couple of friends, I built the frame for this addition using 2x4s for walls and rafters and 2x6s for ceiling joists. One advantage of corrugated metal roofing, apart from low cost, is its light weight. Two-by-four rafters, spaced on 2-ft. centers and overlaid with 1x6 purlins which served as nailers, were all we needed to hold the overlapping sheets.

The maple flooring in this room came out of

a college gymnasium that had been torn down in Jackson. As with all the floors throughout the house, I first covered the slab with builder's felt, then fastened down 2x4 nailers with a rented powder-actuated nailer and masonry nails. I set them face down on 16-in. centers so they would provide ample support and nailing surface for the flooring. In the dining and work room, I relaid the 2-in. wide maple planks just as they had come from the pile unloaded from my pickup, and the result is a scattering of colors as the painted lines of the basketball court appear in random squares across the floor. It's a unique effect, and I'm glad that I decided not to refinish the floor.

This long room has also been fitted with a large, round pocket window that I bought from a housewrecker who was going out of business. For exterior siding, I bought some random-width, locally cut cypress lumber and put up boards and battens. Inside the addition, I paneled with aromatic eastern cedar that I purchased from the same lumberyard. I let it weather outside for six months before installing it. In fact, as time went on, most of the house was paneled in random-width cedar and cypress. Excluding the porch, my house had now grown to 675 sq. ft.

Before we married in 1978, Mindy and I decided to enlarge the house again. So we embarked on a 12-ft. by 24-ft. greenhouse on the south side of the structure, with a 7-ft. by 7-ft. sauna at its west end.

With the kitchen built onto the south side of the smokehouse, a porch on the east, and a double addition off the west side, only the north side remained untouched. But not for long. We added our 12-ft. by 16-ft. master bedroom as the greenhouse was being finished. The walls were paneled with weathered pine boards ranging in width from 12 in. to 17 in. A long, narrow window I'd been saving found its way into the north wall of the bedroom, and I hinged it at the bottom so that it can just swing open for ventilation.

Adding on around the old smokehouse has worked out well, and 1,300 sq. ft. is a big improvement over the space I started with. It would have been difficult to generate the time, money and enthusiasm to do all the building at once. And though I planned each space separately, they work nicely as a whole. □

Ed Nichols is a farmer and furnituremaker in Canton, Miss.

The weathered barnboard paneling used throughout the house, left, looks light against the original smoke-blackened ceiling boards. From this viewpoint just inside the front door, the kitchen can be seen through the doorway at left; the dining and work room is through the door at right. Above, the large pocket window beneath the dining room's snow-covered roof was bought from a housewrecker.

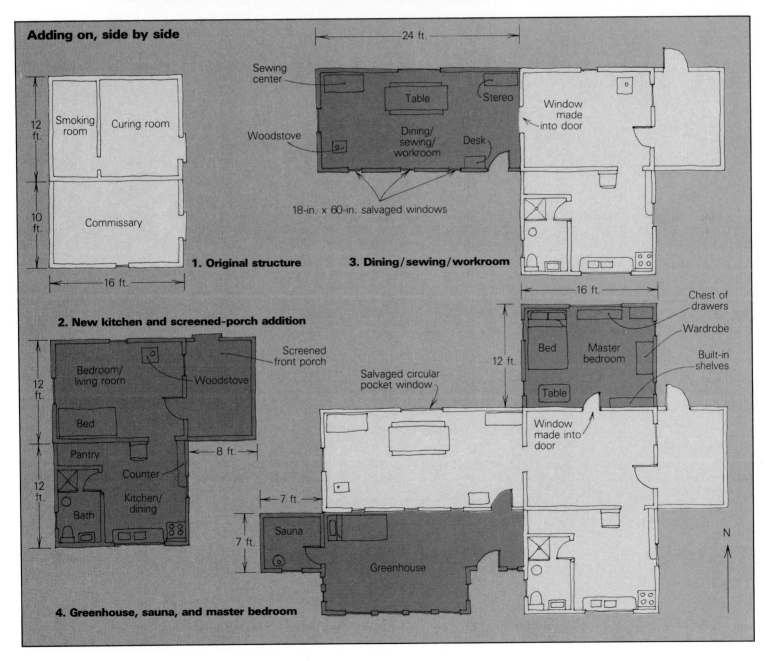

Adding on, side by side

12 ft. / 10 ft.

Smoking room — Curing room

Commissary

16 ft.

1. Original structure

2. New kitchen and screened-porch addition

12 ft. / 12 ft.

Bedroom/living room — Woodstove

Screened front porch

Bed

Pantry

Counter

8 ft.

Bath

Kitchen/dining

4. Greenhouse, sauna, and master bedroom

24 ft.

Sewing center

Table — Stereo

Window made into door

Woodstove

Dining/sewing/workroom — Desk

18-in. x 60-in. salvaged windows

3. Dining/sewing/workroom

16 ft.

Chest of drawers

Wardrobe

Bed — Master bedroom

Built-in shelves

12 ft.

Salvaged circular pocket window

Table

Window made into door

7 ft.

7 ft.

Sauna

Greenhouse

N

Victorian Addition

Energetic clients and a pragmatic approach keep costs down
without sacrificing quality

**West elevation,
original house
with addition**

by Steve Larson

Facing Monterey Bay and backed by redwood forests, Santa Cruz, Calif., flourished in the late 19th century. A nationwide reputation as a seaside resort and a plentiful lumber supply spurred the construction of elegant Victorian homes and buildings on the hills and fields a few blocks from the beach.

Today, this old section of downtown Santa Cruz is a designated historic district, and the once neglected structures are now being valued for their historic and architectural qualities. As a contractor who does mostly remodeling work, I get involved with some of the old places as their new owners bring the sagging buildings back to life, or add on a room or two. One such place is the stick-style cottage that Kit and Kurt Haveman bought in 1976.

Disrepair—The Havemans acquired a house that had been partially converted into a print shop. The front porch had been torn off, and a boxy stucco addition had been built in the front yard for the presses. The plaster was falling off the interior walls, and the exterior hadn't seen a paintbrush in 30 years.

Fortunately, the Havemans had the energy and skills required to put the house back in shape. Over the past four years, they had torn down the addition and restored the porch. The windows are all intact now, some with leaded glass, and they've replaced the crumbling lath and plaster with gypboard.

By the time I met them, their family of seven had outgrown the original ten-room house. They needed a larger bathroom, and studio and storage space for their home-based restaurant-decorating business. They asked me to build a second-story addition.

An appropriate plan—Architect Marilyn Crenshaw worked with the Havemans to develop the addition's design. They planned to extend the existing partial second story toward the rear, and cover the entire house with a broad hip roof that matched the original 10-in-12 pitch (drawing, facing page). This would give them an additional 450 sq. ft. of living space, and would preserve the look of the original house. Low-profile tempered-glass skylights would increase the light inside the house without interrupting the roof planes. The addition would include a larger bathroom, a studio and attic storage. The rear of the addition would be flanked by a deck over the backyard for enjoying the outdoors.

From the outset we knew that the work would have to be done on a tight budget—about $40,000—with well-ordered priorities. Obviously, the first goal would be framing and enclosing the addition. Next, the bathroom and restoring the baby's room would receive full attention, followed by the interior finish work in the studio. A backyard staircase, a ground-floor deck and a fancy deck rail would get whatever remained in the budget. To cut costs, we would use recycled doors and windows wherever we could, and the owners would pull their own permits, order and pick up building materials, and take care of all of the demolition and cleanup.

Securing a permit for remodel work on a historic building wasn't easy. The preservation committee wanted detailed drawings of all four sides of the house, and it took several hearings and a petition signed by the neighbors before the project was approved.

Evaluating the structure—We wanted the house to show little evidence of new construction, so the old and new sections had to blend. This meant that the imperfections of the old house would become our problem as we grafted on the new addition.

Before adding a second story to an existing dwelling, I need to be sure that the framing and foundation underneath are adequate to support the new load. One thing I want to know is whether tilting walls or sagging floors are clues to serious structural flaws, or simply the result of normal settling, lumber shrinkage or minor construction mistakes.

My rule-of-thumb for significant error in an old house is this: up to ¼ in. out of plumb or square for windows, doors and 8-ft. walls, and up to ⅜-in. rise or fall in a 10-ft. run of floor or permanently loaded beam. If the deviations are greater, I hunt for the cause and correct the problem if structural integrity is at all in question. At this stage I often feel like a cross between an archeologist and a detective.

By stringing lines and establishing level marks, we found that the first-floor ceiling was neither flat nor level. It sloped away from the central bearing wall toward the side walls, with a significant drop of ¾ in. at the southwest corner. We got another surprise when we found that the side walls weren't perpendicular to the rear wall. This threw the upstairs platform a full 6 in. out of square.

A close look at the foundation under the

This former Victorian vacation house had suffered years of neglect and commercial abuse. In the photo above, a stucco addition has been removed, and salvaged brackets and balustrades have been installed on the porch. The small photo on the facing page shows the southwest corner before the second-story addition was begun. The elevation drawing at the lower left foreshadows the nearly completed job, above. Trim, permanent deck railings and a coat of paint will finish up the job.

low corner revealed an undersized footing, and a sill plate that was almost completely eaten away by termites. The rest of the foundation was in excellent shape, so we propped up the house (see p. 154) and got ready to pour a new section of the foundation.

Here, we were confronted with a classic dilemma in remodeling. Should we jack up the corner to make it level, thereby lifting the entire dining room, or should we leave well enough alone by fixing the foundation and building to the old lines of the house? It's certainly easier to build on a platform that's square and level, but this advantage was outweighed in this case by another pre-existing condition—the dining room had already been remodeled, and lifting the room would damage the new walls.

My solution was to leave the sag in the downstairs floor but to reduce the slope upstairs to ¼ in. per 10 ft. by progressively shimming the new floor joists. This kind of compromise happens all the time in remodeling. Correcting every problem may be more trouble than it's worth if it means damaging existing architectural features. Compromises are often necessary to create visual harmony between old and new. For example, a new plumb wall next to an old leaning wall can make both look bad. With these things in mind, we decided to live with the out-of-square platform, since the only alternative would be to rebuild the entire first floor so that it would be square.

We formed and poured the new section of foundation, and removed the honeycombed wood. As we replaced pieces of the floor, walls and ceiling on the back porch, we discovered another serious inadequacy.

Framing problems—When they built the house in 1892, the carpenters hadn't put headers over the doors and windows in the one-story bearing walls. Single 2x4s were spanning up to 10 ft. This hadn't caused serious problems yet, but the framing was clearly too weak to support a floor above.

The solution to a problem like this is normally straightforward: open up either the interior or exterior of the wall and insert a new header over each opening. But in this case, I didn't want to open any of the downstairs walls because doing so would disturb the complex trim and shingles on the exterior and the newly completed drywall and cabinetwork on the interior.

Our solution was to install a 4x10 girder on the top plate of each bearing wall. The three girders, which now span all the windows and doorways below the addition, transfer the load from above to supporting studs on either side of the openings and safely on down to the foundation.

To install the girders we had to cut the ceiling joists back 3½ in. where they were resting on the top plates. Fortunately, the original plates were a full 4 in. wide, so the 2x4 joists had about ½ in. of bearing (small drawing, next page, bottom). We connected them to the new girders with framing clips. On top of

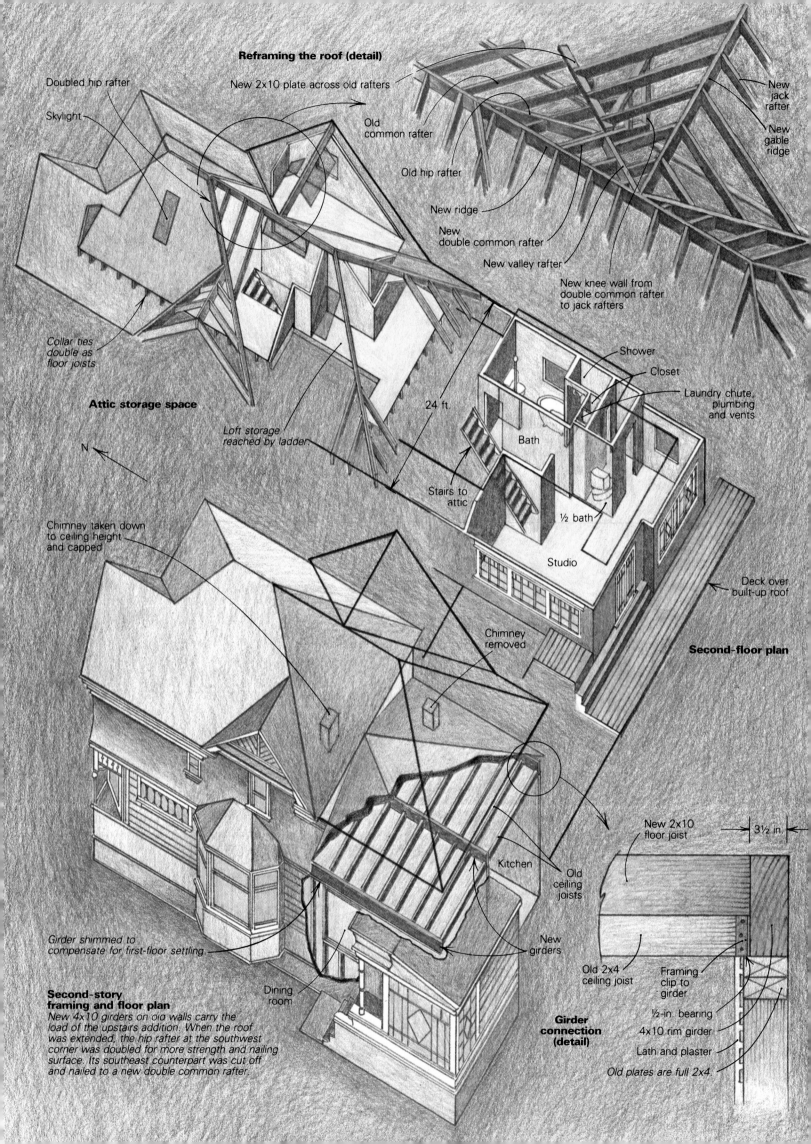

Reframing the roof (detail)

Doubled hip rafter

Skylight

New 2x10 plate across old rafters

Old common rafter

Old hip rafter

New jack rafter

New gable ridge

New ridge

New double common rafter

New valley rafter

New knee wall from double common rafter to jack rafters

Collar ties double as floor joists

Attic storage space

N

Loft storage reached by ladder

24 ft.

Stairs to attic

Shower

Closet

Laundry chute, plumbing and vents

Bath

½ bath

Studio

Second-floor plan

Deck over built-up roof

Chimney taken down to ceiling height and capped

Chimney removed

New 2x10 floor joist

3½ in

Kitchen

Old ceiling joists

Old 2x4 ceiling joist

Framing clip to girder

½-in. bearing

4x10 rim girder

Lath and plaster

Old plates are full 2x4.

Girder connection (detail)

Girder shimmed to compensate for first-floor settling.

Dining room

New girders

Second-story framing and floor plan
New 4x10 girders on old walls carry the load of the upstairs addition. When the roof was extended, the hip rafter at the southwest corner was doubled for more strength and nailing surface. Its southeast counterpart was cut off and nailed to a new double common rafter.

New walls and rafters butt against the old as the addition framing nears completion, right. The former hip rafter at the southwest corner has been doubled to help carry the new loads and to provide a solid nailing surface for the new rafters. Before the house gets a fresh layer of composition shingles, the old roof will be taken down to the skip sheathing and the entire roof frame covered with ½-in. plywood.

these we installed new 2x10 floor joists between the girders, and then nailed and glued a new ¾-in. plywood subfloor in place.

Extending the roof—Tying the new roof to the old framing presented some challenging connections. The hip rafter at the southwest corner was carrying part of the load of the small gable on the west side of the house. Extending the roof would transform this hip into a valley, and as such it would have to support the new load of the jack rafters falling on it. We reinforced it by sistering a new fir 2x10 to the old 2x8 redwood rafter (small drawing, facing page, top).

We butted the new 2x10 ridgeboard to the old one, holding it in place with nails and framing straps, and propping up the other end with a temporary brace. At this point we discovered that the original ridgeboard was out of level; if we continued it our new ridge wouldn't be level with the floor of the new addition. We wondered if we should keep the line of the old ridge, or angle it slightly to keep the ridge level over the addition to simplify roof framing. We decided to go for level, feeling that the discrepancy between the lines of the old and new ridge wouldn't be apparent once we were done. We got away with it.

Things got even trickier at the east side of the house where we planned to add a ridge-high full gable. Part of this new gable would extend over the old roof in the area above the original stairwell and hall. We couldn't disturb the original rafters here because they directly supported an elaborately restored ceiling. So instead of cutting off the old rafters and hanging them to a new, continuous valley rafter, we laid the gable rafters on top of the old roof framing. This was a little complicated. At the line of the stairway wall we cut off the original hip rafter after propping it up with a 2x4 brace for temporary support. Then we added a doubled 2x10 common rafter directly over and partially supported by the stairway wall.

The top section of the new valley rafter, also a 2x10, was likewise butted into the doubled common rafter above the stairway wall. To complete the valley over the stairwell, we laid a 2x10 flat on top of the existing rafters in line with the upper section of the new valley rafter. The jack rafters of the new gable then terminated with a compound miter on top of the flat 2x10, and with standard side cuts at the upper end of the valley.

It was obvious that the original rafters wouldn't be able to support the new load of the gable. We solved this problem by building a knee wall that bears on the doubled 2x10 rafter, picking up the load of the gable rafters and taking the load off the old roof framing.

Replacing the gutters

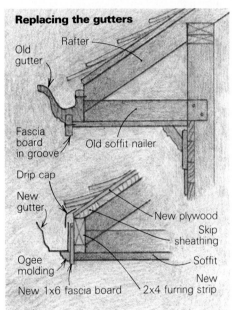

Blending architectural features—To our great relief, the existing exterior walls were plumb, and we tied the new walls directly in line with them (photo, top). To keep the ladder and scaffolding work to a minimum, we framed and squared the wall sections on the new floor, sheathed them with ⅜-in. plywood for shear bracing and shingle backing, and then tilted them into place. We carefully aligned the planes of the old wall sheathing with the new plywood so that the old sidewall shingles would blend inconspicuously with the new ones.

After we completed the framing and roofing, Kurt ripped new cedar shingles to match the old ones and our roofer, Sonny Hankes, applied them over courses of roofing felt in the same pattern as the originals. As the shingles went on, some folks passing by asked us why we were tearing off the old siding. They thought the addition was part of the original house—our greatest compliment.

Gutters—As on many Victorian houses, almost 100 years of exposure to the elements had worn out the redwood gutters. Replacing them would have meant getting kiln-dried redwood custom-milled at a cost of over $12 per lineal foot. This was more than our budget could bear, so we designed a system that let us substitute commonly available galvanized

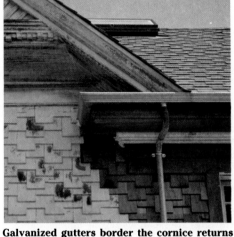

Galvanized gutters border the cornice returns where new construction meets old. The new shingles, ripped to match the original in width, are woven into the square butt pattern that has covered the house for 90 years.

gutters. First we removed all the old gutters, along with the small piece of fascia board that fit into the dado on the gutter bottom, as shown in the drawing above. This exposed the old rafter tails and soffit nailers. We then attached an all-heart redwood 2x4 furring strip to the end of the rafter tails, followed by a 1x6 fascia board.

Before the roofers put down the composition shingles, they installed a 1½-in. galvanized drip cap along the perimeter of the roof, and made sure to bend the edging out far enough so that the back lip of the gutters could be easily slipped under it later.

We treated the new section in a similar way, but without the 2x4 furring strip. Eventually, we plan to add a piece of ogee molding to the junction between the gutter bottom and the fascia board to approximate the original look more closely.

Cornice returns are a common Victorian feature. Nestled under the gable soffit, they form a sort of tiny, hip-shaped roof. In this house, the returns were covered with tin flashing and bordered by the original gutters. The new gutters had a different profile from the old ones, so we couldn't butt new to old at each gable. Nor could the old tin be made to overlap the new gutters.

Rebuilding all four cornice returns (photo above) was my only choice. After carefully removing them with shears, prybars and a reciprocating saw, I partially assembled new units on the ground and then nailed them into alignment with the rest of the fascia board. This way, the new gutters could run continuously around the cornice. We used composition shingles over roofing felt to replace the tin flashing.

Working around the chimneys—The two brick chimneys that rose from the first story into what has now become a second-floor living area weren't tall enough to penetrate the new roof. They would either have to be extended or eliminated, so we brought in a chimney specialist for an opinion. The news wasn't good. The old mortar was cracked, and there were no flue linings. Both of the chimneys were dangerously unstable.

For the fireplace chimney, the solution would have to be to dismantle the chimney down to the firebox and begin anew, either with masonry laid up to modern standards or with triple-wall metal ductwork. Both options

The bathroom blends Victorian style with contemporary materials and convenience. The walls next to the tub, the floor, and the shower (accessible from two sides) are covered with mortar and tiny hexagonal tiles. To protect against moisture damage, the floor was hot-mopped and the mortar tile base sloped to a drain under the tub. Both the wainscoting and the laundry chute (right center of photo, and drawing) are lauan mahogany stained dark.

were expensive, and both involved tearing into the walls of the temporary bedroom on the first floor. This job would cost a lot and make a big mess, so the Havemans decided not to work on this chimney until later. We dismantled it down to the second-floor level and closed off the fireplace.

When we framed the new roof, we made sure that rafter placement allowed clearance for a new chimney, and laid a plywood subfloor over the old flue. We were disappointed that we had to leave this portion of the project undone, but we had to proceed with more pressing tasks.

By completely dismantling the other chimney, which originally vented the woodburning stoves in the kitchen, we created a clear channel from the basement through to the second story. Victorian house plans often included large, multi-storied plumbing wells, which isolated pipe runs and left room for repairs. We decided to make similar use of our much smaller channel.

By carefully arranging the pipes, we were

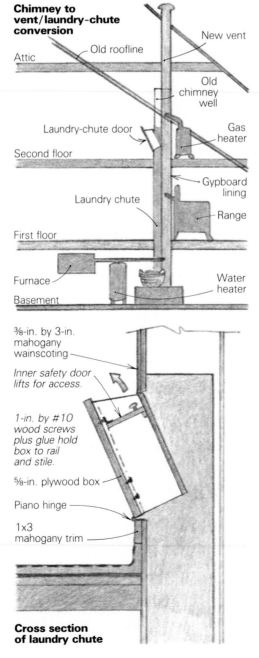

Chimney to vent/laundry-chute conversion

Attic — Old roofline — New vent

Laundry-chute door — Old chimney well

Second floor — Gas heater

Gypboard lining

Laundry chute — Range

First floor

Furnace — Water heater

Basement

⅜-in. by 3-in. mahogany wainscoting

Inner safety door lifts for access.

1-in. by #10 wood screws plus glue hold box to rail and stile.

⅝-in. plywood box

Piano hinge

1x3 mahogany trim

Cross section of laundry chute

able to re-route the bathroom supply and waste lines, and the vents for the studio heater, the kitchen range and the basement furnace and water heater—all without resorting to external plumbing or ductwork, or tearing into downstairs walls (drawing, below left). Painstaking planning allowed us enough room left over for a 12-in. by 12-in. sheet-metal laundry chute from the bathroom to the basement laundry area.

Our building inspector pointed out a potential problem created by this new channel. He emphasized that similar passageways, as well as hidden cavities created by old-style balloon framing, had let fires race through older homes by providing unseen chimneys for flames and toxic gases. Rather than building solid firestops at each floor level, we chose to encase the entire channel with ⅝-in. gypboard to form a one-hour rated fire barrier. We sealed cracks in the gypboard where pipes or ductwork entered with plaster-based patching compound.

The laundry chute was custom made from galvanized sheet metal for resistance to both fire and moisture damage. For fire safety and to prevent small children from falling into the chute, I balanced the plywood and mahogany bin-type door so it would be self-closing (drawing, bottom left). Another door inside the chute provides a second safety barrier—it has to be opened manually by someone tall enough to reach inside the bin.

Working with the owners—The successful completion of a building project depends not only on the technical competence of the builders, but also on the cooperation and communication between the builders and the clients. A good working relationship is even more important during renovation or remodeling because of the surprises that inevitably pop up along the way.

Early in the framing stage we all began to realize that the budget for the project wouldn't cover the non-essentials, and that some of the work would have to be postponed. We were thankful for a realistic priority list, and we stuck to it. Anything completed would be done right, and anything not immediately needed would be left untouched and ready to go when funds permitted.

The owners' active participation was a key element in accomplishing good results. Besides handling the demolition and cleanup, they were always available for consultation and decision making. They also took over the painting, staining and decorating chores.

As the money dwindled, they became more involved in the basic construction. Kurt wainscoted and trimmed the baby's room, and Kit laid the 46,000 plus hexagonal tiles in the bathroom (photo left). In addition, they found salvaged components such as doors, windows, newel posts and light fixtures. The project was a success because of this kind of cooperation, inventiveness and flexibility. □

Steve Larson is a contractor and remodeling instructor in Santa Cruz, Calif.

A Shed-Dormer Addition

Extensive remodeling triples the space of a small Cape

by Bob Syvanen

Adding new space to an old house is seldom as simple as it first looks. Getting the end result to look good is demanding and time-consuming, and the problems that invariably crop up add considerably to the headaches. Working out the basic design and particular construction details on paper isn't so hard, but once the actual work begins, leveling and plumbing the new construction to fit the old structure is a big challenge, especially if years of settling have caused walls to lean and beams to sag. Apart from all these difficulties, keeping the house and site relatively clean and orderly during construction so that life can go on for the clients who are putting up with this invasion adds appreciably to the burden and the time spent.

I faced such a challenge on a recent job. My clients asked me to take their plain 864-sq. ft. Cape Cod cracker box and make it over into a not-so-plain 3,300-sq. ft. house. Though I had considerable freedom with the design, the clients made several specific requests. Chiefly, they wanted about 1,300 sq. ft. of the addition to be on the second floor. There they would set up a large master bedroom, something they had missed since moving to the East Coast from California. Since the house would be occupied during construction, I had to keep the old Cape tight to the weather during the entire process of adding on.

I decided to keep the front roof intact and to build the addition at the back and south side of the old house. The floor plan I worked up (drawing, next page) enlarged the old kitchen and added a dining area, a living room, a bedroom, a bath and a foyer—all on the first floor. I added a three-car attached ga-rage on the north end of the house. Upstairs went the big bedroom (about 500 sq. ft.) along with a bath and access to these via a new stairway. The other part of the upstairs (the space directly above the old house) remains unfinished even now, but will eventually become another bath and bedroom.

The owners wanted to keep these two areas entirely separate, thinking that the unfinished area might become an in-law apartment in the future. To this end, each space on the second

While a two-story addition to this small house was being built, the old roof had to be kept intact until the addition was complete. The 2x10 nailed along the ridge of the old roof serves as a plate for the rafters that extend to the new ridge. Kicker braces for plumbing the dormer wall are still in place.

Plan of old house and additions

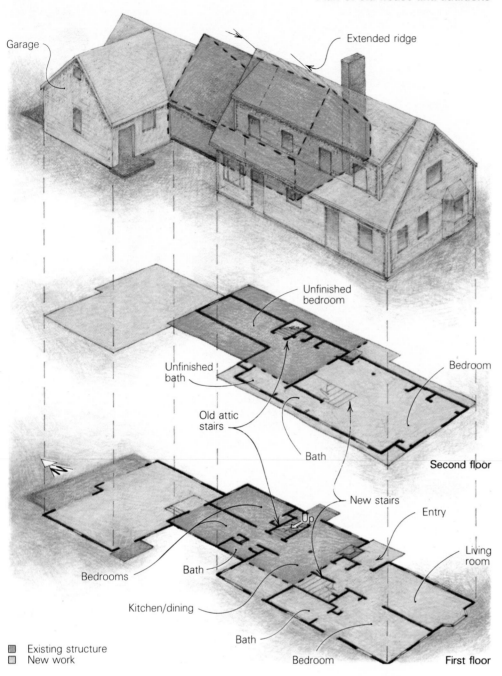

Garage

Extended ridge

Unfinished bedroom

Unfinished bath

Old attic stairs

Bath

Bedroom

Second floor

New stairs

Entry

Up

Living room

Bedrooms

Bath

Kitchen/dining

Bath

Bedroom

First floor

■ Existing structure
□ New work

story has its own way up and down. Excluding the garage addition, remodeling the old house extended the south gable-end wall 30 ft. and added an 11-ft. wide by 18-ft. long section in the opposite direction, along the existing back wall behind the kitchen.

By putting a 40-ft. long shed dormer on the rear of the house, I was able to create the large, open second-story space the clients wanted. Doing this and making the house wider from front to back meant extending the plane of the roof on the front of the house and relocating the ridge so that it would exactly divide the new footprint along its width. The challenge I faced in framing the new roof was to build the dormer big enough for the owners' wants and strong enough for the open floor plan (the ceiling joists had to span almost 20 ft.), and make it look good from the outside. And, of course, I had to do it all without opening the roof to the weather.

Maybe the most trying part of the job was

an uninvited but regular member of the crew named Jasper, a kleptomaniac crow. He seemed to like nail sets best and would pick them right out of your tool belt. We must have lost a dozen nail sets. We even had to keep the truck windows rolled up to keep him from flying off with our ignition keys.

The old attached garage had to be removed from the south-end wall to make way for the addition. But before doing that I had to build the new garage at the opposite end of the old house. Tearing away the garage left a wound in the gable end open to the weather. It also exposed the mudsill, from which I would calculate the height of my new floor. The old and new floors would have to match in height. The old mudsill is a 3x6, the floor joists are 2x8s, the subfloor is ⅝-in. plywood, and the finished floor is ¾-in. hardwood, totaling 11⅜ in. For the addition, the mudsill is a 2x6, the floor joists are 2x10s, the subfloor is ⅝-in. plywood, and there is ½-in. underlayment for

carpeting, totaling 12⅛ in. All floors would be carpeted, so the ½-in. underlayment in the addition would need to be level with the finished floor in the old house. Adding ½ in. for grout under the mudsill, I knew that the top of the foundation for the addition would have to be 1¼ in. below the old foundation wall.

I like to level and seal my mudsills with a bed of mortar between sill and foundation. It's a big help on remodel work to have this half-inch to play with, and can often make the difference between being able to adjust wall height properly and having to live with roller-coaster top plates.

When I told the foundation contractor to set the new foundation parallel to the front wall of the old house, which is also parallel to the ridge, I was thinking ahead to tying the new roof into the old roof, wanting to avoid any torqued planes and a snaky new ridge. Apparently he misunderstood my instructions (or just ignored them), and instead made the gable-end wall of the new foundation parallel to the gable-end wall of the old house. He then squared up his forms so that the new sidewall foundation was perpendicular to its end wall. Just exactly the opposite of what I needed. The garage gable-end had been built completely out of square with its sidewalls. As a result, the foundations for the new sidewalls were so far out of parallel to the sidewalls of the old house that Jasper the crow might have been able to do a better job.

To compensate for the misalignment without calling for a jackhammer and a new pour, I offset the mudsills on the new foundations. But after cantilevering the sill as far off the foundation wall as I dared, I found that it was still about an inch away from being parallel to the front wall of the old house. So I decided that I would just have to tolerate the error, and cope with the consequences when I framed the new roof.

With this problem postponed, I completed the first floor of the addition with little hassle. I took care to level my mudsills, to square the new floor before nailing down the deck, and to plumb the corners of the exterior walls to maintain alignment with the old house.

The next thing I had to worry about was the framing for the 11-ft. by 18-ft. area that would enlarge the kitchen along the back wall of the house. After the addition was fully enclosed, this section of wall would be taken out, but for the time being I was stuck with it. The ceiling joists in this area run from the new back wall to the old back wall of the house. To carry them, I nailed a doubled header to the top plates along the old back wall. To make room for the header (or carrying beam), a 2-ft. wide section of the eave had to be removed and the rafters cut back (photo facing page, left). This left a gap in the roof open to the weather. To cover the gap, I tucked an 18-ft. long piece of building paper under the roof shingles and lapped it over the header. A 20-ft. length of old gutter, hung below the beam, channeled the water run off from the old roof into a length of PVC downspout angled out a window opening of the addition.

New joists, new rafters. The addition's second-story floor joists that tie into the old house (above) are attached to a header nailed to the top plates of the existing wall. To make room for the header, the eaves and rafters had to be cut back. Extending the plane of the old roof without opening it up meant framing an 18-ft. long section of roof with a bottom plate on the deck (right), as though it were a wall. Then the section was raised and braced in position alongside the old ridge. The bottom plate was nailed to the old roof at the ridge, with allowance made to let the new roofing work out flush with the old. A layout error in the foundation was compensated for at the peak by sistering a 2x10 onto the new ridge so it would line up with the already installed gable rafters.

Framing the dormer—With the first-floor ceiling joists and plywood deck in place, I was ready to tackle the dormer framing. I took measurements of the old roof rafters and made a full-size layout on the deck. This layout included the old rafters (many of which would be removed after the framing was finished), new rafters, first and second-floor ceiling joists, the dormer window wall and the interior wall that supports the new ceiling and the old roof. To complete the layout, I added the fascia and soffit. From this layout, I would get the correct angles for making plumb and level cuts on my rafter stock, and the exact lengths for rafters, joists and studs. The full-size layout also let me preview the operations to come and gave me a good sense of how things would go together.

Using the stud height that I had laid out on the deck, I built the 40-ft. dormer window wall with a 6-ft. wide piece of the cheek or end wall at each end (drawing, facing page). This partial return on each side let me brace the new dormer wall at both ends so that it was ready for rafters, and still take my time in filling in the rest of the cheek wall. I set the dormer window wall back 4 ft. from the exterior wall below, and set the dormer's cheeks in 4 ft. from the gable-end walls. To carry the tops of the short rafters, I nailed a 2x8 ledger board to the studs of the window wall 30 in. up from the bottom plate. I think dormer walls look better when they are set back from the edge of the roof. It's more costly to build a dormer this way, but it maintains the integrity of the original roof line, and incorporates the dormer better into the rest of the structure, making it seem less like an ungainly afterthought.

I decided to preserve the plane of the original front roof, and extend it to a new ridge about 4 ft. higher than the existing one (photo

above right). This was a practical measure that would let me take advantage of the existing framing without exposing the old house to the elements. The trick here was being able to extend this plane up to the new ridge without sistering new rafters onto the old ones, which would mean cutting into the roof and removing the old ridge.

To accomplish this, I framed a section of roof to come off the old ridge at the original pitch and in the same plane as the front roof. I began by cutting the 7-ft. long rafters from 2x8 stock, taking the lengths and angles from the layout. Next I nailed a 2x10 plate to the bottoms of rafters (which were set out on the deck), just as if I were framing a stud wall with an oddly angled bottom plate. Then I nailed the 2x12 ridge to the rafters. When this was done, I raised the whole thing into position, and braced it with 2x6s from the dormer deck.

Once the rafter section was in place, I nailed the plate to the existing roof next to the

old ridge, as shown in the drawing next page, top left. Because the rafters underneath the plate would eventually be cut off, I made sure that I got plenty of nails through the plate and into the ridge itself; otherwise, I'd have to depend on the nailing in the old rafter stubs to hold the new roof sturdily in place. I was careful to locate the plate so that its top edge was in line with the top edges of the rafters on the opposite side. This way the new roof deck would flush up with the existing deck, and there wouldn't be a hump in the shingles.

To brace the unsupported rafters, I nailed a straight 2x6 guide on edge to the old roof at each end of the new rafter section and let the ends run to the new ridge. By deducting the thickness of the decking and the thickness of the shingles on the old roof, and by cutting shims to this thickness and nailing them to the guides, I was able to find the right plane for the new rafters to lie in. Since the old roof would have to be reshingled, I didn't worry

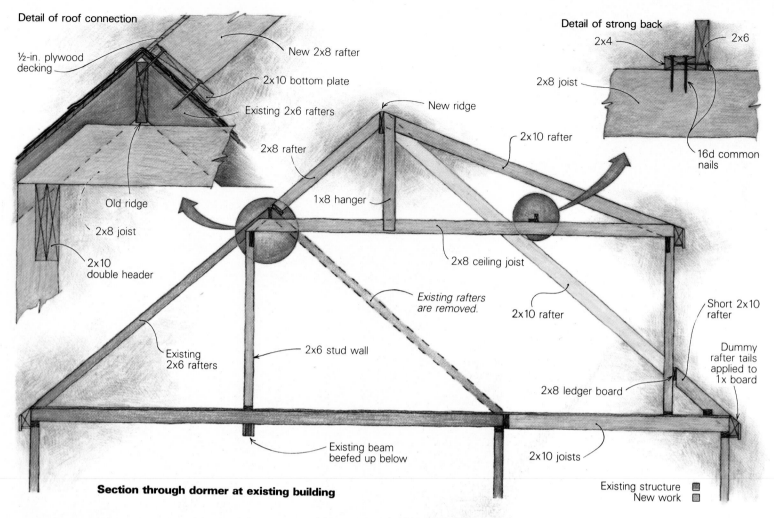

Detail of roof connection

½-in. plywood decking

New 2x8 rafter

2x10 bottom plate

Existing 2x6 rafters

Old ridge

2x8 joist

2x10 double header

2x8 rafter

New ridge

1x8 hanger

2x8 ceiling joist

Existing rafters are removed.

2x10 rafter

Existing 2x6 rafters

2x6 stud wall

2x10 rafter

2x8 ledger board

Existing beam beefed up below

2x10 joists

Detail of strong back

2x4

2x6

2x8 joist

16d common nails

Short 2x10 rafter

Dummy rafter tails applied to 1x board

Section through dormer at existing building

Existing structure ▪
New work ▪

---

much about nailing the temporary guides through the roofing.

Before putting the shed-dormer rafters on, I wanted to be sure the ridge on the extended rafter section lined up with the new gable-end rafters. So I cut a pair of gable rafters, and temporarily set them in place using a 2x4 spacer in place of the ridge. Once again, I got the gable-rafter lengths and angles from my layout on the deck. Then came the moment of truth, the moment I'd prepared for with all the fussing, fudging and plumbing up the frame from the mudsills below. Eyeballing down the 18-ft. length of the 2x12 ridge on the extended rafter section, I was hoping against hope to put the 2x4 ridge block at the new gable rafters dead in my sights. It was a clear miss. The block was 1½ in. off toward the back of the house. The inch I was off at the mudsill had followed me up to the ridge, and it picked up another ½ in. to boot. Not good, but not disastrous either. I had to stick with the gable rafters I'd already nailed in place so I could keep a flat plane on the front roof; I couldn't cheat here. But I could on the dormer side of the ridge. I decided to sister a new 2x10 ridge onto the face of the 2x12 ridge of the extended rafter section and run it all the way to the far gable end. This put the new ridge in perfect alignment with the new gable rafters. Thus, the front rafters all worked out to be the same length, but each of the dormer rafters had to be cut a tad shorter than the previous one as they progressed toward the gable end.

Framing up a shed dormer and introducing

a vertical wall where the rafters ordinarily go means losing the strength and rigidity of a tri-angulated structure. If something isn't done to compensate for this loss, the ridge will sag and the dormer wall will lean out of plumb—if you're lucky. In the worst instance, the ridge (which, with dormer rafters attached, becomes a structural member) can fail and cause the roof to collapse. I solved the problem in this case by framing up a truss-like arrangement that consists of a long 2x10 rafter, a short 2x8 rafter, a 2x8 bottom chord, which functions as a collar tie and serves as a ceiling joist, and a 1x8 hanger, which supports the joist about ⅓ of the way along its 21-ft. span. This 1x8 looks a little like a king post, but its purpose is not to take any compression loading. This restores the triangulation you lose in omitting the rafters and framing up a dormer wall. (In most shed-dormer situations, where joists aren't spanning long distances, the hanger isn't needed.) The joists sit on the double top plate of the dormer window wall, where they extend to the plumb cut on the rafter tails and are well nailed to each rafter.

So each joist would be at the right height when I nailed it to its hanger, I cut a 7½-ft. long 2x4 for a gauge stick. The joist would sit on top of the gauge stick while I nailed the hanger to the joist. To stiffen the joists and to help keep them from twisting and sagging, I ran a *strong back* (detail drawing, above right) across them in the middle of their span between the hangers and the dormer wall.

Because at this point I wasn't ready to re-

move the old roof under the dormer, I couldn't yet install the 2x8 ceiling joists in the 18-ft. long section of roof that was over the old roof. But that part of the structure did need stabilizing, so I nailed a temporary 1x8 tie to each rafter at the dormer wall plate and angled it upward to catch the extended rafter opposite, just above the plate at the ridge. These ties would be replaced with permanent 2x8 ceiling joists to match those in the rest of the dormer, once I built an interior 2x6 stud wall to support the old ridge. Things were now secure enough for me to remove the ridge supports.

The roof framing on the addition was complete at this point, except for the short eave rafters that would extend from the dormer window wall down to the double top plate of the wall below. Instead of measuring these rafters on my deck layout, I picked the correct length for them by measuring them in place. These short 2x10 rafters, at 16 in. o. c., have the same bird's-mouth cut at the bottom as the full-length rafters. They were nailed at the top to the 2x8 ledger on the face of the dormer window wall.

After all the roof trim was on, I shingled the whole roof with GAF Timberline fiberglass shingles. Their texture doesn't show the imperfections that are bound to occur when a new roof meets an old one. A flat shingle lets every bump and depression from the decking below telegraph through.

The old roof section under the new dormer roof could now be opened without fear of wa-

Illustrations: Christopher Clapp

Framing the dormer. The long window wall and the dormer cheeks are set back 4 ft. from the walls below, allowing the original roof plane to show on all sides (photos at right). At this stage, the dormer window wall and cheeks have been framed and sheathed. A ledger board along the bottom of the window wall carries the short rafters. The plumb cuts on the rafter tails have been made flush with the plate, and dummy tails applied, first to a long 1x board, and then to the ends of the true rafters. This makes the rafter tails line up and the fascia and soffit easier to apply, and it eliminates tedious blocking.

ter damage. I stripped the shingles and plywood decking from the old roof section, but left the rafters in place for the time being. Next, I cut and nailed the permanent ceiling joists in this section in place, and took care to level them with the rest of the joists in the dormer. Instead of nailing their inboard ends to an interior wall plate, as I had done with the other joists, I face-nailed them to the existing rafters after mitering their ends at the roof pitch to fit snugly under the deck. Then I reinforced the joists with 1x8 hangers and a strong back, just as I had done in the rest of the dormer. Once these were installed, I removed the 1x8 ties that had held the wall and roof together.

Before removing the old rafters that I had just exposed, I still had to take care of the one disturbing potential weakness in this framing scheme. The juncture at which the 7-ft. extended rafters sit on the plate at the old ridge needed some support, or the roof might sag at that point. I wasn't afraid that the roof would actually collapse, but I did want an extra measure of assurance.

I have taken apart lots of old houses, and my experience and intuition told me that it would be worth the extra time to give this weak link a little extra support against that unpredictably heavy snow load. To do this I built an interior stud wall of 2x6s that sits directly under the ceiling joists where they tie into the old rafters, as shown in the drawing on the facing page. Because this wall had two wide closet doors and a skylight in its 18-ft. length, I notched a double 2x10 header into the 2x6 studs to carry the load of the ceiling joists and rafters above. To get good bearing below, I had to beef up the existing beam that had been installed by a previous remodeler because I doubted its ability to support the increased load.

This framing system had, of course, all been carefully planned out ahead of time, using past experience and common sense. I knew it would work. So when I tore out the old gable-end wall and cut away the old rafters leaving only stubs behind, I didn't bat an eye. Just kept my fingers crossed.

I'm very pleased with the way this job turned out, and as a bonus, Jasper's cache was discovered in a roof gutter across the street. I now have a good supply of nail sets and drill bits, and an extra set of car keys. □

Bob Syvanen is a consulting editor with Fine Homebuilding *magazine. Photos by the author.*

The finished house, seen from the front, appears smaller than it actually is because the extended roofline obscures the new 40-ft. shed dormer at the back of the house.

Rebuilding an Addition

Porches and a room with a bow ceiling enlarge an old house without changing its character

by Nelson Denny with Karen Bussolini

Owners of old houses have special problems when they are faced with the need to repair or renovate. The Coxes of Durham, Conn., were sensitive to the responsibilities of caring for their home, a two-story structure in a historic district, but they had some requirements—mainly, the desire for a large room in which to entertain—that hadn't been considered when the house was built over 150 years ago. They needed to renovate. They also had to repair structural damage between the original house and a dining-room addition built a century or so ago. As designer and builder, my job was to carry out the owners' wishes without violating the historical integrity of the house.

The pedimented gable front of the Cox house faces the town green. The facade has an attic fanlight. The front door is sheltered by a classic columned and pedimented entry porch, and is topped by a half-round light. The dining-room addition created a small ell to the south, toward the back of the house.

The existing house had small, dark rooms with low ceilings. The parlor, 10 ft. by 14 ft., was the largest room. Gutting the house or removing interior walls to create the open space the Coxes wanted would have changed the character of the house, and that was out of the question. The dining-room addition, besides being the source of major structural problems, was too small anyway, and was the logical place to add on.

The Coxes and I decided to remove the old addition, repair structural damage to the main house and build a larger addition to replace the old one. We planned a large room with a bow ceiling, which would open onto a new screened porch in back and a new narrow porch in front. An adjacent room in the main house previously used as a den would become the new dining room (see floor plan, facing page).

The ideas for the narrow porch and the bow ceiling came from my childhood memories. My uncle's Colonial home had a long side porch with columns. It was only wide enough to act as a shelter over the door, good for storing a little stack of firewood or for setting out a rocking chair, yet it was open and inviting. The ceiling I remembered from an early 19th-century schoolhouse in Newtown, Conn. The building was dilapidated and had spread badly, but retained its original bow ceiling. Schoolteacher friends who bought the building tied it back together, repaired the ceiling and wound up with an enchanting one-room home.

We normally experience straight lines and

The Cox house, before (top photo) and after the small dining-room addition was replaced by a larger room for entertaining. The new addition (photographed later in the year) has a screened porch off its rear; a shallow, columned porch facing the street; and a curved chimney cap.

rectilinear spaces. A bow ceiling is a gentle gesture, a way to give a room a special sense of self-containment and comfort. The quality of sound is different in a curved space. A bow ceiling focuses sound in certain areas of the room and leaves others quiet. The effect is restful and elegant. It is also a way to attain the spaciousness of a cathedral ceiling without leaving the design vernacular of an old house. Plenty of space for insulation is another advantage.

In designing details, we had to consider the difficulty and expense of matching the original trim. The job was to be done in the field, without a shop full of fancy molding cutters, and on a limited budget. I considered the weight and texture of the exterior trim and tried to build something compatible out of available stock items. For instance, the old house had gutters built in the roof above the cornice moldings. I was looking for a heavy cornice molding to match the scale of the old ones, and the addition also needed gutters. The solution was to use stock wooden gutters as cornice moldings on the addition. The gutters were expensive and we had to go to Massachusetts to find them, but even so, they were much cheaper than duplicating the old built-in gutters and cornices. And we avoided aluminum gutters, which on old structures inevitably look like an afterthought.

Although old and new roofs were pitched differently, I approximated the gable pediment treatment of the old house on the addition. We built up moldings and made corner boards from regular stock lumber. We lapped new cedar clapboards to the same width as the old pine clapboards on the main house. Twelve-over-twelve windows are still available, although they were not locally stocked and had to be ordered ahead of time so they would be on site when needed.

Inside the addition, the floor is of square-edge random-width oak, butted, screwed and plugged. The owners liked oak trim, which isn't authentic, but has a clean look and ties the other materials in the room together visually. Walls and ceilings were of drywall. The chimney and woodstove hearth we faced with used brick.

Structural problems were concentrated on the inside of the ell where the old addition met the main house. The roof of the old addition had not been flashed where it joined the side wall of the main house, and over the years, water seepage had damaged posts, joist tenons and the sill. Part of the foundation bowed inward. Before we could begin on the new addition, we had to jack up the house a few inches

To fashion the bow ceiling, pieces of ¾-in. CDX plywood were fastened together as forms. Strapping of ¾-in. fir tacked and glued around the curve is a nailing surface for drywall. The forms were attached to the rafters and rafter ties as shown in the detail drawing at the bottom of the page.

and replace the rotted wooden members. We also poured a new section of foundation.

We built the addition using standard frame construction with walls of 2x4s 16 in. o.c., and floors with 2x12s 12 in. o.c. over a 20-ft. span. We ran the new joists front to back so the newly replaced sill would not have to carry any more weight than the old one had. The front and back walls of the addition support the roof. The floors of the front and back porches rest on concrete piers. The front roof is cantilevered, allowing the decorative front porch columns to bear only minor loads.

Laying out the bow—We began by lofting grid lines full-scale on the subfloor. On my plans I drew the shape I wanted with a French curve to the scale of 1:24. Over the drawing I superimposed a grid on a scale of 1:12 and plotted points along the curve. At the tight ends of the curve I superimposed a 1:6-scale grid so that the curve at its extremes would be rendered more accurately. I had considered the spring of the curve in relation to the placement of rafters and window headers, and located these on the full-scale grid laid out on the floor. I wanted a curve that would spring sharply from header height and

flatten out at the top below the collar ties. That meant that it had to start far enough into the room to be able to reach some height without touching the rafters. For this I planned a soffit extending into the room 8 in., the bottom of which was on a level with the rough openings for the windows. A wood ledger strip nailed to the inside of the walls acted as a horizontal reference point and a ledge upon which plywood gussets would rest and form the curve's shape.

Once the measurements were worked out, I transferred them to the full-scale grid on the subflooring. I then snapped a chalk line parallel to

Section through addition with first-floor plan

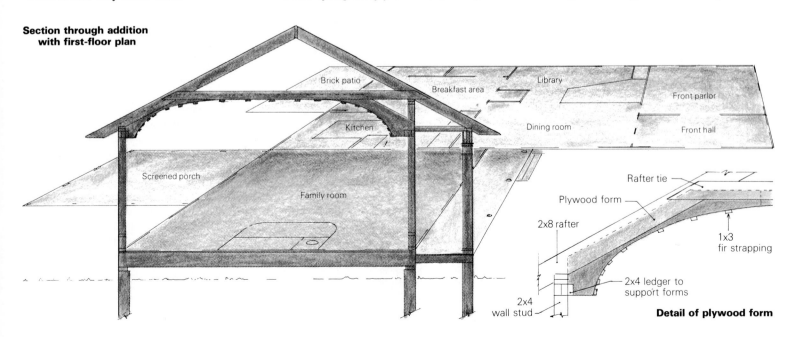

Brick patio

Breakfast area

Library

Front parlor

Kitchen

Dining room

Front hall

Screened porch

Family room

Rafter tie

Plywood form

2x8 rafter

1x3 fir strapping

2x4 ledger to support forms

2x4 wall stud

Detail of plywood form

The completed addition. The curved ceiling creates a spacious room in keeping with the style of the house. The oak soffit that covers the ends of the plywood forms also serves as discreet and elegant trim. Window frames are also of oak.

the end wall to act as a baseline. From there I measured and marked the beginning of the curve and where the rafters and collar ties would fall. I marked the curve's coordinates by hammering a nail into every plotted point on the grid, then pressed a batten around the curve against the row of nails. I used a long piece of ¼-in. by ¼-in. white oak for my batten because it was handy, but anything with a good edge flexible enough to take the curve would have done. Anchoring the batten with another row of nails allowed me to step back and look. When I saw the curve laid out full-size, its top wasn't flat enough to suit me, so I fine-tuned the curve by moving the nails and batten until the shape looked right.

Constructing the bow—I drew a line along the curve for my pattern. From the curve, we cut forms out of ¾-in. CDX plywood. We used narrow pieces of plywood to construct the curved form in sections, and lapped the joints with plywood gussets. We nailed finished forms to rafters and collar ties on each end of the room. The bottom of the curve on each form was notched to fit into position over the strapping at header height. Later on we built over this strapping an oak soffit that covered the bottom ends of the plywood arches and acted as top window trim. When the forms had been nailed and leveled at either end of the room, we ran string lines at

intervals between them. The taut string lines acted as positioning guides for the rest of the forms. After we had nailed them all to rafters and collar ties, we tacked ¾-in. fir strapping to them the length of the room at intervals around the curve. The strapping provided an even surface for drywall and a good base for nailing.

There are a few tricks to bending drywall. Making a curved surface requires more care than does a normal flat wall, but there's no real difficulty to it. We used ¼-in. Gold Bond gypsum board, which is softer than the other major brands. The 4x8 sheets were laid on sawhorses set up outside, then hosed down on only the back side. If the face gets wet as well, the board will split. The back side is the wet side whether you're making an inside curve as we did for the ceiling, or an outside curve.

Don't be discouraged if there is some rippling of the paper surface. The gypsum board will break at the tightest part of the curve, but as long as the surface paper is more or less intact, skimcoating the ceiling with joint compound will hide these minor defects. Skim-coating should be left to professionals who are adept at using long trowels (in the 2-ft. range). Three skim coats should be applied, each lighter than the last. When done correctly, no sanding is needed.

We decided to lay the gypsum board with its long dimension going across the room's width.

Running the sheets around the curve this way allows the joint knife to be pulled with the curve rather than across it (just think about trying to spread joint compound neatly against a tight inside curve with a flat knife). The seams that must run across the curve are at the center of the room, where the ceiling is nearly flat. In this instance, the tapers did such a good job that after the skim coat, no further surface preparation was needed before painting. Normally I would sponge down the drywall to smooth pits and bumps in the joint compound. Washing creates a gesso paste over the surface and doesn't raise the nap of the paper, as sanding does.

Curved chimney cap—The new chimney (bottom photo, p. 90) was used brick over cinder blocks. The curved cap was constructed over curved forms set on the flat chimney top and shimmed to raise the curve to the proper height. The width of the mortar joints was calculated so that no bricks had to be cut to fit the curve. The bricks were set in from each end, working toward the top. To keep standing water from freezing inside the joints and cracking them, the top of the chimney was coated with cement. □

Nelson Denny, builder, lives in Stony Creek, Conn. Karen Bussolini, writer and photographer, lives in Greenwich, Conn.

Southwest Sunspace

How a Santa Fe designer uses thermoformed acrylic to glaze solar additions

by Valerie Walsh

In 1975, passive-solar design was largely experimental. In those days, sunspace additions were called attached greenhouses, and most of them were built from salvaged or inexpensive materials. They looked like glass, lean-to tool sheds. Their primary purpose was to help heat the home, and many owners also grew food in them year round. The early shed-style designs of solar pioneer Bill Yanda were practical and effective. Yet I didn't think that they were aesthetically suited to the adobe-block houses here in Santa Fe. I wanted my sunspaces to harmonize with the soft, sensuous curving forms of the Pueblo-style architecture of the Southwest. I also wanted to go beyond the basic heating and food-producing functions of early greenhouse additions and make my sunspaces pleasant to live in.

Adobe walls are something like live-in sculptures. You won't find in them hard edges, sharp lines and angular corners. Shed-style additions on these houses look out of place. This is why my sunspaces have curved, glazed gables, a design feature I learned to produce by thermoforming Exolite, a double-skinned acrylic panel, made by CYRO (155 Tice Blvd., Woodcliff Lake, N. J. 07675).

In addition to this thermoformed curve, explained in the sidebar on pp. 96-97, I like to use mahogany framing members throughout the sunspace. The curved, laminated mahogany roof beams and the solid mahogany braces add warmth to the addition and complement the well-preserved woodwork that graces most traditional adobe homes.

Structural details—The frost line in this part of New Mexico is at 18 in., so a 6-in. by 12-in. concrete footing is typical. Stemwalls are either adobe, block or frame, insulated on the exterior with a stucco finish. Exposed sills are brick or flagstone with mahogany finished sills on the interior. All of the exposed framing components are mahogany, but I use 6/4 T&G pine roof decking. I generally fabricate most of the woodwork in my shop, then assemble it on site.

The roof is insulated with rigid foam above the decking and then hot-tarred and graveled. I like to slope the top of the sunspace back to the north and not onto the curved glazing or the south glass and wood. I also like to make provision for natural ventilation in my sunspaces. I can meet both requirements by building a sort of clerestory on top of the ex-

Sunspace retrofits don't have to look like additions. This example, in the hills north of Santa Fe, has an adobe-block buttressed stemwall, and thermoformed double-skin acrylic glazing that makes an easy transition from window wall to roof. What makes the sunspace habitable day and night all year long are the insulated curtains in the ceiling below the curved glazing, seen at right. Riding in tracks in the roof beams, the curtains reduce nighttime heat loss in winter, and keep sunlight and heat at comfortable levels during the summer.

isting parapets of the flat roofs common to most adobe houses. Roof beams are carried by the top of this short wall, and screened vents pierce it.

Many solar retrofits rob the rooms directly behind them of the light they once had. My south walls tend to be high, because of the drainage slope back to the north. Summer sun penetration is minimal, but the tall windows flood a greater area of the massive interior walls with winter sun. In addition, the height creates a more spacious feeling, something that's helpful in small additions.

For ventilation, I've used Pella or Andersen casement or awning windows in combination with fixed insulating-glass units. In my next

Shop-built framing members—curved roof beams, posts and headers—await assembly, left. The mahogany sill has already been installed on the new concrete-block stemwall, and the roof-attachment plate has been lag-bolted atop the existing parapet wall. At right, the sunspace has been framed up and the roof decked with 6/4 T&G yellow pine. The roof slopes back toward the house and will drain over the parapet wall to minimize runoff on the sunspace glazing and keep flashing details simple. The rectangular areas between the plate on the parapet wall and the roof of the sunspace will be fitted with hinged vent doors, which when opened will help keep the addition cool. Framing and flashing details are shown in the drawing, facing page.

jobs I'm going to use either Hurd or Weathershield windows, which have a wavelength-sensitive film sandwiched between the two panes of glass for reduced nighttime heat losses. My east and west walls are insulated mass walls with minimal glazing.

The floors are typically brick on sand, or terra-cotta tile on a concrete slab for mass. The interior plan incorporates functional mass, such as hot tubs, and sculpted adobe *bancos* (benches) and planter beds.

Building the mahogany frame—The sunspaces I build consist of the following shop-made parts: finished interior sills, posts, headers, curves and roof beams, nailers, doors, vents, and various trim pieces. On occasion I make up matching interior window units for the north-wall penetrations into the adjoining house.

I build the beams and posts from 8/4 Philippine mahogany. I originally chose mahogany back in 1978 because at the time I could get relatively inexpensive, KD stock that had good strength, stability and decay resistance. Although the price of mahogany has risen since then, I still consider it the right wood for my purposes. Once, when I couldn't get it, I used redwood. It cost me more money, split out frequently and was too soft. It does work well for the potting benches and shelving that I build periodically.

I am looking into special ordering 16/4 mahogany boards to save laminating time. But I'll keep using the 8/4 for the curves. The tighter the radius of the curve, the more wasted wood, even when the templates are laid out as efficiently as possible. A typical 6-in. wide finished curve has to be cut from a 10-in. board.

Posts are usually 4x6s, and the roof beams and curves increase in size as the spans grow

longer. Until last year, I used mahogany for all of my finished sills, but have since switched to brick and flagstone sills, which are more durable. By the time I covered an 8-in. stemwall, 2 in. of exterior insulation and 1¾ in. of lath and stucco plus a drip edge, I had a 14-in. wide finished mahogany sill. At the edge of the bevel, the sill was awfully thin. The intense southwestern sun, heavy rains and frequent snows are hard on wide wood sills.

I order my wood surfaced two sides (S2S), ready to be glued up with Titebond. I don't use waterproof glues, because they're more expensive, and they require more clamps and clamping time. None of the glued joints are exposed to the weather, and I haven't seen any signs of delamination in any of my beams so far.

For added strength the straight beams are reinforced with #10 by 2½-in. screws about every 10 in. The counterbores are then plugged with mahogany. Templates for the curved pieces are traced onto a long wide board and cut into smaller sections. Four matched sections are then temporarily tacked together and cut into curves on the bandsaw. When I assemble these pieces, I overlap the laminae in the curved sections 8 in. I overlap the straight roof-beam sections 12 in., as compression loading changes to bending.

I rout ¾-in. deep by ½-in. wide grooves into the side face of the curved beams for tracks for insulated curtains. I rout these grooves whether or not my client wants night curtains. I started doing this after a client changed his mind, and the grooves had to be routed after the beams and glazing were installed. A painstaking task.

The next step is finishing the wood—sanding and oiling. I currently use Plastique Exterior Tung Oil, manufactured by Komac Paint Co.

(1201 Osage, Denver, Colo. 80201). It is nontoxic to plants and appears to last longer than other oils I've used. I have also had reasonable success with Watco Exterior Danish Oil, Thompson's Water Seal, and Cuprinol. I apply at least two coats of Plastique on all the wood, including trim, before it leaves the shop. When the job is done, I give all the wood another coat or two. I advise my clients to maintain the finish by oiling the exterior trim twice a year and the interior wood as needed, usually once a year.

Site assembly—This begins with attaching the finished mahogany sill to the rough pine sill with two counterbored woodscrews every 12 in. to 18 in. The holes that will not be covered by windows get mahogany plugs. Shimming the sill to get it level is necessary at this point. The posts are lag-bolted into the sills from two opposite sides, offset from one another, like two big toenails. The pilot bores and counterbores are drilled at about 60°. The window jambs cover these holes. Before being set into the ½-in. notch in the sill, the bottoms of these posts are caulked carefully with silicone for a weathertight seal. Then we install the header on top of these posts, caulk at the notches in the header, and fasten it to the posts with counterbored lag bolts. Where two sections of a header butt together, we glue in a spline and draw the sections together tightly. Whenever possible, we make this joint happen over a post.

The header extends about 2 in. to the outside and is kerf-cut to create a drip edge. It also serves as a ledger for the Exolite to rest on. The interior part of the header is beveled slightly to prevent any overhead condensation from accumulating there.

After the sunspace walls are framed up, we

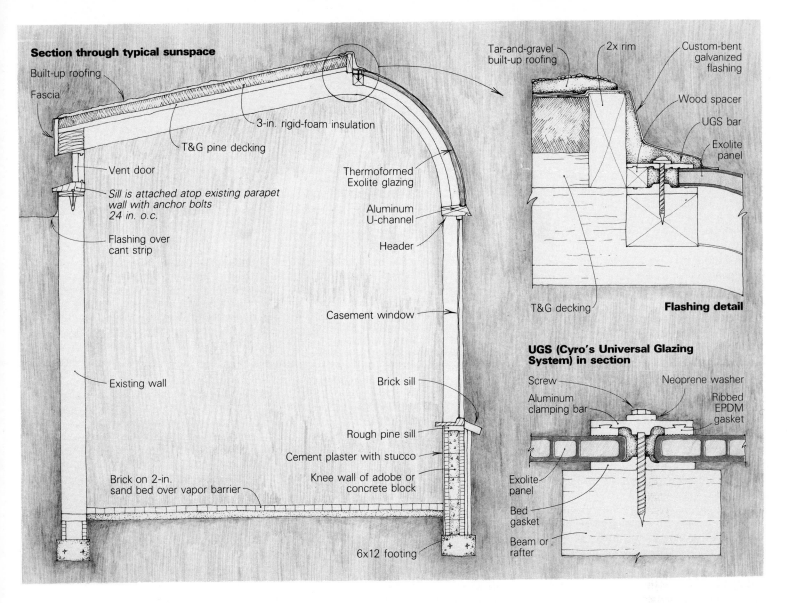

Section through typical sunspace

Built-up roofing

Fascia

3-in. rigid-foam insulation

T&G pine decking

Vent door

Sill is attached atop existing parapet wall with anchor bolts 24 in. o.c.

Flashing over cant strip

Existing wall

Brick on 2-in. sand bed over vapor barrier

Tar-and-gravel built-up roofing

2x rim

Custom-bent galvanized flashing

Wood spacer

UGS bar

Exolite panel

Thermoformed Exolite glazing

Aluminum U-channel

Header

Casement window

Brick sill

Rough pine sill

Cement plaster with stucco

Knee wall of adobe or concrete block

6x12 footing

T&G decking

Flashing detail

UGS (Cyro's Universal Glazing System) in section

Screw

Aluminum clamping bar

Neoprene washer

Ribbed EPDM gasket

Exolite panel

Bed gasket

Beam or rafter

install the curved roof beams. One end of each beam has to be tied onto the south wall of the house; the other end is lag-bolted in a bed of silicone caulk atop the header of the sunspace's south wall.

How the roof beams are connected to the existing house varies from job to job, but as I mentioned earlier, I like to connect the sunspace roof to a short wall above the existing parapet, as shown in the drawing, above left. I prefer to attach the roof beams above the parapet because that adds more height to the interior space and provides an area for the upper roof vents. It also makes for an easy and solid connection.

Further, this lets the sunspace roof drain back onto the roof of the house. The beams are lag-bolted to a sill plate that's attached to the parapet on the roof itself. If I can't build atop the parapet, I expose the existing joists of the house roof, tie into them from the sides, and trim out over the connection. Or sometimes I just attach a ledger board to the north house wall, and fasten mahogany roof beams to it with joist hangers.

Where the sunspace also joins an east or west wall, the end beams are either notched into the plaster wall and lag-bolted in place, or surface mounted, lag-bolted and then plastered up to the beams. Flashing is required

where the sunspace roof dies into an existing east or west wall.

All inside beam edges are rounded over in the shop, leaving only the last inch or so square. After the beams are in place, the square edges left where all the members join together are finished using a ⅜-in. rounding-over bit, taking the curve right around the corner. The edges of the outside faces of the posts do not get rounded, because trim is applied to these surfaces.

Once the frame is up, we oil and then nail down the T&G pine roof decking. On top of this, we install a vapor barrier and then put down a 3-in. thickness of rigid Apache urethane insulation, which is rated at R-25. I generally use a hot-mopped four-ply built-up roof, but have also used mineral roofing (90-lb. roll roofing) or painted sheet metal, depending on roof configuration and budget.

Installing the curved Exolite—Only after the messy hot-tar work is completed do I install the curved Exolite panels. The CYRO UGS (Universal Glazing System) is the one that I use. Exolite sheets must be glazed into the framing system using gaskets. Liquid or mastic systems don't work. Neoprene and EPDM rubber pads have been tested for compatibility with the acrylic. Small vertical sec-

tions may be caulked, if necessary, but only with Dow-Corning #795.

I have been told that CYRO will discontinue all three of their current glazing systems sometime in 1983, and offer one improved system. Before UGS was available here, I fabricated something similar using butyl tape (the type used for installing auto windshields) beneath a 4-in. steel batten. I later learned that butyl products (except for Tremco butyl) are incompatible with Exolite. I've replaced the tape in one of three installations. The other two are still putting it to the test.

To install the UGS, I first stick the rubber pad on the outside of the arch with contact cement. The bottom edge of the curved Exolite fits into an aluminum U-channel that I nail to the extended part of the header. This channel typically comes in 6-ft. lengths, and the joints where the sections butt together have to be caulked carefully. I drill ³⁄₁₆-in. dia. weep holes every 18 in. on the outside of the U-channel and caulk it with silicone where it meets the header. This drives any possible condensation in the Exolite outside.

Installing the curved panels is fairly straightforward once the U-channels are in place. The channel holds the bottom edge of the glazing securely while we fasten it to the curved mahogany beams with the aluminum bar and gasket. I predrill holes in the aluminum batten every 6 in. on the curved sections and every 10 in. for straight portions. I begin bending and fastening the bar from the bottom and work up. This seems to reduce the stress and make a tighter fit. I use #10 by 3-in. self-tapping screws with washers on the curve, where there is greater tension, and #10 by 2½-in. screws for the remainder. The screws should be backed off a half turn after tightening to allow the sheet to expand and to avoid creating potentially damaging local stresses. Needless to say, we drive the 200-some screws with a screwshooter.

I flash the top edge of the Exolite over the UGS where it meets the solid roof, as shown in the drawing on p. 95. This flashing is tough to keep intact if an Exolite panel ever needs to be replaced. Fortunately I've replaced only one set of panels in over six years. These were damaged by a nasty hailstorm. I just replaced the flashing along with the Exolite.

Insulating curtains—Santa Fe has 6,003 degree days, and nighttime insulating curtains for the windows cut down on heat loss enough to make the sunspace comfortable during the evening in cold weather. So far I have installed night curtains only overhead as a partial solution to the heat-loss problem. The vertical glazing needs insulating curtains as well to control the temperature swings, but budgets don't always allow for them.

In addition to reducing winter-night heat losses, the curtains screen out the sun in summer. But using insulating curtains as shades blocks all the light. Best for summer use is a woven exterior shade fabric that diffuses light. Polypropylene is one of few shading materials compatible with Exolite.

I have my insulating curtains made to order in Santa Fe. The interior-side fabric is generally Sierra cloth, a sports-jacket material designed to resist moisture. Some clients choose a southwest Indian print. Next to the Sierra cloth is a space-blanket (Mylar-film) sandwich with a layer of 3M Thinsulate as the filling. Covering these insulating materials on the top side facing the glazing is a light-colored sailcloth that reflects heat. Narrow adjustable-length curtain rods are threaded every 12 in. through the fabric across the width of the curtains—like battens in a sail. These rods are fitted on their ends with small rollers that ride up and down in metal tracks that are housed in the grooves in the curved beams. Some years ago I used to worry about the ⅛-in. gap around the edges of the curtains, afraid lots of heat was getting lost. It was commonly believed then that nearly all the insulating value was lost unless the curtains were sealed tightly at the edges. I know now that the gap is necessary to prevent excessive heat buildup between the overhead acrylic glazing and the closed curtain. Even if it's a light color, the curtain acts as a solar collector and can superheat the air behind the glazing. Without a way to release the heat buildup, the acrylic, which is tolerant of temperatures up to 160°, will begin to sag or deform. □

Thermoforming

Exolite is a double-skin glazing sheet made of acrylic for standard glazing applications, or of polycarbonate, where high-service temperatures and higher impact resistance are needed. The internal ribs of these extruded sheets trap air to provide an insulating value while adding structural strength. Exolite is ⅝ in. thick, 47¼ in. wide and comes in lengths of from 8 ft. to 16 ft. It's light in weight, and costs less ($3.09/sq. ft. in April 1983) than safety glass or tempered insulated glass. Exolite diffuses sunlight softly and evenly, so it is better for plants and easier on the eyes. It can also be cut to size on the job site. But the primary reason I use the stuff is that it can be heat-formed to achieve wonderful curves.

There are disadvantages to using acrylic glazing. It scratches on sight, and you have to handle it very carefully. Chemically, it's incompatible with many cleaning products and solvents, as well as with other building materials. I have nightmares of some housekeeper going at fingerprints on the acrylic with Windex and paper towels. Acrylic glazing also has a large coefficient of expansion. You have to use a dry-gasket glazing system. Figure on ⅛ in. of clearance for each 4 ft. of sheet length.

When I first began curving Exolite in 1978, I was unfamiliar with the process. I just wanted to create curved glazing for my wood beams. To this end, I experimented with a series of $20 Plexiglas strip heaters. With this process I could heat only a narrow line at once. In fact, I was limited to using the 4-ft. panel width as the circumference of my curve, and had to bend each panel across its width, with the ribs running side to side.

I was after a smoother, larger curve with the ribs running top to bottom. After two jobs forming the acrylic with strip heaters, an engineer at CYRO Industries, the manufacturers of Exolite, warned me that this process induced high internal stresses, making the sheet very susceptible to crazing and cracking. He suggested I bend the acrylic by thermoforming: heating the entire sheet uniformly in an oven, shaping it quickly on a form, and then enclosing it in an insulated annealing chamber, where it could cool down gradually, regain its strength and keep internal stresses to a minimum. So I invested in the expensive thermoforming equipment. It has been a learning experience ever since.

Each sunspace job requires about two days for thermoforming the glazing, so I put the whole setup in my woodshop. The thermoforming unit itself is suspended from the ceiling on a hoist. When it's not in use, I store it at ceiling level. The 5-ft. by 7-ft. oven consists of tubular infrared elements in a reflector-backed sheet-metal unit with a circulator fan. Each 1,600-watt quartz tube is 66 in. long. I started out using twelve 4,000-watt tubes and found that I had a serious excess of heat. After a couple of meltdowns, I began to use fewer tubes of lower wattage.

The long edges of the acrylic are thicker than the rest of the sheet to provide firm resistance to the gasket pressure in the installation. These edges must be uniformly curved for a weathertight seal. I discovered that they needed more heat than the rest of the sheet to achieve the uniform plasticity necessary to bend them. If these edges are

too cool for forming, they will wing upward slightly from the plane of the rest of the sheet. This condition would keep me from getting a tight seal and could create leaking problems. It would also stress the acrylic unevenly, possibly causing cracks. Unfortunately the edges of the platform are where the most heat escapes, and the middle of the sheet would get dangerously hot before the edges were ready. I now deal with this problem by running the ribs of the acrylic sheet parallel to the tubes and alternately removing tubes in the center of the oven and adding tubes along the edges. This combination of elements is what has worked the best.

Before the acrylic is heated, the protective plastic film must be removed and the channels blown out clean with an air gun, particularly if the panel has been cut. We always wear soft, clean leather gloves when we handle Exolite. Acrylic shavings from cutting and other stray particles will move up the channels and melt inside if they are not removed before heating. Static electricity can be a nuisance and cause everything to cling to the surface, especially in a woodshop.

Once the sheet is clean, it is carefully placed—not slid—onto the sheet-metal covered platform that sits on sawhorses about 22 in. below the oven. Fire-resistant curtains on all four sides between the oven and the platform prevent drafts and heat loss as the temperature builds to about 350°F. These curtains can be raised quickly when it's time to remove the heated sheet.

The sheet heats up for about four to five minutes before it's ready to be turned over to cook on the other side. The acrylic panel first arches up towards the heater (photo facing page, top right) and then drops down flat to the table when it approaches the flipping temperature. At this point, the material feels like soft rubber, and the channels begin to sag slightly. In thermoforming, timing is critical. If the plastic begins to smoke, it is usually too late to pull it out before it burns and blisters. On the other hand, if it is not hot enough, it will not form properly and must be reheated. Exolite can be reheated repeatedly, but that wastes time. Flipping the half-heated sheet requires care. It can pick up impressions from your fingers, if you don't hold them flat. The sheet must then be dropped into place on the platform—sliding it will cause fine scratches. The second side usually heats up faster than the first.

The bending form—This is made from ¾-in. plywood, with 2x4 bracing, as shown in the photos on the facing page. For the platen, I use ⅛-in. Masonite covered with felt. The brads used to tack the Masonite down will mar the heated Exolite unless they are nailed down flat and then covered with the felt. The upper 2x4 bracing extends several inches beyond both vertical sides of the form to serve as clamping surfaces. At the bottom edge of the form is an L-shaped cleat. It holds the bottom edge of the heated acrylic in place before the clamps are tightened.

Although the Exolite shrinks about 2% when it's heat-formed, I still find it necessary to build my form to a radius 1 in. smaller than the radius of the real curve to compensate for the tendency of the acrylic to spring back slightly after cooling. Split-second timing is imperative for pulling the sheet out while it is hot enough to be formed, yet not too flexible or rubbery to handle. Then comes the adrenaline rush. Four people, two on each side of the oven, have to move like lightning to get the acrylic sheet from the oven onto the form and quickly smoothed down to the curve. They've got about 20 seconds. The hot panel is then quickly covered with a felt-lined sheet of Plexiglas to prevent uneven pressure from the clamps and bars. The Plexiglas cover also keeps the acrylic from cooling down too fast. Room temperature must be steady, and drafts have to be kept out.

Next, we secure 6-in. C-clamps onto the 2x4s that span the width of the form at about 10-in. intervals. We have to be careful here, too. If we apply too much pressure, the acrylic will crush and deform irreparably. If we apply too little pressure, the sheet will not form evenly, and the whole heat-forming process will have to be done over again. As an added precaution against rapid cooling, I cover the entire form, acrylic and clamps, with foam sheeting to insulate it while it takes shape.

Annealing—As soon as the sheet has been bent to satisfaction but before it cools off, we remove it from the form and place it in the annealing chamber—a large box I made from 2-in. thick pieces of Styrofoam. To prevent rubbing and possible scratching, I sandwich the curved panels between sheets of foam, which stay in place during annealing, storing and transporting. In the annealing chamber, all of the curved pieces are covered with a space blanket to further retard the cooling process. After 24 hours of slow, even cooling, the Exolite panels are removed. Now we apply the aluminum terminal sections cap to the bottom edges and the plastic-plug strips cap the top.

I generally do not thermoform the acrylic until I'm ready to install it. This reduces the possibility of damage to the newly curved pieces from hot-tar roofers and from the general job-site shuffle.

Back at the shop, we raise the oven to the ceiling, set the two platforms against the wall, and dismantle the annealing box. The form is stored in the warehouse, and people in the shop go back to working wood.
—V. W.

Walsh's oven for thermoforming double-skin acrylic is a sheet-metal box in which she's installed quartz heating tubes. The unit is lowered by a chain hoist over the platform that holds the panel. Fire-resistant Mylar curtains at the sides prevent heat from escaping. The acrylic panel shown in the photo at top has been heated to the point that it's arched upward. When it sags back down, it's ready to be turned over to cook on its other side. The bending form, shown at right, is made from plywood templates cut to the desired curve; of 2x4 braces, which serve also as clamping ears; and of a ⅛-in. Masonite platen covered with felt (seen in the middle photo). While the acrylic is hot, it's quickly put on the form. A sheet of Plexiglas is laid on top of it to retard heat loss, to protect the Exolite from the clamping battens and to even out clamping pressure (photo right). After the panel has set, it's removed to an annealing chamber so it can cool down slowly, and not develop tension cracks.

The Deck Upstairs

How to combine a deck with a roof that won't leak

by Dan Rockhill

My first rooftop terrace introduced me to the built-up roofing business the hard way. I'd designed a small addition with a nearly flat roof, and I wanted to put a deck on top of it to take advantage of the summer weather, the view and the privacy. I called up the roofing contractors to find out how low the bids would go, and started dreaming of deck furniture.

As the roofers looked over the job, it became obvious that details and prices fluctuated wildly. One wanted insulation on top of the roof sheathing, another underneath; some wanted gravel in the flood coat, and others said gravel was unnecessary. To make matters worse, none of them would guarantee the roof because I wanted to cover part of it with a deck.

I finally got the job done, lost money and learned a lot. Since then I've done a lot of successful and more profitable installations, but I've never stopped keeping a keen eye out for good roof-terrace detailing.

Early decks—Years ago rooftop decks were called promenades or plazas, and were usually found atop fancy commercial buildings. They were covered with a hard and durable surface like quarry tile, laid over a built-up roofing membrane that kept out the water. This type of decking was occasionally used in high-end residential work, but it was too expensive for most ordinary construction.

For a more economical solution, designers looked once again to commercial work, and they came up with the system generally used today—walkboards over a built-up roof. Walkboards, which are simply planks nailed to supports called sleepers, were originally used for scuttleways to reach roof-mounted mechanical equipment on factories, warehouses, office buildings and the like. The sleepers spread the traffic loads, and kept the fragile roofing plies from being crushed.

There are two types of roofing membranes suitable for supporting walkboards or rooftop decks: the tried-and-true bitumen (asphalt or coal-tar pitch) built-up roof, and a modern alternative, the elastomer roof. The built-up roof, with its many layers of hot-mopped felt, is perfect for use on low-pitched roofs because it forms a continuous membrane that keeps out wind-driven rain.

Elastomers are synthetic polymers with elastic or rubberlike qualities. They have gained wide acceptance in commercial work, despite their higher price tag, because they offer excellent flexibility, and resistance to weathering, fire, airborne chemicals, ultraviolet radiation and abrasions. They are also available in a variety of colors. Silicone, neoprene, Hypalon, acrylic and polyurethane rubber are all varieties of elastomers. Some are available in sheet form. Most can be applied as a liquid and finished with a trowel or paint roller. Toxic fumes can be a problem with these products, and you should be sure to pay special attention to instructions involving joining, mixing, curing times and using solvents. Because elastomers are still relatively new to the residential market, many roofers prefer to work with the traditional hot asphalt and gravel, and they continue to install the proven built-up roofs. What I will describe here is how to put a deck over a built-up roof so that the roof won't leak.

The substrate—A rooftop deck has to sit on a structure designed to carry the same loads as the interior floors of the house. Consequently, the members supporting the roof deck should be at least as sturdy as the floor joists below. To divert water away from the building and to prevent ponding, the roof should slope at least ¼ in. per ft. To get this slope, I usually nail tapers ripped from 2x4s to the tops of the rafters, but if the rafters are deeper than required for their spans, it's just as easy to cut the tapers on the rafters themselves.

The roof sheathing is no place to skimp on materials. The deck sleepers could wind up being placed between the rafters, and the sheathing will have to carry this load without flexing. I use ¾-in. CDX plywood over rafters 16 in. o.c., held down with construction adhesive and 8d cement-coated nails. I nail a line of blocks between the rafters to catch the edges of the plywood. For maximum strength, I stagger the joints.

Insulation should go between the rafters, and not between the sheathing and the membrane, where it would gradually get compressed from the deck loads, losing its effectiveness and causing the membrane itself to stretch.

Cants and base—Once the roof sheathing is nailed down, it's time to put on the cant strips and the membrane base. Cant strips are used wherever the plane of the roof meets a vertical surface. They provide a gentle 45° slope for the roofing felts to conform to. Be sure to use them. Felts forced to bend at 90° have a weak inside corner, which will fail before the rest of the membrane. Roofing contractors use fiber cants, or you can rip and stack strips from 2x4s, as shown in the drawing on the facing page, bottom left. The legs of the triangle of a section of cant strip should be 3½ in. long.

Hot-mopping—You can install your own hot-mop membrane by renting a kettle and buying your supplies from a wholesaler, but I don't recommend doing this. Lifting pails filled with 525°F asphalt is a hairy job, nasty and dangerous enough to discourage even the most ambitious do-it-yourselfer. One wiggle of the bucket could spill the smoking asphalt and blister your skin or ruin the finish siding below.

I hire a subcontractor to do the membrane work. This isn't always easy either. Because it costs as much for the roofer to fire up the kettle for one square (100 sq. ft. of roof coverage) as it does for a hundred-square warehouse, many roofers aren't interested in a small job. So specify precisely what you want, then solicit bids. To make sure there are no surprises, don't accept any bids from contractors who don't look at the job in person. At current prices you can expect the roofer's share of a small deck job to be between $400 and $1,000. I also get an agreement before work begins about damage compensation in case a misplaced bucket of hot tar damages part of the building or grounds. Here's how things should go.

Base felt is a heavy, bitumen-impregnated sheet that weighs about 40 lb. per square and comes in 36-in. wide rolls. It is used only for the first layer, and it should be nailed down, not hot-mopped. Nailing it to the sheathing allows some movement between the substrate and the membrane, and makes it a lot easier years down the road to remove the roof if it should need replacing. It has to be firmly attached though, or a stiff wind will put it in the neighbor's yard. Nail it down with roofing nails spaced 6 in. o.c. on the edges and laps, and staggered at 18 in. o.c. in the field.

Membrane—Next, the base is covered with the membrane. It's made up of alternating layers of felt and molten bitumen. The felt acts as a reinforcement, while the bitumen bonds the layers of felt together and forms a waterproof film between each.

Each layer of felt in the membrane sandwich is called a ply. These felts are typically 15 lb. per square, and are held together by a matrix of fiberglass, asbestos or organic fibers. I prefer fiberglass felts because they have terrific

Structure of the roof and deck

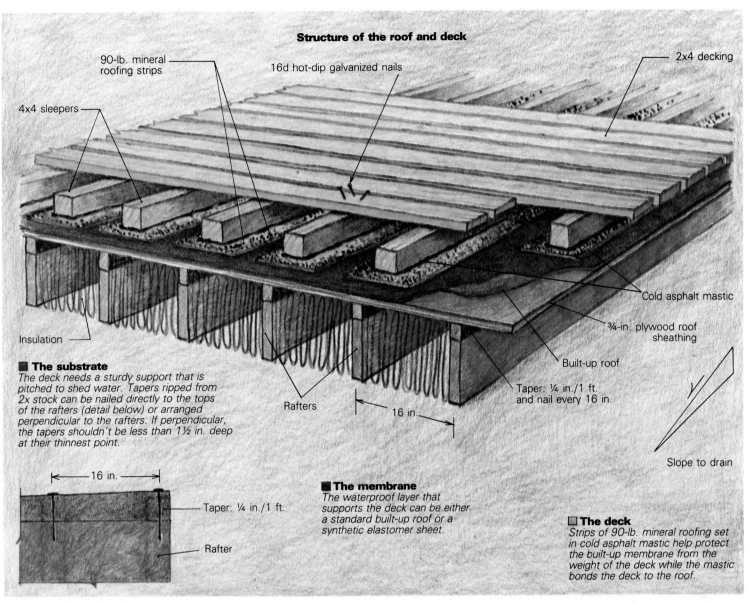

4x4 sleepers

90-lb. mineral roofing strips

16d hot-dip galvanized nails

2x4 decking

Insulation

Rafters

16 in.

Cold asphalt mastic

¾-in. plywood roof sheathing

Built-up roof

Taper: ¼ in./1 ft. and nail every 16 in.

Slope to drain

■ The substrate
The deck needs a sturdy support that is pitched to shed water. Tapers ripped from 2x stock can be nailed directly to the tops of the rafters (detail below) or arranged perpendicular to the rafters. If perpendicular, the tapers shouldn't be less than 1½ in. deep at their thinnest point.

16 in.

Taper: ¼ in./1 ft.

Rafter

■ The membrane
The waterproof layer that supports the deck can be either a standard built-up roof or a synthetic elastomer sheet.

□ The deck
Strips of 90-lb. mineral roofing set in cold asphalt mastic help protect the built-up membrane from the weight of the deck while the mastic bonds the deck to the roof.

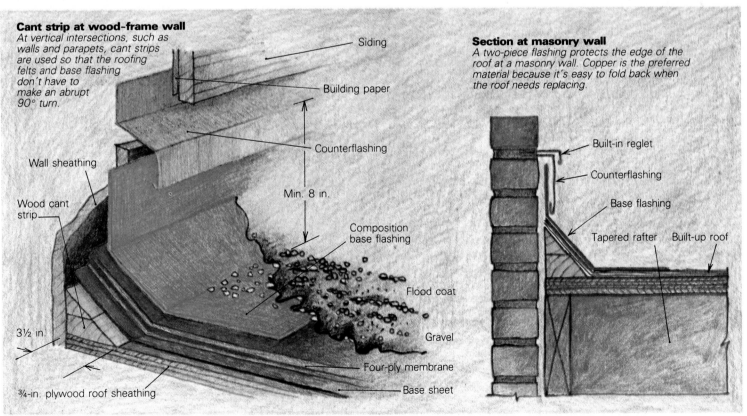

Cant strip at wood-frame wall
At vertical intersections, such as walls and parapets, cant strips are used so that the roofing felts and base flashing don't have to make an abrupt 90° turn.

Siding

Building paper

Counterflashing

Min. 8 in.

Wall sheathing

Wood cant strip

3½ in.

¾-in. plywood roof sheathing

Composition base flashing

Flood coat

Gravel

Four-ply membrane

Base sheet

Section at masonry wall
A two-piece flashing protects the edge of the roof at a masonry wall. Copper is the preferred material because it's easy to fold back when the roof needs replacing.

Built-in reglet

Counterflashing

Base flashing

Tapered rafter   Built-up roof

Illustrations: Frances Ashforth

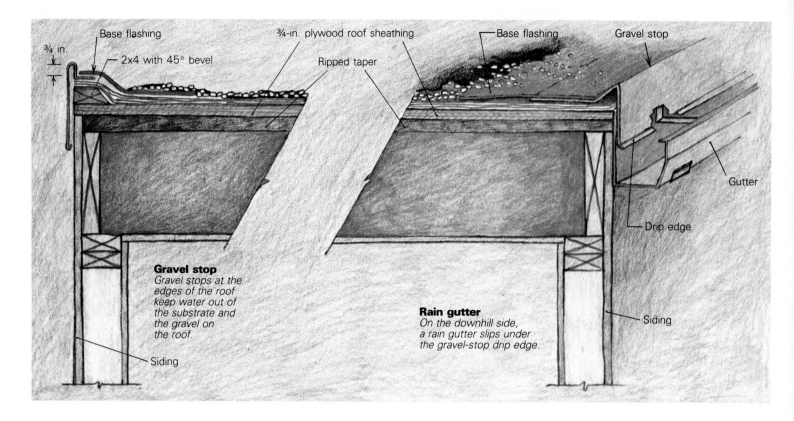

Base flashing · **¾ in.** · **2x4 with 45° bevel** · **¾-in. plywood roof sheathing** · **Ripped taper** · **Base flashing** · **Gravel stop** · **Gutter** · **Drip edge** · **Siding**

Gravel stop
Gravel stops at the edges of the roof keep water out of the substrate and the gravel on the roof.

Siding

Rain gutter
On the downhill side, a rain gutter slips under the gravel-stop drip edge.

strength, won't rot like the organic ones, and save my worrying about the possible ill effects of asbestos.

Plies are laid successively over the base, starting at the low end of the roof and moving up. The first layer is a 12-in. wide strip butted to the roof edge, which is then covered by a 24-in. wide piece and then a full 36-in. wide sheet. Subsequent full sheets are then shingled over one another to leave 11⅓ in. of exposure.

Roofing felt is bonded with a glazing of hot bitumen between each layer; no two layers of felt should touch anywhere on the roof. A three-ply roof is common here in Kansas, but I always specify four plies. The extra layer costs more of course, but I feel that the added lifespan of the roof more than outweighs the greater cost.

Flashing—According to the National Roofing Contractors Association, the most likely place for a roof deck to develop a leak is at the junction of the horizontal and vertical surfaces. The only way for a builder to prevent these potential leaks is to install the right flashing for the particular condition.

You need two types of flashing on a bitumen membrane roof—base flashing and counterflashing. Base flashing is similar to the nailed-on membrane base, but it's reinforced with fiberglass so that it can bend more easily. It comes in 36-in. wide rolls and has to be cut to the appropriate width. Counterflashing, or cap flashing, overlaps and protects the exposed edges of the base flashing.

When the membrane felts are mopped onto the roof, the roofers will lap the felts over the cant strips and a few inches up the walls. The base flashing covers this intersection and extends at least 8 in. up the wall. In parts of the country where snow is likely to accumulate, 12 in. is better. The extra width will make it

more difficult for the snow to work its way behind the counterflashing.

Once installed, the base flashing is counterflashed with a strip of metal folded into a Z pattern, or with shingles or siding if the exterior wall finish permits. If the wall is masonry, you'll have to let strips of metal flashing into a mortar joint. If you can afford it, use copper. It lasts longer than other flashing materials, and when the roof needs replacing, it's soft enough to be folded back out of the way while the new roof goes on, and then be bent back into place.

At the eaves—The next step is installing gravel stops and rain gutters. Gravel stops come in various profiles. They create a clean, waterproof cap at the eaves and keep the loose gravel on the roof from being blown or washed away. At the downhill edge, a gravel stop should overlap a rain gutter. If your roof has a parapet wall, you'll have to install a metal inset through it for water run-off. Your roofer or sheet metal supplier can make this scupper up in the shop.

Top coat—When the base flashings are down, a thick flood coat is mopped over the entire membrane. Gravel is then added to the molten bitumen. It serves several purposes. The light-colored stones refract and reflect sunlight, blocking out destructive ultraviolet rays. This keeps the roof cooler, and reduces temperature fluctuation. The gravel prevents direct abrasion from the weather, and it acts as a weight to hold the plies on the roof.

The part of the roof under the deck shouldn't have a gravel coating. The deck itself will shield the roof. And you don't want any gravel to get between the deck sleepers and the roof as it will eventually work its way through the membrane and cause trouble. For the same reason, don't walk on the gravel-covered membrane.

Decking—Sleepers should be either pressure-treated wood or the heartwood of a rot-resistant species like redwood. Try to locate them over the rafters and be sure to lay them parallel to the roof slope so that the drainage remains unimpeded.

I used to use 2x4 sleepers laid flat, but I've recently begun to use 4x4s instead, because the extra 2 in. of depth makes it easier to fish out the leaves. The extra wood also lessens your chances of driving a 16d nail through the decking and sleepers into the membrane. Since ¼ in. per ft. is an almost imperceptible slope, I don't taper the sleepers to compensate. But if the slope were any greater, I would taper them to make up for the tilt.

Some roofers may want to hot-mop the sleepers in place, but I would advise against having this done. The sleepers usually rot out before the membrane fails, and hot-mopping them to the roof could mean damaging the membrane when the sleepers have to be removed for replacement.

Instead, I set each sleeper in a bed of cold asphalt mastic on top of a 12-in. wide strip of 90-lb. mineral roofing. This strip, mineral side up, is bonded to the flood coat with the cold mastic. When it comes time to remove the sleepers, the cold joint will give way well before the flood coat. The beauty of this system is that the membrane remains intact while the entire structure is firmly glued to the roof.

For the deck itself, I use either treated southern yellow pine or redwood 2x4s, and I space them ¼ in. apart. If the gap is any larger, things like pencils and envelopes fall through the deck with depressing regularity. I nail each plank to my 4x4 sleepers with three hot-dip galvanized 16d nails. □

Dan Rockhill is assistant professor of architecture at the University of Kansas.

Renovations

Attic Remodel

Unused space under a complex roof is turned into a master-bedroom suite

by Glen Jarvis

Circular skylight

Circular skylight

New sloping walls

Existing attic

Tub equipment and water heater

Shower

N

Velux skylights

Tub

4x6 post

Fireplace

Simpson HU 410 hanger

Woodbox

Old 2x4 ceiling joists

2x4 spacer blocks

2x6 joists

Double 2x10 joists

Exposed 6x10 beam

New 2x10 joists at 16 in. o.c.

Living-room wall below

Rooms at the top
The most striking feature of the French Provincial-style house is the huge and complex roof mass (photo at left), much of which was unused attic. To convert this space into a large bedroom suite without altering the roofline, the author installed a row of skylights in the north-south ridge and opened up the space behind them by replacing stud walls and collar ties with posts and beams (rust in the drawing).

Illustration: Vince Babak

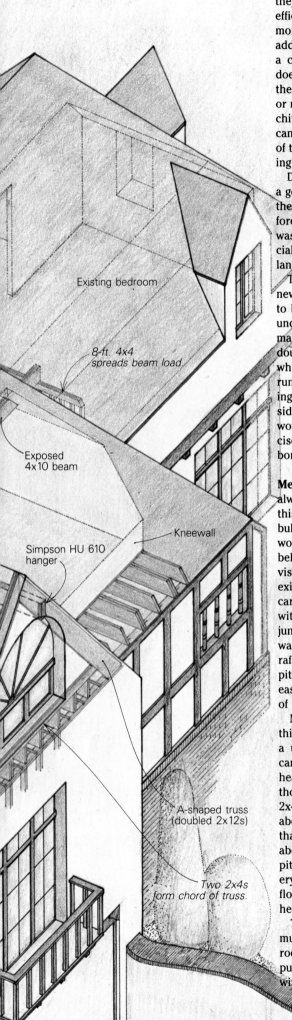

Existing bedroom

8-ft. 4x4
spreads beam load.

Exposed
4x10 beam

Simpson HU 610
hanger

Kneewall

A-shaped truss
(doubled 2x12s)

Two 2x4s
form chord of truss.

Over the last few years, I've done a number of attic conversions. I like them because they so often turn out to be an elegant and efficient solution to the problem of finding more space for a house. Often, for example, an addition to the side or the rear takes too large a chunk of the yard. Finishing attic spaces does require a lot of finicky fitting during both the structural and trim work, but there is little or no foundation or roof work to do. As an architect, I find the process exciting, because I can simultaneously preserve the original form of the house while creating unusual and exciting interior spaces under the sloping roof.

Doing this kind of work, of course, requires a good-sized house to begin with. In my area, there are lots of these, most of them built before 1930. Mayhill and James Fowler's house was built in the 1920s, in the French Provincial style that was popular in this hilly Oakland, Calif., neighborhood after World War I. The Fowlers were interested in adding a new master-bedroom suite, and there seemed to be enough room for a good-sized addition under the unused westernmost ridge of the massive and complex roof. The house has a double ridge line running north and south, which intersects another double ridge line running east and west. The roof is the building's most striking exterior element. From inside the converted space, the attic's height would afford a spectacular view of San Francisco Bay and the Golden Gate over the neighboring rooftop.

Measuring and planning—Unused attics are always murky. I spent a lot of time measuring this one in the semi-darkness of a single light bulb, balancing on the ceiling joists so my foot wouldn't suddenly appear in one of the rooms below. After two or three dusty exploratory visits, I had an accurate framing plan of the existing roof. It turned out that the original carpenters had built the whole elaborate form with 2x4 rafters 24 in. o. c. The result was a jungle of rafters and collar ties, with two stud walls at the north end to carry the weight of rafters dying into valleys. The roofs are pitched at 16-in-12, and the southernmost east-west ridge is 17 ft. above the ceiling joists of the room below.

My job was, first, to figure a way to open up this tangle of framing and, second, to work up a usable floor plan. The first problem that came up was that there was going to be less headroom to work with than I had originally thought. The second-floor ceiling joists were 2x4s, and they couldn't support a new floor above. We would need new 2x10 joists for that. This would raise the attic floor 8 in. or so above the top of the old 2x4s. With a roof pitch like the one we were working with, every inch counted. Just a little over half the floor area would have a ceiling above door height. The rest sloped down to the floor.

The building code (U.B.C.) requires a minimum average ceiling height of 7 ft. in bathrooms and 7½ ft. elsewhere. I was planning to put the bedroom in the section of the attic with the 17-ft. peak, so I wasn't worried about

that. But I wanted to put the bathroom at the north end, and that was close. Fortunately, only the area 5 ft. or more high counts in this calculation. With a 10-ft. ridge line, this area had an average height of 7½ ft.

Structural work—The sequence of operations on this job was to frame up a new floor, reinforce the rafters, and then rough-frame the skylights and windows that we'd planned for the space. We began by checking the building for wind and earthquake loads. Since we weren't planning to change the height or size of the building, the existing walls would be adequate supports. Much of our proposed structural work was pretty complex, though, and we had structural engineer Geoffrey Barrett review our calculations, check the beam and joist sizes and help solve some of the toughest problems.

Not surprisingly, the framing modifications were the main challenge. Old houses weren't built to modern code standards, and when you want to retain original forms, it's often a real trick to merge new work with work that today is officially substandard, but which has held up well for years. Builder Andy Anderson handled all of this very skillfully, beginning with the floor.

We wanted to keep the new joists off of the ceiling below, because they could wreck it if they began to deflect under the weight of the new floor. To manage this, we set the ends of each 2x10 on flat 2x4 spacer blocks on top of the plate, as shown in the drawing at left. This left a 1½-in. gap between the new joists and the existing ceiling, plenty for any conceivable deflection. Anderson nailed the 2x10s off on 16-in. centers, right between the existing 2x4s. A few of the old ceiling joists were deflecting too much and needed a little help. To these, he sistered on a 2x10. The ends of the 2x10s were cut on the angle of the roof, and where they ran parallel to the rafters, he nailed the rafter tail to the joist end.

Once the new floor was framed, the plywood subfloor was glued and nailed down. I like to use construction adhesive, because it reduces squeaks and also stiffens the floor. With this job done, there was finally a good solid platform to work on, and the crew could stop dancing around from joist to joist.

To open up the space, we had to get rid of all the collar ties, along with the stud walls that supported the rafters dying into two of the roof's valleys. Anderson began by installing temporary bracing, tearing out the stud walls, and then sistering new 2x4s to the original roughsawn rafters, so that they could span from ridge to top plate without additional support. The milled lumber also gave us straight walls to nail the gypsum wallboard to.

My new plans called for a series of five Velux skylights in the west slope of the roof, and we installed headers and framed out for them at this point. Later, we stapled kraft-paper backed fiberglass batts between the framing and installed a 6-mil vapor barrier.

We had to install beams where the stud-wall supports had been, but this meant point

loads, and I didn't want to tear up the walls below to install posts. Instead, we figured the best ways to spread the loads out over the bearing walls below.

The most difficult situation was at the south wall, where I'd specified a large, custom-built half-round window with three small awnings under it, to let in a lot of sunshine (photo bottom left). There was no way to transfer the load directly downward, so we created a truss—an A-shaped structure of doubled 2x12s connected at their bottoms by two 2x4 ties. This made a large structural triangle at the edge of the end wall, and the 6x10 east-west beam was fastened to one of the 2x12s with a Simpson HU 610 metal hanger. Near the stairway, this beam, which runs the length of the valley, is supported at the north end by a 4x6 post sitting on floor joists doubled over the bearing wall below. For the 4x10 east-west beam, we set a 4x8 beam on the top plate of the existing attic-level wall, and let the beam rest directly on it. The other end of this beam is hung from the 6x10 with a Simpson HU 410.

The bedroom—The alcove we created under the east-west 4x10 beam seemed the logical place for the bed. It was the right size, and the 17-ft. peak would give it an open and airy feeling. But I wanted it to feel cozy, too, so although we'd been spending most of our time trying to open up space and find headroom, I asked Anderson to frame sloping walls to replace the verticals at the south and east. This balanced the elevations and comfortably enclosed the bed.

We installed a small round skylight near the peak of the roof over the entryway (photo facing page, top right). It lets in some light, but frankly, it's more important as a whimsical touch. It's nice to sit on the bed, look up, and be able to glimpse the sky.

Bedrooms need clothes storage, and we used the area under the northernmost east-west ridge as a walk-in closet. It works well in its own right, but the nicest thing about it is that it keeps the clutter of bureaus and such out of the long sweep of the main space.

At the head of the stairs, a fireplace flue came up from the living room below. We installed a zero-clearance metal fireplace here, and the new walls that enclose the unit also hide the flue from the floor below. The fireplace is near both the bed and the sitting area—the perfect spot for physical and psychological warmth. It's a heat-recirculating unit with an outside combustion air hookup and glass doors. It is quite efficient and light, an important structural consideration.

Next to the fireplace, Anderson constructed

In the completed remodel, the bed sits in an alcove at the south end of the ridge, and the bath is tucked into the low north end. The two new exposed beams in the bedroom would have delivered point loads to the walls beneath their ends, so the framing had to be modified to spread that weight out over entire bearing walls. An A-frame truss over the semicircular window takes the load at the southern end of the north-south beam.

The circular skylight in the peak over the entrance adds a touch of whimsy to what otherwise would have been a large blank wall.

Headroom was a problem in the bathroom, and the shower stall, above, had to be recessed into the rafter and floor-joist cavities to meet code requirements for height and width. The clear-glass enclosure maintains an open feeling, even though the shower encroaches on the entry. The 5x7 bathtub, right, sits against the north wall under a curved tile border that echoes the shape of the window at the other end of the ridge. The view from the tub is of San Francisco Bay and the Golden Gate.

a double-door woodbox. The rear door opens near the stairs, so firewood wouldn't have to be carried across the carpet. It hasn't worked out that way. The Fowler children quickly discovered the possibilities of the double-doored box. It's a great place to hide and to store toys, and it also means that they can open the bedroom door and creep behind the bookshelves and through the woodbox to "surprise" their parents.

The bath—The long, low area at the north end of the attic was the logical place for the bathroom. It had private views and relatively easy access to the plumbing stack below. Also, the drains could be routed down through a closet on the second floor. But there was only a narrow aisle with adequate headroom down the middle of this space. Luckily, you sit down a lot in a bathroom. We tucked the toilet back under the sloping east wall, and ran the dressing table that holds the two lavatories just far enough out from that

same wall that we could install a medicine cabinet and mirror over it.

The 5x7 tub was easy. It would only fit against the end wall (photo above right), and it looked best there anyway. It also allows, through one of the skylights, a spectacular view of the bay in absolute privacy. A small, round skylight in the roof over the tub lets in some reading light. A great place to soak.

That left the free-standing shower (photo above left). Code requires a minimum 30-in. width and 78-in. height. This space just didn't exist, but Anderson created it by recessing the shower's floor and ceiling into the floor joists and rafters. A standard shower stall would have blocked up the aisle visually, and would have made the entrance seem cramped. We used a clear glass enclosure, which doesn't appear to take up important space.

Additional considerations—Before we gyprocked the walls and ceiling, we built a 16-in. high kneewall 12 in. from the edge of the floor

platform. This made finishing easier, and gave us room to run wiring and heating ducts. It also makes the room easier to clean.

One hundred and forty sheets of gypsum board went into this attic, and each one had to be humped up a ladder and in through the new south window. Once they got inside, only one went up uncut. This is where the sheer labor of the job became most evident.

The attic hadn't been insulated, so even the modest amount of fiberglass we were able to stuff between the 2x4 rafters was a big improvement. The Velux windows are doubleglazed and well weatherstripped. We ordered them with exterior shades and interior screens. On warm days the windows can be left open while the shades screen out the sun.

This room probably would be fine without any additional heat, but it was easy to extend an existing duct run behind the kneewall, and we added one register in the bedroom.   □

Glen Jarvis is an architect in Berkeley, Calif.

Garage Remodel

Turning a ramshackle outbuilding into an attractive rental unit

by Mark Alvarez

Small houses are a treat. They're cozy, for one thing; an attribute most of us have not paid much attention to since childhood, but one we appreciate when we're reintroduced. Good ones are elegant, too: Nothing is wasted, and the cooking, living and sleeping areas often flow into each other for an artful impression of spaciousness.

Many little houses are owner-built, and because they have to be so carefully planned, they usually reflect with endearing accuracy the quirks and habits of the person who swung the hammer. Others, like this one, are conversion jobs. Their special charm lies in the fact that they used to be chicken coops or stables. Within the constraints imposed by the original structure, they have to be as carefully planned as a new building if they are to work right. With many conversions, including this one, there's the added responsibility of making sure that the outbuilding-turned-house doesn't stick out like a sore thumb in an already established neighborhood.

When Lesley and Megan Brill wanted to turn the garage behind their Boulder, Colo., house into a rental unit, they asked John Wolff and Tom Lyon to come have a look. Wolff and Lyon bill themselves as "architractors" (see the sidebar below), and handle both design and construction on all of their projects. What they saw in the Brills' backyard was a decrepit old building covered with fake-brick asphalt siding (photo bottom of facing page). They weren't sure at first that the ramshackle structure with its shallow perimeter foundation was worth saving. But there is real economy in finding a way to use an existing structure, and they eventually decided that since the foundation had been supporting the building for 60 years, they could go ahead and build on it as long as they picked up any new loads on interior walls.

Planning—Much of residential Boulder consists of single-family houses on narrow, rectangular lots, often with garages or other outbuildings at the rear. Property owners in the Brills' zoning district have always had the right to add an attached living unit, but detached units were forbidden by zoning regulations, which meant they couldn't turn their outbuildings into residences. Since 1971, though, owners willing to wrestle with a little red tape have been able to undertake such conversions under a special zoning ordinance that allows for something called a Planned Unit Development (PUD).

In many parts of the country, PUD and similar regulations have been passed to encourage large developers to cluster living units and leave more of the land as open space. The great incentive is that it cuts down on the developer's costs for roads and other services. In Boulder, though, the regulations were promulgated in an attempt to encourage appropriate development of the city's already existing residential areas. Home owners and their architects, designers and builders recognized that attached second living units sometimes worked well, but that some additions resulted in huge buildings entirely out of scale with the residential nature of the neighborhoods. They

---

On architracting

When Tom Lyon and I formed our partnership in 1975, our goal was to control our buildings from the first pencil stroke to the last coat of paint with a degree of thoroughness that seemed lacking in much of the construction industry. We created the word "architractors" to convey our dual function as designers and builders.

Since then, our projects have included everything from a Vermont pole house on 13 levels to an experimental two-story Victorian house built in a factory in four sections, trucked to the site and set by a crane. We've completed substantial transformations of a chicken coop, a garage, and numerous residences. We've put wine-cellar cabinets in welding studios, and built greenhouses, towers and additions of every description, with design elements ranging from Queen Anne Victorian to High Tech. Urban infill projects like the Brills', which require tender consideration of the existing neighborhood's fabric, have been of special interest to us.

Through these projects, architracting has served us well. We've been able to apply the lessons of construction to our designs. In general, we are prompted to choose simpler solutions over contrived ones, striving to produce the greatest effect for the lowest cost.

During the early years we didn't write formal specifications for our projects, and drawings were often kept to the minimum required to get a building permit. We have learned that control over the building process is not a substitute for careful planning and decision-making. Tom and I used to build our projects personally, usually one at a time. These days, we often have as many as six or seven projects going at once. We can't always rely on spontaneous ingenuity, and documentation and communication have become increasingly important. We now try to be as thorough as possible with drawings and specifications, but we still make frequent changes in the field. We always seem to be sketching details of such things as porch header trim or a fireplace mantel on a 2x4 at the site. We like working this way. It lets us take construction realities into consideration, and respond directly to the situation at hand.

One of the things we enjoy most about architracting is that it doesn't let us get bogged down in specialized tasks. We both do everything. An average day could involve meetings with clients, drawing, word processing a contract, and framing a floor. Not too long ago I found myself finishing a concrete sidewalk with a trowel in my hand and a bow tie around my neck.

Architracting works best on a small scale, with renovation and custom projects. Remodeling is particularly well suited to design-build because of the surprises you always run into. Clients seem to feel more comfortable with a combined design-build process because they sometimes have trouble making all their decisions at once and like knowing they will be free to make changes. This process, of course, requires time-and-materials billing rather than a fixed bid.

Architracting doesn't work well for big buildings. On large-scale projects, you're running a large crew and dealing with many subcontractors. You don't want many in-process changes. You need a strict, almost authoritarian system. If you build high-rise buildings or 500-unit condominium projects, architracting is not for you. But if you like working on the small scale and developing a responsive and intimate relationship with the building and with the client, the design-build process is excellent. *—John Wolff*

eventually persuaded planners that carefully designed detached living units would often be a better way to go. The adoption of the PUD regulation has led to some interesting salvage and conversion work (see pp. 122-125 of this volume), as designers and builders have turned their minds to creating efficient and comfortable living spaces out of neglected and dilapidated structures.

A PUD proposal has to be reviewed by a number of city departments before a building permit can be issued. The process takes about two months longer than getting a permit for an attached addition. Siting, landscaping, and water and sewer services all have to be approved, along with the design of the conversion itself. The compatibility of the renovation with the rest of the neighborhood is an important consideration.

Before they could apply for a PUD, Wolff and Lyon had to come up with a plan. Two small additions were keys to the success of the project. The first, a roof monitor, opened up the small house vertically and made room for a bright 80-sq.-ft. sleeping loft or study. The second, a 10-ft. by 17-ft. sunspace sunk 16 in. below grade off the south end of the existing garage, became both a solar collector and the main social space in the house. The original 22-ft. by 20-ft. space was arranged to accommodate a bedroom, the kitchen, a dining area, an entryway, a bath, and a small laundry and utility area (floor plan, p. 109).

Construction—The partners began by jackhammering out a trench for the waste line through the rough 6-in. slab that had been poured a dozen years before. To level the floor and beef up support for the interior bearing walls to come, they decided on a topping slab. They began by cleaning the old concrete thoroughly, sweeping off debris, chips and dust. Next, they washed it down with a 10% muriatic-acid solution, and rinsed it well. The night before the new pour, they wet the old slab down. The next day, they mixed a bonding grout of 3 parts sand, 1 part portland cement and enough latex bonding agent (from Fox Industries, Inc., 3100 Falls Cliff Rd., Baltimore, Md. 21211) to form a slurry about the consistency of pancake batter. They coated the slab with this mixture, spreading it out with brooms.

For the topping slab, which averaged about 2 in. thick, they used a 6½-sack mix with a water-reducing admixture available at batch plants, which let them work with less water, for less shrinkage and more strength. They used the garage's walls as forms, and covered the new slab with 4-mil poly for 24 hours to let it cure slowly.

Once the slab had cured, they demolished the south wall, excavated for the sunken sunspace and poured a standard concrete footing and a block perimeter wall. At the other end of the building, the garage doors were removed, and the north wall was reframed to include an entry convenient to the parking area (drawing, p. 109).

The interior walls were framed up next,

The 60-year-old garage, bottom right, was converted to a rental unit, whose three distinct shapes—the original building, the roof monitor and the new sunspace off to the south—suggest the residential design of the neighborhood and let the little house snuggle in comfortably.

then part of the original roof was cut away and the roof monitor was built. The bottom plates of its short 2x6 walls rest on the top plates of new interior walls running perpendicularly below. Its roof rafters are 2x10s. The tongue-shaped extension is a semicircle with a 6-ft. radius. Wolff and Lyon cantilevered three of the monitor's floor joists (2x6s, 16 in. o. c.), adding a doubled one in the tongue's center. They shaped the ends of the joists to the arc, laid and cut the plywood subfloor to the shape, then bent a layer of ⅛-in. Masonite and two layers of ⅛-in. matt board (to match the texture of drywall) around the curve.

The commercial-style tubular-steel loft railing was custom welded in a Boulder shop. The ladder was ordered out of the Cotterman catalog (719 Morton Ave., Aurora, Ill. 60506). It's

Photo: John Wolff

a model 3SS, intended for use in places like loading docks, and was sturdily, if not precisely made. It couldn't be installed so that the rungs were level and the side rails were plumb at the same time. The partners went for plumb. The first few rungs are rebar, and Wolff, who lived in the house for a few months after it was finished, says that they are hard on bare feet. He'd cover them with wooden treads next time. The Cotterman Co. makes a full line of metal and rolling ladders, and Wolff and Lyon consult their catalog frequently.

The floor of the sunspace is brick on a 2-in. leveling layer of sand, spread directly on earth. Wolff and Lyon brought the water line in through this room before laying the brick, and stubbed it up in the built-in windowseat near the dining area. Built-ins are a common element of small house design. Like many others, these also double as storage units, but here they serve another purpose as well. They reduce the need for furniture in the sunspace so that the floor can be kept clear to absorb most of the solar radiation that passes through the windows.

Instead of stripping all the exterior walls, the partners left the 90-lb. asphalt roll siding in place, sheathed over it with ½-in. Thermax and resided with 1x6 pine drop siding. On the inside, they filled the stud cavities with fiberglass batts and installed a poly vapor barrier before hanging drywall. Wolff and Lyon felt that the double vapor barrier would not be a problem in Boulder's dry climate.

Overhead, they ripped off all the old roofing and installed new asphalt shingles over new decking. The 2x10 roof framing of the new sunspace and monitor carries fiberglass batts. Over the kitchen, the original 2x4 rafters were furred down another 4 in., and this small ca-

In the photo above, the tie beam that crosses the house at the intersection of sunspace and original building, and the reveals above and below it, form a sort of skeleton of the demolished south wall of the old garage. Such details don't just articulate the original structure; they help distinguish one space from another within the open plan of the house. At right, the black stovepipe winds its way to the roof, pulling the eye up and into the house. The roof monitor, which has been used as both bedroom and study, adds room and lets in a lot of sunlight. The tongue extending from the edge of the loft borrows a little space from the cathedral ceiling over the kitchen. It wasn't in the original plans for the remodel, but it is the kind of light, whimsical touch that can be so important to the success of a small space.

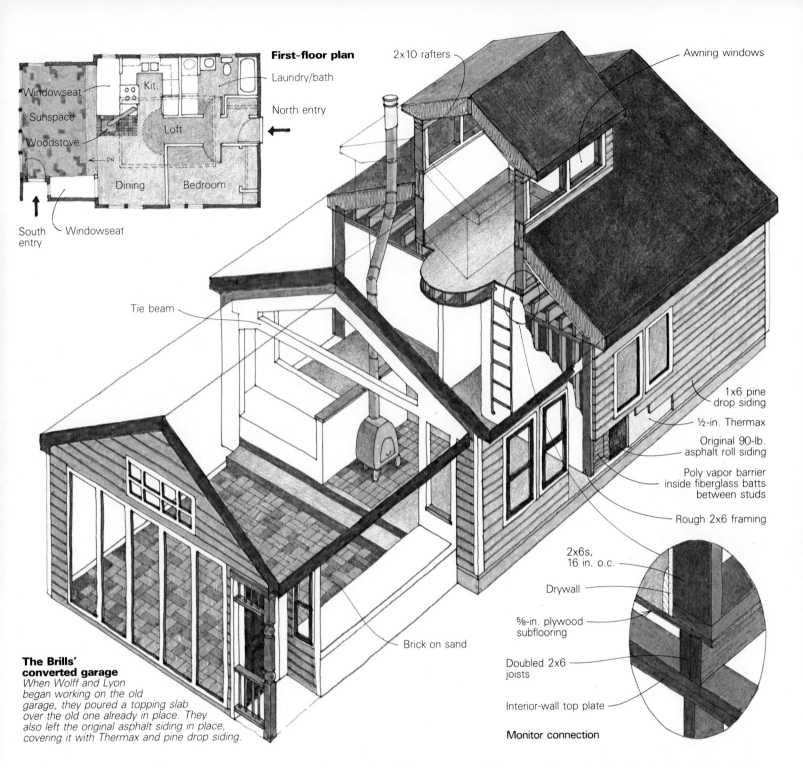

First-floor plan

2x10 rafters

Laundry/bath

North entry

Awning windows

Windowseat

Sunspace

Woodstove

Kit.

Loft

DN

Dining

Bedroom

South entry

Windowseat

Tie beam

1x6 pine drop siding

½-in. Thermax

Original 90-lb. asphalt roll siding

Poly vapor barrier inside fiberglass batts between studs

Rough 2x6 framing

2x6s, 16 in. o.c.

Drywall

⅝-in. plywood subflooring

Doubled 2x6 joists

Interior-wall top plate

Brick on sand

Monitor connection

**The Brills'
converted garage**
*When Wolff and Lyon
began working on the old
garage, they poured a topping slab
over the old one already in place. They
also left the original asphalt siding in place,
covering it with Thermax and pine drop siding.*

thedral section is the least well insulated part of the house.

The electric backup heating hardly ever needs to be turned on. Between the sunspace and scrapwood fires in the stove, the house stays comfortable through most of the winter. In fact, Wolff says that one of the things he would design differently in this house would be a better system for air circulation—the monitor sometimes gets overheated when the woodstove is in use, while the downstairs bedroom is occasionally a bit chilly. A circulating fan and a bit of ductwork would have solved this problem.

How it works—The house is less the result of astonishing virtuosity than of an informed attention to detail. Wolff emphasizes that a small house can feel like a box even when its plan is largely open, unless the living areas are somehow differentiated within the total

volume. The mating of the sunspace and the original part of the building is a good example of how relatively small details can be used to great effect.

The roof of the sunken addition was designed to be both lower and deeper than the roof of the old garage. This creates a peaked reveal where the two roofs meet (photo facing page, left). The doubled 2x6 tension member that was installed when the south wall was demolished completes a pediment-like triangular frame that seems to sit on two other reveals formed where the sunspace's side walls tie into the wider original building. Wolff thinks of this frame and its support as the exposed skeleton of the garage's demolished south wall. They serve as a reminder of the original structure, and more important, they help set the bright, outward-looking sunspace apart from the more private remainder of the house. The tiny building becomes more inter-

esting and enjoyable to live in than just a stretched garage.

The other major interior design feature is the stovepipe, which snakes up through the roof. Its two 45° turns don't seriously hinder the passage of smoke, and as you enter the sunspace, the chimney pulls your eye not just up, but in, introducing you to each level of the house (photo facing page, right).

The different levels work outside, too. The three distinct masses—the original garage, the monitor popping up through it, and the sunspace with its lower roof—create a pleasant cluster that is more appropriate to both the site and the neighborhood than a simple elongation would have been.

The Brills' new house took about seven weeks to build, and it cost them about $45 per sq. ft., a price they probably couldn't have duplicated if they hadn't had the old fake-brick garage to work with. □

Illustrations: Frances Ashforth

Teton Remodel
Making an old house in a cold climate more livable and efficient without changing its character

by Bill Phelps

The old Leek house has been an integral part of the scenery in Jackson Hole, Wyoming, for as long as anyone around here can remember. Its straightforward symmetry, its barn and surrounding tall pines are a picturesque greeting at the south end of town.

The house is only 80 years old, and in many parts of the country its age would not even raise an eyebrow. But in Jackson Hole, those 80 years encompass almost the entire history of permanent settlement.

The Leek house was one of the first frame structures built in the valley (see p. 113), and

The 80-year-old house that was renovated by the author and his crew is one of the oldest frame structures in Jackson Hole, Wyoming. A landmark building in a spectacular landscape and rigorous climate, it commands a view of the Grand Tetons to the north.

over the years it has sheltered an assortment of dudes and cowboys. Faith and Lara, my wife and daughter, and I lived there when we first arrived in Jackson Hole seven years ago. At that time, the house was being used for ranch hands, and I spent my time wielding a pitchfork rather than a hammer. The wear and tear of 80 years was apparent then. The present owners, Kelly and Elizabeth Lockhart, who bought the house in 1982, decided it was time to do something about it, and I was especially pleased when they asked me to help with the renovation.

The Lockharts had three goals for the house. They wanted to make overdue structural repairs, rearrange the floor plan, and improve the energy efficiency. The first two were relatively straightforward, but the third was trickier, because we didn't want to alter the character of the house. For example, we de-

cided to add new insulation to the interior surface of the walls, because most of the siding was still in good shape and we wanted to leave it in place. Luckily, we saw that the sunporch the Lockharts wanted would fit in naturally under two hips we could create by extending the roofline formed by the existing east and west porches across the south side of the house (photos facing page).

Structural work—The structural repairs we made were typical of any renovation. We lifted low spots and patched the foundation. We focused our attention on the south end because it was in the worst condition (3 in. out of level in 30 ft.) and because we were adding on there. The rest of the main floor had its ups and downs, but they weren't as severe, and we felt the difficulties and expense required to level it outweighed the advantage of a perfect-

Photo this page: John S. Huyler

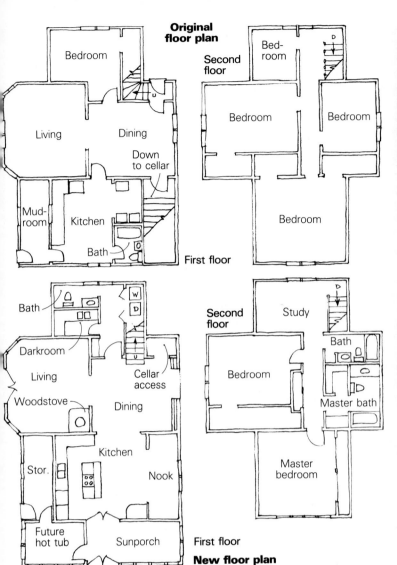

Original floor plan

Bedroom

Living

Dining

Down to cellar

Mud-room

Kitchen

Bath

First floor

Second floor

Bed-room

Bedroom

Bedroom

Bedroom

New floor plan

Bath

Darkroom

Living

Woodstove

Dining

Cellar access

W

D

Stor.

Kitchen

Nook

Future hot tub

Sunporch

First floor

Second floor

Study

Bath

Master bath

Bedroom

Master bedroom

The goal of the renovation was to make the house more comfortable and efficient without changing its looks much or its character at all. Two windows were added to the master bedroom in the south gable end, and a new hip-roofed sunspace incorporated two small existing wings.

ly level floor. After 80 years, the house had no doubt reached its equilibrium.

The Lockharts had decided from the beginning to gut the interior of the house. With help from their friends, they tore into the old lath and plaster, gypboard, insulation, pipes, wires, dust and dried flies. After countless truckloads to the dump and several flat tires, we looked around at the bare bones of that old house and got several surprises. It was my first exposure to 19th-century balloon framing. In some places, 2x4s were just scabbed together to make the required length. The second-floor joists were set on 1x4 ledgers let into the studs. (For more on what you might expect to find behind the walls of old houses, see pp. 60-62 of this volume.) One charred joist space told the story of a close call with disaster. All in all, though, the structure was still sound, and I concluded that it was the sturdy 1x12 board sheathing that was holding it together.

We installed new studs where they were needed, and also added fire blocking between floors in the stud cavities. We installed new headers on the first floor and wherever we enlarged windows. Actually, most of the openings in the house are under gables, and don't bear any of the roof load. On the first floor, they do carry the weight of the second-floor framing, but the 1x4 joist ledger, bolstered by

the rigid 1-in. thick sheathing, seemed to suffice as a kind of continuous header. The ledger also seemed to be doing its job of holding up the second-floor joists, so we just added a few nails through the joist ends into the face of the studs, and left well enough alone.

A renovation this complete makes it fairly easy to change the floor plan. The Lockharts consulted with Jim Engleke, a local architect, and in the design that evolved, the four bedrooms upstairs became two bedrooms, two baths and a study. The kitchen was enlarged, and what had been the entry to the cellar was converted into a breakfast nook. The downstairs bedroom was converted to a half bath, a laundry and a darkroom. The living and dining rooms were left the same (see the floor plan, above).

Insulation—Achieving a balance between energy conservation, solar gain and cost requires compromises in every project. Conserving energy is almost always the most cost-effective approach, and that was the case on this job, too. Large expanses of glass on the south wall would not suit the house, and the budget, although reasonable, had a long list of objectives to meet.

Climate, of course, determines how much insulation you need. In Jackson Hole, the climate is cold, sometimes extremely so. On Jan-

uary 1, 1979, the temperature dropped to −65°F, and one of the main electrical power lines coming into the valley contracted so much that it broke. At the time, rising energy costs had already created doubts about the total-electric dream house, and that night provided a frigid exclamation mark. Temperatures inside poorly insulated houses dropped so quickly that water pipes froze solid in a couple of hours while everyone huddled around the closest woodstove. Jackson Hole averages just under 10,000 degree-days. By comparison, Burlington, Vt., averages 7,876 degree-days and Albuquerque, N. Mex., averages 4,292. There was no question that the old 2x4 stud walls of the Lockharts' house needed a good bit more insulation.

I decided on a system I'd read about, in which the stud cavities are filled with fiberglass batts. Then foam-board insulation is added to the inside of the studs, with 2x2 furring (nailers for gypboard) run on top of the foam board (top drawing, next page). This system has several advantages. The foam board and furring are less expensive than a second stud wall, and require less space. This system also creates a thermal break over headers and studs. The 2x2 furring forms a chase for electrical runs and boxes so that they don't penetrate the vapor barrier. We used reflective foil-faced polyisocyanurate

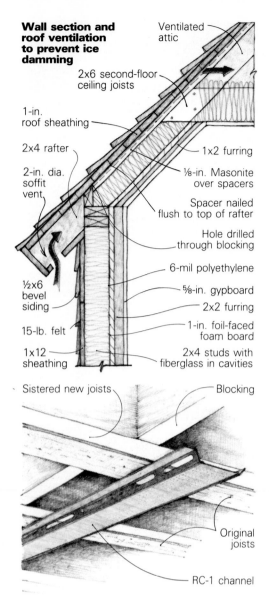

Wall section and roof ventilation to prevent ice damming

- Ventilated attic
- 2x6 second-floor ceiling joists
- 1-in. roof sheathing
- 2x4 rafter
- 2-in. dia. soffit vent
- ½x6 bevel siding
- 15-lb. felt
- 1x12 sheathing
- 1x2 furring
- ⅛-in. Masonite over spacers
- Spacer nailed flush to top of rafter
- Hole drilled through blocking
- 6-mil polyethylene
- ⅝-in. gypboard
- 2x2 furring
- 1-in. foil-faced foam board
- 2x4 studs with fiberglass in cavities

- Sistered new joists
- Blocking
- Original joists
- RC-1 channel

Hanging drywall from sagging joists

foam board, which, with the airspace created by the furring strips, adds R-10 to the system. We installed a 6-mil polyethylene sheet as an infiltration barrier inside the fiberglass batts between the foam-board insulation and the old studs of the exterior walls, primarily to deal with the problem areas around the wall-to-ceiling and wall-to-floor junctions.

In this house, there was another advantage to this approach. The old roughsawn studs varied in width up to ½ in. Using foam board and furring strips made it easy to flush up the wall surface without having to plane or fur out individual studs. The foam panels are 4x8, and we set up a plywood-and-sawhorse bench for measuring and snapping lines. Long cuts parallel to the sides are best made on a table saw to save time; short or irregular cuts can be handled with the same sort of razor knife you'd use on drywall. To install the stuff in an out-of-kilter house, we used standard drywall technique too, plumbing the first sheet and scribing for fit along the floor and ceilings. Foam doesn't have to break over studs, though, because it's so light.

The 1-in. foam board and the vertical 2x2s went on easily using an air nailer and 16d nails. We marked the location of each stud on the floor and at the top of the wall and nailed the 2x2 directly over each one. We were so preoccupied that we didn't stop to think the system through thoroughly. We proceeded to duplicate the out-of-plumb, non-parallel, not-on-layout pattern of the original wall.

After two days we arrived at the kitchen to finish out the insulating and furring. As soon as we began cutting and nailing horizontal 2x6 backing to hang the cabinets, we realized our mistake. We should have run all the 2x2s horizontally at 2 ft. o. c. The drywall would have gone on much easier, we could have made electrical runs without drilling a hole, and we would have saved a few 2x2s.

If the drywall contractor noticed my mistake, he was too polite to let me know. In fact, his installers were pleased not to have to deal with a polyethylene vapor barrier. Sheet-rockers I have dealt with are generally less than enthusiastic about vapor barriers. If the inside corners aren't tucked tightly enough, they frequently have to cut the poly. We taped the joints of the foil-faced foam board, so we had an adequate vapor barrier that was out of their way.

The insulation level we achieved for the walls (R-26) is a little less than I would have liked. We added the highest level we could justify with our budget. Building a second wall or detailing to use thicker foam-board insulation would have cost a lot more for a small additional gain in performance. Instead, we meticulously sealed all the cracks we could find against air leaks, a far greater source of heat loss. We filled all the shim spaces around doors and windows with spray-in foam and stuffed fiberglass insulation in other cavities.

One other problem we encountered while preparing for the rockers was the sag in the old roughsawn second-floor joists. We first tried to remove it by jacking them up with a temporary beam and sistering new joists alongside. This eliminated some of the deflection and gave us a stronger floor, but the sag was still noticeable, and individual joists still varied up to ½ in. on the ceiling below when we removed the beam. The drywall contractor suggested an RC-1 channel (available from U. S. Gypsum, 101 S. Wacker Dr., Chicago, Ill. 60606), which is simply a metal strip. One leg of this resilient channel is attached to the joists, and the other receives the drywall screws (bottom drawing at left). It let us work around the variation in joist thickness, and it also gives the ceiling a greater capacity to absorb the deflection of the floor above. The strips are stiff enough not to give during taping, and since they isolate the drywall from the framing, they cut down significantly on noise transmission. We used ⅝-in. gypsum board throughout the house because it is reinforced with fiberglass and has greater ability to span an uneven surface.

The electrical subcontractor had no difficulty with the 1½-in. space we left him for circuits on the exterior walls. He didn't have to cut the foam, but he did have to attach the boxes to the furring with screws, because

2x2s nailed over foam don't stand up well to hammer blows. He used a router with a ¾-in. straight bit instead of a drill on the 2x2s, and installed a standard protective metal shield over the channel to protect the wire while the drywall was going up. If the 2x2s had been placed horizontally, the circuits almost certainly would have gone in faster.

The remaining areas we had to insulate were the second-floor ceiling and the main-level floor. The existing attic made blown-in cellulose the economical choice over the second floor, and we used 16 in. of it for an R-value of 55. The main-level floor was insulated from the cellar with 6-in. fiberglass batts.

Adequate ventilation between the ceiling insulation and the roof is an absolute necessity in cold climates to prevent ice damming. If insulation touches the underside of the roof, heat loss through the insulation (no matter how thick) will melt snow on the roof. The water then begins to flow down until it reaches the overhang or cornice, where there is no heat loss from below. There it refreezes. Ice accumulates over time until a reservoir is formed above it. Most roofing systems are not able to hold the pond, and water starts leaking down the wall. The way around this is to promote air circulation between the roof sheathing and the insulation beneath it, so that the roof stays cold.

Since the rafters of this house intersected the exterior wall below the ceiling height, we needed ventilation over about 6 ft. from the eaves to the attic. To accomplish this we drilled holes in the blocking between rafters and installed a 2-in. soffit vent in each rafter space. We created a ½-in. air space with sheets of Masonite applied to spacers under the roof sheathing (top drawing at left). The ½-in. space has proved adequate, and the house has had no ice dams. We also cut louvered vents into each gable end.

Windows and a sunporch—The Lockharts wanted to replace the windows with double-hung, insulated units that resembled the old ones as closely as possible. We decided on Marvin windows (Warr Road, Minn. 56763) for several reasons. For starters, we could get them with a baked-on white enamel finish that more closely matched the original windows than clad exteriors would. More important, we could get a matching, single-glazed wood-sash storm window that duplicated the original window treatment and would give us triple glazing. Storm windows are very important over double-hung windows, because double-hungs aren't as tight as other types of windows, and the storm windows act as a buffer against infiltration. Finally, we could buy the storm windows later, thereby reducing the immediate strain on the budget.

The sunporch serves as an airlock entry and a mudroom, as well as an enjoyable sitting room on sunny days. A little less than half of its area has been set aside for a spa that will be installed sometime in the future. As for energy contributions, the sunporch buffers the kitchen wall from the prevailing

Stephen Leek and Jackson Hole

Stephen Leek, the man who built the house I remodeled, was born in Nebraska and arrived in Jackson Hole in 1889, about the time that settlers were beginning to outnumber the trappers and outlaws. He lived in a tent, trapping and hunting through his first brutal winter, and accumulated enough furs and bear hides to purchase a small homestead. He married, settled down to ranching and decided that a log cabin just would not do. Building a frame house required a sawmill, so Leek found a partner and they set one up. Once it was milled, the lumber still had to be ferried across the Snake River and then hauled another seven miles by horse-drawn wagon to the job site. The house he built with such great effort still stands as a landmark in the valley.

For several years, Leek's house was the only lodging available to the few travelers who endured the kidney-jarring stage ride from Rock Springs. Most of them came to hunt elk or to fish, and guiding these sportsmen became Stephen Leek's main business. One of his clients was George Eastman, founder of Eastman-Kodak, who gave Leek a camera and got him started using it. When in 1909 the settlers' ever-increasing demand for land caused the starvation of thousands of the elk that migrated to the valley each winter, Leek's photographs—like the one above, with his homestead in the background—and a personal lobbying campaign in Washington, D.C., led to the creation of the National Elk Refuge in Jackson Hole. And so his house represents more than a pleasant contrast to the modern architectural styles of present-day Jackson. —B. P.

southwest wind and greatly reduces the heat loss from that kitchen wall. On sunny days, the Lockharts can get sun-warmed air into the kitchen simply by opening the French doors and window, but the net glazed area of the sunporch is too small to produce large amounts of extra heat for the house. The sunporch roof was vented to the attic with 3-in. aluminum ducts in the wall and at the east and west sections of the roof with four galvanized J-vents, like the ones that protect bathroom-vent fan outlets.

This renovation, like most, had its share of surprises. It took longer than I planned, and cost more than I estimated. When it was all over, though, the job was a success. Everyone who offered an opinion on the project felt that the house looked better than it had before and that we had maintained the character of the place.

The Lockharts were pleased when their electric bills came in. Their friends and neighbors were amazed at how low their utility bill was (under $60 per month, including lights, cooking, hot water, and the heat not provided by the woodstove). It is gratifying to know that the performance of the house will be even better when storm windows and insulating curtains are added.

Was the job worth the expense and bother? Without a doubt the ranch hands who cut, hauled, stacked, chopped and split ten cords of firewood each year over the last 80 years to heat one floor of this old house would be the first to agree that it was. ☐

Bill Phelps is a passive-solar consultant and builder in Jackson, Wyo. Photos by the author, except where noted.

Transforming an Iowa Farmhouse

An indoor pool for thermal storage, and major structural repairs redeem this abandoned 19th-century wreck

by Arvid Osterberg

Late in the summer of 1978 I asked a fellow architect to walk through the run-down 1860 farmhouse my wife Gayle and I had just bought in Ames, Iowa. When I told him about my plans to repair the house and build a solar addition with a pool, his advice was clear and direct: "Arvid, you could get a bulldozer in here and have it down in a day." I knew that others had been attracted to the Victorian-style house because of its charm and good location, but in the end they too had considered it beyond repair.

Still, the project was attractive. Gayle and I had done remodeling work in two previous houses, and the challenge of rescuing a house that others had passed over was difficult to resist. What made the house even more attractive to me was its excellent southern exposure. The south wing had 44 ft. of south-facing wall, which would be ideal for a solar addition. A long, narrow pool installed along this length would be an excellent heat sink, and would give us a place to exercise during the winter.

After photographing the house and taking some quick measurements of the exterior, I spent a few evenings building a scale study model. It turned out to be extremely useful in evaluating the house's assets and liabilities, and it also helped me to go over ideas with Gayle. When I added the sunspace addition to the model, our enthusiasm grew. We had dreamed of building our own house for years but simply couldn't afford it. Though I was busy completing my dissertation and a third child was on the way, we decided to go ahead with the project and move into the north wing of the house while working on the south section.

I continued to work with the model until I came up with an improved floor plan (facing page). My goal was to make use of what was worth saving, and at the same time to create a more open plan that would take advantage of the warmth captured by the solar addition.

Repairs and a new basement—Once I had complete floor plans and a model, I contacted several contractors for bids. None of them wanted anything to do with the house. They all said much the same thing: Renovating such an old house was too risky, and they preferred new-house construction. So I hired a couple of college students by the hour, bought them hardhats, and took out a building permit and a workmen's compensation policy to protect me in case of accidents on the job. Before long we were hauling out tons of badly deteriorated plaster, wheelbarrow by wheelbarrow.

While the shell of the south wing was being uncovered, I examined the substructure of the house. The original north wing, with its dirt-floored cellar and thick limestone-block walls, was in fairly good shape. The south and east sections of the house, which had been added shortly after the house was built, were in bad condition. Pulling off the old clapboard siding that covered the sills, I discovered a crumbling base wall of stone and brick. Some of the floor joists were actually resting on the ground, and over many years, insects and bacteria had eaten away most of the wood.

All this rotten framing would have to be replaced, and I also wanted to put a basement under the southern section of the house. The solution was to punch a few holes around the perimeter, slide steel beams in under the sills, and then jack the floor up to level while we put in the basement walls. This would be simple

work for a house mover, but the one who agreed to do the job begged off after I'd already dug two openings under the house at his request. His parting advice was to keep digging out a little bit at a time and shore up the floor with temporary supports until I could get footings and walls in place. Fortunately, one of the holes had been dug under a relatively solid section of the south wall, so this is where we started shoring up with posts and braces.

If you ever have to dig a basement under a house, be prepared to move a lot of earth, and to walk hunched over like a troglodyte. We rented a conveyer belt to carry the dirt up out of the hole beneath the ground floor, a better way then the shovel-and-wheelbarrow approach, but we still lost a week to rainy weather.

Another unexpected delay came when we discovered an old cistern. Built under the original kitchen to store water for dishes and laundry, this brick and plaster reservoir had been abandoned and filled with sand. But there must have been a leakage problem because the floorboards and joists in this part of the house were rotten. This made shoring up the house extremely difficult. We made up some temporary joists and supported them with posts and bracing. To speed up the process, I rented a Bobcat to remove the rest of the earth from under the south wing and hired a contractor to put in new floor joists and replace the sill.

This part of the job was a nightmare. Maneuvering the miniature bulldozer between the temporary support posts took nerves of steel, and the additional hand digging was painfully slow. The footings could be poured only in short segments, with equally narrow sections of block wall being laid up between the support

Piet Strydom

The broad southern exposure of the 1860 Victorian-style farmhouse (above) inspired the idea for the solar addition (left), which is linked to the old house by new shingles and siding.

Photos except where noted: Arvid Osterberg

posts. My blocklayer stopped working when the weather got cold, and with the plumbing beneath the house unprotected from freezing temperatures, the waste line froze and had to be thawed and cleaned out in a sobering, if not humiliating, fashion. But finally we got the walls built and replaced the rotted joists and sills with new lumber.

Adding the solar space—The ramps we had cut to let the Bobcat in under the house became, of necessity, part of the excavation for the sunspace foundation. For the rest of the foundation we dug shallower trenches by hand, but the depth of the Bobcat trenches required a stepped footing. The sunspace wouldn't have a basement, but we had to dig down 5 ft. to make room for the pool. To ensure a solid, level base for the pool bottom, we compacted a minimum of 6 in. of sand on the ground between the foundation walls of the sunspace.

Joining a new structure to an old one can be tricky. Because the sunspace, with its long, narrow pool, would extend along the entire south side of the house, my plans called for the removal of the existing south wall. I rebuilt a shaky section of the second floor and then shored up the south wing so that it wouldn't collapse when its wall came down. There were temporary posts and crossbraces everywhere linking the less-than-solid roof and second floor to the new concrete-block wall below. With windstorms and tornadoes frequent events here, I didn't want to take any chances.

Once I was confident about the bracing, we had no trouble removing the studs, siding and windows that made up the original south side. The wall had no sheathing whatsoever, and in places the clapboard was less than ¼ in. thick, reason alone to take it down.

To achieve the open plan I wanted in the living areas adjacent to the sunspace, I needed to span the opening with a large beam. I decided to recycle some old oak barn beams for this purpose, in order to retain the character of an old house. Once the beams were on site, we measured and studied them to assess their structural integrity, and I ended up modifying my design to accommodate the beams I had. Most were weathered and had at one time been infested with insects, so I rented a compressor and a high-pressure hose like the ones used at car washes. Surface by surface, we sprayed off the loose material and dirt on each beam before starting to cut and fit the joints.

Bob Setterburg, whom I had hired as head carpenter for the solar part of the project, thought that we should fasten the beams together on the ground and then lift them into place, rather than trying to install them piece by piece in the south wall. He cut the mortise-and-tenon joints and pegged them together with hardwood dowels. Then we positioned the completed frame on the foundation walls in preparation for hoisting.

We fastened one end of a log chain to the center of the main beam and the other end to a come-along that was in turn fastened to a shored-up section of the attic floor. The bottoms of the posts were securely braced against the floor of the house to act as pivot points. As we started to ratchet the post-and-beam assembly up, we found it was slightly unbalanced, so one of the workers stood on the leading post to even out the weight while we hoisted. I held my breath and hoped the building inspector wouldn't choose this moment to stop by. Once the frame was beyond a 45° position we realized the worst was past, and the man on the

A new south face. Here the new basement under the south wing is complete, as is the foundation for the addition. With temporary bracing installed on both first and second floors, the entire south wall has been removed. The post-and-beam assembly being tilted up was made from recycled barn beams and will span the open space between the addition and the original house.

First-floor plan

Guest bedroom

Study

Living

Woodstove

Kitchen

Dining

Sunspace addition

Illustrations: E. Marino III

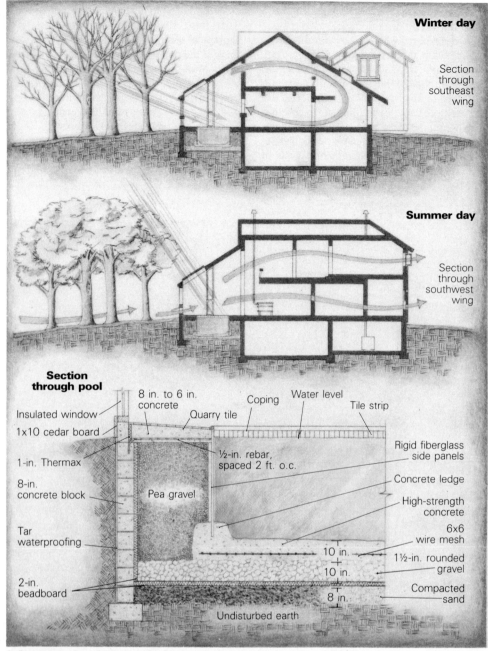

Section through pool

Insulated window
1x10 cedar board
1-in. Thermax
8-in. concrete block
Tar waterproofing
2-in. beadboard

8 in. to 6 in. concrete
Quarry tile
Pea gravel

Coping
Water level
Tile strip

½-in. rebar, spaced 2 ft. o.c.

Rigid fiberglass side panels
Concrete ledge
High-strength concrete
6x6 wire mesh
1½-in. rounded gravel
Compacted sand

10 in.
10 in.
8 in.

Undisturbed earth

Solar mass, insulation and air circulation make the solar addition work effectively. The open plan promotes convective distribution of sun-warmed air in winter (top) and allows for cross-ventilation in summer (center). Water, gravel, cement and tile in the pool (above) make up the thermal mass, and insulation cuts heat loss.

Winter day

Section through southeast wing

Summer day

Section through southwest wing

The roof slope of the original south roof was extended to cover the sunspace addition.

The quarry tile, gravel fill and concrete surrounding the 7,500-gal. pool (photo facing page) increase its heat-storing capabilities. Opening up the space adjacent to the addition lets the rest of the house share the sun's heat.

beam was able to step off without a major shift or movement occurring. Once the barn beams were in place, we fastened them to existing rafters and floor joists with spikes and lag bolts.

Framing up the lean-to sunspace was relatively straightforward. I had decided that for the sake of compatibility with the old house, the existing slope of the south wing's roof should be continued in the addition. We were able to rest the rafters for the addition on the top of the beam, and nail them directly to adjacent old rafters. The only snag was compensating for eccentricities in the old house. High winds, snow loads and just plain age had caused it to shift out of level and to twist out of plumb, particularly on and above the second floor. Bob took a great deal of care in checking dimensions, restoring framing members to plumb and level, shimming and adjusting. The addition had to be built to exact lines because of all the glass panels we'd be installing.

Skylights—Finding details and instructions on skylight installation was difficult. Leaks and heat loss through roof-mounted glass were my major fears, but I felt that the skylights would be an important part of the design for summer heat gain into the pool water and winter sun penetration into adjacent living areas. My first design called for large skylights sized to match the width of the windows below. But when I began pricing glass I discovered that standard-sized sliding glass door replacement panels (33 in. by 75 in.) cost about half as much as the slightly larger non-standard units.

One of the main advantages in positioning the skylights at the lowest point on the roof is that the glass panel can be treated as a large shingle: You don't need to build a curb, and flashing the bottom edge of the glass is greatly simplified because there's no roofing below it.

Bob and I decided to let the addition's 2x10 rafters serve as framing for the skylights. While we were framing and sheathing the roof, we installed headers at the top and bottom of each opening. Then we laid each 1-in. thick insulated glass panel down on a bed of black glazing tape. Another layer of tape followed, except along the bottom edge, which would later be covered with an angled strip of aluminum flashing. To hold the glass in place, we screwed cedar battens down along the top three edges. Cedar shakes were then installed, covering the battens and overhanging the top three edges of each glass panel by about 1 in.

This glazing system, with its loosely fitting furring strips, started to give us trouble when warm weather set in. On hot days the glazing tape softened, causing the glass to slide down ever so slowly. To remedy the problem we removed the shingles and furring strips, then moved the skylight back up into position and reinstalled the furring strips, using longer screws. This worked fine for a couple of weeks

Piet Strydom

until more hot weather caused the problem to recur. This time I installed a steel angle bracket at the bottom of each skylight to hold it, and we've had no trouble for over three years.

The pool—Once the house was closed in I breathed a sigh of relief. In 10 weeks we had leveled up the original floor on the south side of the house, completed a new basement, removed the old south wall, added a sunspace, and re-roofed and re-sided the entire house. I hired a contractor to install the exercise pool and heat sink, choosing a system based on rigid fiberglass side panels and a poured concrete base (section drawing, facing page).

Before installation began, I leveled the sand and put 2 in. of rigid insulation on the three exterior foundation walls and over the packed sand base. The contractor added 6 in. of gravel to the base and fastened the fiberglass panels together with special bolts and reinforcing bars. Then he set up reinforcing mesh across the pool bottom and poured the bottom with a 10-in. wide concrete ledge all around the sides. We used pea gravel to backfill around the pool, then poured a rough concrete floor for the rest of the solar addition, which I later covered with quarry tile.

Performance—I equipped the pool with a standard filtration system, adding an override switch in the living room so that I could operate the pump and filter independently of the timer. The timer turned out to be a good idea, because I've discovered that the pump and filtration system need to operate no more than four hours per day, not nearly as often as the installer recommended. Stagnation and algae are obviously less of a problem indoors, so I've also saved on chlorine.

Technically speaking, the solar addition is a direct-gain system rather than a sunspace because it can't be closed off from the rest of the house. The 7,500 gal. of water in the pool act as a heat sink. The concrete, gravel and tile that surround the pool also contribute to its thermal mass. As might be expected, it takes a while to raise the temperature of this substantial mass. But once warmed, the water is slow to cool down, and gives back heat for a long time. From mid-May to mid-September, the water temperature fluctuates between 70°F and 80°F. The pool water cools off in the fall and can dip into the 50°F range by mid-winter, too cold for swimming. I think the temperature drop is attributable mostly to night-time heat loss. We haven't tightened up the north wing of the house yet, and enough cold air comes in to offset some of the addition's solar gain. Another factor is heat re-radiated from the water out through the windows of the addition. We bought a clear cover for the pool that has hundreds of air bubbles trapped between two layers of plastic. It floats on the water and reduces heat loss slightly in addition to controlling humidity build-up during the winter, a common problem with most indoor pools. I'd also like to install insulated window shades on the solar glazing to reduce heat loss.

After two winters, I bought a natural-gas-powered heater to keep the pool water warm enough for swimming. Thanks to the insulation we installed around and underneath the pool, we're losing very little heat to the ground. I discovered that we need to operate the pool heater only about 4 hours per day in midwinter to maintain 80°F water. And even on the coldest winter days, the tile in the kitchen and around the pool stays warm enough for stockinged feet. For exercise and relaxation, the pool is great, especially when the weather is bad and no one wants to go outside.

To get heat from the solar addition into the rest of the south wing, I made large wall openings on both levels. Convection loops (drawing facing page) are the most direct way to distribute heat passively. Warm air from the addition rises to the second floor of the south wing; as it cools, it returns to the first floor on the north side of the house where it can then be drawn into the sunspace. By monitoring the water temperature and using the water heater, I can keep the addition's temperature high enough to maintain the convection loop well into the night—a benefit that most low-mass solar additions don't offer.

We heat our passive-solar house for about half of what most of our neighbors pay for homes of similar size. And during the summer, we don't need an air conditioner because the open plan provides good cross-ventilation, taking advantage of natural breezes. □

Arvid Osterberg is an associate professor of architecture at Iowa State University.

Rock-Bottom Remodel

How an architect turned an old garage into his house and office

by Ira Kurlander

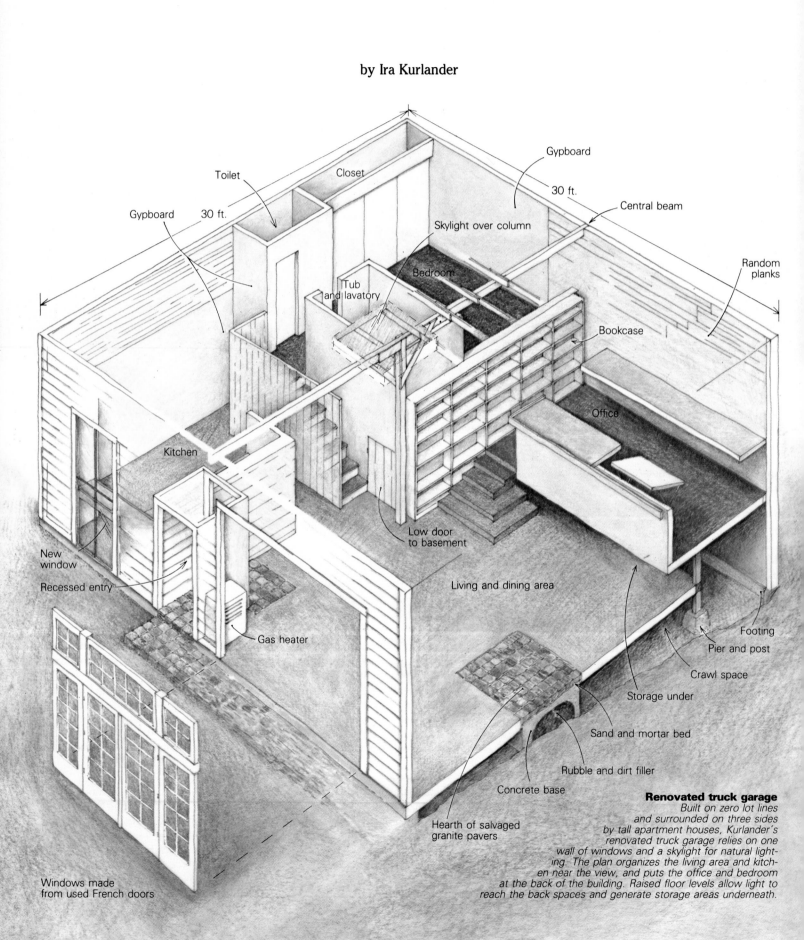

Toilet

Closet

Gypboard

Gypboard

30 ft.

30 ft.

Central beam

Skylight over column

Tub and lavatory

Bedroom

Random planks

Bookcase

Office

Kitchen

Low door to basement

New window

Recessed entry

Living and dining area

Gas heater

Footing

Pier and post

Crawl space

Storage under

Sand and mortar bed

Rubble and dirt filler

Concrete base

Hearth of salvaged granite pavers

Windows made from used French doors

Renovated truck garage
Built on zero lot lines and surrounded on three sides by tall apartment houses, Kurlander's renovated truck garage relies on one wall of windows and a skylight for natural lighting. The plan organizes the living area and kitchen near the view, and puts the office and bedroom at the back of the building. Raised floor levels allow light to reach the back spaces and generate storage areas underneath.

Sometimes the most challenging design problems an architect gets are those with the most limitations. I'd purchased a piece of inner-city property with a 900-sq. ft. outbuilding at the back of the lot, and wanted to convert it into my office and residence, so that I could rent out the main house to help pay the mortgage. But this old truck garage, built in the 1920s, had an uncommon set of restrictions that I'd have to design around.

Three of the four 30-ft. long walls of the building were located on property lines, and the law required them to remain windowless. Inside, the 13-ft. ceiling was too low to allow a second floor, and a column occupied the exact center of the building. To make matters worse, the garage had already been converted into a dingy, poorly organized dwelling. Last, local codes and my $7,000 budget meant that I wouldn't be able to increase the size of the building. My only alternative was to rearrange the interior spaces.

A multi-level floor plan—I gutted the building, and while I sorted and stacked the reusable materials, I pondered my options. Given a choice, people will move toward the part of a room that offers natural light and an outdoor view. I could put windows only on the south wall, so I located the living and dining area and the kitchen in that sunny part of the building (drawing, facing page).

Taking advantage of the fact that the low-pitch shed roof was highest to the north, I arranged the interior like a theater, with rooms far from the windows lifted above the main floor to get an unobstructed view and more light. The office is 30 in. higher than the living area, separated from it by a low wall that defines the space and provides a needed measure of privacy. In plan, the office may seem isolated, but the view of the garden from the drafting table makes this workspace seem larger, and more a part of the rest of the house.

I placed the bedroom in the darkest corner at the highest possible level (60 in. above the main floor). For convenience, I located the bathroom on the same level. I built some badly needed storage space into the area between the slab and the bedroom floor, reducing the number of head-bumping joists by spanning the widely spaced 4x6 beams with extra-strong 2½-in. tongue-and-groove decking. Someday, the washer and dryer will be located in this generous storage area. If I could get a window into it, I would be tempted to convert it to a second bedroom.

The only walls in the house that actually

Three pairs of recycled French doors fit together to fill the original garage-door opening. Waxed hardboard floors in the living and dining area, above right, are inexpensive and easy to clean; they give a pleasant earth-tone background to the area rugs and cobblestone hearth.

A broad cobblestone step, right, sweeps across the courtyard and links the garden to the doorway. The recessed entry offers shelter, and makes the interior of the small house seem spacious by contrast.

Illustration: Christopher Clapp

reach the ceiling enclose the toilet. The other rooms are open, and share light and ventilation, yet they remain clearly separate from one another. From the living area, it is impossible to see the mess in any of the other rooms, and the whole house can be tidied up quickly for clients or guests.

Because the local zoning code prohibits outside additions, I wasn't able to extend a typical roof projection over the front porch. Instead, I recessed an entry into the building, creating a sheltered area where I could fumble for my key while holding a bag of groceries. Because of the entry's small size (3 ft. square and 6 ft. 10 in. high), the interior of the house seems generous and expansive when you open the door. In fact, the space inside is larger than the courtyard, and the bottleneck entry makes the contrast still greater.

Windows for the south wall—The old double-door garage opening was about 12 ft. wide by 10 ft. high. I wanted to fill this space entirely with windows. Since a two-story building was located only 22 ft. to the south, the more height the windows had, the more sunlight they would let in. My first thought was to install a gas-station garage door with glass panels, but it was impossible to find one—at least one I could afford.

Instead, I decided to use French doors that I had collected from various remodelings. I combined three pairs, all of different widths, to create a low-budget window wall. The final arrangement (top photo, previous page) has a Palladian formality.

The framing for the new window was simple—4x4 posts from subfloor to header, with the two widest doors hung in the middle. I fixed the midsized pair in place on either side of the operable doors and ran the narrowest pair across the top. One full door was mounted sideways over the two center doors, and the last door was cut in half to fill the remaining gaps. For the time needed to replace a few broken panes plus the cost of the posts and trim, I had 120 sq. ft. of glass.

I needed an operable window with maximum ventilation for the kitchen. I took the easy way out and had a new aluminum casement made. It's the same height as the living-room window and runs all the way to the floor (photo facing page), thus opening the small kitchen to the garden outside.

The skylight—The lack of windows in the house tempted me to pepper the roof with skylights. But it's been my experience that lots of skylights with just a few windows is not a good combination; the skylights emphasize the lack of a view and suggest the feeling of being at the bottom of a well.

I decided to get by with a single skylight, placed right over the center column. Its location in the center of the house anchors the rambling collection of levels around the post, and transforms this obstacle into a unifying element. The skylight also helps to balance the

light that comes in from the one window wall. One-quarter of the skylight is directly over the bathtub, giving this interior room a glimpse of the sky and the tall trees in the courtyard.

The 2-ft. o.c. roof joists favored a dome skylight either 4-ft. or 8-ft. square. I chose an economical 4-ft. square double-dome, and during noisy rainstorms and in cold weather, I am glad to have less skylight and more solid roof. Only one problem remains—the neighborhood raccoons have discovered that the skylight is a warm place to congregate.

Interior finishes—The original roof beam and joists are barely adequate for their spans, and 50 years had resulted in visible deflection. I chose to leave these members exposed, since covering them would have added considerable weight to the structure and cost a lot of money to boot. To strengthen and match the existing framing, I added roughsawn knee braces at the central post. Two of the interior walls were then partially sheathed with random-size planks salvaged from neighborhood debris bins. Fitting the various lengths and widths was time-consuming, and the many small cracks had to be caulked. But the only costs were for nails, caulk and the frequent saw sharpenings necessitated by cutting nail-embedded boards. These boards looked shabby at first, but when they were painted white, things came together. Work like this is best done by an amateur—I think it would drive a good carpenter crazy.

As an inexpensive substitute for a hardwood floor, I glued 4x8 sheets of ¼-in. tempered hardboard to the ¾-in. plywood underlayment. When it is machine waxed, this material's dark brown color acquires a depth and sheen that make a pleasing background for furniture and rugs. Unfortunately, the floor's location just off the courtyard garden means that lots of outdoor grit gets ground into the finish, and the hardboard needs power waxing and polishing three times a year to maintain its looks. Next time, I'll try a urethane-type coating as a sealant before waxing, for greater protection against moisture and scuffing.

The entry area and the hearth required a sturdier floor. Luckily (for me), streets in San Francisco's old produce market were being torn up, and the original granite cobblestone pavers were free to those who'd haul them away. I laid them on their sides in a bed of dry sand mixed with cement, so that they could be pushed around and leveled as needed. When the arrangement was satisfactory and the dry mortar joints were at an even height (about 1 in. below the top of the pavers), I topped off the mortar joints with sand and poured water over the surface. The sand kept the mortar mix from splashing, and retained moisture while the grout joints cured. After a week, I swept off the stones and vacuumed the loose sand out. Surprisingly, installing the pavers was the easiest part of the remodel. Later I added more pavers to the courtyard, making a broad step across the front of the house that includes both the French doors and the entry (bottom photo, previous page). Big design gestures like this make a small place feel larger.

A top-loading cast-iron stove from the 1890s helps heat the house and brightens up a windowless wall. Steps beside the bookcase-wall lead to the office, which has been left open to take advantage of the view, natural light and ventilation.

As seen from the top of the bedroom stairs, a custom casement window opens the kitchen to the garden and lets in fresh air. Second-hand cabinets and appliances behind the kitchen wall are in keeping with the whitewashed paneling and sideboard, both made from salvaged planks.

The heating system—Since so few of the walls in the whole place reach the ceiling, an old freestanding gas heater is adequate for heating most of the house. An 1890s cast-iron stove (photo facing page) is the one thing I splurged on. Its Victorian decoration has great style, and although it's not airtight, it's still quite efficient. Its top-loading door, originally meant for coal, is handy for loading short lengths of wood and is neater than side-door designs that drop ashes on the hearth. And its mica windows let the firelight shine through.

Electrical—The entire electrical system was redone from scratch by a licensed electrician. To save his time (and my money), I had him run the wiring in exposed conduit and boxes along baseboards and beams. Later on I added a plug-in light track to the living-area ceiling for more lighting flexibility.

I like this exposed system, but if I'd had more time and money, I would have made custom metal cover plates to hide the punch-out sides of the electrical boxes. The present combination of plastic cover plates on metal switch boxes is unappealing.

Summing up—My only real regret is that I didn't install enough insulation. Next time I re-roof, I'll add a couple of inches of rigid foam on top of the 1-in. rigid fiberglass already installed, and when the time comes to renew the exterior siding, the walls will get a full 3½ in. of fiberglass batts.

The two most important lessons I learned from remodeling the garage were about economy and planning. Rather than diminishing the finished product, the strict budget made me search out alternative materials, which in turn set the style of the house. Having a flexible approach, I was able to switch from high-tech gas-station doors to traditional French doors. Instead of buying a sideboard for the dining area, I built one out of the same salvaged planks I used on the walls.

Hiding the kitchen behind a storage wall let me use an odd assortment of castoff kitchen cabinets. Likewise, the exposed roof joists and the view through the skylight make the old pedestal sink in the bath seem less obtrusive. I also avoided getting bogged down in hiding vents and flues. As long as the space is open and interesting, used materials and simple solutions to mechanical problems aren't distracting.

The open plan has indeed become a cliché of contemporary architecture, but sometimes it does make sense. This house has the same square footage as a four-room Victorian cottage I used to live in. But even though the cottage had lots of windows and a good view, its hallways and boxy plan made it a tight maze compared to my transformed garage.

Trying for maximum light and openness within such demanding restrictions created pleasant, livable spaces, which I think is the ultimate goal of good architecture. □

Architect Ira Kurlander practices in San Francisco, Calif.

Interior photos: Michael Nichelson

Renovating a Carriage Barn

Salvaging an old building makes sense, even if it means fighting through yards of red tape

by Craig F. Stead

Recently, my wife and I found ourselves owners of an 1899 Victorian house. To the rear was a two-story wooden carriage barn of just over 1,000 sq. ft., with a large attached chicken coop and a car shed. Our lot was in downtown Boulder, Colo., a rapidly growing city of 100,000. Urban renewal and rehabilitation had been underway in the area for several years, and new streets, parks and crosswalks had been built. Large old shade trees dotted the parkways, and most of the yards had mature fruit trees and lilac bushes around other Victorian houses.

Boulder has a tough planning department. Our lot was zoned for a duplex dwelling, or—under a special review process—two separate dwellings, called a Planned Unit Development (P.U.D.). Most developers naturally were operating under the duplex zoning rather than getting tied up in the expense, hearings, and paperwork that a P.U.D. required. They would just build a larger addition onto the back of the original house, then pave the rear of the lot for parking. Adding gravel along the sides of the lot cut down on maintenance. This approach saved time and money, and undeniably provided housing for people who needed it, but it was an aesthetic disaster, and it obliterated the backyard. Tenants had to lug beach furniture to the roofs to get in some outdoor relaxation. We decided to take a different approach.

On the line—Between our two buildings was a beautiful backyard filled with old fruit trees, flowers and bushes. As the site plan (right) shows, our corner lot gave us good access to both structures and plenty of on-street parking. A building with its walls right on the edges of its property is said to have zero lot lines. The carriage barn was so far to the rear of the lot that its back and side walls were actually over the lot lines. It was a perfect setup for a Planned Unit Development in which the lot would be split between the two buildings, giving a yard to each. We planned to convert the carriage barn to a three-bedroom residence.

The fact that the barn had zero lot lines let us allocate to it a plot of only 2,500 sq. ft., because the lack of setbacks meant that all of the lot that wasn't built on was usable backyard space. Where public policy favors increasingly dense city areas, as it does in parts of Boulder, allowing zero lot lines must be seriously considered. I think the standard 10-ft. setbacks on all sides of a structure waste a lot of land in most urban settings. Setbacks from the street and at a

house's sides aren't much used. They do provide for ventilation, light and access to the walls, but these considerations can be accommodated by thoughtful design and the careful use of easements. Our rear wall was adjacent to an alley, so there was no trouble there. For the sidewall, I had to get a 5-ft. access easement from my neighbor. Without this easement, the fire code would have required a solid wall with a one-hour fire rating, but with it I would be able to install the windows necessary for the natural ventilation of the house. The chicken coop had been built 5 ft. into the neighbor's yard, so I traded the easement rights for the removal of the encroachment.

Slowly through the system—The rear wall was 3 in. over the lot line into the city-owned alley. To get clear title to it, I had to file a vacation proceeding with the city council. It took six months. Once we got the title, a re-survey of the carriage-barn walls showed an error in the

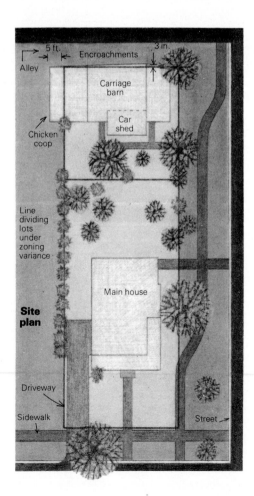

Site plan

original survey. The wall was an inch farther into the alley than we'd thought. A second vacation proceeding. Another six months. This time, I asked for an extra 3 in. in case I needed the room to re-side or insulate the wall sometime in the future. I learned from this year-long process the obvious lesson that it is important to verify the accuracy of your survey when you are dealing with a zero lot-line structure. Also, if you are requesting an easement or a vacation of land, build in a margin for error if you can.

The Planned Unit Development process required all the elements of a formal subdivision. Survey, plans and lawyer's fees alone ran about $5,000, and I spent almost a month of my own time preparing and submitting documents to the city. It was a lengthy procedure, entangled with red tape. In approaching the planning department with my proposal, I found it helpful to have clear structural drawings, a good plot plan, and a complete legal description of the lot lines, easements and encroachments. We had working drawings prepared by a contract draftsman from our sketches and design ideas. The professional drawings made a good impression on the city staff, and helped me get approvals more quickly than I might have otherwise. Several city departments got involved before we could get a building permit, and I found that hand-carrying documents and constant phone contact was necessary to move the proposal smoothly along.

Getting to work—I have come to realize that renovating an existing structure can substantially reduce construction costs. To my way of thinking, this kind of salvaging is the cheapest way for someone with a limited income and some basic construction skills to obtain a beautiful home. I have also found that by doing a large part of the work myself, I can afford the fine finish details and top-of-the-line appliances and fixtures that normally wouldn't be within my budget.

In approaching any project involving conversion of an existing structure, you must evaluate the soundness of the building and decide how to fix any structural defects. Most important are the condition of the foundation and the soundness of the wall and roof framing. The carriage barn had been built on a laid-up stone foundation 12 in. deep—typical for a building of its age in this area. About 2 in. of uneven settling had occurred along the rear wall at the alley, where the soil was exposed to water runoff

Craig Stead

Bruce Miller

The carriage barn, above, was at the rear of the shady, flower-filled yard. It had been built over its own property lines, and extended several inches into the public alleyway, where the child is standing. Nonetheless, it was a perfect subject for a building-code variance that let Stead salvage and renovate it while splitting his lot in two. The completed carriage house, right, sits on a well-planted plot of 2,500 sq. ft. By doing most of the work himself, Stead saved enough to be able to afford fine finish materials and landscaping improvements.

from the eaves. In my experience, foundation problems most often occur from uncontrolled water drainage, which results in frost heaving and shifting. Areas without gutters and below-roof valleys and downspouts are where foundation cracking and settling are most common. Brick houses are most seriously damaged by foundation deterioration because of cracking of the mortar joints in the walls. Wooden structures have more flex, and can withstand more settling before structural problems appear.

The 2 in. of uneven settling had not damaged the barn's structure, and I needed only to level things up and then pour a 6-in. deep reinforced concrete beam and a drainage curb along the old foundation. The roof of the main structure had always been maintained, so the rafters and joists hadn't rotted or warped. The second floor of the carriage barn had originally been a lightly framed hayloft. It was sagging and bouncy,

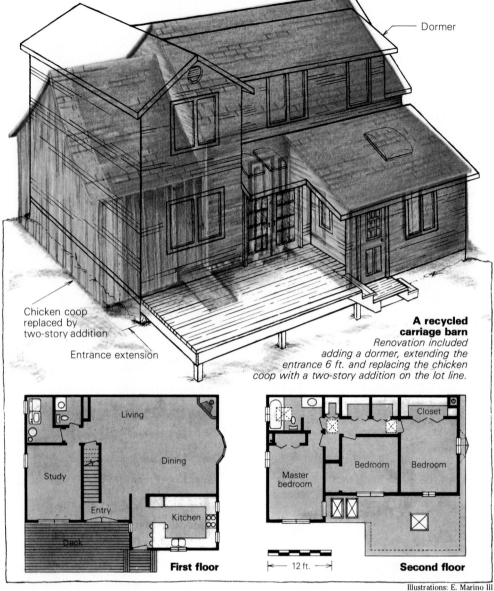

Dormer

Chicken coop
replaced by
two-story addition

Entrance extension

**A recycled
carriage barn**
*Renovation included
adding a dormer, extending the
entrance 6 ft. and replacing the chicken
coop with a two-story addition on the lot line.*

Living

Dining

Study

Entry

Kitchen

Deck

First floor

Closet

Bedroom

Bedroom

Master
bedroom

|← 12 ft. →|

Second floor

Illustrations: E. Marino III

but I would be able to correct the problem by jacking up each joist, and scabbing on another 2x10 alongside.

Demolition—I tore down the attached chicken coop because of its encroachment on my neighbor's property, but I would have gotten rid of it anyway. Unlike the barn, it had been poorly built, and was sagging badly. Rather than take it apart one board at a time, I used a worm-drive circular saw with a carbide-tipped nail-cutting blade (Oldham makes a good one) to cut it into strips and chunks. This saved a lot of time in demolishing a roof with three layers of shingles on top of its sheathing. I just sawed between the rafters from ridge to eave, and then tipped the pieces into a waiting truck to be hauled to the dump. With the chicken coop gone, I framed up a two-story addition, with its west wall right on the property line.

Deciding how much of an older structure to save is important. It's tempting to let bowed walls stand to decrease the cost and trouble of replacing them, but the unfortunate result is often higher labor costs for running rough electrical, plumbing and heating systems. My own policy, after seven years in the home renovation business, is simple: When in doubt, tear it

out. Complete all necessary demolition early in the project so you have a clean, open area to work in.

Several years before, I had worked on a crudely built kitchen addition. To strengthen the wall, I replaced the studs one by one, a very tedious process. Then I tried to jack up and reinforce the roof, which turned out to be too weak to take the strain, so I had to replace the whole thing. I could have done a better job twice as fast if I had torn the kitchen down to the foundation and rebuilt it properly. Take your time and evaluate your structure carefully in the initial phases of a project to determine how much should be demolished. If you lack the experience to make a proper assessment, hire a renovation contractor as a consultant to work with you on this part of the job.

Efficient design—All remodeling seems to have one key problem that dictates many of the design features. Fitting in the stairway is a common one because certain dimensions and spatial relationships are required by code. You may have to try several designs to find the best solution. In my case, the carriage house needed adequate head room, access to a bath and bedroom on the second floor, and a straight run to

conserve space in an efficient first-floor plan. All this simply wouldn't fit, so we extended a section of the front by 6 ft. to give us room for a stair and entryway, which also acted as a small but effective passive-solar collector.

Renovation work often involves designing a workable traffic pattern. One way to see the effect on usable floor area of walkways in a house is to shade all walking and door clearance areas on a blueprint, and then see what's left for furniture. Use 3 ft. as a comfortable walking width, and distance between fixed elements. If over 50% of your plan is for walkway, then you have a bad design, and will have problems locating furniture so you don't trip over it. I used the staircase and entry as a central point in our traffic flow, and connected the various floors and functions along short halls (see floor plan). This maximized the usable floor area and minimized waste space.

We ran into another space problem. There was no room under the carriage barn to run plumbing, heating and wiring. So I built a two-story utility core containing the bathrooms, a utility room, the furnace and the power service. This approach kept the major plumbing and electrical lines together and significantly reduced the cost of roughing them in.

Keeping it warm—Older structures are notorious for high heating bills. Energy efficiency was thus a top priority in the design and construction of the carriage house. I wanted some solar benefits without a solar display that would have been out of character with the neighborhood. The result for the 1,700-sq. ft. house was an $18 gas heat bill for February 1981, lower than the bills of some comparably sized solar houses in Boulder.

We accomplished this level of energy efficiency in various ways. We wrapped the whole structure with 1-in. thick, foil-faced, urethane foam board to seal the old siding from draft infiltration, and to add more resistance to heat loss. Canned urethane foam sealed off foundation drafts, window leaks and framing gaps. We caulked all windows, corner boards, siding junctions and door frames. I kept a caulking gun handy, and I plugged any cracks that were open to the wind. We installed lots of double-hung, south-facing Thermopane windows. Heat collected by the entry and stored in its stone floor traveled by convection up the stairwell to warm the second floor. In summer, the top sash of the second-floor windows can be opened, and the entire house acts like a chimney, venting the rising hot air.

I built in a high-efficiency, prefabricated fireplace with glass doors, outside combustion air vents, an adjustable flue damper and a recirculating blower. I used a Preway Heat Mizer fireplace. It works well, but I think the blower is too noisy. The fireplace alone can heat the house on the average winter's evening.

We insulated the north wall heavily. I also planned for no north-wall windows and to build 4-ft. deep closets along the north side of the second floor. These closets also provide a sound barrier against noise in the alley. I installed a high-efficiency, spark-ignition furnace with a flow-through humidifier and an automatic set-back thermostat. The furnace was carefully sized to match the heat loss of the house, and worked out at 100,000 Btus per hour.

We installed a dishwasher that incorporated its own water heater so that the main hot-water tank temperature could be placed on a minimum setting. The hot-water heater is in the utility core with the bathrooms and the washing machine clustered around it. This way, hot water is instantly available wherever needed, and line heat loss has almost been eliminated. I insulated all hot-water pipes from the heater to the point of use. I put dimmers on all main-floor light switches, with the exception of the stairwell light.

My experience with this project shows that you can get a remarkably high level of energy efficiency with rather ordinary and direct methods carefully implemented during construction. But I'm also convinced that an accidental convection loop contributed significantly to the low heating bills.

Serendipity—After living in the house for a few winter months, I noticed that warm air seemed to be distributed by means of natural convection. I investigated. The kitchen is three steps down from the living room, so heat generated in cooking rose into the living room to warm it. The forced-air ductwork had been installed in the back of the second-floor closets, and it fed the living room through ceiling registers, and the bedrooms above through floor registers. I found that warm air from the fireplace, which collected on the living-room ceiling, flowed into the ceiling heat registers and out of the floor registers in the bedrooms. The living room never overheated when the fireplace was in use, and the rooms of the house remained at a relatively constant temperature without the need for circulating blowers.

Having saved a considerable amount of money by salvaging an existing structure and doing a lot of the construction work myself, I splurged on the finishing details which are so often compromised because of cost overruns or

ignored in the rush to finish. Solid oak-front cabinets, high-quality bath and kitchen fixtures, indirect and track lighting, and durable, good-looking floor coverings all contributed to an attractive finished product.

Landscaping helps to blend the structure into the lot and the neighborhood. I installed gutters all around the house and drained downspouts away from the house to ensure that the old shallow foundation would stay dry.

The results of the project were very satisfying. The planning department of the city of Boulder even gave it an award. Conversion costs, excluding land and my labor, were $53,000. Two of us worked about six months to complete the job. Salvaging the carriage barn instead of demolishing and replacing it saved us about $15,000. And the neighbors like the way the house fits into the setting and how it improves the neighborhood. □

Craig Stead specializes in renovation. He now lives in Putney, Vt.

Glass, a stone floor and its orientation make the entry an effective passive solar collector. Heated air rises to warm the upstairs. The same principle carries air heated during cooking from the kitchen (left) up three stairs to the dining and living areas. Photo: Bruce Miller.

Converting a Store and Stable

Structural repairs and a reorganized interior create living and studio space for two artists

by Robert Hare

In January of 1980, my wife Lorraine and I bought a building for $3,700 at a city auction. Built in 1850, the 50-ft. by 60-ft. brick block originally contained a stable and dry-goods store on either side of a drive-through passageway. Upstairs, there were two floors divided into lots of small rooms. Located on a south-facing hill overlooking the old Delaware & Hudson canal in the historic Rondout district of Kingston, N. Y., this building and many of its neighbors had long ago been abandoned by merchants and middle-class tenants. The auction was the first of several steps taken by the city of Kingston to revive this once-lovely area. But when Lorraine and I were first shown around by the city's property manager, there were no signs of revival—just a bunch of old, boarded-up buildings. Ours (top photo) was one of them.

The building had been condemned in 1969, and its backyard was clearly the unofficial neighborhood dump. A section of the flat roof had caved in because of leakage and rotting timbers, and there was more rot everywhere on the second floor. There were gaps and cracks in the walls where the mortar between bricks had disintegrated. Nevertheless, I knew that this wet, dark, crumbling place held great possibilities for us.

Lorraine and I are artists, and we had been looking for living and working space for well over a year, with no luck. We had some money but couldn't pay regularly on a typical mortgage. And we wanted to live within a couple of hours' drive of New York City. So this old building 90 miles up the Hudson seemed to have lots of potential: plenty of space, proximity to New York, a southern exposure, and an interesting, historic neighborhood full of neglected buildings waiting to be reclaimed. I had done some general contracting and could see transforming the space into studios and large, open rooms.

What sealed the deal was the discovery that we might get some financial aid from a New York State Historic Preservation grant. Break-

An abandoned shell. **Built in the mid-1800s, this brick building, top, held a stable and dry-goods store on its ground floor, with a two-floor rooming house above. Leaks in the roof and general neglect caused the structural and cosmetic deterioration that led to its sale at auction in 1980. The front of the original dry-goods store was restored along with the rest of the building's facade, above, in compliance with Historic Preservation grant guidelines.**

ing this aid loose of its bureaucratic ties to federal, state and local agencies nearly did us in, but we eventually got enough money to cover the cost of a new roof, new windows, new floor joists and masonry repairs. The funds came with certain constraints, the chief one being that the building's facade had to be restored to its original appearance.

Drawing up plans—I decided to draw up the plans for the renovation myself, calling in architect Anita Yuran to approve them. From the beginning, I planned to use the stable and hayloft as my workshop and sculpture studio. It was an open, ground-floor space with large, barn-type sliding doors front and back. The hayloft above would be office and storage space. Lorraine's painting studio was originally going to be in the old feed-and-grain store—the other large, open space on the ground floor. But then we decided to add two big skylights to the roof and to locate her studio under one of them, on the floor above my studio. This way, she would have more privacy from the street and be closer to our second and third-floor apartment and our new baby. All the studio space would be concentrated on one side of the building, and the dry-goods store could be made into a rental apartment.

Since we really didn't need as much living space as the building's three floors afforded, we decided to remove the southwest corner of the third floor to create a large, two-story space that would serve as kitchen, living room and dining room. This large space would also benefit from the solar heat coming through one of the skylights. What remained of the third floor would become bedrooms and bath (drawing, facing page).

Masonry repairs—Before any construction could begin, the building had to be gutted, cleaned and made structurally sound. A demolition crew came in and removed 60 yards of trash every day for two-and-a-half weeks. What came out were windows, walls, rotted

Black-and-white photo: Robert Hare; Illustration: Vince Babak

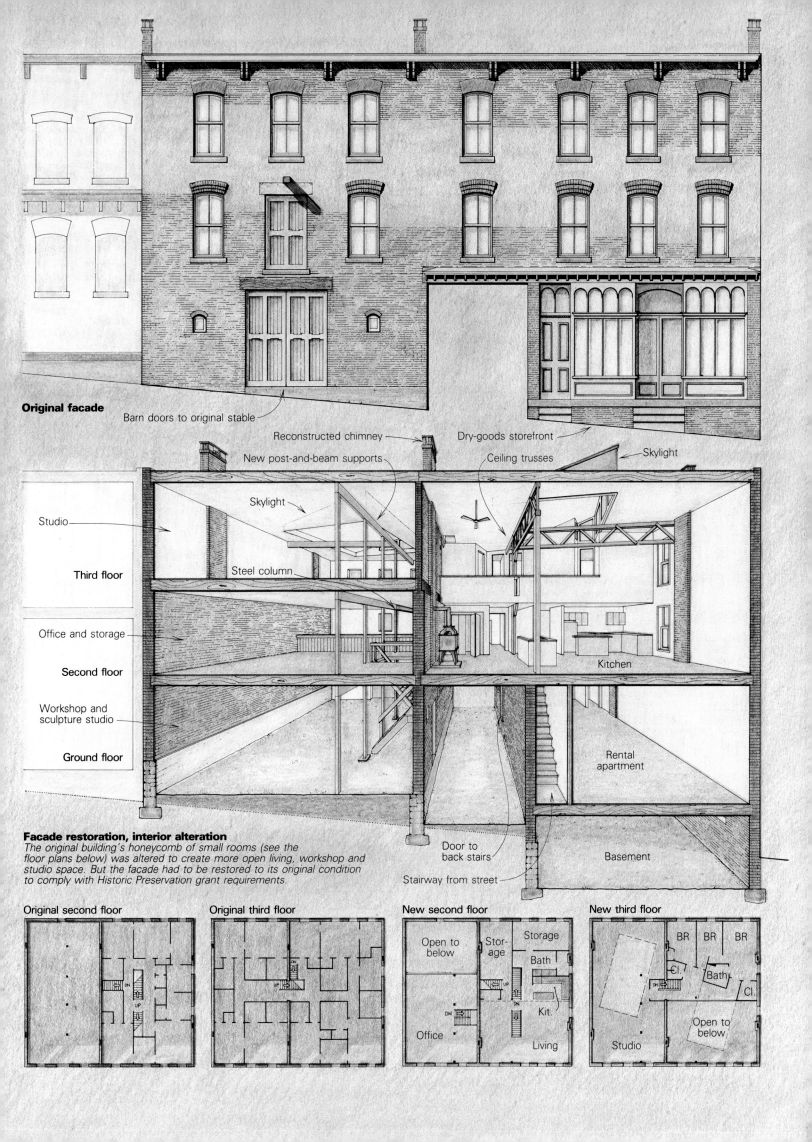

Original facade

Barn doors to original stable

Reconstructed chimney

Dry-goods storefront

New post-and-beam supports

Ceiling trusses

Skylight

Studio

Skylight

Third floor

Steel column

Office and storage

Kitchen

Second floor

Workshop and
sculpture studio

Rental
apartment

Ground floor

Door to
back stairs

Basement

Stairway from street

Facade restoration, interior alteration
*The original building's honeycomb of small rooms (see the
floor plans below) was altered to create more open living, workshop and
studio space. But the facade had to be restored to its original condition
to comply with Historic Preservation grant requirements.*

Original second floor

Original third floor

New second floor

New third floor

Open to
below

Stor-
age

Storage

Bath

BR   BR   BR

Cl.

Bath

Kit.

Cl.

Office

Living

Studio

Open
to
below

Opening up. Breaking through the second-floor ceiling created the high, open room that serves as living, dining and kitchen space. Top left, trusses fabricated from 2x stock are bolted to a 5x12 post and support the roof joists. The supports visible through the opening in the brick wall will hold the roof joists above the painting studio, bottom left. Facing page: The sun and a woodstove provide ample heat for the upstairs apartment; ceiling fans move the air around. Bedrooms and a master bathroom are beyond the balcony on the third floor.

floor sections and garbage from inside and outside the building. When the crew was done, we were left with a fragile brick box open to the sky. In short, not much.

What had really caused most of the damage to the building was that the drains through the rear parapet had been allowed to clog with leaves. The resulting pond on the low-pitched roof eventually led to leaks and rotting roof timbers.

All exterior walls were built three bricks, or 12 in., thick, but over the years water and freeze-thaw cycling had taken their toll on the old mortar. Large sections of the rear brick wall had to be rebuilt before any other renovation work could be done. The masons removed a huge, V-shaped section of badly buckling brick over the rear end of the passageway and then rebuilt it with salvaged brick and 8-in. cement block. The block wall took the place of the two inner brick layers, and a face course of brick was laid up outside it, with face ties mortared into block joints for added strength. Using the 8-in. wide block behind a face course of salvaged brick made the best use of our limited brick supply, and also meant faster work for the masons.

Inside the house, the block and all exterior walls were later covered by insulation board, furring and drywall. The southeast corner of the building and two other wall sections were also rebuilt with brick, as was the top 18 in. of the building on two sides and back. We also replaced the sill under the storefront and steps with new pieces of bluestone, a locally quarried, slate-like rock.

To keep the long walls from bowing in the future, we installed a ¾-in. thick tension rod across the entire width of the building. It penetrates the walls, and big, circular ¼-in. thick plates act as washers beneath giant nuts outside the building.

Near the bottom of the exterior walls, especially in the passageway, bricks had over the years been pried loose and carted off. Such scavenging had left the innermost brick layer intact, however, so we had only to reconstruct the two outer layers.

The building's six chimneys had been built only a single layer thick by simply leaving out the center bricks in the 12-in. thick walls. We dismantled them and constructed new chimneys around 8-in. ceramic flue liners.

Structural carpentry—Shoring up the floors and what remained of the roof was our next project. We started in the basement, jacking up sagging joists, then slipping in lintels and

Construction photo: Robert Hare

posts and nailing them fast as permanent supports. On the top floor, no jacking was necessary because only about a quarter of the roof joists remained.

On the south side of the building, where our apartment would be, we had removed the second and third-floor bearing walls that supported the roof. To span the opening and support the roof, the architect designed a pair of trusses that I built from 2x lumber. Using a crane that I had designed for moving sculpture, we managed to snake the trusses in through a window and onto the second floor. From there we erected scaffolding to lift the first truss at its center, using come-alongs.

I had to perch 30 ft. up in the air to set the street-side end of the truss into the pocket the mason had built into the exterior wall. The truss needed a push to set it home. The men on the inside end pushed, and the wall moved as the truss nudged its pocket. An image of the truss, the wall, the ladder and me in a pile on the sidewalk flashed through my mind. But the wall held, the truss was mortared and bolted in place, and it hasn't moved since. We bolted its other end to a 5x12 post that carried to a brick wall below the second floor. We used this installed truss and a scaffold to lift the second truss into place.

Once the trusses were up, we reframed the roof with 2x10s, nailed down a deck of rough 1x lumber, and built the two skylight sheds. They face due south and hold insulated vertical glass. Since the skylights wouldn't be visible from the street, we were able to get them approved by Historic Preservation officials. The building isn't oriented exactly along a north-south axis, so the solar monitors, as I call them, are angled, rather than square with the roof joists. This angle lets the sun fall on the two-story high brick wall between our apartment and our studios, so we can store some passively gained heat.

Finishing up—Most of the building's windows were either missing or beyond repair, so we had a local millwork shop make Thermo-

pane replacements. Our grant called for replicas of the original windows, so we couldn't use standard double-hung units. Fortunately, all 26 of the curved-top sash that we needed were the same size, so their per-unit cost worked out to be less than we would have paid for factory-made casement windows of similar size.

Restoring the building's facade also had to be done according to Historic Preservation standards. This meant repointing the brick with old-fashioned lime mortar and returning the front of the dry-goods store to its original condition. In spite of its shoddy look when we bought the building, most of the wood in the storefront turned out to be sound. A new panel below the display window, new paint and new glass were all that we needed.

The rest of our renovation proceeded with few snags. Extremely cold weather brought everything to a standstill for a week in January, but throughout the rest of the winter the carpenters, plumber, electrician, drywall taper, painters and floor-sander shivered and worked with me on what sometimes seemed an impossible project.

I couldn't act as the legal general contractor because of funding-related regulations. So we hired Core Builders as general contractors, and they hired me as job supervisor and finish carpenter. My working every day with the crew proved to be a great advantage. Because I was always on the site, I was able to deal with design problems as they arose. As a result, we never had to pay for new work to be ripped out and rebuilt. Although it is often difficult for the general contractor to have the owner on the job, this project worked out well for us all. We kept our costs down to $18 per sq. ft., the contractor made a profit, and we all parted friends.

Given all of the changes we made for $18 a sq. ft., some of the corners we cut really made a difference. I wrote the specs to building-code minimums but still managed to satisfy the Historic Preservation people. The finish schedule for the interior included only a primer coat, and we used salvaged plumbing fixtures because old ones were not only cheaper but to our eyes better designed. We bought kitchen cabinets without doors (a 50% savings), which I made and installed later. A close friend and metal monger gave us all the structural steel—a two-story steel column and a 20-ft. I-beam—which we used in the old stable to help support Lorraine's studio. The 45 commercial green enamel reflectors we used as light fixtures were salvaged from the dry-goods store—the last tenant had been an electrical contractor. This cut the cost of our electrical fixtures by two-thirds.

I'd often work all day on the building and come home to refinish woodwork and rewire lights with Lorraine at night. Working long

hours does take its toll, and I eventually reached a point where I was so tired that I let some details slide to get the job done sooner. When the roof was being rebuilt, I was three floors below working on the old storefront. So I didn't find out until it was too late that the flashing was being tarred together, rather than soldered, as I had called for in my specs. The roofer insisted that the tar would hold, and I didn't have the energy to stop the job. So now the roof sometimes leaks around one of the chimneys, and we're still hassling with the roofers over this.

The hardwood floor in our apartment was another problem. I wanted to lay the new floor directly on the old one, but the original floor was in such poor condition that we couldn't lay the new wood perpendicular to the old as is usual. The contractor suggested putting down a ⅜-in. plywood subfloor, but I thought that laying the boards diagonally across the old floor would give the required strength and stability. We couldn't do either within our budget, so we laid the new floor parallel to the old, and it isn't as smooth and tight as it should be.

Shrinkage of the framing lumber wasn't something we had anticipated either, but because the building was so damp when the renovation began, many of the old joists have shrunk at least ¼ in. We've actually heard the building creak from time to time, and there are some fissures in the drywall and spaces under a few baseboards. These flaws haven't affected the structural integrity, though, and we'll cover the gaps when we do the final painting and finish work.

Most of our visitors are so surprised by the light and space of our living room that they overlook the details. We've lived in this building for more than three years now, and we're still delighted every time we walk up the stairs and see those double rows of arched windows. The big room is easy to heat with our woodstove and the sun. I've rigged up a four-layered insulating blanket for the solar monitor, which keeps the building warmer on winter nights and cooler on summer days. Ceiling fans are used to push warm air down to the floor. The brick mass and the new insulation in the walls also help to moderate the temperature. The bedrooms get excess heat from the big room via the balcony. Although we have a gas hot-air backup system, it is seldom used.

The studios are wonderful and efficient workspaces. At first all that uneven direct light was a problem for Lorraine, but eventually we built a large rolling easel, which she can move around the studio to get the best lighting situation at the moment.

We've still got a certain amount of work ahead of us: closet shelves, caulking, painting and sealing the brick wall. But we're not in a great hurry to do it. At the moment we're enjoying working and living in a large, beautiful, affordable space. □

Robert Hare works as a sculptor and cabinetmaker in Kingston, N. Y.

The kitchen has stock cabinets and a work island, and is tucked underneath the balcony that overlooks the living room. One of the roof's two skylights, with its adjustable insulated curtain, can be seen above the top floor.

Opening Up an Attic
A skylit stairway brings light and space
to an upstairs apartment

by Ira Kushner

From the outside, the 60-year-old house I worked on last year in New Haven, Conn., looks like most of the other wood-frame houses on the block (photo above left). But inside, the space has been completely re-organized, and what was once a dark, dirty attic (photo above right) is now a master-bedroom suite with bathroom, den and a sky-lit stair leading up to it from the second floor.

The project began one day while I was sit-ting with a friend, talking houses. We decided it would be a good idea to take an old two-story house and convert it into two apart-ments (the second-floor apartment would have its master-bedroom suite in the attic). As it turned out, about a month later a couple that I knew found just such a place, and we started to talk. Sam and Sue were interested in a duplex conversion, and Sam wanted to help out with the project on weekends and after work. We agreed that in return for acting as the general contractor and handling much of the carpentry work myself, I would get the downstairs apartment at a reduced rent.

The whole house required renovation, but working on the upstairs apartment was the most challenging part. We determined right away that we could indeed convert the unused attic into a bedroom. Though in shabby shape, the attic was structurally sound, and the idea of a having master-bedroom suite un-der the eaves was attractive. The major prob-lems would be overcoming the cramped feel-ing of the space and connecting both levels with a new stairway. There was already a staircase up to the attic at the back of the house, but it was narrow and rickety—fine for an occasional trip, but not very convenient for everyday use.

I saw the need for an open, all-wood stair-case to the attic, and for an operable skylight for proper ventilation. The owners wanted a master bedroom big enough for a queen-size bed and a large closet, a bathroom with bare essentials (a vanity, toilet and shower) and a den that could also serve as a guest room. And they wanted all this on the attic level.

With their approval, I began to draw plans. At first, I wanted to cut out part of the second-floor ceiling to create a 10-ft. by 7-ft. open space between the two floors. After talking with the city building inspector, I changed my

mind. Cutting through all these joists, he ex-plained, would require heading them off with a composite beam of two or three 2x10s and carrying the load down to the basement with 4x4 posts. This would mean more work and money than we could afford. I decided to open up the space anyway, but to leave the original joists exposed and intact. Fortunately they were in good shape and relatively free of twists and splits.

Gutting the interior—Since the house had never been insulated and the old walls were in poor condition, I knew that the plaster and lath would have to be removed from all exteri-or walls to expose the cavities between studs. Demolition began. I had planned to leave the plaster ceilings as they were, and with this in mind, I cut through the plaster on the second-

A workable shell. This 60-year-old, two-story house in downtown New Haven had a sound exterior (top left), but inside, a thorough reno-vation was needed. Top right, the attic with corbeled chimney in its original state, before it was converted to a master-bedroom suite.

floor ceiling to make the opening for the balcony and the stairway. I'm sure that all contractors must make this mistake at some point—thinking that to save time and money you leave the old plaster intact wherever possible. Eventually I removed about 95% of the plaster and lath, stripping ceilings and walls down to the joists and studs. This was messy, demoralizing work, but getting it done and cleaning up the building at an early stage turned out to be the best way to proceed. The drywall crew had an easy time of it because they didn't have to fiddle around trying to match gypboard to plaster.

Exposing the framing had other benefits too. I discovered that the house had been balloon-framed, a construction method that has been almost entirely replaced by platform-framing each story. All the exterior wall studs were as long as the building was high, extending from the sill atop the foundation to the top

plate in the attic. Two-by-six floor joists were supported by ribbon boards let into the studs on both sides of the house.

Structurally, the house wasn't as strong as it should have been. In some places, all that supported the 2x6 floor joists across the building's 22-ft. width was a flimsy 2x3 interior bearing wall. You could see the ceiling sag whenever someone walked on the floor above. We solved this problem by doubling up most of the joists, and by replacing the 2x3 wall with three 2x10s spiked together. This we supported with 4x4 posts, which rest on footings in the basement. To satisfy the building code, we had to add blocking between the studs in the exterior wall at each floor level. The blocks serve as firestops and also strengthen the balloon frame.

The structural support for the opening between the second floor and the attic was provided by leaving most of the original floor

joists intact (photo below left). Three joists had to be cut to create headroom for the new staircase. The resulting open corner is supported with a 4x4 post.

In the attic, the exposed rafters, which were set on 2-ft. centers, were in good condition. The collar ties, which had been nailed to every other rafter, were for the most part warped and split. Since the ties would be exposed in the finished space, I replaced them all with new 1x8s.

The tongue-and-groove fir floorboards in the attic were sound, but I couldn't see refinishing the floor. There were shrinkage gaps between most of the boards, and there was enough dirt lodged in the wood to make sanding a disagreeable and unhealthy job in that cramped space. So we nailed down ½-in. particleboard, which later got covered by carpeting in the living space and sheet vinyl in the bathroom.

From attic to living space. The plan, below right, called for new stairs and an opening between floors, with a skylight above. Bottom left, the original ceiling joists span the 10-ft. by 7-ft. opening. The 4x4 post supporting the ceiling will also carry one corner of the stair landing, designed as a torsion box (drawing, below left). Part of the skylight's rough framing is seen above the worker's head. Bottom right, the master bedroom has been framed and sheetrocked. Low space along the sides is for storage. New collar ties were left exposed to gain headroom.

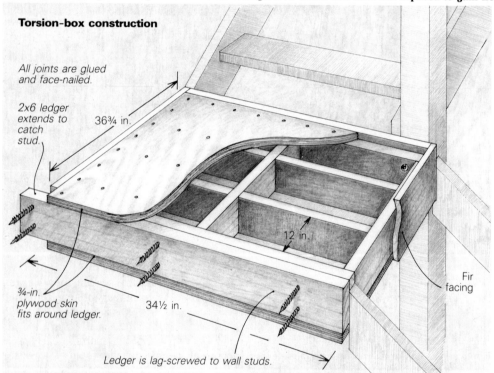

Torsion-box construction

All joints are glued and face-nailed.

2x6 ledger extends to catch stud.

36¾ in.

12 in.

¾-in. plywood skin fits around ledger.

34½ in.

Fir facing

Ledger is lag-screwed to wall studs.

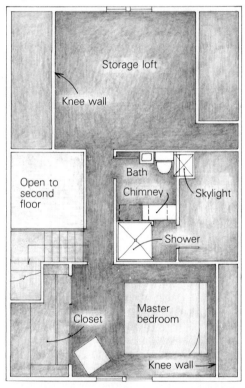

Storage loft

Knee wall

Open to second floor

Bath

Chimney

Skylight

Shower

Closet

Master bedroom

Knee wall

The converted attic and the main floor of this renovated upstairs apartment share the open space between levels. The skylight is in the roof above the opening. The custom-made staircase rests on a torsion-box landing that doesn't require support at each corner, enhancing the open plan.

New work—I had trouble fitting everything into the attic bathroom. Originally I had planned to install the shower under the sloping chimney, but this would have pushed the bathroom wall out into the hallway. Thus the shower had to go on one side of the chimney, with the toilet and sink on the other. I installed a small (21-in. by 28-in.) operable skylight in the roof to act as a vent.

Because the areas where the attic ceiling meets the floor weren't very usable for living space, I framed up knee walls along both sides of the attic to create closet and storage space. I called in the plumber and electrician, and their work was fairly straightforward. The only major problem arose when the plumber wanted to cut 2-in. holes in several 2x6 joists. This was not a problem for the plumber, but it was definitely a problem for the joists, which were at the limit of their span. I had him re-route the pipe run slightly and designed a soffit in the kitchen ceiling to hide the pipe.

When all the framing in the attic was done, we stapled 5½-in. thick batt insulation between the rafters, then nailed 1-in. thick rigid foam board over them, for a total value of R-19. Once the exterior walls had been insulated with 3½ in. of fiberglass, the drywall crew came in. They got all the rock up on the second floor and attic in one weekend; by the end of the next week all the taping was done.

To save time and money, we had decided to use No. 2 pine 1x4s for baseboards and all window and door trim. The results were good. Mitering corners with this straight stock was a breeze, and the clean, simple lines added to the informality of the open plan. We were able to re-use most of the original interior doors, but the front and rear entry doors had to be replaced with solid-core doors to meet building-code requirements.

The skylight—Finally it was time to tackle a part of the project I feared. I'm not fond of heights, so I was a bit concerned about climbing a 30-ft. ladder to do the rooftop skylight installation. But after giving the installation instructions a thorough read, I discovered that I could do nearly the entire job from inside the house. Good news. As it turned out, the entire process, from cutting through the roof to installing the step flashing, took less than four hours.

Stair and landing—Installing the staircase was another job I was apprehensive about. Custom-made at a local stair shop, the stairway was delivered in two sections. I was to build the landing that would connect the two units and then assemble these three separate parts in place. I discussed the problem with Charles Jones, a carpenter friend, and we agreed that it would be a good idea to construct a torsion box for the landing. The in-

herent strength of this type of construction made it possible to leave one corner of the platform unsupported (photo above).

To make the torsion box, I first built a 34½-in. by 36¾-in. frame of 2x6s, with a center stringer and blocking every 12 in. (drawing, facing page). I used plastic-resin glue in all the joints and face-nailed them with 16d nails. I covered the top and bottom of this grid with a skin of ¾-in. plywood, using glue and 1⅝-in. drywall screws. The plywood overhangs the frame by 1½ in. on the wall side of the platform; these 1½-in. lips fit on the top and bottom of the wall-mounted 2x6 ledger, which is lag-screwed into the studs. The only other support for the box is the 4x4 post that holds up a corner of the opening between floors. After fastening the box to the post and the ledger, I test-fitted the two stair sections to the platform. Happily, I got a tight fit, so all I had to do was counterbore the stringers top and bottom and fill the holes with dowel plugs. I covered the two exposed sides of the box with fir boards for appearance, then applied several coats of polyurethane.

The skylit opening between floors, with its custom-built stairway, is the focal point of the apartment. The light and openness gained on both levels have transformed what would have been a drab, cramped space. ☐

Ira Kushner lives in New Haven, Conn.

Rescuing an Old Adobe

How an architect reclaimed a duplex by drying out the site and stabilizing the foundation

by Paul G. McHenry, Jr.

Repairing and remodeling an old adobe just north of downtown Albuquerque proved to be one of my most extensive and challenging jobs. Originally an outbuilding of the Madison Dairy, the structure was used as a milk barn from around 1915 to the early 1930s, when it was converted to a duplex. Poor soil conditions and an inadequate foundation caused serious settling problems. Over the years, its walls and floors had been subjected to stop-gap repairs, none very satisfactory.

By 1976, when the current owner first contacted me, repairs were sorely needed. A retiring deputy director of the Peace Corps, she wanted to convert the duplex into a more spacious house with a guest wing that could also be used as a rental apartment. This remodeling, however, could be dealt with only after the building's structural problems had been solved. The severe settling of walls and floors had broken plumbing lines, caused cracks you could see through, and made windows and doors difficult or impossible to open.

The existing duplex units were small, and included only the bare essentials. To make each unit a comfortable dwelling, we had to

make substantial additions (see the floor plan on p. 136). To the west unit we added a master bedroom, a bath and a kitchen; the old bedroom became a study. To the east unit, which was the larger to begin with, we added only a bathroom and a pantry. On the south of the duplex we built a pair of large spaces that would be common area for both apartments. One would be an enclosed garden or peristyle, open to the sky above and tucked in between the two kitchens. The other common space would be a great room, which would connect with both kitchens and enclose the garden on the south side.

I was disturbed by the possibility that the two common spaces would compromise the privacy of each unit. I've always viewed communal spaces with great suspicion, because I've found that most people like to define their own domains very distinctly. To guard against this, and in anticipation of the time when the owner would rent the other unit, I sized the entries to the great room to accept standard doors. With the doors in place, the spaces could be allocated to either side.

The garden presented its own problem. In

the desert Southwest, spaces of this size and shape can get unpleasantly hot in the summer and cold in the winter. So we planned for a future solar greenhouse roof when the circumstances and the budget permitted.

The garden was finished and landscaped, but unfortunately our predictions of excess heat and cold turned out to be correct. A year later, we built a slightly pitched built-up roof over the garden using a solid covering on the north side and a plastic greenhouse roof on the south slope. This was a definite improvement, but the garden was still too hot in the summer. Two years later, we solved the problem by redesigning and rebuilding the roof, this time providing only clerestory windows to the south.

Fixing the foundation—The first order of business was to determine the precise condition of the foundation and wall structure. We did some exploratory excavation, and discovered that the building had been built on a 6-ft. to 8-ft. thick layer of heavy clay, almost of pottery grade. The clay beneath the house had been kept damp by poor drainage and leaky

plumbing, and you could liken the situation to floating a building on a bowl of gelatin.

Our diggings further revealed that others before us had tried to rescue the sinking foundation. One unsuccessful remedy had been to pour a concrete apron against the foundations in certain areas. But the aprons had served only to trap the water that was leaking from the plumbing lines, making the settlement problem even worse.

The original foundation was only as wide as the wall. It was soft and crumbly in places, giving credence to the possibility that the footings were made with lime concrete rather than with portland cement. Lime concrete—probably a money-saving move on the part of the builders—was used early in this century.

We decided to replace the plumbing system entirely—an approach that had been tried before, judging by the jungle gym of abandoned and rusted pipes we found below grade. There was even a waste line that had tilted in the wrong direction and wouldn't drain.

We decided first to dry out the site by installing gravel drains that led from the foundation into two new dry wells. First we removed the concrete aprons. We dug the wells about 8 ft. deep through the clay bed and into a permeable layer of gravel and sand, then filled each well with river gravel and sand. The drains would carry off rainfall concentrations, and the time required for construction, during which the plumbing wouldn't be used, helped dry out the site. By the time we finished the renovation, the drains and dry wells had effectively carried away much of the excess moisture that had accumulated around the foundation over the years.

Next, we undercut those parts of the footings that were badly cracked. At these junctures we poured deeper, wider footings to give adequate support to the walls above, and to resist further sinking. In the location that had settled the worst (it had sunk almost a foot), we found four concrete floor slabs, one poured on top of the other. In one case the would-be remodelers had poured a new slab atop the old one without even bothering to remove the linoleum.

Repairing the walls and windows—The 10-in. thick adobe walls were basically sound in spite of the settlement problem, and contained unexplained wood members, both horizontal and vertical. Perhaps they were put

Originally built as a dairy barn and then converted in the 1930s to a duplex, this old adobe structure (facing page) was remodeled by the author and made into a residence and rental unit. The house sat on a bed of clay that was kept wet by leaky plumbing and poor drainage. The foundation sank year by year into the ooze. While doing exploratory excavations, the crew found a concrete buttress poured against the footings (above right), apparently some other builder's attempt to arrest the sinking. After repairing the plumbing and installing new drains to dry out the site, McHenry's crew dug under portions of the old foundation wall, formed and poured new footings (right). These remedies have prevented further settling.

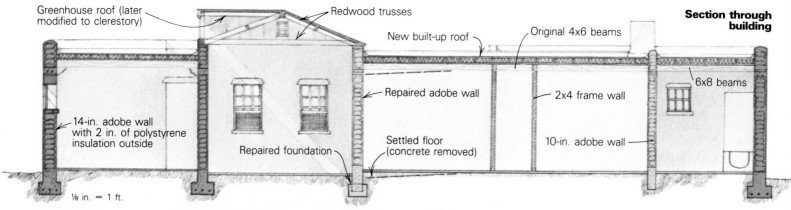

Greenhouse roof (later
modified to clerestory)

Redwood trusses

**Section through
building**

New built-up roof

Original 4x6 beams

6x8 beams

Repaired adobe wall

2x4 frame wall

14-in. adobe wall
with 2 in. of polystyrene
insulation outside

Repaired foundation

Settled floor
(concrete removed)

10-in. adobe wall

⅛ in. = 1 ft.

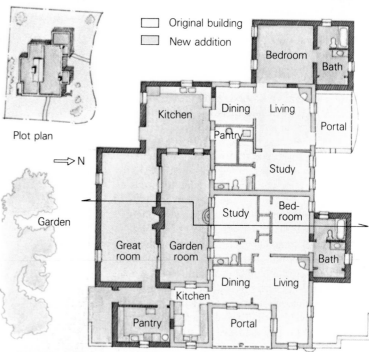

Original building

New addition

Plot plan

⇨ N

Garden

Bedroom

Bath

Kitchen

Dining

Living

Portal

Pantry

Study

Study

Bed-
room

Great
room

Garden
room

Bath

Dining

Living

Kitchen

Pantry

Portal

there as repairs for settling walls. This is not a standard practice, and never was. The settlement in one area had caused cracks through the repeated layers of stucco. Subsequent erosion and crushing of the adobes meant that some portions of these walls had to be torn out and rebuilt.

Adobe walls are rumored to provide great insulation. This isn't true, but their thermal mass does yield a good comfort factor, moderating the wide daily temperature fluctuations in the Southwest. The 10-in. thick walls (a standard adobe brick size for many years) has a steady-state R-value of about 3.5, whereas a 2x4 frame wall, insulated with rock wool, has an R-value of about 12—but without much thermal mass. To insulate the adobe walls, we decided to spray 2 in. of polyurethane foam directly onto the outside of the exterior walls after removing the old stucco. This spray-on insulation, when of the proper density, can be parged over with stucco in the usual way.

Most interior walls were wood frame, with lath and plaster on each side. Like the floors, some walls had settled badly. Moisture had rotted the lower parts of these walls and attracted termites. So out they came. We had to shore up the roof temporarily while some of the bearing walls were torn out and rebuilt.

The interior plaster was badly cracked from settling and then further disturbed by our alterations to doors, windows and mechanical-electrical systems. Patching plaster cracks is difficult because the patches are hard to hide on smooth surfaces. You have to remove all the loose material, but this always seems to loosen more, and the process goes on and on.

We were tempted to rip down all of the interior plaster right down to the adobe brick walls, and on some walls we did. But our old-time plasterer figured out a way to save much of the old plaster. He nailed poultry netting to all surfaces and applied two coats of gypsum plaster, which provided a good sound surface. The first coat strengthened and filled the surface, and a second thin coat provided a smooth surface that matched the original plaster treatment. With this work complete, we painted all the interior walls an off-white.

The roof was supported by exposed 4x6 pine beams. The 1-in. wood deck above this was covered with several generations of 90-lb. mineral felt roofing, built-up roofing and gravel, which we had to strip off and replace. The insulation value of all this was virtually nil. While the roof beams were well below current standards for their spans, deflection was minimal, and from all appearances, they were supporting their load quite adequately. But they were covered with multiple layers of paint, stain and varnish and well sprinkled with nail

The clerestory windows above the garden room (photos facing page) were added after the owner found that the open garden got too hot in the summer and too cold in the winter. The clerestories moderate solar gain and heat loss, and make the garden room comfortable year round. The top left photo shows the interior of the garden room, and the amount of sunlight admitted at noon in mid-March.

holes and scars, perhaps from some previous use, which made them unsightly. They couldn't be cleaned by normal methods, so we resorted to sandblasting to strip all the coatings back to the natural wood. While sandblasting is generally a no-no in restoration work, it was an appropriate procedure here because it emphasized the wood grain (by gouging out the softer early wood and making ridges of the denser late wood).

The windows were, and always had been, a disaster. They were ordinary, multi-lite barn sash, hinged casement fashion to a simple wood box frame, which was flush with the wall on both sides. The sash swung inward, and screen wire was tacked to the exterior of the box frame with screen mold and brads. This simple solution, arrived at by some well-meaning handyman in times past, had serious drawbacks. The head on the exterior had no provision for a drip edge, and rainwater followed the head piece into the interior. No drainage slope or even stops were designed into the sill, so water ran off from the wall above, collected at the sill, where it had warped the wood, and flowed inside.

I decided at the outset to replace all the windows because they just couldn't be fixed. The existing openings called for non-standard size units. Fortunately, all of these could be the same size, so the quantity would put the cost of a special order within the bounds of our budget. To unify the new additions with the old house, we used the odd-size sash throughout. The only exception was in the garden room, where damaged sections of the wall had to be removed and larger windows could be installed to supply needed light.

The original box frames of the windows were, for the most part, solid, so I decided to remove only the sills. These I replaced with stained redwood sills on the exterior, slanted clear of the wall for drainage, and brick stools on the interior. The 2½-in. brick stools turned out to be an attractive and durable surface for house plants and other things. The new windows were bronze-colored anodized aluminum double-hung sash, mounted to the exterior surface of the existing frame. They were double glazed, and their location, with the new sills, corrected the drainage problems.

Heating and electrical—The existing heating system consisted of two gas-fired wall heaters, which were inadequate. The Albuquerque climate, along with the thermal lag of the adobe walls, makes a quick-response heating system most desirable. Central forced air will do this best, if placing the ductwork for return and supply isn't a problem. In this case, it was a problem because of the concrete floors, which were to be left intact. There wasn't any room for return-air ducts in the ceiling either. Finally, we settled on a hot-water radiant baseboard system. This would heat each space, and wouldn't require removing a lot of concrete floor for the installation.

The building's electrical system was a dreadful tangle of antique wiring, and most of its insulation had died of old age. In many restora-

tions it is possible to use portions of the original wiring, but in this case it made more sense to abandon it all, and rewire to modern standards. New wiring in an adobe house can be quite simple. We buried new plastic-sheathed cable (rated for direct burial) in grooves easily cut in the adobe walls with a claw hammer. A covering of plaster conceals the runs and makes things fireproof.

A new floor—The existing concrete floor was adequate, and our original plan was to make use of it. The small number of cuts required to accommodate the new heating piping and the plumbing systems would be covered with carpeting or sheet vinyl. At midpoint in the construction, however, the owner decided that she wanted brick floors instead of concrete. This meant we had to jackhammer out all of the old slabs, and place a bed of sand as a base for the brickwork.

Brick floors (fired brick, not adobe) are a good choice for adobe homes. Despite FHA requirements that brick floors be laid on a concrete slab at least 2 in. thick, my experience shows that they can be laid down economically on a sand bed over a vapor barrier without losing any firmness or stability. The bricks are laid tightly against one another without mortar. The resulting surface is smooth and level.

We removed minor burrs at the edges and corners of these wire-cut bricks by either rubbing the surface with another brick in a sanding motion, or with a rotary floor sander. Sanding mellows out the surface texture and helps fill any voids. But too much sanding will abrade through the fire-hardened skin of the brick and expose the soft inner core of clay. We finished the floors with several coats of an oil-base varnish, the first one thinned with mineral spirits to ensure good penetration into the surface of the brick. This sealing process protects the floors from spills and leaves a surface that's fairly easy to clean.

As with all restoration-reconstruction projects, the question arises at the end, was it really worth it, or would it have been better to clear the site and start fresh? The endless hassles with original features gave rise to hundreds of on-the-spot decisions that turned out to be mostly right. The final effect was that the new additions blended perfectly with the old, and the house retains an ambience that would otherwise have been lost.

Five years after the job was completed, the owner quit watering the flower garden outside the great room. The clay below the soil dried out, and despite the massive footings and all our precautions, the south wall settled. Awful cracks appeared in the walls and ceiling. We installed crack monitors across the crack (they can measure as little as 1 mm of movement), and dug two French drains in the neglected garden. After a few weeks the walls stopped settling, and we patched the cracks in the plaster. Things have been fine since then. □

Paul McHenry is a builder and architect in Albuquerque, N. Mex. Photos by the author.

Illustrations: Victor Lazzaro

When we first noticed the Isham house on one of our frequent drives through the east side of Providence, R.I., it held no appeal for us. The windows were boarded up, fire or smoke damage was evident on all three floors, and the front door and most of the window sashes had been nearly demolished by firemen in an effort to gain entry and vent smoke during the blaze. Still, buying such an ugly duckling would give us a workable shell at minimum cost; careful design, restoration and remodeling would produce an attractive home that could be resold at a substantial profit. With this in mind, we contacted the owner and arranged to get a closer look.

Entering a fire-damaged building is a

Photo: Louis S. DiGaetano

gloomy experience. It is advisable to come prepared with a powerful flashlight, gloves, good boots, and a jackknife for digging into beams to assess the depth of the damage. You have to watch your step since the fire may have weakened the floor. That wasn't the case here, though. The basement was untouched, and the floor on the first level still sound.

The blaze had probably started in the kitchen, by far the most severely damaged part of the house. Flames had licked out the kitchen windows at the back (south side) of the house and climbed all the way up to the roof, leaving a trail of charred shingles. Fortunately, the roof itself had escaped damage. Inside the house, the kitchen,

Rebuilding a Fire-Damaged House
Restoration and innovation produce a modern, livable house rich in historical detail

by Louis S. DiGaetano and Kathleen Haugh

The restored stairway and entry contrast dramatically with the fire-damaged area shown at the top of the page. The arched doorway leads to the kitchen.

dining room, rear hall and front entrance foyer had been burned. The fire had stripped away plaster on some ceiling and wall areas, especially in the kitchen and the dining room, exposing the framework. This was the only evidence of possible structural damage. We noticed some burned areas in the two rear bedrooms and the bath on the second floor, but the rest of the house—including the entire third floor—had received only smoke and heat damage. Soot blackened the walls, and the heat had curled and cracked both paint and wallpaper.

We visited the house twice. Looking it over the second time we tried to ignore the fire damage and determine the positive characteristics of the building. Under all the soot there appeared to be a richly detailed entrance hall, highlighted by a large fireplace, an unusually placed bay window, and diamond window lights over the bay window and the front door. The spindles and railing on the main staircase to the second floor were completely intact, and a clerestory stained glass window between flights had miraculously escaped destruction. The second floor had a workable layout of four bedrooms and one bath. The three rooms on the top floor were appealing mainly because of the penetrating gable slopes in the ceiling.

We found the neighborhood an additional plus: Nearby houses were neat and well-cared for, a fact that would increase the resale value of our renovation work. After buying the house, we were surprised and encouraged by its historical significance. A bit of research at the Rhode Island Historical Library and some help from the Providence Preservation Society revealed that this house had been designed by Norman Isham, a renowned regional architect and scholar. We eventually found a complete set of original drawings (the first-floor plan is reproduced at right), confirming that the house had been built in 1900 for one Abbie B. Slader and her servants. Certain details in the design of the house led us to believe that she must have been an older woman—perhaps a widow. The position of the fireplace and oddly angled window bays at the front of the house on both first and second floors gave her a complete view of the street from her hearthside seat. The more formal rooms (for receiving and entertaining guests) were at the front of the house, as was customary in those days, with kitchen, back stair, and third floor areas being left to the servants. Isham's attention to detail, especially in the parts of the house to be viewed by the public, was excellent. With our vision improved by this historical background, we noticed additional ornate casework both inside and outside the house. There were even pendants at the gable ridges, which turned out to be the remains of finials that had been sawn off at the roofline.

Convinced that there was a well-built, richly detailed and historically significant house beneath the obvious mess we had seen, we decided to make the purchase and get to work.

The new design—While acknowledging the importance of architectural restoration, we feel that contemporary lifestyles require new spatial arrangements. After all, the requirements of a young family today are quite different from those of a widow and her servants over 80 years ago. Formal parlors and large dining rooms must give way to family rooms and all-purpose play areas for children. Our aim was to restore and preserve the historical details of the house, with particular attention to its more public areas, while redesigning the interior so that we'd have a marketable property once the job was done.

The kitchen, for example, had originally been strictly an area where servants worked. It had been remodeled at a later date without consideration for efficient work-flow. We needed to make it more versatile, and less isolated from the rest of the house. Our plan called for an open, arched window between kitchen and dining room, and a bay window that would open the view to the back yard. We also wanted to remove a partition so kitchen floor space would be more open and useful as an area for work, eating and children's play. Relocating the rear entrance would make room for a washer and drier.

Extra storage space and closets were needed throughout the house. Our revised plan for the first floor (drawing, right) included new closets in the front and rear entries, a pair of built-in cabinets in the dining room and completely new cabinetwork in the kitchen. On the second floor, we planned to connect two small adjoining bedrooms, creating a master bedroom with extra space for closets, a dressing room and a new bathroom. The two bedrooms and bathroom down the hall could be left as they were, except for framing in a common-wall doorway. Each had its own separate hallway entrance, and the added wall space would increase the existing closet area. Work on the third floor would mainly involve repairing the fire damage and improving the existing bathroom.

These designs for remodeling the interior would produce only a few exterior changes: a small octagonal window and a large bay window in the kitchen, a repositioned back door and a slightly altered window pattern. Otherwise the unaffected public facades were to be restored to what they were before the fire. This would be challenge enough, considering the extent of the damage.

Ripping out—Once the new design decisions were made, it was time to begin dismantling and ripping out the building. We decided to contend with interior repairs and remodeling before tackling the exterior work. Demolition is in the best of circumstances an unpleasant and dirty task, and it was made even worse by the sheer quantity of burned items.

As is true with any type of restoration work, we had to tread lightly. Even though they were badly burned in some cases, important details such as moldings, door and window casings and stair spindles had to be removed with great care. Otherwise the invaluable architectural elements that give the house its unique character would be lost. We've found in the past that moldings need not always be removed, even though the walls surrounding them will be stripped of plaster. Leaving them in place saves time and is probably the safest strategy, since the possibility

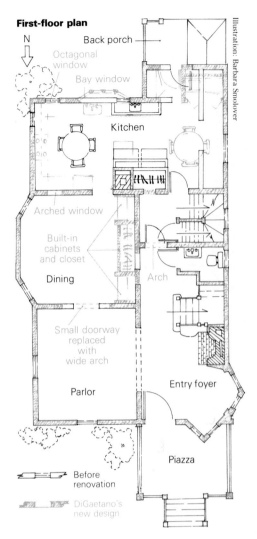

First-floor plan

N

Back porch

Octagonal window

Bay window

Kitchen

Arched window

Built-in cabinets and closet

Dining

Arch

Small doorway replaced with wide arch

Parlor

Entry foyer

Piazza

Before renovation

DiGaetano's new design

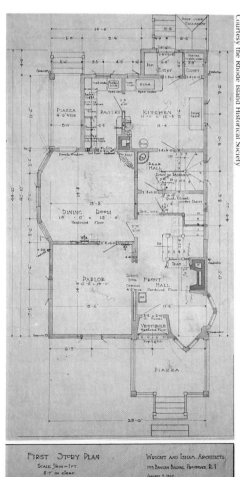

A narrow arched doorway, above, connects the kitchen to the back of the entry foyer. Whenever possible, original casing was left in place, but temporarily pried away from the wall to accommodate the new plaster. A plastering crew, hired to enclose both rebuilt and newly constructed walls, used special equipment, like the stilts shown at right, to speed the work.

of damage is greatest during removal. With the molding or casing left in place wherever possible, we pick out the plaster from behind it with an awl or screwdriver. When the wall is re-plastered, the molding can be pried away slightly until the job is done and then forced against the finished surface with new nails. If casework must be removed, we use a taped hacksaw blade to cut troublesome nails. The alternative—trying to pull frozen molding nails—usually causes the old wood to shatter or split.

After deciding which details could be left in place and which ones had to be removed, we were ready to strip the plaster. A sidewalk ice scraper, with its stiff, broad blade, is an excellent tool for removing plaster right down to the lath (photo, above left). At this time we also removed the wall sections that had to come out as part of the more open remodeling plan.

Cleaning out the inside of the house revealed the extent of the fire damage, especially at the back of the house on the first floor. To remove the char from the framing lumber, we sand-blasted, using the finest grade sand possible and a rented machine. We proceeded cautiously, since even fine sand under pressure can quickly reduce a floor joist to dust. To our surprise, the joists were made of oak, and even after sand-blasting they more than met their load requirements. To dispel any lingering odor of burnt wood or smoke, we sprayed all the joists with several coats of shellac sealer.

Removal of paint and wallpaper began immediately and lasted through the entire job. Heat from the fire had partially lifted the paint from surfaces all over the house, so a total strip job was required. We removed all the doors and delivered them to a stripping company. That

was the simple part. Painted woodwork was stripped in place; we used either chemicals or heat guns (but not in combination), relying on a wide variety of scraper blades and plenty of elbow grease to remove the softened finish. Fumes from old lead-based paints are dangerous, so whoever was doing the work had to wear a toxic fume mask.

The staircase presented a special problem. We realized it would be difficult and aggravating to strip the rounded spindles in place. Fortunately a close inspection revealed plugs on the underside of the handrails; removing them gave access to the bolts connecting the handrail to the newel post. We numbered all parts, disassembled the posts, rails and spindles, and sent the whole lot to be dipped clean. From past experience we knew that key numbers had to be scratched into the wood if they were to remain visible after stripping.

Removing the old wallpaper was tedious and time-consuming. Many of the upstairs rooms had three separate layers of paper, with several coats of paint thrown on for good measure. We scored the paper with a utility knife and used a rented steamer to loosen the materials as we removed it layer by layer, section by section. The plaster wall we finally exposed was typically rough—turn-of-the-century plasterers used horsehair as a binder in walls that would be papered. To clean the surface, we scrubbed all the walls with TSP (trisodium phosphate), using a stiff brush, and then applied a skimcoat of joint compound. Then we sanded the wall, applied a finish coat of joint compound, and sealed the surface with two coats of primer.

Our remodeling scheme for the top floors wasn't as extensive as for the first floor, so we

couldn't justify completely gutting these areas merely to repair smoke damage to walls and ceilings. Fortunately, there are companies that specialize in cleaning up smoke-damaged buildings, and we decided to subcontract the job to these experts. The process is extremely labor-intensive: Walls, ceilings and casework have to be scrubbed down, using special chemical cleaners. The results were acceptable; soot-blackened areas were rendered a dull grey. Once again, we sprayed several coats of shellac sealer over the affected areas to seal in the remaining discoloration and odor and provide an even base for the finish paint. As a final step to eliminate any trace of smoke smell, the subcontractors fumigated the house with deodorant.

Exterior repairs—Although the back of the house had sustained the greatest damage in the fire, repairs were necessary over the entire exterior surface. Our first task was to remove the damaged window sashes, take measurements and order new ones. We specified spring-type aluminum jambs as replacements for the existing weighted sashes. The new bay window for the kitchen was a stock unit, which we installed after cutting and reframing an opening in the back wall.

Although none of the structural framing had been damaged by the fire, the entire rear facade had to be reshingled. On the east and west sides of the house, we noticed that the flared second-story detail had suffered water damage over the years. We removed the damaged shingles to expose the wall sheathing in both these areas. Our advice to anyone else who undertakes such a job is to make a plan for coping with the resulting mess. We didn't anticipate the massive volume of scrap material that quickly accumulated as we tore off the old shingles.

We raised scaffolding so we could work on the siding, and this allowed us to inspect the vergeboard and corner brackets and finials at the roofline. All were damaged enough to warrant replacement; we removed this casework so it could be duplicated in the shop. We also confirmed that the finials at the gables had apparently been cut off, leaving only the pendant detail below. After we had studied an intact finial from another Isham house, we made new finials and installed them, using the same mortise-and-tenon joint at the ridgeboard that we found in the original construction. The corner brackets and vergeboards were likewise rebuilt and replaced.

Interior remodeling—Our plans for the inside of the house called for several important changes on the first floor. Before we gutted the damaged walls and framing, we noted an arched doorway connecting the entrance foyer to the dining room. Although we subsequently replaced this doorway with a much-needed closet, the arch provided a template that we incorporated in new doorways and openings. Using the arch motif in building larger doorways and openings between rooms allowed us to create the more open plan we desired, while still maintaining a style consistent with Isham's original design. With a string-and-pencil compass, we marked arcs corresponding to opening widths on ½-in. plywood sheets. The arches were then cut out in pairs with a saber saw, and 2x4 blocks were nailed between each pair of arches. The blocking provided a nailing surface for the covering layer of gypsum lath and attachment to the header and jack studs. In some cases we had to shim the gypsum lath out from the new framing so that the new wall would be flush with the existing wall sections. (The original framing lumber had been full dimension, while our new 2x4s measured only 1½ in. by 3½ in.) The old lath we had salvaged was good shim material; sometimes we cut plywood strips in various thicknesses to make up the space.

In addition to replacing the narrow doorways with wider open arches, we made several other changes to tailor the living space to modern family requirements. As mentioned earlier, we built a closet into the entry foyer (opposite the stairway) and added matching cabinets in the dining room. Using the fluted pilaster detail beneath the stairway as a model, we had similar pilasters milled to frame the dining-room cabinetwork. The result, shown in the photos below, successfully creates historically compatible detailing—a priority in this formal room.

Completely new cabinetwork was also required in the kitchen. We used ½-in. exterior plywood for sides and bases; clear pine for rails, stiles, door frames, and drawer fronts. We built the base cabinets right onto the kitchen wall, but upper cabinets were made as individual units and then screwed in position. Our design for the upper cabinets called for arches in the glass-paneled doors. This carryover of the arch motif makes the kitchen a more integral part of the house—one of our primary design goals. The

small octagonal window that we added in the kitchen's south wall was yet another way of giving more continuity to the first floor. We located the window directly opposite the arched opening in the kitchen/dining-room wall in order to accentuate the length of the house, tying the front to the rear.

On the second floor, work centered around the master bedroom suite. In building the new bathroom (adjacent to the existing bath), we removed all of the oak parquet floor to make room for bathroom tile. We used this old but sound flooring downstairs in the living room to replace a fire-damaged floor section. In general, re-using materials from other parts of the house is practical and time-saving in restoration work. We removed the basecap molding from the entire third floor and re-used it on the first floor. (The top floor wasn't the focal point of the restoration, and could have less costly stock molding.) Old casework from inside closets can also be transferred to the more public areas where it is needed. We weren't able to replace all the first-floor casework in this way, but our savings on custom millwork were considerable.

We enlarged the master bedroom by removing a partition, creating access to the adjacent room, and relocating closet space to the area next to the new bath. This became the dressing room. The reorganized space would provide the new owners with a private area separate from the children's rooms, yet close enough for comfort and convenience.

Plumbing and electrical service—The fire had probably been caused by an electrical malfunction, and an examination of the existing service revealed a tangle of old and new wiring. We

decided to rewire the entire house and update the existing service to 100 amps, both for safety and to provide adequate power for a contemporary home. During the remodeling process we worked closely with the electrician. Sometimes, tearing out and resurfacing a wall can prove less costly (in time and money) than having the electrician snake his wires.

Like many old houses, ours lacked general lighting. We built recessed incandescent fixtures into the kitchen and hallways, and recessed wall washers in the entry to highlight the fireplace. In other rooms we installed switched outlets to provide the convenience of switched lighting without unnecessary overhead fixtures.

The plumbing system, like the existing forced-air heating system, was reworked. All new water pipes and new soil pipes for the kitchen and second-floor baths were required. We also installed new ducts to bring heat to the redesigned parts of the second floor.

Plaster and finish work—The time had come to enclose all the new construction (and several first-floor wall sections we had to rebuild) with a finished wall surface. To achieve compatibility with the original interior finish, we decided to use the Imperial Gypsum Veneer System, subcontracting the job to a plastering crew (photo previous page). First they fit and screwed gypsum lath to the wood framing and covered all joints with fiberglass mesh tape or metal corner beads. Then a coat of Imperial plaster was applied—a very thin layer, followed the next day by the finish coat. The total plaster thickness ranges from $\frac{1}{16}$ in. to $\frac{3}{32}$ in., yielding an unusually hard (3,000 psi), smooth surface that can be successfully used to join new and old plaster sur-

An arched window in the kitchen/dining-room wall, above, links the remodeled kitchen with the rest of the house, breaking down the formal barriers inherent in the original design. The octagonal window, added for the same reason, extends the line of view through the kitchen and into the backyard. Another unifying feature is the fluted pilaster frame of the recessed dining-room cabinet, left, modeled on the original pilaster in the stairway (photo, p. 138). The front doorway, with its diamond light detail, can be glimpsed beyond the arched opening.

Photo: Douglas Hale

faces. Due to differences in rigidity and expansion characteristics, Imperial plaster can't be used as a skimcoat over old plaster. Instead, we used gypsum joint compound to improve these wall and ceiling surfaces. Careful supervision ensured proper fitting to casework left in place.

After plastering, we first replaced the salvaged casework. Restoring the original detail required a blending of old and new custom reproductions and stock moldings. By combining the various types and using a portable router, we were able to duplicate the original intent. We rebuilt the original front door, a victim of the fireman's ax. The brass hardware was repaired, polished and replaced. The stairway was rebuilt and the diamond lights above the entryway windows and doorway were rebuilt and reglazed. Finally we indulged ourselves by commissioning a stained glass window for the front door, incorporating the street number.

All the floors had to be sanded and refinished. The sanding required a light touch, since the coarse belt on the power sander could easily abrade through the oak parquet veneer (there were pine boards on the third floor). We chose Watco Floor Finish, applied by pouring the material on, spreading it over the bare wood with a brush or rag, and wiping off the excess. The finish can be reapplied at any time (varnish and polyurethane require sanding before reapplication). It penetrates into the pores of the wood and hardens into a tough, low-luster finish.

Painting—Before making any decisions about painting the exterior of the house, we talked with a color consultant from the Rhode Island Historical Society. Our objective was to create an authentic color scheme that would also be compatible with the building's current surroundings. After careful consideration and many tests, we settled on dark brown oil stain for the shingles (a prime coat on the new wood and two coats over the entire surface), a semi-gloss café au lait for the exterior trim and woodwork, and burgundy porch and deck enamel as an accent color for particular decorative elements (doors, window sashes and finials)—the results are shown in the photo at left.

Inside the house, we refrained from making a commitment on the color scheme until we had found a buyer. This isn't always possible, but we were fortunate in being able to resell at this stage. Early resale works positively for both parties, since we offer appliance and lighting allowances plus advice on painting. The new owners decided to use tile pavers as the finish floor surface in the kitchen and chose to install a restaurant range with a custom-made, stainless steel hood.

Selling the house just as we were finishing the job had another obvious benefit—a decisive conclusion that freed up funds for subsequent projects. The creative and financial rewards for six months of hard work were proof that restoration and contemporary design can go hand in hand. □

The restored front entry. The carved portico detail was stripped of paint, then primed and finish-coated with burgundy porch and deck enamel—the accent color used on doors, window sashes and finials. Trim and other woodwork was painted with semi-gloss café au lait (oil base), and dark brown oil stain was used on the shingles.

Louis DiGaetano and Kathleen Haugh, of Providence, R.I., are partners in an architectural design and construction business.

A Remodeled Bath

A better plan, a greenhouse window and some bold blue tile give a dingy bathroom a brand-new look

by Dennis Allen

My friend L. Dennis Thompson bought a small stucco house in one of Santa Barbara's older downtown neighborhoods. Dennis is an architect, and he immediately began to make lists of the remodeling jobs he wanted to do. They ranged from plumbing repairs to skylights, porches to second-story additions. But because he's working on a tight budget, the projects had to be assigned priorities, with some scheduled as more distant dreams.

Ironically, the job that got done first wasn't the highest on the list. He decided to tackle the bathroom right away because he was made an offer he couldn't refuse—free labor. I was teaching my annual tile-setting course at the local university extension program, and I was looking for a suitable site for hands-on in-struction. Dennis assured me he could have plans and materials ready in two months.

Superficially, the bathroom looked fine. It had been hastily upgraded to help sell the house. A huge mirror covered one wall, and thin wood paneling had been applied around the tub. But there were gaps between the strips of paneling—a lousy wall covering for a damp location. A cheap carpet covered the old vinyl floor, and the toilet occupied the most prominent spot in the cramped room. Beyond it stood an antique vanity. The room had only one small window, and Dennis wanted a lot more light. So the challenge was to turn an adequate bathroom into a light-filled space, and to give a group of student tile-setters a range of experiences.

Planning with constraints—To reduce costs, Dennis wanted to keep plumbing modifications to a minimum. His new plan kept the supply and drain lines in nearly the same place, but switched the location of the vanity and the toilet (drawing, below). This made the vanity the center of attention and tucked the toilet behind a low privacy wall.

The room needed more floor space, but there wasn't any easy way to claim it. The adjacent rooms didn't have any extra square footage to give up, and the setback limitations of the local building code wouldn't allow any footings beyond the existing foundation. The solution was a room-wide bay window with a wide shelf supported by knee braces. Since this bay is defined by the building department

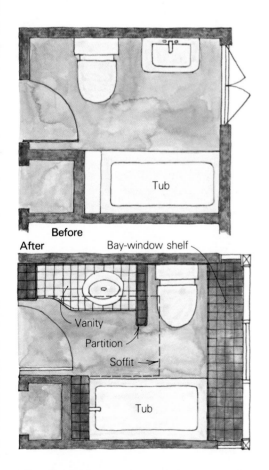

Before

After

Bay-window shelf

Vanity

Partition

Soffit

Tub

Tub

Blue tile winds its way around the room in this view from the bay window. The soffits create a coffered ceiling, and mask the dropped header made necessary by the bay window. The old wall mirror was removed and trimmed to compensate for the lowered ceiling, and the scrap piece saved for the medicine-chest door.

Shower framing
A 2x framework under the blue tile, photo above, made room to run new plumbing supply lines without disturbing the wall behind it.

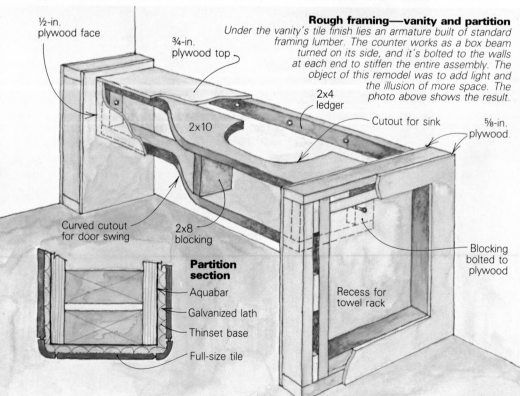

½-in. plywood face

¾-in. plywood top

Rough framing—vanity and partition
Under the vanity's tile finish lies an armature built of standard framing lumber. The counter works as a box beam turned on its side, and it's bolted to the walls at each end to stiffen the entire assembly. The object of this remodel was to add light and the illusion of more space. The photo above shows the result.

2x4 ledger

Cutout for sink

⅝-in. plywood.

2x10

Curved cutout for door swing

2x8 blocking

Partition section

Aquabar

Galvanized lath

Thinset base

Full-size tile

Blocking bolted to plywood

Recess for towel rack

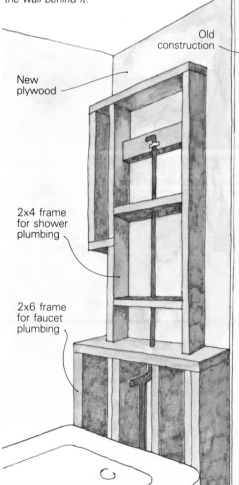

Old construction

New plywood

2x4 frame for shower plumbing

2x6 frame for faucet plumbing

as just another cantilever, it doesn't violate the setback code.

Dennis picked a cobalt-blue tile to establish the color in the room. He wanted it to march along the wall above the vanity, over the partition wall and then wrap around the corner and onto the bay window shelf. To balance this dazzling blue, he chose creamy white tile for the vanity itself and around the tub. He decided that both color tiles should be 4¼ in. square, which would create a strong, grid-like pattern in the room—if everything could be made square and plumb.

To keep from having to trim too many tiles, Dennis drew elevations of the room, at a scale of a half-inch to the foot, showing all the fixtures and every tile in place. The drawings were a lot of work, but they were worth it. They helped both of us to lay out the framing to accommodate the tiles, and to anticipate the detail problems before the place filled up with eager students of the tile trade.

Demolition and new framing—Only one piece of the existing bathroom survived the remodeling—the wall-size mirror over the vanity. We hired a glass company to remove it and cut it down to a size that would fit into the new space. We used the 1-ft. wide scrap that resulted to make a door for the medicine cabinet (photo, p. 143). With the mirror out for fitting, we gutted the bathroom down to the studs, and opened up the exterior wall for the bay window.

The horizontal members that support the bay window (photo right) are essentially floor joists, only at sill height, and they are supported by 2x4 knee braces. These braces are tied to the cripple studs by plywood gussets. The result is a rigid framework that may seem overbuilt, but with two rigid surfaces—stucco finish on the outside and tile on the inside— we didn't want the kind of movement that results in cracks.

The bay faces southeast and catches plenty of sun, so we gave its sill a 1½-in. mortar bed for a bit of thermal mass. The major opening in the bay is finished with three Pella windows. They have double-glazed, snap-in panels, with translucent glass on the inside. The shed roof and ends are fitted with custom-cut pieces of clear safety glass. When the landscaping grows enough to provide some privacy, Dennis plans to replace the translucent glazing with clear glass.

Shower solution—There is a closet between the tub and the hallway, and we didn't want to disrupt the existing framing. The problem was where to run the plumbing for the shower head. Dennis solved this one by detailing a furred-out frame that butts the existing wall, and holds the shower supply line and the tub faucet (photo and drawing, facing page, right). Its dimensions were worked out to allow full tiles wherever possible. This solution left the closet intact, and created a pleasing ceramic sculpture reminiscent of a high-tech office building. The nook near the wall is a good place to store shampoo bottles.

Vanity and partition—In a room this small, all of the parts are interdependent. The low partition wall not only screens the toilet, but also serves as a towel and magazine rack and holds up the end of the vanity top. The vanity, in turn, is a box-beam on its side, and it firmly anchors the partition (photo and drawing, facing page, left).

The thickness of the partition was determined by the width of one full tile plus two quarter-rounds. At its core is a 2x4 frame covered with ⅝-in. plywood. It's best to use kiln-dried lumber for this kind of framing because green lumber will shrink away from the outer layer of tile, creating voids between the two that at the very least will crack the grout. A layer of moisture-barrier paper covers the plywood, followed by a thinset mortar base about ¼ in. thick to bring the wall out to the right dimension for the tile.

I like to use Aquabar B paper (Forti-Fiber, 4489 Bandini Blvd., Los Angeles, Calif. 90023) for the moisture barrier in this kind of work. It's a sandwich of two layers of kraft paper with an asphalt-emulsion center, and it gets high marks for water resistance. It's more pliable than builder's felt, making it a lot easier to fold around angles and projections. Also, it doesn't bulk up at corners the way felt does.

The thinset base hangs on galvanized expanded metal lath. This stuff comes in several weights. I used 3.4 lb. per sq. yd. I specify galvanized lath for wet locations because in many of the bathrooms that I've remodeled, the non-galvanized lath behind the old tile is often close to total disintegration. Although it's nearly impossible to recognize visually, expanded metal lath has a right-side-up. On a vertical surface, the cups in the lath need to slope upward, away from the backing. You can check the lath's orientation by rubbing your hand over it—when you've got it right, the upstroke will feel relatively smooth, while the downstroke will grab at your fingers.

Like the partition, all the tiled surfaces in the room have a thinset bed on lath over plywood. We used bent-over 5d galvanized box nails to secure the lath, and we spaced the nails about every 8 in.—close enough to eliminate any springy spots.

Tiling tips—To begin setting the tile in this room, we marked a line one tile above the top lip of the tub. We carried this index line all around the room, and tacked 1x2 guide boards to the walls just below it. My ten students laid up most of the tile in one weekend. Some mixed thinset, some cut tiles and smoothed edges and some laid up the courses. It was chaotic but marvelous, and I was amazed how ten people could work harmoniously in such a small space.

The tiles that we used have tiny lugs built into their edges to ensure uniform spacing. The danger here is that they will occasionally overlap one another, producing a high tile in an otherwise smooth wall plane. A good way to prevent this problem is to cover the windows and hold a drop light directly above the tile. The raking light will create exaggerated

Virtually the entire exterior wall was removed and reframed to form a greenhouse bay window. To stiffen the structure, triangular gussets tie the horizontal members and their knee braces to the cripple-wall studs.

shadows next to the protrusions, allowing you to correct the position of the tiles before the mortar sets.

The most difficult part of the tiling was laying the curved section in the face of the vanity top. Dennis and I cut lots of little pieces, 1 in. wide, to lay like piano keys around the curve. We used a water-cooled, diamond-blade saw for this, but I wish we'd had a newer blade. The thicker the band of diamond chips on the blade, the cleaner the cut, and our blade left ragged edges that had to be smoothed down with a stone. We gave the tiles a day to set, and then grouted them (see *FHB* #17, p. 75).

The completed bath is now the most delightful room in the house. The bay window warms up the room at an early hour, and makes it a pleasant place to pry open your eyelids in the morning. Plants do well on the window shelf, and the room contributes a bit of solar heat to the rest of the house when the bathroom door is left open. The large mirror and the bay window team up to create a surprising increase in the amount of light and perceived space.

If Dennis were to do it again, he'd do a few things differently. First, the room needs a heat source other than the windows. It's warm during the day, but chilly at night. Also, he's had second thoughts about the flooring. He finished the floor with oak strips, stained to match the floors in the rest of the house. Hardwood floors in the kitchen and bath are okay for the fastidious, but guest bathers sometimes fail to mop up their splashes, and some of the strips are beginning to cup.

The total cost of the project was almost exactly $7,000, which included replacing some of the old galvanized water pipes under the house with copper ones. Besides getting the bathroom he wanted, Dennis saved about $800 by using student labor. □

Dennis Allen is a contractor who lives in Santa Barbara, Calif.

Illustrations: Frances Ashforth; Photo this page: L. Dennis Thompson

Bathroom Built-Ins

Precise alignment and production techniques are the key to building overlay doors and drawers

by Rob Hunt and Robert Robertson

Overlay drawers and concealed hinges give the cabinet in this master bathroom its sleek lines. Production techniques made the work go surprisingly fast, with no sacrifice in precision.

On a recent remodeling job, we designed and built all the cabinets for a master bathroom, creating clean lines and unrelieved surfaces by covering cabinet stiles and rails with overlay drawers and using concealed hinges on all cabinet doors. Our clients had found themselves with several spare bedrooms after their sons grew up and moved out, and they decided to convert one of these rooms into a spacious, comfortable bathroom—something they had always wished for but couldn't afford while their sons were still at home. They wanted individual dressing areas with built-in vanities, upper cabinets and floor-to-counter drawer units, all in teak. And they wanted teak trim everywhere in the new bathroom—door jambs, casings, around the mirrors and cabinets and around the tops of the walls.

Our job as architectural woodworkers would have been fairly straightforward, had it not been for the fact that a couple of inexperienced carpenters had made an awful mess of the framing and drywall, leaving everything out of square and out of plumb. The cabinet-maker who had originally contracted to do the trim and built-ins tried for two weeks to make things fit. His third week on the job, he threw up his hands and went off on a bender, never to return.

The careless framing and sloppy drywall work made the job a daily struggle for us too, and we ended up spending three months on it. Several tight spaces had to be filled with cabinets or built-in chests of drawers. In two instances, we had to assemble the cabinets in place because adjacent walls were so askew that a pre-assembled cabinet couldn't have been moved in and scribed to fit.

Since there wasn't a straight wall in the place, it was hard for us to make the trim details consistent around the room. A lot of planning was necessary to compensate for all the previous mistakes so the trim would work out right. We started by establishing a level line all around the room. This line would eventually become a 5-in. wide teak band 8½ ft. above the floor. Most of the door and corner trim would die into this horizontal band. We installed the vertical pieces first and then applied the band, shimming it out here and there because the walls were uneven.

The owners had decided on tile floors. Wherever tile would come in contact with trim, we made sure that the trim was plumb so that the tile setter could maintain even and parallel rows of tile. This job had 2-in. square tile that came in big square sheets backed with plastic mesh, and we knew it would be hard to fudge very much on the grout joints to compensate for out-of-level trim.

Where we couldn't put up trim before installing tile, we used temporary grounds so the tile man would have a real edge to work to. Later we pulled these down and applied teak trim. To prevent stains, all of the teak was sealed before the tile was installed.

Trim work—Teak is nice to work, but it sure can dull sawblades and jointer knives. I wasn't prepared for all the resharpening we had to do. We began by belt-sanding all the teak to remove the mill marks. Later we touched up and slightly eased the edges with some sandpaper on a rubber sanding block.

We installed the door jambs first, taking care to plumb both directions and to make the door opening the same size from top to bottom. (We were using all custom-order doors so we didn't worry about exactly what size the openings were, just that they were consistent from top to bottom.) Next we installed the

teak casings. To close the joint between jamb and case, we glued and nailed them in place. All trim that wouldn't have to be removed later, such as mirror trim, was glued to adjacent pieces of trim.

To get good adhesion when gluing teak, you have to wipe the mating surfaces down with acetone before applying the usual yellow (aliphatic-resin) wood glue; this removes some of the oily resin from the surface fibers to allow better glue penetration. Cleaning, gluing and wiping up the mess is a slow process, but makes for better joinery.

The vanities had to be built in place because their casework had already been started when we arrived. We made the face frames in the shop and then installed them on the cases. The chest-of-drawer cabinets (photo facing page) we built in our shop and then installed. The cabinets over the chests of drawers were built without face frames, which we nailed on after installation.

Careful planning—When we build cabinets, we always do shop drawings, elevations of the cabinets without doors and drawers, showing

the face-frame members. On these drawings, we indicate how the pieces go together, with notations that show on which side the doors are hinged and how much they overlap the face frames. Above or below the elevations, plan views show how the front meets the case, with notations showing how much the front overhangs the partitions and ends. The elevations and plans are usually drawn at 1:12 scale (1 in. = 1 ft.), which is easy to convert in the shop and small enough to present the information on a manageable piece of paper. Special details are drawn at a larger scale—sometimes even full size. We use the elevations to dimension the face frames, and the plans to get dimensions for the cases.

Before drawing up your design, you've got to consider the style of your cabinets, the type of hinges and drawer guides you plan to use, and the width of reveals (spaces) you want between doors and drawers. Then you can determine the size of face-frame members. We try to make the face-frame stiles (where there will be drawers) wider than the plywood case sides by an exact plywood thickness (⅜ in., ½ in., ⅝ in., ¾ in.) so that we

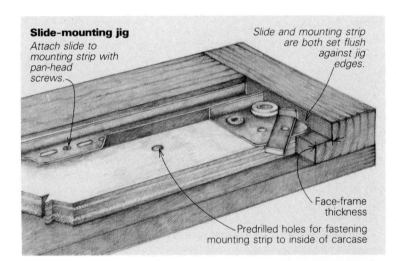

Slide-mounting jig
Attach slide to mounting strip with pan-head screws.

Slide and mounting strip are both set flush against jig edges.

Face-frame thickness

Predrilled holes for fastening mounting strip to inside of carcase

Time-saving techniques. Drawer slides were mounted on plywood strips using the jig shown in the drawing. Then the strips were screwed to the carcase sides. Above, a pneumatic stapler cut down face-frame assembly time and eliminated the need to clamp the joints while glue dried. At right, the boxwood face frame has been installed on a plywood carcase and trimmed with solid teak. Since the face frame has been sized to match the strip thickness, the slides align perfectly with their openings.

Achieving the overlay fit. Above, veneer strips shim drawer fronts as they are pressed against staple points in the boxes, creating registration marks for permanently fastening front to box with screws, as shown at left.

can mount the drawer slide on a plywood strip on the workbench. In production cabinetwork, it is much easier to get everything aligned if you can mount the piece of plywood with its attached slide directly to the inside of the cabinet (glue and nails), rather than trying to screw the slide to the cabinet itself as was shown in *FHB* #9, p. 32.

When our drawings were done, we made cutting tickets for the face frames. These are detailed lists describing each stile and rail, with dimensions and the location and sizes of mortises and tenons. We mortise-and-tenon face-frame members, so we add ½ in. to the drawing dimensions for the tenons. Then we cut the mortises and tenons and assemble the face frames by gluing all joints, pulling them tight with clamps and stapling through the back of the frame (through the mortise cheek into the tenon) with a pneumatic stapler.

Gluing all joints and using a pneumatic stapler and nailer is at least twice as fast as nailing or driving screws by hand, and we haven't noticed a difference in quality. Another plus is that the power nailer countersinks and drives in one step, and the surface is free of hammerhead dings—all you have is a tiny hole.

Because plywood sheets as they come from the manufacturer are not always square, we first rip the sheets to width and then check the ends for square before crosscutting. We cut all of the plywood up at the same time, label each piece, and put the pieces in piles: one pile for each cabinet. Then we lay out and make all of the special cuts and dadoes. We use a jig for the router to cut dadoes and rabbets across the grain. Grooves and rabbets with the grain are done on a router table.

When the pieces are all made, we assemble

the cases without glue and check their overall measurements before we finally glue and staple the parts together. The back is put on, glued and stapled. Cut square and fit snugly in the rabbeted back of the cabinet, the back piece squares up the box securely when it's glued and nailed. This makes it easier to position and install the face frame, which we glue and then clamp in place while joining frame to carcase with gun-driven nails.

Once assembled, everything is sanded. We belt-sand the face frames to make all of the joints flush, then finish-sand and ease all edges by hand.

Next we made the drawers and doors. Instead of making drawers with an integral front (*FHB* #9, p. 36), we made the drawer boxes first, and applied the hardwood fronts later. This allowed us to align and position the drawer fronts after installing the cabinet and drawer boxes, ensuring that the reveals between the drawer fronts were correctly aligned and uniform in width.

For drawers that have ½-in. clearance between the inside edge of the face frame and the drawer side, we usually use KV 1300 slides (Knape and Vogt Manufacturing, Grand Rapids, Mich. 49506). The overall drawer width is 1 in. less than the opening.

We made the drawer boxes from No. 2 or No. 3 1x12 white pine, which we first ripped and crosscut to rough size. Then I jointed one face and we thicknessed the stock to ⅝ in. Finally we jointed one edge, ripped the stock to finished width, and then crosscut the pieces to exact length.

The dadoes that house the drawer back and the rabbets that hold the front of the box were quickly cut on a router table, using a ⅝-in. bit. Depth of cut is important as it affects the overall width of the drawer.

To complete the cutting for drawers, we ran the grooves for the drawer bottoms with the dado blade on the table saw, and then cut out the bottoms themselves.

To assemble the drawers, we first put glue in the dadoes and rabbets; then we put the bottom into one side, attached the front and back and added the remaining side. Since we cut joints for a snug fit, we usually have to use a rubber hammer to get things together. A couple of staples through the joint makes clamping unnecessary.

Before the glue sets up, though, we check squareness with a framing square. This is a critical check when you are installing drawers with side-mount slides. We use a block plane, if necessary, to make the fronts and backs flush with the sides on the top edge. Then we round over the top edges of the boxes with a ¼-in. round-over bit, being careful not to round over the outside edge of the box front, so that when the drawer front is attached, the edge between the drawer front and the drawer box is close and tight.

Next we install the slides on the drawers. With KV 1300s, you mount the slide flush with the front and parallel to the bottom edge of the drawer. We drive one screw through the vertical slots at each end of the slide and into the side of the drawer. These slots allow some leeway for adjustment once you mount the mating slides on the inside of the cabinet.

If everything is right, the drawer will be flush with the face frame on both sides. If not, we scribe the front of the drawer box on the top and bottom edge so it will be flush with the cabinet face, and then taper it to the line on the jointer, avoiding the staples. You could also trim this taper with a hand plane.

When assembling drawers, it's a good idea to drive nails or staples from the sides into the front, rather than from the front into the sides. This way you won't nick your plane iron or jointer knives when you're trimming the front. When each drawer box fits right, we drive the rest of the screws into the slides.

Fitting overlay doors and drawer fronts— Nothing can ruin the looks of a pricey cabinet job more thoroughly than misaligned drawer fronts and doors. The overlay fit design we had decided on for the bathroom cabinets is achieved by allowing only a very narrow spacing between all drawer fronts and cabinet doors, so proper alignment was especially important. We usually do all the installing and fitting with the cabinet upright, but before the top of the cabinet is put on. This way we still have easy access to the inside of the case.

For the bathroom cabinets, we used ³⁄₁₆-in. thick plywood shims to get uniform vertical reveals between cabinet doors and drawer fronts, and ¹⁄₁₆-in. veneer shims to produce the horizontal reveals, as shown in the photo at the top of the facing page.

The first step in achieving the overlay fit is to stand the cabinet upright and slide the bottom drawer box into its hardware in the bottom opening. Then the solid drawer front is aligned on the face frame against its shims. By pushing the box up against the front and shooting two staples from the inside through the box and into the front, we joined front to box with the right alignment. Then we removed the drawer carefully (since only two staples held front to box) and fastened both parts together by driving flathead screws through the box and into the front (photo facing page, bottom). With the bottom drawer complete, we replaced it in the cabinet, then placed a shim on its top edge to space the next front. And so on up the front of the cabinet. It's important to have the cabinet sitting upright rather than on its back when installing the fronts, so that the drawers have their final gravity fit.

Some of the cabinets had to be built in place, and their tops were already attached before we installed the drawers. So when we got to the topmost drawer, it was impossible to staple the box to the front from the inside. Instead, we shot some staples through the front of the top drawer box before sliding it into the cabinet, then nipped them off just above the slides. Pressing the teak drawer front against the installed box caused the staples to make index marks in the front, which we used to align front and box when screwing them together.

Concealed hinges—To avoid having hinges interrupt the visual flow of line and plane, we used Grass concealed hinges (Grass America Inc., 1377 S. Park Dr., Kernsville, N.C. 27284) for all cabinet doors. The popularity of concealed hinges has grown in recent years. Several brands are available, but we've used only the Grass hinge. It has many advantages. The door can overlay the stile any amount on the hinge side as long as it is 1 in. or more. After installation, the doors can be taken off simply by loosening one screw on each hinge and separating the two parts, much as you would separate a butt hinge. It's easy to install, once you've done a few. The hinge has good spring-loaded action, and at $6 a pair, costs less than most concealed cabinet hinges.

There are a few things you have to watch out for when using these hinges, though. They're not well suited to plywood doors because they require a 1³⁄₈-in. dia. hole to be drilled ⅝ in. deep in the back of the door. Though this is fine in solid stock, in plywood you could easily bore into a void. The 1-in. or more overlay on the hinge side can also be a limitation, as it sometimes makes for awfully wide stiles. You've also got to have at least a ³⁄₁₆-in. reveal between doors on the hinge side. Another problem is that there are no locating bumps on the back of the fixed leaf, so it is hard to know where to screw the hinge to the face of the cabinet. One solution we've tried is to cut the heads off a couple of screws and temporarily hold them in their holes with duct tape. They should stick out of the back of the hinge just a little so that when the door is held in the proper place against the face frame, you can give it a tap with your hand and leave indentations where you will bore pilot holes in the face. Since we use these hinges in large numbers, we're going to weld some screw heads in a pair of hinges to make a permanent set of alignment hinges.

The hinges we used for these cabinets require a 1³⁄₈-in. dia. hole drilled ⅝ in. deep, with its center ⁹⁄₁₆ in. away from the door edge. This means that your bit will exceed the width of the door by ¼ in. We use a brad-point bit that we modified by filing its point off. You could also use a Forstner bit. Either way, you have to chuck your bit in a drill press to bore this hole, and I wouldn't recommend drilling them out by hand, or even with a portable electric drill. Butting a scrap piece of ¾-in. thick stock tightly against the door edge where you'll be drilling prevents tearout. It's also important to use an accurate depth stop, since you'll need to drill to within ⅛ in. of the front face of the door (assuming your cabinet doors are ¾ in. thick). For the same reason, we had to file off the center point of the bit. □

Rob Hunt and Robert Robertson own Water St. Cabinets and Furniture, in Bastrop, Tex.

Top, concealed hinges are the key to the overlay cabinet doors, and they must be mounted in precisely drilled holes. At right, tile and teak combine to give the finished master bath its simple, yet elegant, appeal.

Remodel Plumbing
How to connect the new pipes to the old ones

by Steve Larson

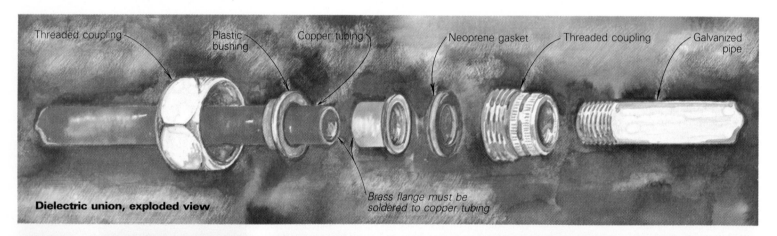

Threaded coupling — Plastic bushing — Copper tubing — Neoprene gasket — Threaded coupling — Galvanized pipe

Dielectric union, exploded view

Brass flange must be soldered to copper tubing

Sound connections. New copper lines can't be joined directly to old galvanized supply lines, or both metals will corrode. The solution is to use either a dielectric union (drawing, top) or a brass union. In the center of the photo, a dielectric union-to-steel nipple screws into the leg of a galvanized tee. Coming off the same tee is a brass nipple/brass union/copper tubing transition. New galvanized pipe is tied into an existing galvanized line with a tee fitting, nipples and union (drawing, right).

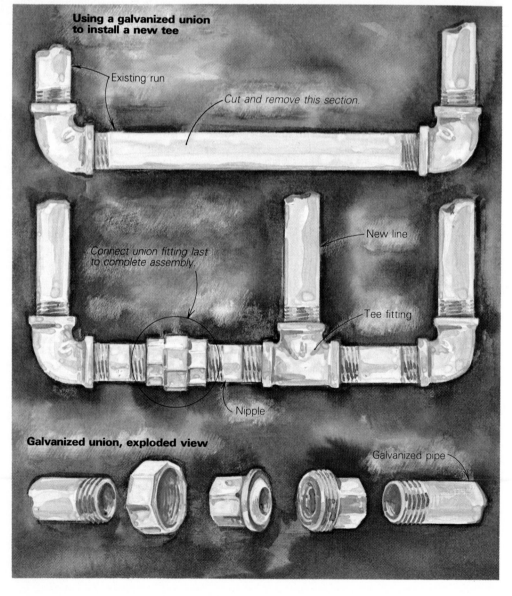

Using a galvanized union to install a new tee

Existing run

Cut and remove this section.

New line

Connect union fitting last to complete assembly.

Tee fitting

Nipple

Galvanized union, exploded view

Galvanized pipe

At some time in just about every remodeling job, new plumbing has to be joined with the old. You might be replacing a corroded supply line, plumbing a bathroom addition or relocating the lines for a remodeled kitchen. Most plumbers agree that remodel plumbing is far different from doing new work. Sometimes it's as simple as connecting new fixtures to the old lines, but often it's an excruciating exercise in Murphy's Law. The old-pipe diameters aren't the same as the new ones, the pipes aren't made of the same materials and your workspace is ideal for a dwarf contortionist. Fortunately, these are common problems, and those who have been down this road before have figured out some good solutions. This article is a stew of advice, products and tools that can make your remodel plumbing connections work out for the best.

Checking out the old system—Before hooking into the old system, you have to look at what's really there. Check for obvious leaks and look for traces of rust or corrosion on the outside of galvanized fittings. Reduced water flow and rusty tap water are signs that the water-supply system may be ready to rupture. A rust-weakened pipe that might otherwise last for years will often break apart with the first torque of the pipe wrench.

Restricted flow can be caused not only by rust buildup but also by non-corrosive mineral deposits. But in either case, when you start knocking around the old pipes you will often dislodge enough crud to clog things up somewhere else. Make sure that the existing drain lines are working well and that they are properly vented and sloped before you tie into them. Your new work may be fine, but if it overloads a dying system, you'll be the one to inherit the problems.

Tapping into supply lines—If the old supply lines are in good shape, choose a place to tap into them that's close to your new fixtures. You'll also want to make sure that your tap-in location is easy to get at so that you won't lose time working in cramped quarters.

Most older homes have galvanized water-supply pipes, but I recommend using copper tubing for all new supply lines because it will last longer than galvanized and it's easier to cut and assemble (see *FHB* #10, pp. 40-41). Some plumbers have switched completely to plastic pipe and fittings, since two new materials—chlorinated polyvinyl chloride (CPVC) and polybutylene (PB) can even be used for hot-water supply lines. But plastic supply lines haven't been approved by many local building codes, so you'll have to check your municipal regulations before using them. For drain, waste and vent (DWV) lines, I always use plastic for economy and ease of work, and there's little code resistance to this.

If the old line is galvanized pipe, you'll have to cut into it with a hacksaw or a reciprocating saw. If the line is copper, use a tubing cutter. In a tight space, a compact tubing cutter is indispensable for breaking into a copper line. Lacking this, you'll have to use a hacksaw

blade. In any case, make sure the water is turned off before you cut the line, and have a bucket handy to catch the drain-off.

If you're joining new copper tube to existing galvanized supply lines, the dissimilar metals will corrode each other unless you use a dielectric union. This special fitting separates the two types of pipe with a non-metallic gasket (drawing, facing page, top). For the same reason, support copper tubing with brass, copper, plastic or plastic-coated hangers.

A dielectric union in a grounded water pipe will break the ground circuit—the gasket inside the union won't conduct electricity. So this circuit must be reconnected by bridging the dielectric union with clamps and ground wire. Some local codes require a continuous ground wire, so it's important to check with your building inspector.

Another way to join copper and galvanized supply lines is with a brass union and nipple (photo facing page). The brass doesn't corrode in contact with copper or galvanized steel, so it's a good transitional material. Again, codes vary, so check with your inspector for the preferred coupling.

Dielectric unions have a flange that must be soldered to the copper tubing. So that you don't overheat the gaskets, remove them before soldering. And when you solder tubing in place, always keep a spray bottle of water within reach in case something starts to smolder. Otherwise, by the time you crawl out from under the house, you might need a fire truck to put out what one quick squirt could have quenched—and the water is probably turned off too.

If you choose to continue using galvanized pipe, a galvanized union will allow you to insert a tee with minimum dismantling of the old lines (drawing, facing page, bottom). You'll have to cut a small section from an existing straight run of pipe using a hacksaw or reciprocating saw. Again, pick a location that's accessible. Ideally there should be some play in the old pipe so that you will be able to push or pull the line slightly to get your final fit. If the old line is rigidly held in place, you'll have to be more exact in fitting nipples and tees into the section you've cut from the old pipe. Remember to add ⅜ in. to ½ in. for each threaded connection. The last connection will be the two halves of the union itself.

Threading pipe in place—If you're working on galvanized supply lines, you'll probably have to cut and thread pipe in place. The alternative is to remove an entire existing section to alter or replace it. If your workspace is cramped, or if the old pipe is too corroded to take new threads, you'll save time and aggravation by simply replacing it. But in many cases cut or broken galvanized pipe can be threaded in place using a ratcheted pipe threader (photo right). It holds the die in a ratchet assembly and requires only 1¼ in. of clearance around the pipe.

Most plumbers own several pipe threaders, but they're expensive, so you might want to rent one from a contractor's tool yard. Even

with the best tool, threading a pipe in place can be a knuckle-busting proposition. Apart from working in cramped quarters, you have to keep the pipe from wiggling around, as it usually wants to. The best way to do this is to clamp or block the pipe against nearby framing members, or to hold it in place with a pipe wrench. Another trick in tight spaces is to replace the threader's standard handle with a shorter section of ¾-in. threaded pipe.

Flexible connectors—When a new house is being plumbed, water heaters are normally joined to the hot and cold lines by means of rigid pipe and standard unions, but I find it a timesaver to use flexible water-heater connectors. They easily bend to reach a repositioned heater, or one with an intake line in a different location. Where I live, in earthquake country, I strap the water heater to the frame of the house, especially when I'm using flexible connectors. And if the heater doesn't have a temperature/pressure-relief valve, install one in the hot line at the top of the heater or at the specifically marked outlet on the heater itself.

The offset closet flange is another helpful fitting for remodel plumbers. It allows you to change the mounting position of the toilet slightly by rotating the flange. If you need to move a toilet a few inches one way or another to gain some clearance, if you're installing a new unit with different wall-to-flange dimensions, or if you want to avoid chopping into a floor joist, this is the fitting to use.

Tying into the DWV system—The traditional way of plumbing drain, waste and vent lines is with cast-iron pipe. Pipe sections have a bell-shaped hub at one end, and a small ridge called a spigot at the other. The spigot fits into the hub, leaving a small gap that is packed with oakum (an oily, rope-like material) and sealed with molten lead (photos p. 153, left and bottom right). Working with cast-iron pipe is difficult under the best of circumstances, but dragging it around under a house or through a hot and dusty attic while remodeling can be a nightmare.

Fortunately, plastic pipe (ABS schedule 40

A ratcheted pipe threader needs only 1¼ in. of clearance around the pipe, making it ideal for threading pipe in place. For extremely tight spaces, the handle can be replaced with a short section of ¾-in. threaded pipe.

Photo this page: Steve Larson; Illustrations: Barbara Smolover

A snap cutter is used for cutting cast-iron drain, waste and vent (DWV) pipe or clay-tile sewer pipe. Integral cutters break through the pipe as the chain is tightened. In this photo, a plumber is adjusting the tension of the chain before snapping the pipe by bringing the scissor handles together.

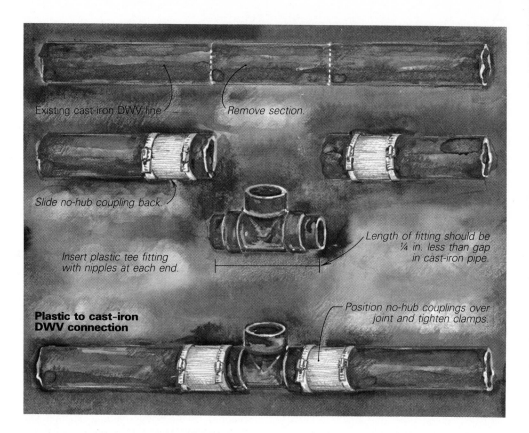

Existing cast-iron DWV line

Remove section.

Slide no-hub coupling back.

Insert plastic tee fitting with nipples at each end.

Length of fitting should be ¼ in. less than gap in cast-iron pipe.

Plastic to cast-iron DWV connection

Position no-hub couplings over joint and tighten clamps.

or PVC-DWV) can be substituted for cast iron in nearly all residential applications (check with your building inspector). Runs of exterior DWV line are an important exception. Sunlight can cause the plastic to decompose, and extreme temperature changes can cause it to expand and contract enough to break its seal with the roof flashing or with horizontal branch lines. Our local codes allow plastic vent lines on the exterior of the house if they are coated with two coats of latex paint.

If you're joining new plastic waste lines to an existing cast-iron system, you'll probably have to cut the metal pipe at some point. I know plumbers who have used a hammer and cold chisel for this job, but I don't recommend this approach. The best tool to use for cutting cast-iron or clay sewer pipe is the soil-pipe cutter, also called the snap cutter. You can usually rent one at the tool yard or plumbing-supply store.

Most snap cutters have a heavy chain that you tighten around the pipe until the cutting discs in the chain snap the pipe in two (photo above). The snap cutter almost always makes a clean cut, but occasionally old pipe will break unevenly. Another snap usually solves the problem. Whenever I can't afford a mistake, I use a reciprocating saw with a metal-cutting blade. A masonry blade will cut clay sewer pipe in similar fashion.

New plastic pipe can be joined to old cast-iron pipe with the no-hub coupling, a neoprene sleeve that is clamped around the plastic and iron pipes with adjustable, stainless-steel collars, as shown in the drawing above. The collars are just larger versions of the hose clamps used on auto radiators. You tighten them with a nut driver or a screwdriver (the former tool does a faster job). The neoprene sleeve fits over the ends of both pipes, and

tightening the collars makes the connection watertight. Because the seal on a no-hub coupling relies completely on the compression of the neoprene sleeve, it's important to clean or file the outside of the old pipe to remove rust, dirt or other projections.

The outside diameter of 3-in. or 4-in. cast-iron DWV pipes will usually be about ¼ in. smaller than the outside diameter of plastic DWV pipes. You can often deal with this discrepancy by cranking down tighter on the cast-iron side of the collar, but in some jurisdictions the building inspector will want you to use Mission couplings. These are identical to the no-hub coupling except that they have a stepped sleeve that accommodates the slight difference in pipe diameter.

Pipes with substantially different wall thicknesses, such as clay to cast iron, are often joined with a Calder coupling (photo facing page, top right). This connector is similar to the no-hub coupling, but is used with adapter bushings, or donuts, of different sizes.

If you run into a situation where you need a Calder coupling but can't lay your hands on one right away, you can wrap a strip of inner tube around the smaller pipe until you've bushed it out to the diameter of the larger one; then join the pipes with a standard no-hub fitting. If the pipes are roughly horizontal, make sure that the strip of inner tube starts and stops at the top of the pipe. This trick isn't sanctioned by code, so you should use it only as a temporary measure.

Plastic pipe has been around long enough so that you may come across an existing plastic DWV system in renovation work. An easy way to tie into such a system is with a glue-on saddle tee. Just cut a hole in the existing pipe (make sure it's the same size as the inside pipe diameter of the tee), swab the tee fitting

with glue and then temporarily hose-clamp it in place until the glue sets.

Testing your work—A thorough inspection of any remodel plumbing is essential, since a leak can damage the home and ruin the furnishings. Once, in the middle of an upstairs remodeling job, I learned a lesson that I won't soon forget. I'd installed some new copper supply lines, and before heading home for the evening, I turned on the water and checked them thoroughly for leaks. There weren't any, so I left the supply system on. But an over-heated solder joint let loose a few hours later, and several hundred gallons of water spewed out all night long. Luckily, it flowed into an area we were planning to remodel anyway.

Now whenever I'm plumbing upstairs, I use air pressure instead of water to test new lines. The idea is to isolate the new plumbing from the old, cap off any openings, attach an air-pressure gauge and pump up the system with an air compressor or a bicycle pump. Pressure test gauges are available at plumbing-supply outlets, and they accept a ¾-in. nipple. I leave the gauge on for a few hours (local code says 15 minutes). If the system loses pressure, I know I've got a leak. I locate it by squirting a detergent/water solution on each pipe joint. Instead of spewing a stream of water, a leak will blow bubbles. This lets me find leaks without producing puddles. If a joint leaks, I don't have to drain water out of the lines to resolder.

For final hookups between new fixtures and the old system, you'll have to rely on the standard test of running water through the lines and watching for leaks. □

Steve Larson is a building and remodeling contractor in Santa Cruz, Calif.

Cast-iron and clay waste lines are connected with a Calder coupling. A thick bushing fits over the smaller pipe to equalize the different outside diameters.

Adding drain, waste and vent lines. Most new DWV lines are plastic, but in old houses, they need to be joined to existing cast-iron pipe. At left, lead is melted with a torch, then poured around the oakum-packed joint between the cast-iron bell housing and nipple of the waste line, above, to seal it. Then a plastic sanitary tee fitting will be plumbed onto the cast-iron nipple with a no-hub coupling. A neoprene sleeve will seal the joint.

Capping a Foundation

One man's method for raising wood sills built too close to the ground

by Roger Allen

Many older homes were constructed with wooden sill plates too close to the damp ground. The primary reason for capping a foundation is to correct this situation by raising the sill. While this isn't the sort of task most homeowners would consider doing themselves, it is not as difficult as one might think. If the ground around the house can't be lowered, then with proper planning and careful workmanship, it's usually possible to raise the foundation.

In capping, siding is removed to expose the studs, and while the house is supported with temporary beams or house jacks, the studs are shortened to accommodate the cap. Then a new foundation is poured on top of (and in some cases, around) an existing foundation (drawing facing page, top.) Minimum clearances between sill and grade allowed by building codes vary, but 6 in. to 8 in. is the general rule. Reinforcing steel (rebar) and anchor bolts are included as in any other foundation. The new anchor bolts are an additional benefit of capping since many older homes were constructed without them.

The type of reinforcement used depends on whether the existing foundation is brick or concrete. In capping a concrete foundation, horizontal rebar and vertical dowels are added into the existing foundation, as shown on the facing page, top right. The size, amount and placement of this steel should be determined by an engineer. To cap a brick foundation, a saddle cap is constructed to strengthen the brick. This method requires the cap to encompass the brick foundation with a minimum of 3 in. of concrete on the sides. The height is determined by the necessary clearance above grade. Horizontal rebar is added to each side and to the top. In high caps a second horizontal piece may be required on top. A saddle tie, which is a piece of bent reinforcing steel, joins the horizontal pieces. The saddle tie is placed at approximately the same distance required of anchor bolts (generally every 4 ft.).

Capping a brick foundation has additional benefits. Old bricks and mortar tend to be more absorbent than new concrete, and capping prevents the bricks from acting as a wick, absorbing moisture from the ground and transferring it to the framing. It also adds reinforcing steel where there was none, and anchors the house to a solid wall of concrete.

Getting the house off its foundation—Moving the structure poses obvious problems. How do you pour concrete on top of a concrete wall

that supports the house? How do you support the house when necessary framing is removed? And how do you pour concrete into that dark, underground world of spiders and snails, where a human can barely crawl, let alone work?

If the challenge of working under such conditions does not entice you, think of the money you will be saving. To cap 120 ft. of a foundation with an 8-in. wide and 12-in. high cap, you'll need about 3 cu. yd. of concrete. At a cost of $55 per cu. yd., that means $165 for concrete. You may need $100 more for a concrete pump, and another $100 for reinforcing steel, anchor bolts and miscellaneous hardware. Forming lumber could run yet another $100, and one or two helpers on the day of the pour perhaps $100 more. If you consult an engineer, it could cost you another $100. All this adds up to $665. I have seen estimates as high as $8,000 for the same job. Perhaps spiders aren't so scary.

Because the existing sill must be removed where the foundation is to be capped, temporary supports must be constructed. It is wise to cap a foundation in several sections and avoid supporting the entire house at once. I generally study how the house is normally supported and duplicate this support as closely as possible. This is one case when you should always overbuild your bracing. If you have any doubt as to how strong the temporary supports should be, consult an engineer or an experienced builder.

Support procedures—Where the floor joists run perpendicular to the foundation, a beam (usually a 4x8) can be run underneath them a few feet in from the foundation (figure 1A). The posts (one post every 8 ft. is usually enough) should be set on a solid pad in undisturbed soil. The pads must be large enough to distribute the load over the ground without sinking. On very solid earth, precast concrete piers make excellent pads. Heavy blocks of wood or timbers will often suffice, but in some cases I have had to dig a hole 4 in. deep by about 18 in. square to pour a concrete pad.

House jacks and shim shingles can simplify the installation of temporary supports. When the old framing is removed, the house will settle a little. To minimize settling, I aim for a snug fit of the temporary support posts. House jacks can be used in place of or in conjunction with the posts to snug the beam up to the floor joists. Shim shingles tapped between the posts and beam also help to ensure a tight fit. Support posts should be plumb and checked periodically for

leaning. Be sure that all the posts and beams are secured strongly enough with diagonal bracing to withstand collisions from workers.

When the joists run parallel to the foundation, another method of support is called for. In this case a rim joist will be carrying the load when the studs beneath are removed or shortened. If the rim joist is not doubled, it should be at this time; to prevent tilting, add blocking to the adjacent joist (figure 1B). The distance between the temporary support posts will be determined by the allowable span of the joist. If the joist is doubled and nailed securely, it will increase the allowable span to about 6 ft. in a standard platform-framed, two-story house. When the house is supported this way, repairs must be made in sections between the supports.

If you want to repair the whole wall at one time, place 4x8 beams every 6 ft. perpendicular to the rim joist and support them at either end, as in the drawing on the facing page, bottom right. This technique allows longer spans of new sill to be installed at one time, but you have to remove more exterior siding than may be necessary, and you have to work around twice as much support timber. Nevertheless, it may be the best or the only technique for a particular job. Don't feel limited to only one technique for supporting a house. Many times a combination works well.

Removing existing sills—Once the house is supported, cut the existing studs to the proper height to accommodate the raised foundation. It is often easier to remove the exterior siding and work from the outside, but before choosing this approach, consider that exterior siding left in place makes an excellent concrete form; stucco also works well. On a concrete foundation, if there is adequate work space on the inside, leave the siding on and remove what is necessary after pouring the concrete. On a brick foundation, this consideration is irrelevant because the existing foundation must be encompassed on both sides.

The old studs must be cut off very straight. When the siding is left, a Sawzall is generally the tool to use, but making a straight and square cut with a Sawzall is difficult. Skilsaws cut square but in the cramped quarters you may be working in, Skilsaws are unwieldy, often dangerously so. A good sharp handsaw (and some elbow grease) is often the best choice.

Before cutting the studs, connect them with a well-nailed tie brace to keep the studs from moving once they lose the connection with the old

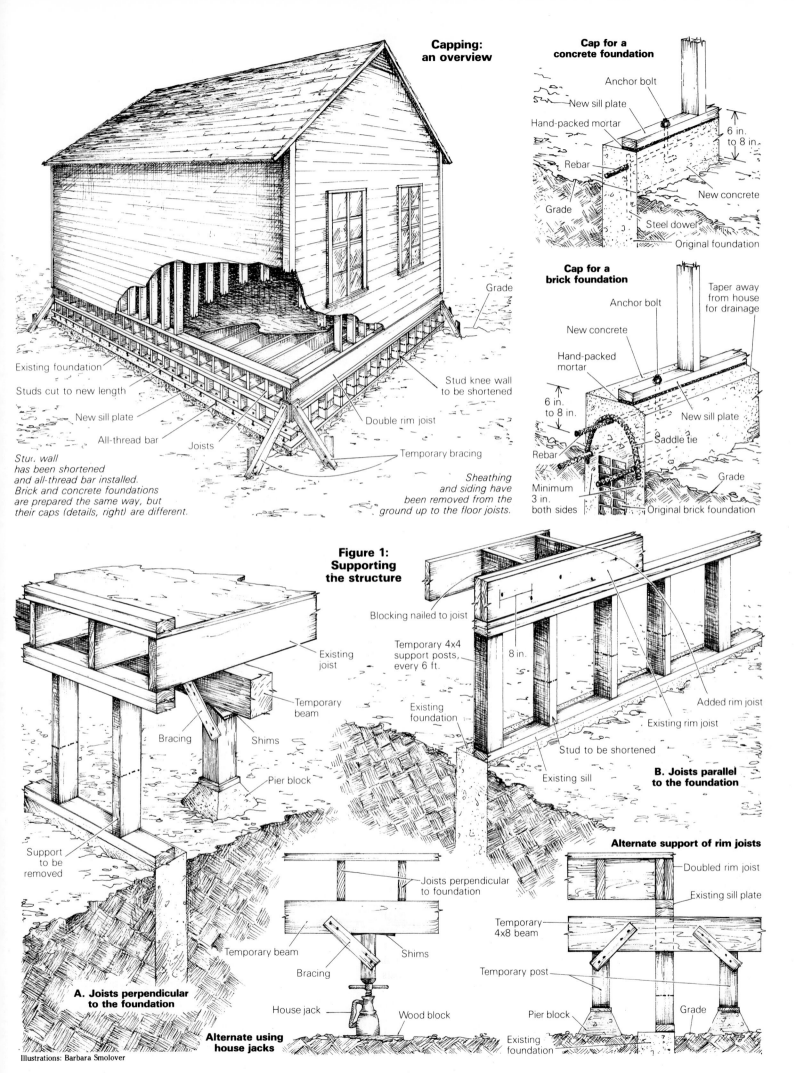

Capping: an overview

Grade

Existing foundation

Studs cut to new length

New sill plate

All-thread bar

Joists

Stud knee wall to be shortened

Double rim joist

Temporary bracing

Stud wall has been shortened and all-thread bar installed. Brick and concrete foundations are prepared the same way, but their caps (details, right) are different.

Sheathing and siding have been removed from the ground up to the floor joists.

Cap for a concrete foundation

Anchor bolt

New sill plate

Hand-packed mortar

6 in. to 8 in.

Rebar

New concrete

Grade

Steel dowel

Original foundation

Cap for a brick foundation

Taper away from house for drainage

Anchor bolt

New concrete

Hand-packed mortar

6 in. to 8 in.

New sill plate

Rebar

Saddle tie

Minimum 3 in. both sides

Grade

Original brick foundation

Figure 1: Supporting the structure

Blocking nailed to joist

Temporary 4x4 support posts, every 6 ft.

8 in.

Existing foundation

Added rim joist

Existing rim joist

Stud to be shortened

Existing sill

B. Joists parallel to the foundation

Existing joist

Temporary beam

Bracing

Shims

Pier block

Support to be removed

A. Joists perpendicular to the foundation

Joists perpendicular to foundation

Temporary beam

Bracing

Shims

House jack

Wood block

Alternate using house jacks

Alternate support of rim joists

Doubled rim joist

Existing sill plate

Temporary 4x8 beam

Temporary post

Pier block

Grade

Existing foundation

Illustrations: Barbara Smolover

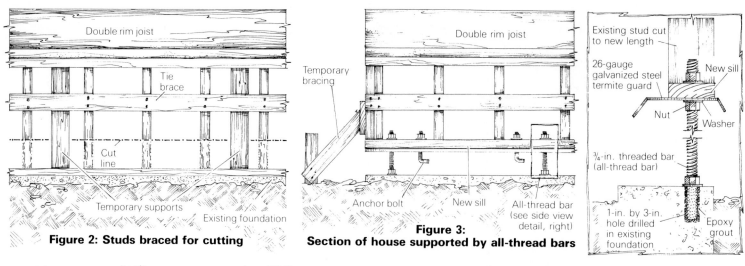

Double rim joist

Tie brace

Cut line

Temporary supports

Existing foundation

Figure 2: Studs braced for cutting

Temporary bracing

Double rim joist

Anchor bolt

New sill

All-thread bar (see side view detail, right)

Figure 3: Section of house supported by all-thread bars

Existing stud cut to new length

26-gauge galvanized steel termite guard

New sill

Nut

Washer

¾-in. threaded bar (all-thread bar)

1-in. by 3-in. hole drilled in existing foundation

Epoxy grout

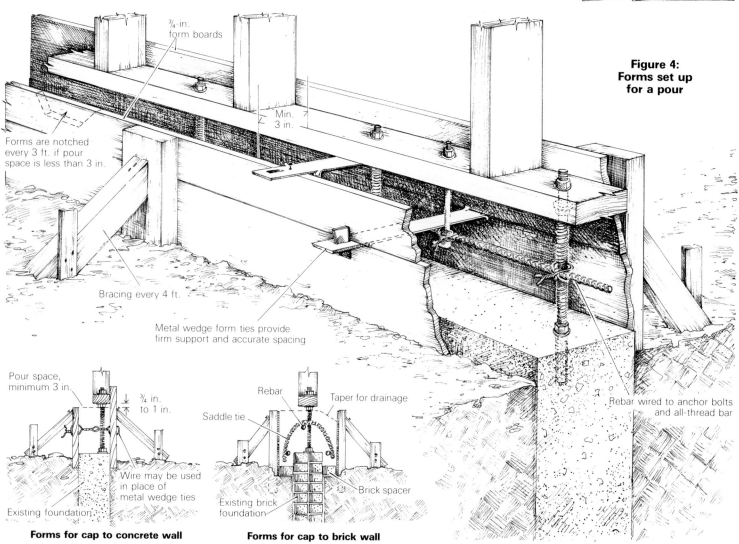

¾-in. form boards

Figure 4: Forms set up for a pour

Min. 3 in.

Forms are notched every 3 ft. if pour space is less than 3 in.

Bracing every 4 ft.

Metal wedge form ties provide firm support and accurate spacing

Rebar wired to anchor bolts and all-thread bar

Pour space, minimum 3 in.

¾ in. to 1 in.

Wire may be used in place of metal wedge ties

Existing foundation

Forms for cap to concrete wall

Rebar

Taper for drainage

Saddle tie

Brick spacer

Existing brick foundation

Forms for cap to brick wall

Foundation capping: a step-by-step summary

1. Note the presence of water lines, sewer lines, meter boxes, wiring, and other obstacles that may affect the placement of temporary and permanent supports.
2. Support the house where capping is to be undertaken.
3. Nail a tie brace to studs above cut line.
4. Remove the old sill so your sawblade won't bind when cutting the old studs.
5. Cut old studs to proper height.

6. Install anchor bolts and all-thread bar to a pressure-treated sill.
7. Nail new sill to bottom of cut studs.
8. Drill holes in old foundation for all-thread and rebar if needed. (This may precede step 7 if workspace is limited.)
9. Grout all-thread into old foundation and tighten the nuts on the all-thread between the old foundation and the new sill. Remove temporary supports.

10. Hang rebar.
11. Build forms.
12. Pour concrete.
13. Vibrate.
14. Allow concrete to cure.
15. Hand pack mortar under new sill.
16. Remove forms.
17. Tighten anchor bolts.
18. Remove temporary bracing.
19. Replace siding if it has been removed.

sill. This step, shown in figure 2 on the facing page, is especially important where the siding has been removed.

Installing a new sill—Once the studs have been cut and the lower parts removed, nail the new sill to their bottoms. Select a good straight pressure-treated sill. When the sill is cut to expose a cross section, the lumber should be green all the way through. If you see blond lumber, the pressure treatment was not thorough. Use only well-treated sills—you won't want to do this job a second time.

It may be easier to drill the holes for the anchor bolts before the new sill is nailed to the bottom of the studs. Take care not to place a bolt where a stud will fall. The size and spacing of anchor bolts depend on local requirements. In areas prone to earthquakes, anchor bolts are commonly placed 4 ft. apart, and no more than 1 ft. from corners, ends, or unions in the sill. Elsewhere, 6-ft. spacing is the norm. Common anchor bolts range in size from $\frac{1}{2}$ in. to $\frac{5}{8}$ in. by 8 in. to 10 in.; $\frac{1}{2}$ in. by 10 in. is typical.

If termite-proofing sheet metal is to be added, fasten it tightly to the bottom of the sill before drilling and nailing. Drill through the sheet metal first using a hole saw attachment. Yes, this does wear the sawblades out fast.

If large sections of foundation are to be capped in one pour, all-thread bar should be installed. All-thread bar, or threaded steel rod, is metal stock threaded its entire length. It is available in various sizes from hardware stores or concrete accessory companies. At the same intervals that one would place a support post, the all-thread bar should be run from a 1-in. diameter hole drilled 3 in. deep into the old foundation through the top of the new sill, as shown in figure 3. Pack grout or an epoxy equivalent into the gap between the $\frac{3}{4}$-in. rod and the larger hole to ensure a firm connection with the old concrete. Place nuts and heavy washers at the bottom of the bar on top of the old foundation and directly under the new sill. When the nuts are tightened, the all-thread will secure the nailed sill firmly to the framing above and prevent it from sagging. When they are properly installed, the all-thread bars support the house and the temporary posts can be removed.

All-thread bar must be installed plumb or it will not carry the house properly. Although the all-thread bar is adequate to support the house in short sections, it does not supply any shear strength; it only carries a load from directly above. It is also necessary to attach temporary diagonal bracing to the corners of the house, as shown in figure 3.

If there is enough room above the new sill, the all-thread can be added after the sill is nailed in place. Otherwise insert it into the sill before installation. Holes in the softer brick foundations may be drilled with masonry bits and a normal electric drill. For a concrete foundation, considering that many holes have to be drilled, you can rent a Roto-hammer—a combination jack-hammer and drill—from most equipment yards. Remember to drill the holes in the sill and foundation $\frac{1}{4}$ in. larger than the bolts to allow some leeway for installation.

Forming the cap—When the new sill is nailed to the bottom of the shortened studs and the all-thread is in place and tightened, it is time to install the rebar. The all-thread is a handy place from which to hang it. If the wall is to be poured in sections, the steel should extend 24 in. beyond to provide an effective tie to the next section when it is poured. If vertical steel is used, it should be inserted into holes at least 3 in. deep in the old foundation and grouted.

Because not much concrete is usually involved in pouring a cap, forming is relatively simple. Often all you have to do is to brace boards that are nailed in place to wooden or metal stakes. If the exterior siding is left in place as a form, make sure that weak points, such as the union of two pieces of siding or a crack in the stucco, are strong enough. If not, beef them up.

When the cap is to lie only on top of the old foundation and not encompass it, the outside form will rest tightly against the old foundation's side. If the siding has been removed, these form boards can be nailed with duplex nails to the framing above. Duplex nails should be used on all forms to allow for easy removal. The inside forms will also rest against the old foundation and require wood or metal stakes and form ties or wire for proper support (figure 4).

When the cap rests only on top of the foundation, leave space at the top of the inside form for pouring the concrete. Usually the size of the sill in relation to the size of the wall will allow for this space. If more space is required (3 in. is the minimum) notch the form at 3-ft. intervals at the top and build a funnel for the concrete to fall into the notch. If a termite guard has been added, you can temporarily bend the edge upward and out of the way before pouring the concrete.

A cap for a brick foundation requires a minimum 3-in. spacer every 4 ft. at the bottom of the form. Bricks work well for this purpose. After the concrete is in place and has been vibrated, use a small trowel to taper the exterior top away from the house for drainage.

Many people assume that because a cap will hardly be seen there is little reason to make it look good from within. Consequently, there is a tendency to build sloppy-looking forms on the interior side. But let me caution you: Sloppy-looking forms are often weak. Straight, neat forms are much easier to brace properly.

Pouring concrete—Most of the hard work is now over and the most exciting part is about to begin: the pour itself.

For small sections of foundation work, sacks of concrete can be mixed in a wheelbarrow and distributed via shovel or bucket. For larger amounts, a ready-mix truck should deliver your calculated amount. Always add at least 10% to the estimated load to allow for the inevitable tipped wheelbarrow. If the volume of concrete is very large or the workspace too awkward to drag buckets of concrete, you'll have to hire a concrete pump. Hire a grout pump and use concrete made with pea gravel, a concrete mix with aggregate no larger than $\frac{3}{8}$ in. The mix costs about $10 more per yd., but it allows you to use a smaller and less expensive concrete pump—the grout pump. A grout pump has the added advan-

tage of smaller hoses, which means less weight to drag around under the house.

Concrete pumps and concrete are usually ordered from separate companies—plan ahead to synchronize the two. Even so, on the day of the pour, one is likely to be late. Don't panic, it always happens. It is far better, however, to have the pump arrive early so it can be set up before the concrete arrives.

Before you begin to pour, be sure that the operator of the pump understands your instructions as to starting and stopping the pump. Learn early what the delay between your instruction and his response will be. If you are far under the house, another person can relay your commands. I can recall several times I was almost buried in overflowing concrete because a pump operator was talking to a neighbor or eating his lunch. If you have calculated the volume of concrete as closely as you should have, you don't want it wasted.

A critical aspect of pouring is to make sure that no spaces are left unfilled in the forms. The concrete must be vibrated so it settles everywhere. Vibrating guards against the weakening effect of a honeycombed wall. There are several methods of vibrating. An electrical vibrator, designed specifically to be placed into the concrete on large pours, is rarely necessary for capping. One good technique for capping is to tap the sides of the forms with a hammer, as well as packing the concrete from the top with a stick. Another way is to remove the blade from a Sawzall and place the shoe of the Sawzall against the outside of the form; when running, the Sawzall acts as an excellent vibrator.

Vibrating increases the stress that the poured concrete puts on the forms, so the forms should be watched as carefully when vibrating as they were during the pour. If the bracing seems inadequate, stop pouring or vibrating and shore up the weak sections immediately.

Because concrete shrinks as it dries, a small gap would be left under the new sill if the concrete were poured all the way to the bottom of the sill and then allowed to dry. To solve this problem, leave a $\frac{3}{4}$-in. to 1-in. gap between the newly poured concrete and the bottom of the new sill. After the concrete has cured, you can hand-pack mortar into this space. If the gap were smaller, filling would be more difficult.

All concrete spilled onto the forms and stakes should be cleaned off before it hardens, making it easier to strip the forms. Many a worker has cursed his lack of foresight while struggling to pull stakes or to pry boards that are embedded in hardened concrete. You can pull off the forms the day after the pour, but I usually leave the temporary supports in place for a couple of days to allow the concrete to cure and attain its full strength before accepting the weight of the house. After the concrete has cured and the hand-packed mortar has hardened, the anchor bolts should be tightened. If siding was left on the outside as a form, it should now be raised to the proper level above grade. Your house now sits high and dry. □

Roger Allen is a general contractor in the San Francisco area.

Renovating a Chimney

New flue liners convert fireplaces for woodstove use

by Joseph Kitchel

Installing new flue lining in an old chimney is somewhat akin to digging a basement under a finished house—it's not impossible, but it's a lot easier to do beforehand, during the original construction. Unfortunately flue liners were invented a long time after many chimneys had been built, and the older the chimney, the greater the need for new liners. Cast from fireclay or fireproof terra cotta, they provide a safe, effective exit route for smoke and combustion-related gases. Unlined chimneys are hazardous, ineffective and troublesome by comparison.

The chimney we had to work on was part of a common wall in a three-story Brooklyn rowhouse, built between 1860 and 1870. Although it served three fireplaces, we planned to eliminate the one on the third floor and convert the other two for woodstove use. This meant installing two separate flues in the chimney space, one for each stove. We decided to begin the job on the second floor, adding the first-floor flue sections at a later date.

Getting set—Before starting a job like this, it's important to know the type of stove to be used, because the location of the stove's exit pipe determines where you install the thimble fitting in the new flue. I had decided on a Lange 6303A/B, a Danish woodburning model with an exit pipe that can be adapted to run from either the back or the top of the stove. I chose to use the horizontal exit, since this would allow me to install the

thimble in the first flue section rather than farther up on the chimney wall. A tile or slate hearth would be added after the new linings were installed, so I took this into account when determining the height of the stove pipe and the location of the thimble fitting.

I also wanted to install the cleanout door in the same bottom flue section. Most chimney cleanouts are in the basement, but since this was a second-floor installation, I thought it best to locate the cleanout on the same level. The cleanout door is now hidden behind the old cast iron cover plate I removed from the original fireplace. It was one of three such covers provided for fireplace-to-stove adaptations, and I incorporated it in the rebuilt chimney to retain a bit of the appearance of the original fireplace.

Another important decision in planning is whether to use round or square liners. Smoke rises in a swirling motion, so the corners of square flues become cold spots where creosote and soot can accumulate. Consequently round flues are generally considered to be superior, even though they are more expensive and a bit more difficult to install. Round linings are manufactured in 24-in. sections, with inside diameters ranging from 6 in. to 18 in. (even sizes only). Since our stovepipe was only 4½ in. wide, we chose 6-in. linings. Transporting and handling the flue sections requires a gentle touch, since the castings are extremely brittle. The only other materials we needed for the job were

portland cement, sand and white cement (added in small quantities to the face mix to approximate the color of the old mortar).

Before beginning the actual work, I covered the floor around the chimney with some foam rubber carpet padding followed by overlapping sections of vinyl-covered canvas wallpaper. Unconventional as it might sound, I've found these two protective layers an ideal combination: The vinyl-covered canvas sheds water (and mortar), while the foam cushions the floor against the inevitable falling bricks. Chimney reconstruction is messy, especially when a substantial number of bricks must be removed, as was the case here. Protecting the surrounding work area from the ravages of the job is well worth the effort.

Digging in—Our plan was to install the flue liners in the old chimney passageway and then brick them in, restoring the wall to its original appearance. First we had to remove the facing brick layer to expose the inside of the chimney. A hammer and a sturdy, narrow cold chisel are the best tools for this job. To cope with the occasional stubborn or awkwardly placed brick, I also kept a pry bar close at hand. Generally, the old mortar was brittle and could be chipped away easily. Working from floor to ceiling, we removed the chimney wall in a staggered pattern so that the re-laid bricks wouldn't look so conspicuous. We saved all of the face bricks to use again. The entire brick wall had been

The first step in installing new flue liners is removing bricks from the second-floor fireplace to expose the chimney cavity. Hammer, railroad spike and pry bar are essential tools. A vinyl-covered canvas dropcloth over rubber carpet padding protects the floor. At right, Kitchel aligns two pieces of angle iron, which will be cemented in place across the face of the cavity to reinforce the chimney before the new liner is installed.

painstakingly cleaned of plaster at an earlier stage in the renovation, and its rosy pink color would have been very hard to match with new brick. Besides, there was always the expense of new brick to consider, and the trouble involved in hauling it up to the work area.

Inside the chimney we found thousands of brick fragments. Some had been built into the chimney to achieve the turns and separations between old flue channels. Others were simply the result of our chiseling work or age-related crumbling. All this rubble had to be removed so the cavity would be clean when we installed the new flue sections. An old railroad spike turned out to be a good tool for cleaning off the bricks. Its wide head was easy to hit and its broad, flat point broke the soft mortar away quickly.

The original chimney was constructed so that the flue of each fireplace started in the center of the chimney. As it progressed upward, the flue had to angle to the right or left to pass the fireplace above and thus make room for its flue. We wanted to keep the new flue sections as straight and plumb as possible, to make the chimney safe and efficient, and also to make the masonry work easier. Since we planned to eliminate the third-floor fireplace and its flue, both new flues could run straight up, with no sidesteps or bends. We located the first-floor flue on the extreme left side of the chimney; the flue for the second floor would run straight up the middle, and the resulting space on the right could be used as a tunnel for some electrical cables. In general, old chimneys provide a very good vertical tunnel through which wiring or plumbing can be run; keep in mind, however, that adequate separation between the conduits (in the form of airspace and solid masonry) must be provided to prevent excessive transfer of heat.

Even though we didn't plan to install a second stove on the first floor for some time, we needed to build both linings into the chimney from the second floor up. Then we could later complete the job from the floor below without disturbing the second-floor brickwork. With this in mind we dug out the chimney cavity to a point 14 in. below the second floor.

Installation and reconstruction—Although conventional mortar mix is available for bricklaying jobs like this, we are used to concocting our own mortar from one part portland cement to three parts sand. Our mortar board, a piece of exterior-grade plywood bordered with 1x2s, was set directly on the canvas dropcloth.

We cemented two 4-ft. lengths of 3-in. by 3-in. by ¼-in. angle iron across the cavity opening below the second floor. Positioned parallel to one another (the L pointing up) and joined to the cavity wall, these iron beams form a reinforcing baseplate for both flues. We set the first-floor liner between the Ls and surrounded it with a course of cement blocks, building the cavity up level with the second floor.

Because both the cleanout door and the stovepipe thimble are designed to fit into a square flue liner, we had to use an 8-in. square liner as the base section for the second floor flue. Cutting openings in the ceramic pipe to receive these fittings (photo top right) is a delicate job. You can

The first section of liner is cut to receive the thimble fitting, a tricky business since the ceramic material is very brittle. Closely spaced holes are first drilled along the cut-line; then the waste piece is knocked out with a hammer and chisel, as shown.

After the cavity has been built up to floor level, the first flue section can go in, left. The square opening at the bottom of the flue will receive the cleanout fitting. When both flue sections are in place, the chimney is bricked in around them, starting with a layer of cement blocks, right. The round flue section will eventually be connected to a new lining from the floor below; the square section in the foreground is for the second-floor lining. The back walls of old chimneys like this one usually require parging, or stuccoing over, before the new lining and interior brickwork can be laid in.

A round flue section is cemented to the square base, left. To ensure a good fit, a square piece of wire lath with a hole cut in the middle is set in the mortar between the two liners. Right, joints between round liner sections are sealed completely with mortar. The remaining interior brickwork extends to within an inch or so of the liner, allowing room for heat-induced expansion. Face ties in the last interior course will be bent into the face course as the wall is rebuilt.

A plywood sheet, top, temporarily replaces the third-floor hearthstone. The face course below has been relaid using the original bricks and repointed to match the style of the original chimney. Above, bolts sunk in the reconstructed face course just below the third floor secure a new chimney girt to the wall. This will support a new section of floor that replaces the third-floor hearthstone.

use a rotary saw equipped with a masonry blade for the straight cuts. We made the round opening by drilling closely spaced holes with a masonry bit and then carefully chiseling out the tile between the holes.

The next step was to brick in the chimney around both liner sections. Again we used cement blocks, since they wouldn't be visible and were easy to position and level. The solid masonry around the hearth would also hold the heat well.

Laying the first round flue section on top of the square base section was a bit like fitting a round peg in a square hole. To make the joint secure, we cut a 6-in. hole (the round pipe diameter) in a square piece of wire lath and placed it between the sections. Then we covered the joint with mortar and bricked in the cavity to within an inch or so of the liner. We filled this space with loose, dry rubble on the theory that the liners could expand and contract more freely, thereby minimizing the chance of cracking. Bricks were soaked in a bucket of water before we laid them into the wall. The extra water held by each brick lets the mortar cure more slowly, providing a stronger bond that won't powder with age.

In laying up successive flue sections, we established a working plan: First, we'd check the back wall of the cavity for loose joints. More often than not this course of brickwork (the face brick of the room next-door) would need parging (stuccoing over). Then we'd set the new liner section in a bed of mortar on top of the lower section, lay up the bricks around it until we were one course above the top of the liner, and repeat the operation. Since the first liner of the left-hand flue had been set 14 in. below the first liner of the right-hand flue, the joints of the liners were automatically staggered. We laid up all the liners and their supporting brickwork first, inserting face ties in the last layer of back brick to ensure a good bond with the face course.

In reconstructing the chimney face, we had to work into the irregular pattern deliberately created when we removed the brick. Whenever we could, we matched color and texture in fitting the new brickwork into the old. We even tried to imitate the rather haphazard pointing style of the original wall. The mortar had to be allowed to slump a little in the joint before being struck off flush with the brick face. If voids appeared, we left them. This took a little self-discipline, but the result was successful.

When we reached the ceiling of the second floor we had to remove a brick arch, which supported the marble hearthstone of the third-floor fireplace. This arch had originally been installed so that the hearthstone did not touch any of the floor joists. To make it safer and easier to work on the third floor, we temporarily covered the gap left when the hearthstone was removed with a sheet of ¾-in. plywood. Later on, when the masonry work was complete, we could frame in a new section of the floor, since no stove or flue was planned for this level. With all this in mind, I sunk three bolts in the reconstructed chimney face just below the floorline to hold the new chimney girt that would support the flooring, as shown at left.

Work on the third floor went smoothly. We

moved our cushioned dropcloth upstairs before tearing out the bricks and continuing to lay in the flue sections. We stopped just short of the ceiling. This was also the roof of the building, and we didn't want to disturb the brickwork at this juncture because the flashing joint between chimney and roof was fine—the bricks were all sound and the flashing didn't leak. We figured we'd just be asking for trouble by disturbing the seal. Instead, we decided to leave the face course of bricks intact and remove only the interior cross-bricking that divided the original flues. These interior partitions had to come out in order to keep the new flue sections running plumb, since the chimney narrowed slightly near the roofline and the two original right-hand flues jogged to the left. Working from the inside, we cleared out as much of the chimney cavity as we could reach before we went topside to complete the operation.

On the roof—The chimney wall continued above the roofline, separating our flat-roofed building from the higher gable-roofed building next door. Above the flashing, we discovered that the brickwork was not in very good condition; even the wall on either side of the chimney needed to be rebuilt. We carefully dismantled the damaged areas and cleaned out the chimney cavity above the roofline. Now all we had to do to finish the job was to install the remaining flue sections and to rebuild the chimney and wall around them.

To protect against downdrafts caused by wind deflecting off the gables, a chimney should extend well above the roofline. We built ours up about 3 ft., topping off the two flues with the bell end of a sewer-tile section and a wall-capping tile. Decorative chimney tile manufactured specifically for this purpose is four to six times more expensive than the substitutes we used. (The wall-capping tile has perforations cast into it, since each cylindrical section is meant to be divided in two. We used the paired pieces together to make the final flue piece.) High temperature resistance would not be a consideration here, since the stoves we were planning to install have internal baffles that prevent most of the heat from going up the chimney along with the smoke.

We extended the tiles about 16 in. above the brick line and topped the brickwork with a sloped cap, mixing the mortar just as we had throughout the job. The exposed chimney had been quite weathered before we rebuilt it, so we decided to give the entire chimney face above the roof line a stucco finish, as additional protection from the elements.

We completed the lining and rebuilding in November 1980 and quickly installed the woodstove on the second floor. Since then, the heating bill for our gas-fired steam system has been reduced by about two-thirds. We still have the option of putting another woodburning stove in on the first floor—and the satisfaction of having improved an old chimney without altering its own original character. □

Joseph Kitchel, of Brooklyn, N.Y., is a prop builder, cabinetmaker and renovator.

The chimney cavity, top, hollowed out at the roofline in order to accommodate the two flues. Only the top part of the chimney has been removed; the flashing joint where chimney meets roof remains intact. Center, flue-pipe installation proceeds on the roof just as it did inside the house, the only difference being that some of the adjacent wall has to be rebuilt as well. Once the final flue sections have been bricked in, the chimney gets a sloped cap, above, so that water will run off. The stucco finish on the exposed brick provides additional protection from the elements.

Staircase Renovation

Loose, tilted flights signal trouble underfoot, but even major problems can be fixed with screws, blocks and braces

by Joseph Kitchel

There seems to be a great deal of reluctance among renovators to tackle any kind of stair rebuilding. I have seen many beautifully renovated homes with sagging staircases, loose balusters and makeshift railing supports. People who wouldn't think of leaving cracked plaster cracked or sagging floors unshored will put up with staircases so crooked they would make a sailor seasick, and squeaks so loud they wake the whole family at night.

Procrastination and lack of understanding of the mechanics of stair construction are at fault here. No one seems to know quite where or how to start, or who to call to do the job. To be sure, attacking an ailing stair takes courage, resolution and perseverance. It is one of the dirtiest and most disruptive renovating jobs.

The stairway is the spine of the multistoried row house. It links the sometimes minimal area of individual floors into what can be a spacious and accommodating floor plan. Because changing the stairway can seriously affect the physical flow of people and spoil the aesthetics of the whole interior design, it is far better to renovate than redesign or reposition.

Parts of a stair—Each step consists of a riser, the vertical portion that determines the height of each step, and the tread, the part on which you step. The dimensions of steps must be consistent within flights, though they may vary from one flight to the next. Variation within the flight will break the stair-user's physical rhythm and cause tripping. Tread widths may vary in the bottom two or three steps of the main flight for aesthetic purposes, and at the top of a flight, where pie-shaped steps are needed to negotiate a curve. Riser height, however, must not vary.

The newel post, usually decorated with paneling or carving, supports the railing at the bottom of the flight. Though it gives the impression of being heavy and sturdy, after years of being swung around by ebullient children, it has probably loosened enough to sway from side to side or lean out toward the hall. The vertical supports of the railing, aligned more or less behind the newel post and marching upward with each suc-

cessive step, are balusters or spindles, which are dovetailed into the treads.

Keeping the balusters from slipping out of their joints on the open side of the staircase are the noses, continuations of the molding that forms the front edge of the treads. These noses are removable and not part of the tread itself.

On each side of the stairs are the stringers, which hold the risers and treads. The stringer attached to the wall is usually routed or plowed out to receive the steps; this is called a housed stringer, and it produces a strong, dust-tight stairway. The outside stringer may be open or closed. Stringers may be simple, laminated with other pieces to form the curves of the stairs, or partially concealed by decorative filigree.

Were you to remove the plaster under the staircase, you might find two or three 4x4s or 4x6s running the length of the flight—one nailed to the inside of the outside stringer, one centered beneath the steps, and perhaps an-

Photos: Jeff Fox

other nailed to the inside of the stringer attached to the wall. These are the carriages, the members that add extra support. At the bottom, the carriages ideally rest on top of the stairway header, a joist that frames the stairwell end. They are sometimes attached to the inside face of the header. (This was the cause of failure in one flight I repaired. The weight of the stair forced out the toenails holding the carriage.) At the top, the carriages attach to the face of the upper-story header joist or, in the case of a curved flight, to angled braces running from notches in the wall to the upper floor joists.

Other elements of stair construction visible from beneath the flight are the wedges or shims driven between steps and stringers. Tapping these wedges tight or adding wedges made from shingles or building shims can do a great deal toward tightening up a staircase.

Diagnosis and dismantling—Problems with stairs fall into two categories. The simpler ones concern the railing, balusters, newel post and railing supports—the superstructure. Trouble here, though relatively easy to repair, can be symptomatic of more serious problems in the steps, carriages and stringers—the substructure.

Before you remove any plaster, explore the failings of the flight. If the steps are loose and tip toward one side, then the carriage or stringer on that side has weakened. The cause may be rotting, breaking, warping and splitting, or the carriage may have separated from the stringer.

Another symptom of major deterioration is a series of gaps or cracks along the ends of the treads or risers where they fit into the stringer. These rifts may occur on either side of the stairs, but are most often on the wall side, suggesting that a center or outside carriage has shifted downward, skewing the flight toward the center of the stairwell.

Large cracks in the plaster at the top or bottom of a flight are a good sign that the carriages have come loose from the headers. However, cracks generally parallel to the carriages or crisscrossing their length may indicate that vibration has caused the plaster to loosen and the keys to

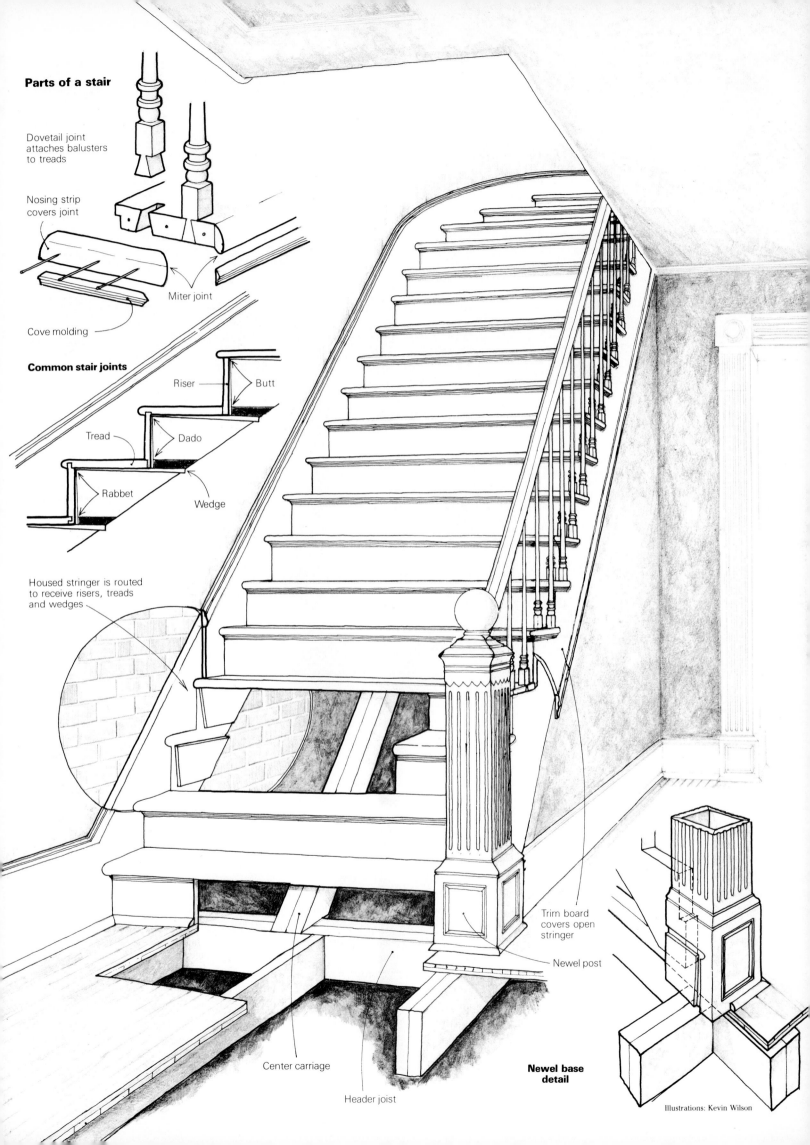

Parts of a stair

Dovetail joint attaches balusters to treads

Nosing strip covers joint

Miter joint

Cove molding

Common stair joints

Riser

Butt

Tread

Dado

Rabbet

Wedge

Housed stringer is routed to receive risers, treads and wedges

Trim board covers open stringer

Newel post

Center carriage

Header joist

Newel base detail

Illustrations: Kevin Wilson

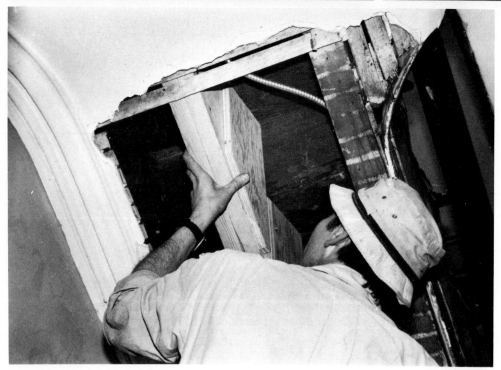

Substructure repairs are major problems and should be tackled first. To correct a distorted stringer, author Kitchel, above left, strips stairs of treads and risers. Plaster has been removed from beneath the stairway previously, and the resulting debris cleared away for a dust-free work area. The jack between wall and stringer provides lateral support until the stringer has been repositioned and reattached, and all steps have been renailed. Above, a carriage pulled away from the joist can be reattached with an angle iron made from ⅛-in. plate attached to the header with ⅜-in. bolts. The carriage usually rests on top of the stairway header, but occasionally it is attached to the inside face. Left, support blocks of ¾-in. plywood fastened with Sheetrock screws minimize deflection.

spindles, may have been purely cosmetic. Remove them so that all parts of the stairs may be properly aligned.

Substructure repair—You should now know the causes of your stair failure; tackle the bigger ones first. If a carriage is rotted out or cracked, tear it out and replace it. If it is intact but springy, it may be undersized; laminate a new beam or a steel reinforcing plate onto it. Solutions at this point must be as individual as the problems. But by far the most common failings are bolts and nails which have worked loose, allowing carrying elements to pull free from walls and header. In this case, mending plates made from ⅛-in. steel work well.

If you must raise or remove carriages, first free them from each riser and tread; otherwise, the attached superstructure will loosen as the skewed members are jacked up. To remove treads and risers, pry them apart at joints or cut through the nail shanks if pulling is impractical.

For major repairs, jack the stringers or carriages into place in a manner that won't damage the superstructure and will keep it from damaging you. To give the jack or brace a level bearing surface, attach angle blocks cut to the slope of the stairs with clamps or screws.

break off, which is a much less serious repair.

If your stair has a decorative plaster molding running along its wall side, a continuation of the ceiling cornice, don't despair. This can be saved if it is not badly damaged and is still attached securely to the wall. To dismantle, carefully cut through the plaster and lath along the molding with a masonry blade in a circular saw, cutting parallel to the stair edge of the molding, leaving the molding intact. Plan this cut so that plaster or Sheetrock can be rejoined to this edge.

To further assess causes of stair failure, remove nearby plaster and lath. You may not have to remove all of the ceiling covering if the plaster isn't bad and if the problem is localized. Take time to clean up all the resulting plaster dirt. Debris allowed to accumulate on the flight below makes moving your stair platform difficult and dangerous, and will also worsen the

spread of dust throughout the rest of the house.

If necessary, remove noses and balusters, but label all parts first. Assign each step a number (I usually start at the bottom) and tape this number to the outside of the step and to its adjacent nose molding and spindle.

Using a screwdriver or chisel, gently pry the noses away from the stringer. They're usually finish-nailed in two or three places. You'll see the dovetail joint that connects the spindle to the tread. Tap the spindles out at the bottom and pull them down out of the railing.

Examine the joint between riser and tread to judge how to handle repair of squeaks or gaps. The joint may be a dado, a rabbet or simply butted and nailed. Past repairs, such as wedges driven into the gaps between riser and tread, fillers in the spaces above the treads along the wall stringers, or braces along the railing or

If the wall stringer has come loose from a masonry wall, reattach it by raising it to its proper position and nailing it with cut-steel masonry nails of sufficient length to go well into the wall. Wear goggles. A better method is drilling through the stringer and into the masonry with a carbide bit, and tapping in a lead sleeve; a lag bolt and washer expand the sleeve and tighten the stringer to the wall. If it's a frame wall, lag screws alone will hold stringers to studs.

If the outside stringer has twisted or warped, and is pulling the treads out of the wall stringer opposite, remove the treads and risers and force the stringer in toward the wall. Get the necessary leverage by temporarily bracing from the outside of the stringer toward the partition wall opposite. Screwing or bolting the stringer to the accompanying carriage will correct matters.

With the supporting members repositioned, now attend to the steps. Repair split treads and risers by removing them, lapping a piece of plywood over the back of the split, and gluing and clamping overnight. If you glue and screw the lapping piece you may forego clamping, and can replace the piece immediately. If the very edge of the nose is split, insert dowels from the edge to reattach it, being careful not to split the riser's dado or rabbet joint.

After you've corrected stringer and carriage problems and each tread and riser is back in place and renailed to the outside stringer, strengthen the steps by nailing step blocks to the center carriage. Why this wasn't done originally has always puzzled me. From a piece of ¾-in. plywood cut a step block to fit under each tread, and place it firmly against the back of each riser. Nail or screw the blocks to the side of the carriage, and then nail through the face of the tread and riser into the edge of the blocks. Trim the bottom edges of the blocks to conform to the angle of the carriage. I usually alternate the blocks on opposite sides of the carriage, but they all may be attached to the same side if the staircase is narrow and you can't get between the center carriage and the wall. Nailing blocks on both sides of the carriage is overkill, but add them wherever extra support is needed.

At this time a test run up and down the stairs will tell you where additional nailing and bracing are needed. For all face nailing in treads and risers, I use 6d or 8d finish-head, spiral flooring nails. For nailing where it doesn't show, I prefer 6d or 8d rosin or cement-coated box nails. I find 1½-in. or 2-in. Sheetrock screws driven with a variable-speed drill useful where hammer space is limited. Screws often add more strength than nails, because they pull things together and don't require pounding, which may disturb the alignment of nearby areas.

If risers, treads or stringers are to be refinished separately from the spindles, consider doing this now. Stripping, sanding and painting are easily done with the upper parts out of the way. Before finish is applied, set and fill all nails.

Superstructure repair—Newel-post problems are best dealt with after all other structural problems are solved. Although removing or loosening the newel post may be necessary to work on the carriages or stringers, it can usually be left in place to support the railing.

Newels are usually attached to the bottom step with a threaded rod, and to the railing with a hanger bolt. (Hanger bolts have wood-screw threads on one end and machine-screw threads on the other.) On the machine-screw thread of the hanger bolt is a star nut, which can be turned through the access hole with a screwdriver or needlenose pliers after the bolt is in place. (A plug fills the access hole later.) For extra strength screw into the railing from the inside of the newel post.

Straighten or tighten a shaky newel post by shimming under its bottom edges and renailing or screwing it to the floor. For greater support, try one of these repairs using a threaded rod. First, remove the newel post. Bolt a threaded rod to a bracket or wooden block so that the bolt fits flush with the bottom of the block. Screw the block and rod assembly to the floor, then slip the newel post over them and reattach it. To repair the post without removing it, attach two brackets under the tread of the first step as

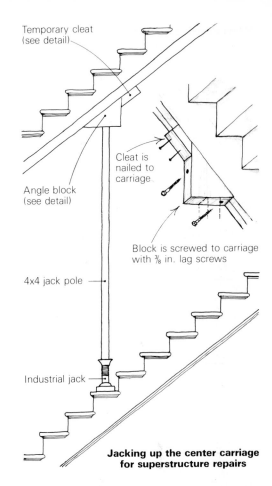

Temporary cleat (see detail)

Cleat is nailed to carriage

Angle block (see detail)

Block is screwed to carriage with ⅜ in. lag screws

4x4 jack pole

Industrial jack

Jacking up the center carriage for superstructure repairs

Building a Stair Platform

Before you renovate your staircase, you'll need to build a stair platform. Part of the reason stair repair is so difficult is that there is no place to stand, no way to get up to the job.

The exact dimensions of the platform depend upon your stairs. To make the platform, set a straightedge, level, on the fourth or fifth step from the bottom of your main staircase. The height of the platform is the distance from that step to the floor; its length is the distance from the back of that step to the front of the bottom step. Check these dimensions at different locations on various flights of your staircase. Sometimes rise and tread dimensions or angles of incline vary from flight to flight, but not usually. Then cut and attach legs and braces as shown in the drawing.

The platform should be wide enough to hold your stepladder comfortably, but narrow enough to allow passage on the stairs when it's in position. The platform will probably fit your neighbor's stairs, and you can use it when repainting your own stairwell; it is therefore a tool to retain after renovaton. You might consider making it collapsible for easier storage.
                                                                    —J.M.K.

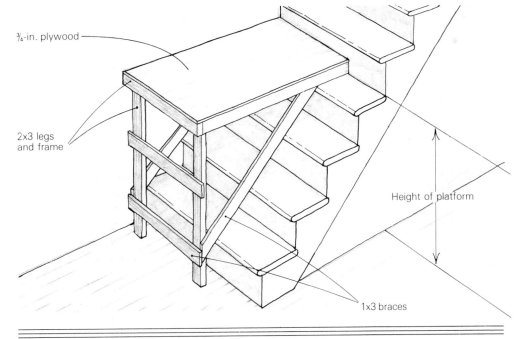

¾-in. plywood

2x3 legs and frame

Height of platform

1x3 braces

Newel-post attachment

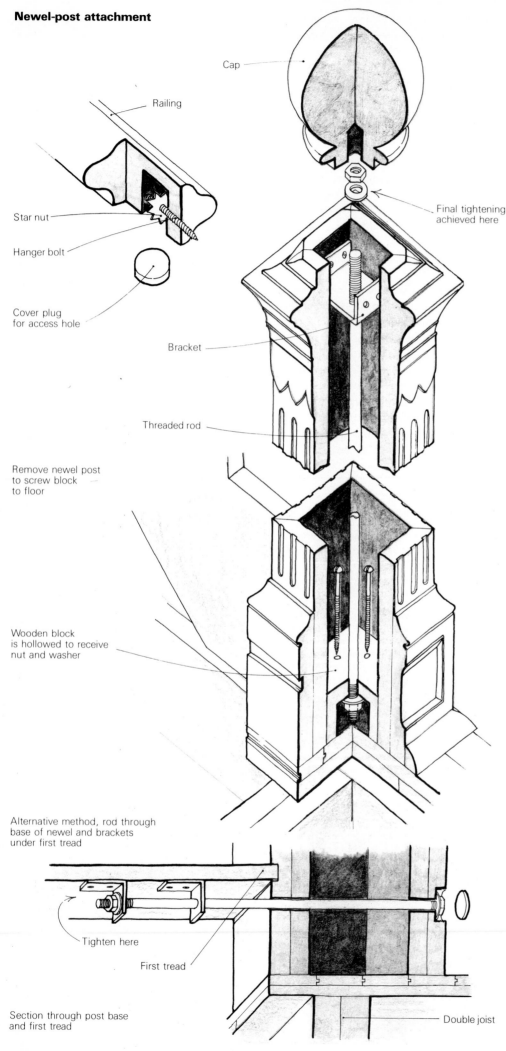

Cap

Railing

Star nut

Hanger bolt

Cover plug
for access hole

Final tightening
achieved here

Bracket

Threaded rod

Remove newel post
to screw block
to floor

Wooden block
is hollowed to receive
nut and washer

Alternative method, rod through
base of newel and brackets
under first tread

Tighten here

First tread

Section through post base
and first tread

Double joist

shown at left. Drill a hole through the base of the newel post to align with the holes in the brackets. Insert a threaded rod through the holes, bolt at both ends, and fill the access hole with a plug.

To replace the spindles, first coat both ends with white glue. Insert the top end of the spindle into the railing underside first, then slide the dovetailed end into its tread slot. Shim the joint wherever necessary, from underneath or from either edge, securing it with a finishing nail through the dovetail into the end of the tread. I find a rubber mallet useful when replacing spindles, because it will not mar the finished surface of the wood.

As you proceed from bottom to top, occasionally check the alignment of the railing and make adjustments by trimming or lengthening the spindles. Temporary braces hold the railing in place until all spindles have been installed and the glue is dry.

You can lengthen spindles (or adapt spindles from another stair) by adding a short piece of dowel. Drill into the top end of the spindle, and glue and nail the piece of dowel in. When the glue is dry, rasp and sand the dowel to the contour and taper of the spindle tip. Stain to complete the match.

When the final spindle has been inserted, the small bracket that originally connected the top of the rail should be reattached, or a new one made to fit. This prevents lateral movement of the rail and will hold the spindles in their correct positions as the glue dries.

Refinish the noses before you attach them. If you remove old nails by pulling them through from the back with a pair of nippers, you'll avoid the splitting that usually occurs when the nails are pounded back through and pulled from the face. Glue the noses and nail them twice along the side and once through the miter where nose meets tread molding.

Replacing the ceiling under the flight is the final step; use lath and plaster or Sheetrock. If your stairs curve, use short sections of wire lath to recreate the original curve.

Take care to keep all nailing surfaces in the same plane. This can be done with two straight-edges; one the width of the ceiling area, from the outside of the stringer to the wall, and the other as long as possible to run the length of the flight. Use building shims where necessary to keep furring strips in the correct plane. Determine your plaster line in relation to any plaster molding along the wall and to the bottom edge of trim pieces that adorn the outer carriage. I usually let the beaded or molded edge of this outer trim protrude below the plaster line. Existing pieces of plaster or plaster molding to be replaced may be drilled and secured with screws before touch-up spackling or painting. □

Joseph Kitchel, of Brooklyn, N.Y., is a prop builder, cabinetmaker and renovator.

Expanding a Kitchen, Step by Step

In renovation, one thing always leads to another

by Eric K. Rekdahl

Renovation work is full of surprises. Even in simple-looking jobs, digging into one area will invariably expose unanticipated problems in another, which in turn will force you to rearrange something else. Good renovators are clever enough both to anticipate some of the trouble they're likely to run into and to know that lots more will show up. They are flexible enough to improvise when plans go awry, and imaginative enough to take advantage of situations as they arise. Technical skills are also important to minimize tedium and frustration.

When Dick and Renie Riemann acquired their 1928 Tudor Revival house, designed by the architect John Hudson Thomas, they also inherited a kitchen with 48 sq. ft. of floor space and 5½ ft. of countertop, separated from the dining room by two doors and a pantry (drawing, below). The refrigerator was in the laundry, a sagging foundation was causing the floor to droop, and inadequate framing had cracked the plaster.

The Riemanns wanted a modern, functional kitchen with a family eating area and a desk for planning. They wanted an open, informal space, with enough room for guests to chat with the cook. The obvious solution was to eliminate as many walls as possible, streamlining the maze-like circulation created by the pantry, kitchen and laundry room. They also wanted to enlarge the kitchen by enclosing an area north of the laundry wall that was covered by an overhanging second-story bedroom floor.

Laundry wall—The area was broken up into so many small rooms that we hardly had space to set up our equipment and move around. By removing the non load-bearing walls (D, G and E in the drawing), we created a good-sized working area. This was straightforward work, except for a problem we had anticipated: The cast-iron drain from an upstairs toilet ran through wall D. We disconnected the plumbing and removed the pipe. It would have to be relocated later.

Then we tackled wall B, the laundry's north wall. It was framed with a 2x4 stud wall, which carried 4x6 floor joists for the bedroom above. Instead of removing the wall and replacing the top plate with an 8x10, we kept the double 2x4 top plate and sandwiched it between two rough-

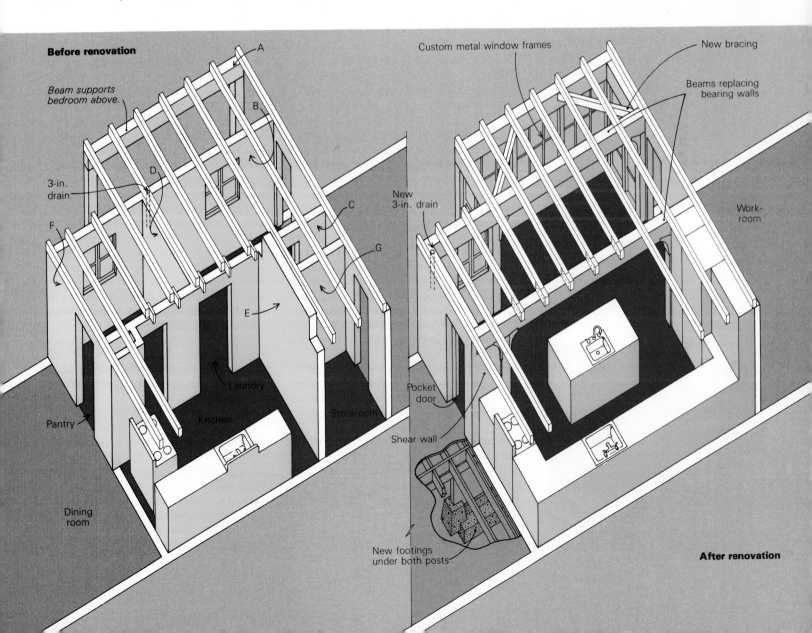

Before renovation

Beam supports bedroom above.

3-in. drain

Pantry

Dining room

Laundry

Kitchen

Storeroom

A

B

C

D

E

F

G

Custom metal window frames

New bracing

Beams replacing bearing walls

New 3-in. drain

Work-room

Pocket door

Shear wall

New footings under both posts

After renovation

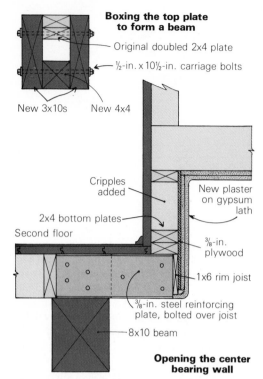

Boxing the top plate to form a beam

— Original doubled 2x4 plate

— ½-in. x 10½-in. carriage bolts

New 3x10s   New 4x4

Cripples added

2x4 bottom plates

Second floor

New plaster on gypsum lath

⅜-in. plywood

1x6 rim joist

⅜-in. steel reinforcing plate, bolted over joist

8x10 beam

Opening the center bearing wall

Opening up the north wall of the kitchen revealed 10-in. long 2x6s supporting an upstairs wall (below). These were replaced with steel plates and 4x6s, as shown above. At the south side of the kitchen (bottom), joists were attached without cripples or blocking.

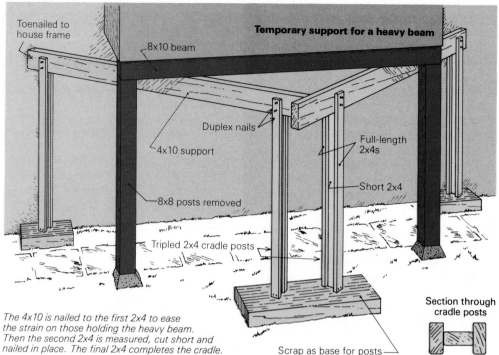

Toenailed to house frame

8x10 beam

Temporary support for a heavy beam

Duplex nails

4x10 support

Full-length 2x4s

Short 2x4

8x8 posts removed

Tripled 2x4 cradle posts

Scrap as base for posts

Section through cradle posts

The 4x10 is nailed to the first 2x4 to ease the strain on those holding the heavy beam. Then the second 2x4 is measured, cut short and nailed in place. The final 2x4 completes the cradle.

sawn 3x10s. This way we could use the old framing as bracing while using the same sandwich approach to beef up the posts at the beam ends. After the 3x10s were bolted in place, we removed the stud frame. To complete the beam we bolted a 4x4 between the 3x10s, flush with their bottom edges (drawing, above left).

The upstairs bedroom floor joists extended 4½ ft. beyond the laundry wall to rest on an 8x10 beam (A in the drawing on the previous page), supported by 8x8 posts just beyond a concrete path. Extending the exterior wall to include these posts and beams would gain about 50 sq. ft. of kitchen space without affecting the house's original roofline or proportions—an opportunity we couldn't resist. But we would need to remove the 8x8s temporarily so we could pour a stem-wall foundation and a slab floor.

To support the 8x10, we used two 4x10s extending from the side of the house and meeting at a point beyond the beam (drawing, above right). We supported the 4x10s on four posts, each built up out of three 2x4s. We first nailed one 2x4 to the side of a 4x10. This took most of the weight off whoever was holding the heavy beam, so measuring and cutting the second 2x4, which would sit at right angles to the first to form a saddle for the heavy timber, was easy. The third 2x4 was nailed up full length and parallel to the first to cradle the 4x10.

Once the foundation work was done and the slab poured, we replaced the 8x8 posts, removed the temporary supports, and fitted custom metal window frames in the new wall.

Central wall—Once we finished the north wall of the laundry, we moved on to the area's central bearing wall (C), just north of the small original kitchen wall (E). Removing the plaster ceiling, we were astonished to find cantilevered 2x6 joists only 10 in. long carrying the load of an upstairs bearing wall (photo, center left). Had the 4x6 joists for the bedroom over the laundry been 8 in. longer, they could have carried the

offset upstairs wall without a problem. We could only surmise that some change in plans had produced this structural anomaly. As it was, the 2x6 rim joist was carrying most of the load. Since we were changing the rim joist's end bearing, we needed to extend the 4x6s the extra 8 in. to carry the upstairs wall.

To do this, we bolted half the length of ⅜-in. steel plates, 5½ in. wide by 15 in. long, to each face of the 4x6s. We then bolted 8-in. 4x6s between each set of plates, and nailed a 1x6 rim joist to the ends of these extended beams (drawing, above left). The floor joists over the kitchen had been face-nailed to the studs of the upstairs wall without blocking or cripples beneath them, which we added before nailing up a skin of ⅜-in. plywood to tie everything together.

At the south wall of the kitchen, the same floor joists had been face-nailed to the roof rafters with no bracing (photo, bottom left). Where the joists didn't line up with the rafters, cripples had been inserted at the angle of the roof. I think it was just the lath and plaster that held them in place. We added blocking under each joist to form a new soffit, and nailed a ⅜-in. plywood gusset to the blocking, cripple and joist for rigidity. Then we could get back to the storeroom/kitchen wall (C in the drawing).

The wall's load had been evenly distributed, requiring only modest footings. Our plan to replace the framing with an 8x10 beam spanning 12 ft. meant larger footings to take the two concentrated loads.

A 4x6 carried the 2x8 floor joists under the wall. It was supported in turn by 4x4 posts on isolated piers about 4 ft. on center. The crawl space was barely a foot high at its east end, and the whole thing was clogged with heating ducts, so the easiest approach was to take up the flooring and excavate from above. We undermined about half the bearing of the pier closest to each point of concentration, poured concrete under both, and incorporated them into new footings about 2½ ft. wide by 4½ ft. long and 10 in. deep

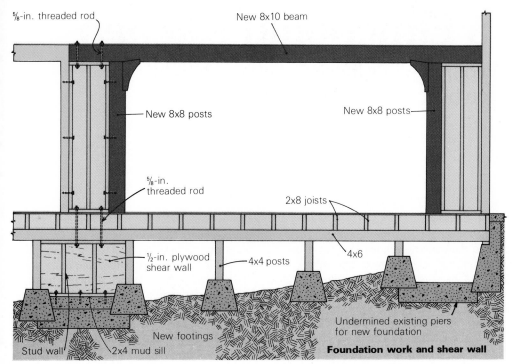

⅝-in. threaded rod

New 8x10 beam

New 8x8 posts

New 8x8 posts

⅝-in. threaded rod

2x8 joists

½-in. plywood shear wall

4x4 posts

4x6

Undermined existing piers for new foundation

New footings

Stud wall

2x4 mud sill

Foundation work and shear wall

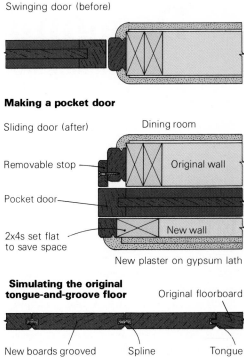

Swinging door (before)

Making a pocket door

Sliding door (after)

Dining room

Removable stop

Original wall

Pocket door

2x4s set flat to save space

New wall

New plaster on gypsum lath

Simulating the original tongue-and-groove floor

Original floorboard

New boards grooved

Spline

Tongue

(drawing, above). We realized we now had an opportunity to add a shear wall tied directly to the ground to keep the house from racking, so we formed a stem wall on the new west footing directly below the 4x6 beam with anchor bolts and a 2x4 mud sill. We then incorporated adjacent 4x4 posts in a short 2x4 stud wall 12 in. o.c. under the 4x6. Before sheathing it with ½-in. plywood, we ran two ⅝-in. threaded steel rods to the bottom plate of the new west shear wall on the kitchen floor level, binding the new 8x8 post and the 8x10 beam together into a racking panel that carried right down to the new footing.

Pocket door—Fixing our last nagging problem brought our structural work full circle. The house had settled so much that the swinging door between the pantry and the dining room wouldn't pivot more than 90° before it hit the floor and jammed. When it opened into the pantry it was in the way of the stuff stored there. We decided that the best solution was to build a pocket sliding door. So we framed up a new wall in the former pantry out of 2x4s, face side out, covered with gypsum lath and new plaster (drawing, top right). This left us plenty of room to install the original door on its new sliding track, and enough space in the corner to tie up another loose end, the waste line from upstairs.

Re-routing the drain produced three new problems. First, because the upstairs flooring and 4x6 floor joists were to be the finished downstairs ceiling, we had to run the drain line above the upstairs floor. Thus the use of a back-flush toilet, which flushes back rather than down. Its 3-in. drain is about 2½ in. above the floor, and allowed us a 10-ft. horizontal run (at a fall of ¼ in. per ft.) before we would have to penetrate the floor. Our pocket-door corner was 7 ft. away from the toilet, well within range.

Second, some of the flooring under the old toilet needed to be replaced, and numerous calls to lumberyards revealed that 1x6 roughsawn V-joint, tongue-and-groove fir was not a stock

item. We decided to simulate the original material as best we could by using 1x6 rough fir. We would chamfer the edges on a table saw and groove them for splines with a router (drawing, above right). It turned out that 1x6 rough fir wasn't stock either. So I found myself standing at the lumberyard in front of a bandsaw where they were resawing 8x16 fir beams. All I wanted was two 1x6s, 12 ft. long. The operator sent one of his helpers to locate a 2x6, which he brought back on a forklift, and within minutes I drove away with my custom-milled, roughsawn fir planks.

Third, we had to patch the 4x6 beam that had been hacked away by the plumber installing the original drain. This beam would be visible in the new ceiling, so we carefully chiseled and planed a square recess around the damage, then let in a

patch of rough 2x6 with similar grain. This we secured with glue and finish nails.

Our simple-sounding assignment to open up the room for more space led us inexorably to everything from foundation work under the house to installing plumbing on the next floor. We found serious structural flaws that had to be remedied, and had ourselves created conditions that would have been unsafe if we hadn't followed through properly. We'd worked around the unavailability of materials, and had taken advantage of opportunities to improve the structure of the house as we went along. Most renovation work is like that.   □

Eric Rekdahl is a partner in the design/build firm of Rekdahl & Tellefsen in Berkeley, Calif.

In the expanded kitchen, the new carved beams and brackets echo details found throughout the house. Red oak cabinets by Robert Zummwalt harmonize with the oak flooring and trim.

Designing a Functional Kitchen

Planning around your family's lifestyle and work habits will get you beyond standard solutions

by Sam Clark

The key to kitchen design is movement—how people move through the house; how supplies, tools and foods are moved in the kitchen itself; and how people use their arms, legs, eyes and hands as they prepare meals and clean up afterwards. A small, simple kitchen designed in harmony with this movement will be a more inviting and efficient place to work in than the most lavishly equipped showplace laid out with standard formulas and stock cabinets.

Siting—Begin with how the cooking area will fit into the house. Siting the kitchen in the house is as important as siting a house on the land. No interior design can compensate for a lack of light and air; so the first step is often to take down walls, add windows or move the kitchen to a brighter part of the house.

Remodeling a kitchen often means reorganizing the house plan (drawing facing page, bottom). Consider the chief activities of your home, such as cooking, eating, visiting, entertaining, sleeping, studying, playing, listening to music, cleaning, reading, coming in and going out. Your kitchen design to a large extent will determine how these activities mesh.

In some cases the best relationship between two activities or spaces is the same for most households. A kitchen entry near the garage, for example, is always ideal. Indoors, the dining table should be near the cooking area.

But on many questions, family needs will differ. The dining area is a good example. If your entertaining tends to be informal, you might want the dining table to be in the kitchen or open to it. Guests can help cook, and the cleanup crew need not be excluded from after-dinner conversation. On the other hand, you may prefer a separate and more formal dining room. It isolates the cook, but it also isolates kitchen mess. The same considerations apply when you decide whether to include a conversational sitting area in the kitchen.

Decorating magazines often recommend a kitchen play area for families with small children, but segregating the play area would be much better for many families. Similarly, the stereo, the laundry, a homework and hobby area, or a TV might either fit well in your kitchen or disrupt it. In general, a more open and inclusive layout works best when the family is small or relatively well disciplined, and when there is a quiet den to retreat to.

Siting and layout have a more telling effect on how pleasant and functional the kitchen will be than any decorating you might do. If your funds are short, spend first on the layout, and be stingy with the cabinets, appliances and fixtures. You can always upgrade the equipment later.

Three principles regulate the internal design of the kitchen work area, or indeed any work place: storage at the point of first use, grouping counter space and equipment into work centers, and ordering these centers according to work sequences.

Storage—Most people store things by category. The beans are stored with the flour because both go in canisters. Corned-beef hash and chicken noodle soup go together in a larder because they come in cans. In an efficient plan, though, foods and equipment should be stored where they will be used first. You rinse dried beans and dilute canned soup, so both should be stored near the sink. Flour is usually scooped dry right into a large mixing bowl, so it should be kept near the bowls. The canned hash goes straight into a skillet—store it at the stove. Think the same way about utensils. Saucepans are usually filled with water first, so they might well be stored at the sink. Griddles belong near the stove.

Many items, such as knives, can openers, mixing bowls, cooking oil, and salt and pepper, are used at two or three different stations. It makes sense to store them in several small stashes rather than in one central spot.

Work centers—Since different kinds of kitchen work call for different tools, supplies and work surfaces, the kitchen should be divided into distinct work centers, set up to make the basic jobs as convenient as possible. Though the centers have been defined many ways, I find it most useful to picture three basic centers: the *cleanup center* at the sink, the *mix center,* and the *cooking center* at the stove.

The *cleanup center* (**A**) is for dishwashing and for cooking tasks that require water. Its focus is the sink, which should have about 2 ft. of counter on the dirty-dish side (a good place for this is an inside corner where two counters meet) and at least 20 in. of counter on the clean-dish side. It also needs either a built-in dishwasher (24 in. wide and 34½ in. high) under the counter, or a large dish drainer, which can be built in above the sink. A trash can should be nearby. All the soaps, pot-scrubbers and sponges you use for washing dishes are kept here. A set of drawers or wire bins for potatoes, onions and other non-refrigerated produce is nice if there's room.

Though tableware is often stored in a separate serving center, dishes you use every day really belong near the sink. The chore of putting clean dishes and pots away in cupboards and drawers all over the kitchen is archaic and unnecessary. If you have a dishwasher, build racks or shelves for clean dishes within arm's reach. If you wash by hand, a draining dishrack built above or to one side of the sink can be designed to hold most of the daily dishes and basic bowls and saucepans. This will give you a place to put rinsed dishes away wet, eliminating the need to dry or drain them first. Given this arrangement, washing dishes by hand will take about the same effort as loading and unloading the dishwasher, so you may decide to do without a dishwasher and use its space beneath for storage.

The *mix center* (**B**) is the place where ingredients are combined. Think of the mix center as your main work surface. It should be roughly 3 ft. to 5 ft. long. Bowls, whips and whisks, electric mixers and blenders, measuring tools, baking dishes, spices, shortening, oil, baking powder and grains are among the items properly stored here.

The *cooking center* (**C**) is the third major work area. It encompasses the stove, and attendant utensils—griddles, skillets, spatulas, hot pads. The cooking center also needs a work surface and a heatproof area to set down hot dishes. It's the place to store oil, some spices and the foods that go straight onto the burners or into the oven. You will probably need additional counter space here, either all on one side of the stove or in sections on each side. Often the cooking center is expanded to create a second large work area for preparing big meals and to make space for a second cook to work. I like a large butcher block here, and perhaps a compost drawer (photo, p. 173, top) for easy cleanup.

Sometimes a large counter between the sink and stove, equipped with portable trivets and cutting boards, can serve as a combined mix and cooking center. This is an excellent plan for one orderly cook or for tight layouts, as long as a kitchen table or sink counter can be requisitioned when you need extra space.

Many books and magazine articles assign the refrigerator to the mix center. This gives

Three work centers.
The cleanup center (A) is at the sink. It includes either a dishwasher or a large dish drainer over the sink, as shown. Foods and tools used first at the sink are stored in the cleanup center. The mix center (B) is a counter where recipes are usually put together. Often it is next to the refrigerator. Mixing utensils and staple ingredients belong here. Open shelving makes it easy to locate what you need. The mainstay of the cooking center (C) is the stove. Frying pans are kept here, along with the food that goes directly into them. In the photo below, the pots and pans hang from an overhead rack. All of the kitchen centers have accessible storage areas.

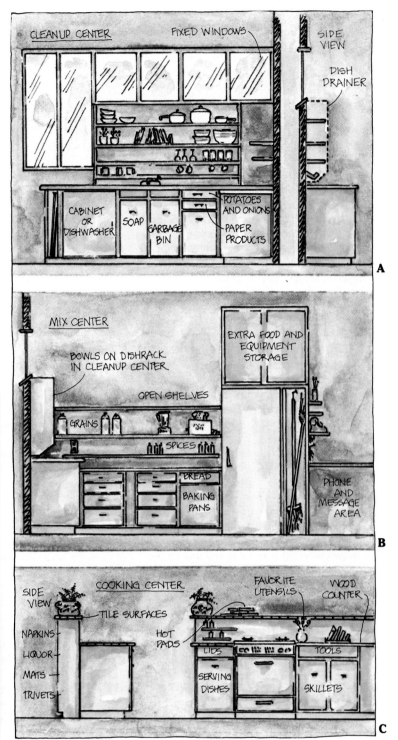

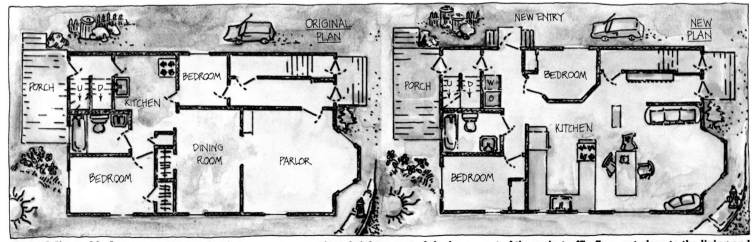

Remodeling a kitchen may mean moving it to a more convenient, brighter part of the house, out of the main traffic flow, yet close to the living and dining areas. In the original plan, left, the kitchen is far from the dining room, in a dark, cramped corridor between the entry and the rest of the house. In the new plan, right, a well-lit kitchen with ample counters is open to the dining and living spaces; and a new entry simplifies the path in and out.

Photos: Wendy Page; Illustrations: Barbara Smolover

the kitchen layout a nice symmetry: three centers, each with its own major appliance. But functionally, the refrigerator—along with a 12-in. or 18-in. counter on its handle side to make loading and unloading convenient—can be separate as long as it is not too far from the work stations. Treating the refrigerator as a fourth layout component gives you much greater flexibility because it multiplies the possible configurations.

If space allows, two small additional centers may be useful. A *serving center*, located on the table side of the stove, can hold serving bowls and spoons, napkins, tablecloths, or placemats, trivets and the like. Heatproof counters are handy here. Mounted on casters, a serving center can double as a serving cart. A *planning center* with a desk, cookbooks, a phone, a message board, pencils and mail slots is also nice to have if a small spot at the edge of the work area is available.

You'll also need spaces at the work centers for small appliances, bread, snacks, a radio, coffee and tea, and liquor. Sometimes subcategories of this kind are elaborated into additional centers such as a bar, a hobby center, a canning center, a recycling center, a snack center and so on, making the kitchen needlessly large and destroying its efficiency. I think it's best to keep things simple. Stick with the basic centers, and use special drawers, shelves or racks as subcenters.

Work sequences—When possible, arrange the work centers to correspond to logical work sequences. The drawings below show the travel path for preparing a cooked vegetable in two different layouts. In the one on the left, the path is short and logical from the back door to the table. In the one on the right, it is not. No sequence will work perfectly for all types of kitchen work, but a good order to strive for might go thus: from back door to refrigerator to sink center to mix center to cooking center to table.

Layout methods—Many books and articles on kitchen planning suggest arriving at a design by collecting "kitchen ideas" the way kids collect baseball cards; eventually you have a complete set. I like a different approach. Get a notebook, put a comfortable chair in a corner of your current kitchen, and watch what happens. Observe who does which jobs. Identify which tasks seem simple and straightforward, and which clumsy and time-consuming. Notice when people rub their backs in pain, when they reach comfortably, where collisions occur. Determine which jobs now require extra steps, and which can be completed with just a few. Kitchen researchers used to compare layouts by listing or photographing every reach, bend, search and step. Without going to the lengths they did, you can use careful observation to evolve your new or improved kitchen.

Based on these observations and your other ideas, write a program—a list of your design goals. It should include the ways you want your new kitchen to be different from your present one. Here's an example.

Cooking area: more storage; space for two cooks at once; space for freezer; direct access to yard and car.

Desired special features: very sunny; spacious feeling; family encouraged to help out; guest and cooks not isolated—guests help out.

Activities to be included in kitchen: phone; meal planning; laundry; canning; desk.

Things to be excluded: street noise; TV noise; formal visiting (separate parlor desired); older children's noisy play.

Dining: all meals in kitchen; seating for five daily, up to ten maximum with guests; dine on south wall, overlooking garden; no view of street from table.

Cost: money, $6,500 max.; time, ten weekends at ten hours of work each, or 100 hours.

Disruption: No more than a month of living in dust, but up to three months with some details incomplete.

Next, begin drawing possible layouts, locating the kitchen within the home, and the work centers within the kitchen. Include all areas inside and out that may be involved or related to the design. Beware of the standard U, L, galley, island, and peninsular layouts you see in all the kitchen books and decorating magazines. These conventions were devised over 30 years ago as guidelines for evaluating kitchens in mass-produced housing. They usually result in decent, general-purpose designs, and you can learn from them. Just don't be bound by them. In remodeling, for ex-

ample, trying to achieve a standard U or L could force you to move walls, stairs, doorways or plumbing that could just as well stay in place.

Beware also of the well-known triangle rule. The work triangle was developed around 1950 at the University of Illinois as a test for layouts in tract housing. According to the studies done there, the distances between the three

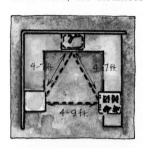

major appliances (the sink, stove and refrigerator) should be within the limits shown at left. If they are longer, the cook will take unnecessary steps. If they are shorter, the kitchen will be congested, and the work areas too small. Many people base their kitchen layout entirely on this idea. I think that intelligent storage and well-thought-out work centers are much more important.

Although standard design conventions are helpful rules of thumb, they shouldn't be followed slavishly. Draw your possible layouts as freely, playfully and loosely as you can.

Evaluating layouts—Evaluate your plans by comparing each with your design program and with the notes you made during observation. Fasten push-pins at the main stations of your plans, then wind yarn from point to point as you imagine performing various cooking and cleanup sequences. The length of yarn you use gives you a scaled measurement of the hypothetical distances traveled, so you can check the efficiency of each design for a given task.

Designing work centers—Design the work centers by making a series of elevation drawings in the same scale you used for the plans. Refer again to your initial program and to the notes you made during your observations. This is where the principle of storage at the point of first use comes into play. The design of the centers should reflect the specific ways in which each will be used. First plan the work surface itself. Most kitchen designs force us to work standing up, assembly-line style. If there's room, plan one or two places where a tired or meditative cook can work sitting down. An old-fashioned kitchen table, for example, isn't just a spot for informal meals. It also lets two or three people work sitting down and facing each other instead of staring at the wall.

In each area, find the counter height that leaves your back straight and your arms comfortable while you work. Have someone measure from your elbow to the floor while you stand straight with your upper arm vertical and forearm horizontal. For most people, a counter two or three inches below this point will be just about right for washing dishes, making sandwiches, and for most cooking activities. For kneading bread, rolling out dough, mixing heavy batters, or working with

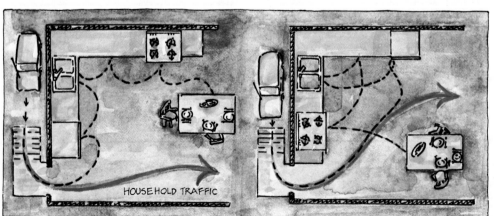

Planning for efficiency. **Both of these layouts look fine until you trace the travel paths for a typical kitchen task. Then the superiority of the arrangement on the left becomes evident.**

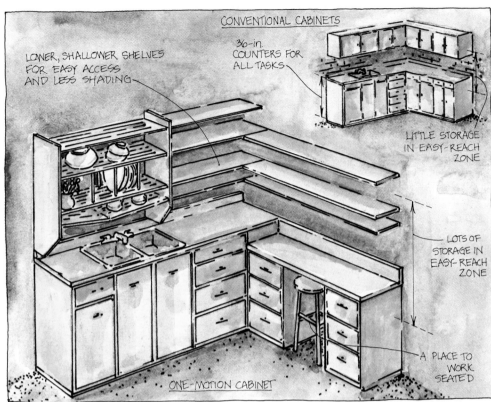

Sensible counters and cabinets are built for convenience. Storage is designed for specific contents, counter height is tailored to the task, and drawers make it easy to retrieve things. Most of the storage space in standard cabinets is hard to reach. All counters are the same height, and there are no special accessories like the composting drawer and the knife slot in the photos at left.

long-handled tools, the counter should probably be 6 in. to 7 in. below the elbow, especially if you bake regularly. This will leave the stove and sink counters a few inches higher than the mix-center counter.

Consider your counter surfaces carefully. Raw or oiled wood is good for chopping vegetables, but not for chopping raw meats (because of potential bacterial contamination). Tile will resist heat at the stove. Plastic laminate, polyurethaned wood and other non-porous surfaces are convenient at the mix and sink centers. Remember that you can always use trivets or cutting boards on top of a counter that won't stand up to heat or chopping. Just make sure that the sink counter won't be damaged by water.

Next, plan storage. If the first rule of work-center design is storage at the point of first use, the second is to give prime locations to items used most often. While it's nice to have all your bowls handy, it is essential to have your favorite one or two immediately at hand. Arrange things so that these everyday items can be put away and retrieved without wasted movement. Items you use constantly should be available with a single motion if possible.

A knife slot at the back of the counter (photo above left) is a good example of one-motion storage. The reach is short, there are no doors or drawers to open, and the knives, at hand height, are accessible without your having to stoop or stretch. The rack is fully visible, and selection is easy. The knives are handle up, so that you can grasp the one you want with the grip required for its use.

Remember that all storage isn't equal. Some spots are harder to get at than others. Any-

thing above 20 in. and below 60 in. (roughly between the knees and the shoulders) can be reached comfortably. The drainer, the knife rack, open shelves at or a little below eye level, and other racks just above counter height are one-motion locations. The bottom shelves of enclosed overhead cabinets and the top one or two drawers below the counter are almost as handy. You have to open something, but there's no bending or stretching. Lower drawers and higher shelves are accessible, but you have to stoop or reach to get at them. The top shelf and bottom drawers, which are outside the 20-in. to 60-in. field, are quite inconvenient. The worst spot of all is on fixed shelves behind doors in base cabinets, because finding something there inevitably requires a lot of shifting of the stored items and fumbling in the dark.

The drawing above contrasts standard and functional kitchen storage. In conventional kitchens, the best storage spot—the back of the counter—is the one place no storage is provided. Overhead cabinets usually start about 54 in. above the floor, which is at the top of the area easily reached by the average person. A typical base cabinet has one good storage spot, the top drawer. Most of its contents are buried in the deep fixed shelves.

A more functional model might look something like the one-motion cabinet in the drawing above. It would have narrow open shelves at the back of the counter, perhaps up to head height, or racks designed for specific contents. Almost everything below counter height would be in drawers, on rolling shelves, or on racks mounted to the inside of cabinet doors. This was the model developed by the Cornell

Kitchen, the most advanced and also the most ignored of the 1950s research kitchens.

Locate the most used items first. Then find storage for the items used regularly but not constantly. Finally, deal with the turkey pan, waffle iron and other infrequently used items.

A good test of the designs you draw in elevation is to imagine performing work sequences, movement by movement. Picture each reach, step or grasp, each opening or closing of a door or drawer. Think where your hand will be at the exact moment you need a tool—this is the ideal storage location. These imaginary movies are analogous to the string diagrams you performed on your layouts.

A kitchen designed in this way does not just save time; it changes what it feels like to work in the kitchen. Your movements as you cook become more economical, deft and sure. Work bounces and jerks less, and flows more. Because cooking becomes more artful and graceful, the work becomes a pleasure in itself.

The kitchen you design this way may look odd. It will probably have fewer doors than other kitchens, and more drawers. It will have more racks, bins, and other special storage setups. The various counter heights may give it a less streamlined look. However, it will cost less, because it will have been designed for function, not show. Perhaps most important, it will have been designed for the way people move through your house, and the way you and your family cook and clean up, so it will work better for you. □

Sam Clark is a carpenter and author of the book The Motion-Minded Kitchen, *published in 1983 by Houghton Mifflin.*

Custom Kitchen Planning

A designer's thoughts on renovating the home's most complex room

by Matthew Kaplan

The kitchen is the most difficult room to design. No other area contains such a crush of objects—from cereal boxes to sinks—and such a stew of human activities. Deciding which objects must be accommodated is one of the first steps in kitchen planning. At the same time, refrigerators, ovens and other mechanical helpers should not encroach on the largest and most important spaces, which belong to the people who cook, work and dine there. Planning a kitchen renovation to meet their needs means that both construction options and personal preferences must be recorded, organized and integrated.

Before I begin designing a kitchen, I interview the owners to find out what they will need. Their old kitchen is thoroughly analyzed and often reveals characteristics that can be useful in the new design, such as hobbies, collections of plants, or small dining areas. The most important element in developing a custom-tailored room is a detailed, written description of the owner's ideal kitchen. Obviously, later on compromises will be made for lack of money or lack of space, but I have found it better to modify, revise or even eliminate features than to add on in the latter stages of planning.

The kitchen form—As an aid in developing a written description, I ask my clients to fill out a kitchen form similar to the one shown on the right. It is organized from the general to the par-

Within this 15-ft. by 15-ft. kitchen there is an informal dining area, an island counter, the usual battery of appliances, a pastry counter and a wine vault housing 1,000 bottles.

THE KITCHEN FORM

Use of space—Describe in detail all functions.

Sewing/ironing/	*Desk*
laundry	*Play area*
Bar/dining-room	*Other*

Major appliances—Makes and models to be chosen during preliminary design phase. Underline those you would include.

Range	*Dishwasher*
commercial-features	*trim panel*
residential-features	*Sink*
Ovens	*number of*
double or single	*compartments*
gas or electric	*faucet action*
venting required	*spray, pop-up drain*
self-cleaning	*soap dispenser*
color, size	*chopping board*
doors - glass vs. solid	*garbage disposal*
Cooktop	*Grill*
gas	*Freezer*
electric	*Compactor*
commercial	*Washing machine*
residential	*location*
Refrigerator/freezer	*front or top loading*
ice maker	*Dryer*
color, size	*gas*
side by side	*electric*
top or bottom freezer	
trim kit	

Small appliances—Those you own or plan to purchase. Will they be displayed or concealed?

Toaster	*Electric knife*
built-in	*chargeable*
portable	*nonchargeable*
Toaster oven	*Can opener*
Coffee maker	*electric*
Coffee grinder	*manual*
Mixer	*drawer-mounted*
Food grinder	*wall-mounted*
Blender	*T.V.*
Ice crusher	*Radio*
Yogurt maker	*In-counter motor for*
Scale	*combination*
Ice-cream maker	*appliances*
Deep fryer	*Other*

Storage types—Concealed or displayed.

Foods	*Canisters for staples*
stored in quantity	*Spices*
and used daily	*location*
packaged, canned,	*Paper goods*
jars, bottles	*Tea, coffee*
Bread	*Wine, liquor, aperitif*
storage location-	*Pots, pans*
special drawer	*Fondue set*
Potatoes and onions	*Glassware and dishes*
type of storage	

Decorative

Wall	*Stained glass*
applied fabric	*Plants*
graphics	

Other considerations

Intercom	*New doors and*
Smoke detector	*windows*
Burglar alarm	*Air conditioning*
Fire extinguisher	*Lighting*

ticular, from the description of functions to the housing of kitchen equipment and supplies.

Use of space. If the kitchen is complex, it is also the most versatile space in the house, and you can't spend too much time discussing use. It is used for cooking and dining in traditional ways, for kibitzing over coffee with neighbors, and even for paying bills and doing homework. If there are young children, incidentally, now is the time to take their presence into account so that you can design tamper-proof storage areas and safe play areas.

Major appliances. Consider large appliances next because, after spaces for people, these take up the most room. Many people decide to buy new appliances when renovating kitchens. Although the information about types, sizes and special features is not crucial in the early stages of planning, it's important to order appliances as soon as possible. By setting up delivery dates about two months before the anticipated completion of the project, you may avoid price increases and you'll expedite construction. If an incorrect model is sent, it can be returned at once and little harm will be done. If you are planning to include custom cabinet work, the cabinetmaker can ascertain exact sizes and note the location of appliance seams that might affect cabinet detailing. Electricians and plumbers can determine in advance what connections will be necessary. The disadvantages of ordering appli-

This kitchen was designed so that two cooks could work there simultaneously. All the details—from appliance choices to activities—were discussed before plans were drawn.

Above, cleft slate was used for the countertop (left) because of its beauty and durability. Although it is expensive and heavy, hot pots cannot damage it. Two maple cutting boards were recessed in the slate. Under-counter drawer space was designed to accommodate the owners' needs. Floor-to-ceiling pantry and cabinet (right) was designed to accommodate all sizes of pots and pans.

Cabinets and Countertops

Cabinets and Countertops—Cabinet design requires a bit of head-scratching. For the kitchen shown on these pages the clients wanted a tone of warmth and elegance. The cherry gave the warmth; the molding, the elegance.

Once we had decided upon the molding profile shown below, I thought about joinery. I had intended to mill the profile into the rails and stiles, joining the corners with a mortise-and-tenon joint and coping the ends of the rails to the profile of the stiles, giving a good fit with lots of gluing surface. But a molding so ornate made coping impossible. I decided to join the stile and rail with a spline joint, and add the door molding afterwards.

After several hundred feet of cherry molding

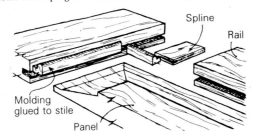

Spline

Rail

Molding glued to stile

Panel

had been milled to my specifications, I realized that it would dwarf the panels. After many experiments, I decided to cut down the molding, using just the curl. I think it works—a little spicy, but light-handed.

The slate countertops are held in place by gravity. I ran a bead of silicone on the top of the ¾-in. plywood frame and used black silicone between slate edges, but otherwise used no hardware—no L-braces or joining plates—to attach slate to wood. Although the top of the slate is cleft and quite irregular, the bottom is finely cut and perfectly flat.

Cooking surfaces built into wooden cabinets can be problematic and dangerous because extreme changes in temperature or moisture are hard on wood. To isolate the cooktop's intense heat, I lined its opening in the cabinet with Transite insulation board and then fitted a specially fabricated stainless-steel liner. Because this insulation board has asbestos fibers, cutting it with a saw will put these fibers into the air and your lungs. Instead of cutting, I suggest wetting and scoring it repeatedly with a utility knife until you can snap it easily. □

—*Peter Dechar, a cabinetmaker in Brooklyn, N.Y.*

ances early are the possibility of theft if no one lives in the building, or that they'll be in the way during construction.

Selections of major appliances are influenced by how the owner will use the appliance, performance of the appliance, size and capacities needed, gas or electric hookups, optional accessories wanted and durability. The choices are narrowed down until they coincide with the space available, the location of utility lines and the kinds of finished surfaces planned for the completed kitchen. Here are some points to consider in deciding on appliances:

Commercial ranges are expensive and take up too much space; their purchase is unjustified for most households. Domestic ranges are the best bet, especially easy-to-clean models with trim that overlaps the countertop.

Double ovens allow for simultaneous preparation of dishes that require different cooking temperatures. The height of the double ovens is flexible; I like to position the top one so that its open door will align with the countertop. This allows for the easy transfer of hot dishes.

Cooktops are often used in conjunction with double ovens. I recommend cooktops 30 in. long because they consume little counter space and their shallow depth allows more drawer space underneath. The standard height of cooktops is about 36 in., but I place them slightly lower, from 32 in. to 34 in. This height allows easier stirring and a better view into deep pots. Because many cooktop dishes need short cooking times and high temperatures, I favor gas cooktops over electric. Either type should have removable trays under each burner and removable tops for easier cleaning.

A dishwasher with the fewest buttons is the best choice. Not only will it be less expensive, but most of the buttons on complex models are seldom used anyway.

Sink styles are nearly infinite, and selection depends upon the cook's preferences. Heavy-duty sinks are worth the extra money. Stainless-steel sinks pair nicely with plastic laminate counters, and synthetic stone sinks work well with slate, granite or marble counters. Sink height depends on the height of the principal cook; best in general is the 32-in. to 34-in. height I recommend for cooktops. A lever-type faucet is

handy because you can turn it with your wrist if your hands are dirty. Pop-up drains obviate having to fish in hot, greasy water for drain plugs.

Washers and dryers stacked vertically conserve space, an advantage in small rooms; side-by-side machines under counters also create unobtrusive laundry areas.

Small appliances and storage. After locating major appliances and cabinets, think about any special equipment you'd like to have close at hand. It's useful to know if an extensive collection of small appliances will require additional outlets or if a blender needs an in-counter motor. Some people are crazy about their spices and like to display them in special racks. Others want to have such staples as potatoes and onions close at hand. These specifics are important once work begins on preliminary drawings, because the counter space must accommodate all the equipment and supplies that will be used there.

Lighting. Make sure that working surfaces are broadly illuminated. Although I prefer the warm light of incandescent bulbs, newly developed warm-white fluorescent tubes are worth considering. They use less electricity, burn cooler and

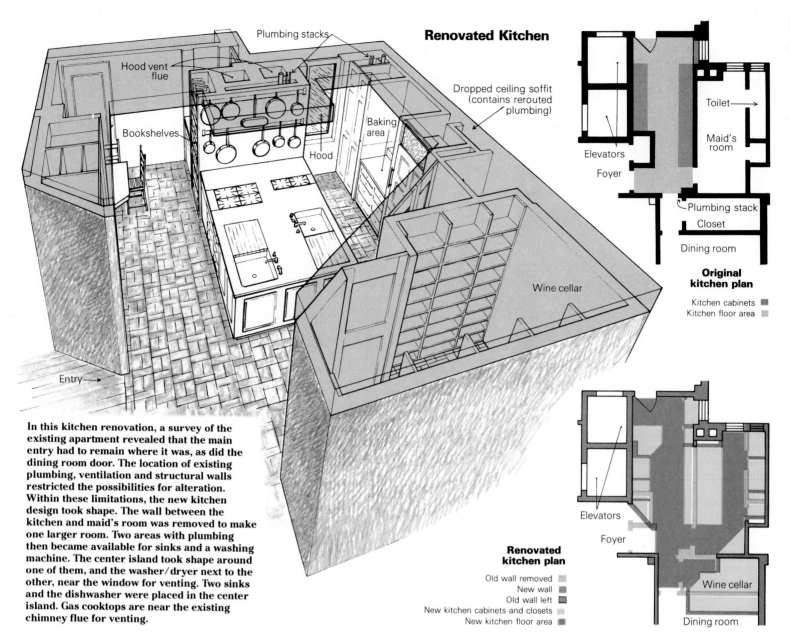

Renovated Kitchen

Plumbing stacks

Hood vent flue

Bookshelves

Hood

Baking area

Dropped ceiling soffit (contains rerouted plumbing)

Wine cellar

Entry

Toilet

Maid's room

Elevators

Foyer

Plumbing stack

Closet

Dining room

Original kitchen plan

Kitchen cabinets
Kitchen floor area

Elevators

Foyer

Renovated kitchen plan

Old wall removed
New wall
Old wall left
New kitchen cabinets and closets
New kitchen floor area

Wine cellar

Dining room

In this kitchen renovation, a survey of the existing apartment revealed that the main entry had to remain where it was, as did the dining room door. The location of existing plumbing, ventilation and structural walls restricted the possibilities for alteration. Within these limitations, the new kitchen design took shape. The wall between the kitchen and maid's room was removed to make one larger room. Two areas with plumbing then became available for sinks and a washing machine. The center island took shape around one of them, and the washer/dryer next to the other, near the window for venting. Two sinks and the dishwasher were placed in the center island. Gas cooktops are near the existing chimney flue for venting.

provide more diffuse light. If you want light fixtures inside vent hoods, use commercial housings to seal out moisture and to contain the glass bulb should it break.

Surveying the space—Photos of the existing kitchen layout are helpful during schematic drawing stages, so take them as early as possible. Photos record stylistic elements such as intricate plaster work, wood moldings or paneling that may affect the final design, if you are trying to preserve the style.

After measuring the kitchen, document the composition and condition of existing surfaces and the locations of existing mechanicals, such as plumbing, electrical wiring and vents. Information about these systems is easy to get: Where were the old appliances, fixtures and the lines that served them? To be sure I remember the location of mechanicals, I'll often sketch in the systems on Polaroid photos while I'm on the site. But to know for sure what is behind the walls, it's sometimes necessary to cut into them. By determining the routes of mechanical systems early, you know the parameters of dif-

ferent design solutions. For example, you may not want to move sinks and dishwashers across a room if it means installing a new system of drain pipes to accommodate them. Although pipes and wiring are flexible to a degree, some choices are prohibitively expensive. Cutting into walls for a look can be crucial, for surprises uncovered after construction begins can make meticulously drawn plans useless.

Schematic drawings—From the filled-in kitchen forms and the survey you'll have enough information to begin drawing a number of kitchen schematics. There are as many methods of depicting kitchen space as there are books on the subject, but I prefer to draw a basic floor plan from the survey and to sketch various alternatives on tissue-paper overlays. I prefer a scale of ½ in. to 1 ft. Any larger size requires an inordinate amount of drawing, and anything smaller produces drawings without much detail.

The order of allocating space roughly follows that of the kitchen form, beginning with the movement of people. Main corridors must always be wide—3 ft. to 3½ ft. is minimum—so

that people returning home with groceries or passing while cooking have enough room. If several cooks will be working together, all the corridors should be at least 3 ft. wide.

Venting and waste line requirements have a lot to do with appliance location. Sinks, washing machines, gas cooktops and electric ovens require venting to the outside and should be placed as close as possible to a wall or a chimney vent (shown in the drawing above). Gas ovens and refrigerators are the most flexible to place.

Counter space is always a battle at the end, for each major appliance must have a counter next to it. Calculate drawer and shelf space when you sketch what each wall of cabinets and appliances will look like. Pantries and floor-to-ceiling storage cabinets save space and are more convenient to use than conventional cabinets.

Where confusion about the drawings persists, chalk final plans on walls or floors. This way you can walk around in the space and live with it awhile before beginning construction. □

Mathew Kaplan is an architect who practices in Brooklyn, N.Y.

Rehabilitating a Duplex

Two partners turn a dreary, inefficient up and down into a passive-solar side by side

by Rich Lopez

John Marshall and I have been friends for years. In 1980, we decided to become partners and create living units for each of us. We bought an old up-and-down duplex on an 8,300-sq. ft. Boulder lot, with the idea of renovating it.

The building was not only ugly (inset photo, right), it was a wreck. The downstairs unit was the basement, and the ceiling was so low down there that we started to call the place the Hobbit hole. Unlike the cozy Hobbit holes in Tolkein's books, though, this space was cramped, dark, windowless and wrapped around the furnace room. There was no soundproofing in the ceiling, and anyone downstairs could hear every step upstairs, not to mention muffled conversations. The upstairs unit was no prize either, but it was more livable. It contained two bedrooms, a full bath, windows and a large redwood deck.

I wound up with the basement when we moved in, and the first night I was shocked when I heard the furnace switch click on, followed by the loud hiss of natural gas entering the combustion chamber. Suddenly there was an explosion as the gas ignited only 10 ft. away. The only thing that made living intimately with the furnace tolerable was the thought that we'd be under construction in three months—six at the most. Wrong. It was over a year before we got started, and I could stand living underground for only half that time. We switched after six months.

We each lived in the basement a lot longer than we wanted to. As a result, we concluded that the goal of the remodel would be to create two separate living units that would be so alike that we could flip a coin after they were finished and both be happy with the outcome.

Planning—Although the house as it stood made no use of them, the site had many things we'd been looking for. I'm an energy planner with an office in downtown Boulder, and I liked the southern slope for its solar potential, an interest John, who is a lawyer, began to share as time went on. We both liked the location for its proximity to downtown and to the historic Mapleton

The house that Lopez and Marshall bought (inset) had been remodeled several times during its 50-year lifetime. Architect David Barrett retained as much of the original structure as possible while changing its layout completely and making it energy efficient. Lopez and Marshall have resorted to their backup electric heat only during a cloudy five-day below-zero spell.

The first task was to demolish much of the original building. After insulating part of the old foundation and pouring new slabs, builder Peter Wendorf laid up the block partition wall between the two new units.

Financing details

We wanted FHA approval on our plans for several reasons. First, with a government-insured mortgage, we could get a better interest rate at the bank. Second, an FHA-approved mortgage is assumable—an important consideration these days, even though we don't contemplate moving.

The biggest problem with obtaining FHA approval was fitting our concept of rehabilitation into the FHA program guidelines. FHA encourages rehabilitation, but the administrators at first saw our project as a demolition, not a rehabilitation. We saw their point, but we sat down with them to explain why they were wrong. We carefully went over the goals and policies of the FHA rehab program and showed how our project satisfied each point. They finally agreed, and we got two FHA-insured, 12% $55,000 mortgages from a local bank.

Our construction budget also included two City of Boulder Rehabilitation Loans of $20,000 each at 9.5% interest for 15 years. To qualify for these rehab loans, the money for which comes from a consortium of Boulder banks, the house in question has to have been built before 1950 and have serious code violations. We easily qualified, with violations for wiring, minimum insulation and plumbing. The legislation also requires retaining at least 75% of the exterior. We complied by keeping six of the eight exterior walls. Builder Peter Wendorf later told us we saved about $8,000 in materials by not razing the building. Approaching the project as a rehab was the key to being able to finance it. —R. L.

Hill area, with its large trees and beautiful homes. And there were spectacular views of a rock formation called the Flatirons to the south.

We began by using the book *A Pattern Language* (Oxford University Press, 1977), a tool that architects and designers use to organize a client's priorities and to define a site's attributes. Along with John's brother Tom, who is an architect, we used the book to help us identify what we really wanted in the renovation, and to incorporate the passive-solar elements we wanted into the design. As a result of all this, Tom worked up a preliminary design that added a mirror image of the existing floor plan on the adjacent lot and doubled the size of the old building. We soon found that this went beyond the practical limits of our budget. When I first walked into the bank to discuss construction loans, I had a set of concept drawings for a 3,000-sq. ft. remodel and addition neatly rolled up at my side. I was so shocked to hear the loan officer talk about $50 to $60 per-square-foot costs that I never even bothered to spread them out. A $150,000 to $180,000 project was simply beyond our means. That was when we decided that we needed to work closely with a local architect during the design process to keep our dream houses within a reasonable budget.

I'd known David Barrett, a Boulder architect and principal in Sunflower Architects and Environmental Designers, for some time. We hired him with the understanding that his job was to take our wish list and make it economically and structurally realistic.

The result, which stressed flexibility and spacial quality, was a simpler and smaller design than the one we'd envisioned. Several factors influenced the design. First, we didn't want to be roommates; we wanted to be neighbors. We

wanted separate, private homes. It was clear that the only way to achieve the equality our experiences in the Hobbit hole had made us yearn for was to change from an up-and-down to a side-by-side configuration. Each 1,562-sq. ft. unit in Barrett's plan (drawing, facing page) would mirror the other, but we wouldn't be enlarging the footprint much, and we wouldn't be expanding onto the adjacent lot.

Second, we all wanted to blend the new house into its neighborhood, and to keep in mind the view, the sun, the winds and the trees on the lot. We wanted to obtain and store as much seasonal solar gain as possible, and we had a site that offered natural berming to the north and a gentle slope to the south.

Third, we decided that even though we had to make huge changes in the original house, we'd retrofit and reuse as much of it as we could. Our reasons were partly philosophical, partly aesthetic—old materials look nice and it's a shame to waste them—but our decision to incorporate as much of the old house as we could was mostly economic (see the sidebar at left).

Fourth, the limitations of our budget meant we would have to be very clever in our use of space. We solved many design problems by bringing in the builder, Peter Wendorf, to work with us. Builders usually don't have the opportunity to participate in the design process, but this definitely helped us avoid a lot of unnecessary expense. It also established a relationship that gave us enough design flexibility to deal with problems as they came along.

Design—Early in the design process, Barrett took an inventory of the materials in the old building and decided what could be reused. He even prepared a demolition drawing (facing page, top right), something we'd never seen before. The old house was a heavy masonry building, but for our purposes, the masonry was in the wrong place. It was outside the meager insulation in the walls and was useless as thermal mass. In fact, it was conducting heat from inside to outside. One of Barrett's and Wendorf's most important jobs was to rework and relocate the masonry to expose it to the sun while isolating it from exterior temperature variations.

The original house was laid out wrong for our purposes. The entrance was to the east, and there were few windows to the south. Barrett moved the entries to the north, and opened up the south side with a total of 255 sq. ft. of glass (including skylights). He designed the units to have cathedral ceilings in each bedroom, separate dressing areas, and open living room, kitchen and dining areas with partial separation by half-walls, as shown in the drawing.

David wanted thermal mass behind the south glazing to pick up and retain as much of the sun's heat as possible, but because of the spectacular vista, a standard Trombe wall wasn't appropriate. Calculations showed him that a vari-

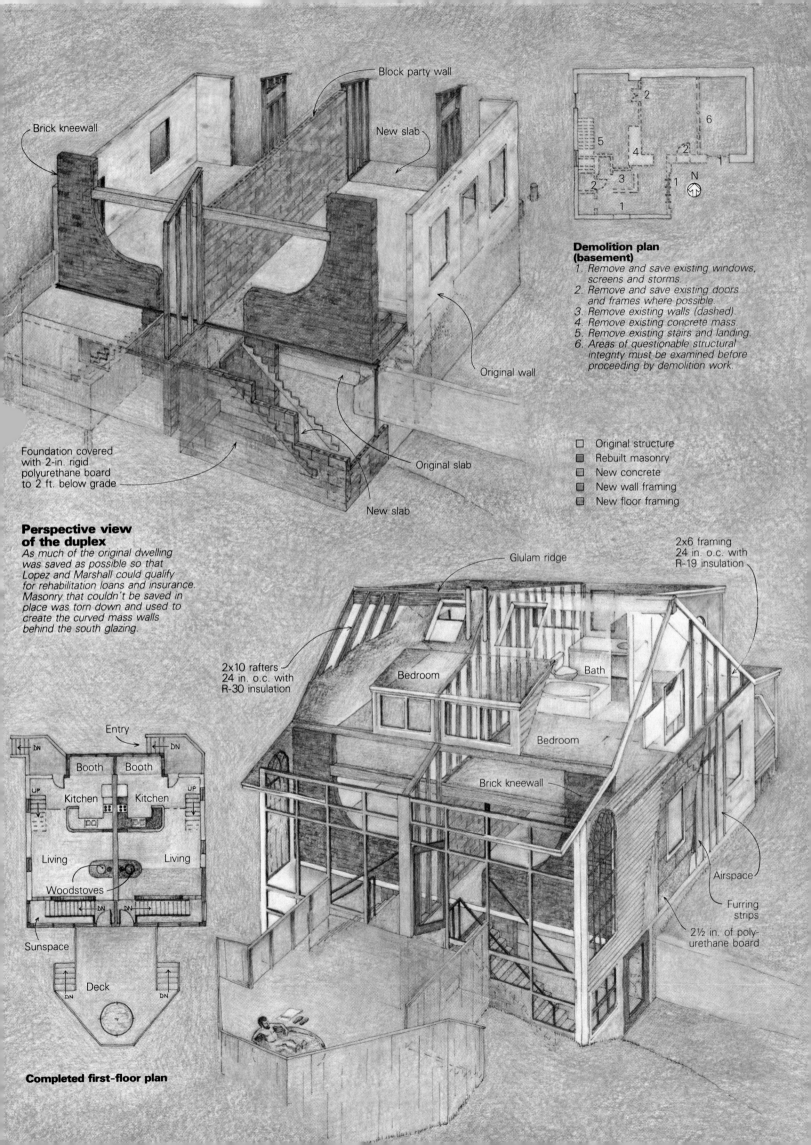

Brick kneewall

Block party wall

New slab

Original wall

Original slab

New slab

Foundation covered with 2-in. rigid polyurethane board to 2 ft. below grade

Demolition plan (basement)
1. Remove and save existing windows, screens and storms.
2. Remove and save existing doors and frames where possible.
3. Remove existing walls (dashed).
4. Remove existing concrete mass.
5. Remove existing stairs and landing.
6. Areas of questionable structural integrity must be examined before proceeding by demolition work.

☐ Original structure
◼ Rebuilt masonry
☐ New concrete
◼ New wall framing
☐ New floor framing

N

Perspective view of the duplex
As much of the original dwelling was saved as possible so that Lopez and Marshall could qualify for rehabilitation loans and insurance. Masonry that couldn't be saved in place was torn down and used to create the curved mass walls behind the south glazing.

Glulam ridge

2x6 framing 24 in. o.c. with R-19 insulation

2x10 rafters 24 in. o.c. with R-30 insulation

Bedroom

Bath

Bedroom

Brick kneewall

Airspace

Furring strips

2½ in. of polyurethane board

Entry

DN

Booth   Booth

UP   Kitchen   Kitchen   UP

Living   Living

Woodstoves

DN   DN

Sunspace

DN   Deck   DN

Completed first-floor plan

ation would still leave us with more than enough mass, so he designed the curving kneewalls of recycled brick that frame the view and are the focal points of our dwellings (photo above).

To end up with separately owned, separately financed homes, we had to subdivide the lot by obtaining PUD approval from the City of Boulder (see pp. 106-107 of this volume). Also, to obtain FHA financing for each of us separately, we had to subdivide the lot and form a homeowner's association. We summoned all our skills to push this project through necessary legal and bureaucratic channels as quickly as we could. We often hand-carried the financial applications and building-permit papers from desk to desk downtown, and we both worked hard to convince FHA officials that the project complied with their guidelines.

Construction—To create two adjacent units oriented to the south, we had to demolish most of the existing structure. Although according to Wendorf, it probably would have been easier to raze the entire building and start from scratch, we wanted (and needed) to salvage and reuse as much of it as possible, especially the stone foundation and the brick walls.

Wendorf began the demolition by carefully removing all the interior non-bearing walls. In the basement, this lead to the discovery of a huge granite boulder tucked behind brick and wood-frame partitions. His crew had to jack-hammer it out. Next, the exterior brick walls were dismantled, virtually one brick at a time. The 50-year-old bricks had been laid up in two wythes, and the inside edges of each were like new and suitable for reuse. Wendorf and one helper used chisels to break them free, and John and I spent many hours pulling usable bricks out of the piles they left and stacking them.

The house had been remodeled three or four times before, and the rafters were sagging under the weight of three layers of roofing. This was no problem, because they were coming down anyway. When Wendorf pulled up the oak flooring on the first floor for salvage, he found that it had been laid on sleepers over a sagging floor below. He removed all the original joists and rebuilt the floors.

Once the demolition was complete, reconstruction began. Barrett and Wendorf didn't want to excavate too deeply next to the stone foundation because they were afraid of destabilizing it. They went down to 2 ft. below grade and insulated the rock with 2-in. polyurethane board. Wendorf then poured a new 4-in. insulated slab to the south of the existing one, so that both units would be the same size. He also poured a small slab for the new entry and dining nooks to the north and another slab under the proposed deck to the south.

Next, he laid up a cinder-block wall between the two units, and salvaged bricks were recycled into the new mass wall. The brick walls on the east and west were insulated with 2½ in. of foam board over a furred-out ½-in. airspace. Half-inch plywood sheathing went up next, followed by 6-mil plastic and 1x6 shiplap cedar siding. Wendorf sealed sills and door and window jambs with polyurethane foam. On the north and south, the walls were framed with 2x6s and filled with fiberglass batts. The 2x10 roof was insulated to R-30.

Partway through construction, we realized we could have great views from our bedrooms and more headroom by adding dormers to the south-sloping roof (photo facing page, left). Because we were all working together, making this change to our plans was quick and easy.

There was one more really noticeable change to the original plans. Next to the curving brick walls, perhaps the most striking features of our project are the 100-year-old arched windows with curved panes on the ends of our sunspaces (photo facing page, right). The windows once graced Denver's Mayflower Hotel, which was torn down in 1975. I found them in a Denver salvage yard, Barrett incorporated them into the design, and Wendorf popped them in place.

While the two living units were to be identical in size and mirror images in shape, the finish in each is different. In the west unit, which eventually became John's, we decided to leave the brick exterior wall exposed. In my unit, the brick wasn't in very good shape, so we plastered over it. I also installed a slate slab beneath the

The walls of the existing building were torn down brick by brick, and recycled into curved mass walls (facing page) that would absorb direct solar radiation. Some changes in the design were made as the project progressed. The bedroom dormers (above) were added when Lopez and Marshall realized they would yield more headroom and better views than the skylights originally specified. Lopez found the arched windows (right) in a salvage yard.

stove and flagstone from the back yard against the wall behind it. It looks nice, and it keeps the block wall from soaking up quite so quickly the heat I want kept in my house.

We were involved with the day-to-day coordination with the builder, making many on-site decisions. During construction, we did a lot of non-skilled work: cleaning up the job site; collecting, cleaning and stacking the bricks; making numerous trips to the landfill. Toward the end of the project the budget was running low, so we did a lot of the finish work.

Framing the two units took three months. The whole job was finished in six months, at a cost of just over $50 per sq. ft. The house has performed very well. We've both been comfortable in our spaces, and the thermal performance has been better than Barrett predicted—more than a 35% solar contribution to our heating load. We've calculated that night insulating curtains over the south glass would give us a 65% solar fraction, but they would cost over $1,000, so we probably won't install them soon.

Because we were so involved in it, our project seemed to develop a life of its own. The energy surrounding it carried us through the inevitable rough patches, and when we were done the result exceeded even the lofty expectations we had in the conceptual stages. □

Rich Lopez is the Energy Coordinator for Boulder County, Colo.

Photos except where noted: Mark Christensen

Index